The Function of Public International Law

Jan Anne Vos

The Function of Public International Law

ASSER PRESS

Springer

Jan Anne Vos
XYNTHEZYX
Nijkerk
The Netherlands

ISBN 978-90-6704-860-6 ISBN 978-90-6704-861-3 (eBook)
DOI 10.1007/978-90-6704-861-3

Library of Congress Control Number: 2013930140

Published by T.M.C. ASSER PRESS, The Hague, The Netherlands www.asserpress.nl
Produced and distributed for T.M.C. ASSER PRESS by Springer-Verlag Berlin Heidelberg

Printed on acid-free paper

Springer is part of Springer Science+Business Media (www.springer.com)

Foreword

Since the late 1980's international legal scholarship has been shaken up by incisive anti-foundational critiques as voiced by *inter alia* David Kennedy and Martti Koskenniemi. Following the tradition of critical legal scholarship, these critiques demonstrated the indeterminacy of foundational legal concepts in international law and the openness and reversibility of international legal arguments. The insights from critical legal scholarship provoked strong and contradictory responses. Some embraced them as tools for emancipation, that could be used to disclose the political agendas pursued in the name of an objective and neutral international legal order. International law, in this view, should be re-politicized. Others, however, regarded critical scholarship as undermining the international rule of law; as a project that may be well-developed in terms of analysis and deconstruction, but also as a project that threatens international law's independence from politics as well as its ability to civilize conduct in international affairs.

Jan Anne Vos' *The Function of Public International Law* is an ambitious attempt to transcend the terms of the debate between critical legal scholars and 'mainstream' international lawyers about the relation between law and politics. Vos basically accepts the validity of the critique voiced by critical scholarship. In terms not dissimilar to Koskenniemi's basic concepts in *From Apology to Utopia*, Vos argues that international legal argument oscillates between two mutually exclusive positions or frameworks. The first is the framework of obligation, which holds that rules of international law restrict a pre-given freedom of states. The other is the framework of authorization, which holds that international law confers upon states the normative power to act. According to Vos both frameworks suffer from the same problem: they cannot be upheld consistently. As a result, international legal argumentation has a tendency to constantly shift from one position to the other, even though both positions cannot be valid at the same time. Vos illustrates the workings of both frameworks in general theories of law, international theory, the sources of international law, the law of international organizations and concepts such as *ius cogens* and *erga omnes*.

For Vos, however, the radical indeterminacy that follows from his analysis does not mean that international law is irrelevant or overtaken by politics. On the contrary: Vos regards the dilemma situation that results from the mutually exclusive and internally contradictory frameworks as a precondition for the proper working of international law. International law, in his view, is not a system of rules laying down standards for conduct, but rather a system which forces states (and other actors) to continually constitute and reconstitute international society through practical reasoning. Within this reformulated framework, Vos regards international law and international politics as mutually constitutive; as part and parcel of the never-ending constitution of international society. For him this is, to use the title's wording, the function of public international law.

As I stated above, the approach taken by Vos is ambitious. Vos is not afraid to turn established readings of international law and legal theory on their head nor to come up with independent and original interpretations of some classics in international law and legal theory. Moreover, he does not shy away from developing his own framework of international law and from giving examples how this framework could be (or could have been) applied in practice. The unconventional nature of Vos' approach will most likely spur debate and controversy. In a way, however, this is exactly what the book seeks to achieve. After all, the book itself is part and parcel of what it analyzes, the ongoing debate on the constitution and reconstitution of international society through practical reasoning; through argumentation, critique and counter-argumentation.

January 2013

Wouter Werner
Professor of Public International Law
VU University
Amsterdam, The Netherlands

Contents

Chapter 1
Introduction

1.1 Oppositions

The structure of public international law is commonly characterized in terms of its opposition to the structure of the internal law of the State. Whereas the structure of the internal law of the State is vertical, the structure of public international law, in view of the absence of authority above States, is horizontal. Within that structure, the function of public international law—the legal effect that rules of public international law have on the members of international society—is commonly understood in terms of an opposition between two frameworks: rules of public international law either limit the freedoms to act of the members of international society (limiting form) or confer powers to act on the members of international society (conferring form). These frameworks may be regarded as two forms in terms of which the concept of public international law governs relations between States.[1] In either form, rules of public international law are regarded as coterminous with the common good of international society.[2]

In the late 1980s, critical theory of public international law deconstructed the concept of public international law—in its limiting form—by identifying the opposition, informed by the liberal doctrine of politics, between the requirement that rules of public international law bind States and the requirement that rules of public international law emanate from the freedom to act of the members of international society. In order to accommodate both requirements, international legal argument must contain within itself both 'descending' and 'ascending' strands. Because those strands are mutually exclusive—a rule of public

[1] On the centrality of this definition and its attraction for reform, see Kennedy 2000, p. 343.

[2] In relation to the limiting form: *Reservations to the Convention on the Prevention and Punishment of the Crime of Genocide*, Advisory Opinion of 28 May 1951, Dissenting Opinion of Judges Guerrero, Sir Arnold McNair, Read and Hsu Mo, ICJ Reports 1951, 15, 46: 'It is an undeniable fact that the tendency of all international activity in recent times has been towards the promotion of the common welfare of the international community with a corresponding restriction of the sovereign power of individual States.'

J. A. Vos, *The Function of Public International Law*,

DOI: 10.1007/978-90-6704-861-3_1,

international law cannot simultaneously restrict the freedom of States to act and emanate from the freedom of States to act—international legal argument has been analyzed as incoherent and political.[3] From that point of view, the concept of public international law was regarded as unsuitable to govern, heteronomously, relations between autonomous States. While the concept of public international law may have been intended to regulate international politics, the outcome of the critical analysis is a reversal of the relationship between public international law and international politics. In order to avoid nihilism, critical theory of public international law suggested that the concept of public international law might alternatively be understood in terms of practical reasoning: a conversation about what should be done here and now in international society.[4] If the ground structure of international society is solely formed by international politics, the question remains, however, how practical reasoning differs from international politics.

Ironically, by identifying the incoherence of the concept of public international law—formed by the opposition between incompatible requirements, critical theory of public international law simultaneously created a new opposition: between itself and what it termed 'main stream' public international law. Adhering to critical theory of public international law meant equating international life with international politics. Adhering to mainstream public international law meant reconciling the concept of public international law and the concept of sovereignty.[5] Trusting the concept of public international law entailed dismissing critical theory of public international law.[6] Conversely, seeing mainstream public international law as in any event driven by international politics implied, perplexingly, regarding critical theory of public international law as idealistic.[7] Apparently, the dichotomy between mainstream public international law and critical theory of public international law could only be resolved by converging on international politics, to the detriment of the concept of public international law.[8]

It may be possible, however, to mark out a role for the concept of public international law in international society and to re-establish the relationship between the concept of public international law and international politics, by revisiting the horizontal structure of public international law and the function of public international law, which shape the opposition between mainstream public international law and critical theory of public international law. To that end, it will be argued first that the structure of the concept of law underlying the concept of public international law has always been understood as vertical rather than horizontal. This vertical structure, it will be argued secondly, has always been understood in terms of the opposition between the limiting framework and the

[3] Koskenniemi 2005, pp. 17–23, 58–69, 563–589.

[4] Koskenniemi 2005, pp. 533–561.

[5] Kennedy 2000, pp. 346–347.

[6] Scobbie 1990, pp. 339–352.

[7] Zemanek 1997, paras 5–8.

[8] Korhonen 1996, pp. 1–4, 9–22.

conferring framework. Thirdly, it will be argued that a synthesis of these frameworks can be achieved, which intertwines the concept of public international law and the concept of international politics and establishes a connection between these processes and the members of international society.

Focusing on the vertical structure of the concept of law underlying the concept of public international law involves addressing the complex relationship between law and institutions. The vertical structure of the concept of law is inseparable from the institution of the State, which produces the internal law of the State.[9] The structure of public international law is, of course, axiomatically described as horizontal, but this description is derived from the absence of authority above States.[10] From the absence of an institution like the State above States the structure of public international law is inferred. The dichotomy between mainstream public international law and critical theory of public international law is, in part, informed by this structural difference. Whereas mainstream public international law sees the structure of public international law as horizontal, critical theory of public international law relies on the vertical structure of the domestic analogy, as implied in its identification of descending and ascending strands. Moreover, describing the concept of public international law in terms of governing relations between States implies a hierarchical relationship to the extent that States are thereby characterized as subjects of public international law. It is merely to the extent that States are characterized as legislators of public international law,[11] that the structure of public international law is seen as horizontal. From the perspective of critical theory of public international law, the simultaneous characterization of States as legislators and subjects of public international law leads to an ascending strand—from States as legislators to rules of public international law—and to a descending strand—from rules of public international law to States as subjects of public international law.

Apart from critical theory of public international law, the concept of public international law has also been criticized by social idealism. Social idealism, as formulated by Allott, severed the link between law and institutions and connected the concept of law instead to the concept of society. Criticizing the concept of public international law as the law of an international 'unsociety', Allott formulated the concept of law as inherent in society and, *mutatis mutandis*, the concept of public international law as inherent in international society. At the same time, Allott drew attention to the function of (public international) law by formulating it in terms of the delegation of power-rights to the members of (international) society. This description of the function of (public international) law, it may be noted, inscribes itself within a vertical structure.

---

[9] Kennedy 2000, pp. 346–347.

[10] Mahiou 2008, pp. 39–40.

[11] *Reservations to the Convention on the Prevention and Punishment of the Crime of Genocide*, Advisory Opinion of 28 May 1951, Dissenting Opinion of Judges Guerrero, Sir Arnold McNair, Read and Hsu Mo, ICJ Reports 1951, 15, 31–32.
Lauterpacht 1936, p. 54.

In order to transcend the dichotomy between mainstream public international law and critical theory of public international law, these three approaches—social idealism, mainstream public international law, and critical theory of public international law—may all be seen as situated within the vertical structure of the concept of law underlying the concept of public international law. Identifying the vertical structure of the concept of law underlying the concept of public international law allows proceeding to the function of public international law. Where mainstream public international law provided the limiting form, subsequently deconstructed by critical theory of public international law, social idealism provided the conferring form, rejected by mainstream public international law. The argument to be unfolded will consist of showing the incoherence of either form when viewed separately, and showing the possibility of their synthesis, which fuses structure and function, law and politics, as well as society and institutions.

While the perspectives of social idealism, mainstream public international law, and critical theory of public international law all seem to indicate vertical aspects of the structure of public international law, the function of public international law as such is addressed most explicitly in social idealism. There, it plays a key role, as it is directed at transforming the concept of public international law as the law of international 'unsociety' into the law of international society. According to the law of international unsociety, States, in the absence of a rule of public international law restricting that freedom to act, would have an extreme freedom to act as they please, which could even extend to a freedom to commit acts of genocide. In *Reservations to the Convention on the Prevention and Punishment of the Crime of Genocide*, the ICJ inferred, famously, from the special character and the origins of the Convention on the Prevention and Punishment of the Crime of Genocide that 'the principles underlying the Convention are principles which are recognized by civilized nations as binding on States, even without any conventional obligation'.[12] Subsequently, this statement informed the reasoning which identified the concept of obligation *erga omnes*[13] and the reasoning which endorsed the concept of peremptory norm of general international law (*jus cogens*).[14] It would appear that the Court was saying there that States do not have a freedom to commit acts of genocide because civilized nations have recognized the principles underlying the Convention as binding on States. This would mean, however, that, but for those principles, States would have such a freedom to act. That is the kind of freedom to act that Allott would seem to have had in view when characterizing the concept of public international law as the law of international unsociety. In the reasoning of

---

[12] *Reservations to the Convention on the Prevention and Punishment of the Crime of Genocide*, Advisory Opinion of 28 May 1951, ICJ Reports 1951, 15, 23.

[13] *Case Concerning the Barcelona Traction, Light and Power Company, Limited (New Application: 1962; Second Phase),* Judgment of 5 February 1970, ICJ Reports 1970, 3, paras 33–34.

[14] *Case Concerning Armed Activities on the Territory of the Congo (New Application: 2002; Jurisdiction of the Court and Admissibility of the Application)*, Judgment of 3 February 2006, ICJ Reports 2006, 3, para 64.

the ICJ, that freedom to act is restricted by the recognition by civilized nations of the principles underlying the Convention as binding on States. When referring to the origins and the special character of the Convention, the Court seems to have assigned a legislative effect to General Assembly resolution 96 (I), notwithstanding the position of principle—adopted in ICJ jurisprudence—that General Assembly resolutions in themselves are not binding.[15] From the perspective of critical theory of public international law, the pertinent point is that the descending strand—the identification of the principles underlying the Convention as binding on States—is not supported by an ascending strand—the exercise of the freedom of States to act directed at the formation of those principles. Rhetorically, the Court established this link by differentiating between States and civilized nations and connecting General Assembly resolution 96 (I) to the general principles of law recognized by civilized nations. Social idealism, on the other hand, counters such an extreme freedom to act by reverting to the conferring form. From that perspective, the members of international society do not have initial freedoms to act, but may only act when public international law, as the law of international society, delegates power-rights to them. While seeing the concept of public international law as inherent in international society, however, social idealism also dissociates the concept of public international law from international society, because the function of public international law is defined as hierarchically superior to the members of international society. The opposition between social idealism and mainstream public international law essentially consists of the opposition between the conferring form and the limiting form.

1.2 Structure: The Lauterpacht View and the Lotus View

In the previous section, the three steps of the argument to be unfolded were outlined in a preliminary way. This section deals with the first step—the point that the structure of the concept of law underlying the concept of public international law is vertical. In the previous section, the vertical aspects of critical theory of public international law and social idealism were pointed out and, with respect to mainstream public international law, it was suggested that it might contain both horizontal aspects (States as legislators) and vertical aspects (States as subjects). It is important to realize, however, that both the view of States as legislators and the view of States as subjects imply a vertical structure of mainstream public international law. This may appropriately be demonstrated by analyzing the contrast between the vertical approach to the concept of public international law adhered to by Sir Hersch Lauterpacht in *The Function of Law in the International Community*

[15] *Legality of the Threat or Use of Nuclear Weapons*, Advisory Opinion of 8 July 1996, ICJ Reports 1996, 226, para 70.

and the horizontal approach to the concept of public international law adhered to by the PCIJ in the *Case of the S.S. "Lotus"*.

In *The Function of Law in the International Community*, Lauterpacht argued that the doctrine of the inherent limitations of the judicial function was inconsistent with general principles of law and with a view of public international law as a legal system. Obligatory judicial settlement should therefore be regarded as inherent in the concept of law, including public international law. Accordingly, it may be said that *The Function of Law in the International Community* was not primarily concerned with the function of law, but with the judicial function. Nevertheless, as background to his discussion of the judicial function, Lauterpacht set out his view as regards the function of law:

> The function of law is to regulate the conduct of men by reference to rules whose formal (…) validity lies, in the last resort, in a precept imposed from outside.[16]

In conjunction with his argument in favor of obligatory judicial settlement, Lauterpacht argued that the concept of law, including public international law, must necessarily be situated within the concept of community, understood in terms of the rule of law. From that perspective, Lauterpacht postulated that the initial premiss of the concept of public international law might be formulated as 'the will of the international community must be obeyed' (*voluntas civitatis maximae est servanda*), situated within a 'super-State of law'.[17]

Lauterpacht developed these views while rejecting the view of the so-called 'special character' of public international law—special in comparison to the internal law of the State—as a law of coordination as opposed to subordination.[18] The contradictory fact that in such a horizontal system States could impose themselves as judges upon other States meant, according to Lauterpacht, that obligatory judicial settlement constituted an inherent element of the rule of law within a community.[19] Furthermore, it was part and parcel of the judicial function, according to Lauterpacht, to determine when to rely on the formal completeness of the law (recourse to a residual principle of freedom in the absence of a restriction) or to derive a material solution from general principles of law so as to achieve justice.[20] Somewhat inconsistently, Lauterpacht concluded that the future development of public international law was located in its approximation to the internal law of the State.[21]

It may be inferred from this description of Lauterpacht's views that, according to Lauterpacht, the concept of law necessarily has a 'vertical' structure, which means that rules of law are situated not only outside but also, hierarchically, above

[16] Lauterpacht 1933, part I, para 1.

[17] Lauterpacht 1933, part VI, para 19.

[18] Lauterpacht 1933, part VI, paras 13–17.

[19] Lauterpacht 1933, part VI, paras 18, 20–21.

[20] Lauterpacht 1933, part II, Chap. V.

[21] Lauterpacht 1933, part VI, para 22.

the subjects of the law and operate downwards in respect of them. This is indicated in particular by his idea of the super-State of law, which encompassed the maxim *voluntas civitatis maximae est servanda.*

Lauterpacht's approach may appropriately be contrasted with the horizontal approach to the concept of public international law famously adhered to by the PCIJ in the *Case of the S.S. "Lotus"*:

> International law governs relations between independent States. The rules of law binding upon States therefore emanate from their own free will as expressed in conventions or by usages generally accepted as expressing principles of law and established in order to regulate the relations between these co-existing independent communities or with a view to the achievement of common aims. Restrictions upon the independence of States cannot therefore be presumed.[22]

To what extent is this view similar to and/or different from the approach put forward by Lauterpacht? Let us first identify a similarity. The PCIJ formulated the function of public international law in terms of 'governing relations between States', which comprised 'regulating relations between co-existing communities' and 'the achievement of common aims'. Likewise, Lauterpacht formulated the function of law in terms of 'regulating the conduct of men'. It may thus be observed that both the Lauterpacht view and the Lotus view formulate the concept of (public international) law in terms of rules and regulating. The Lotus view further characterized those rules in terms of their binding quality. Both the Lauterpacht view and the Lotus view therefore depict the concept of (public international) law as hierarchically situated above the subjects of the law and operating downwards ('governing', according to the PCIJ) in respect of the conduct of men or relations between States.

Let us now turn to the difference between the Lauterpacht view and the Lotus view. The PCIJ reasoned that the rules of public international law, in the form of conventions or usages generally accepted as expressing principles of law, must emanate from the free will of States, because States are independent. While the PCIJ spoke in terms of governing and regulating, it emphasized at the same time the independence and free will of States. It never seemed to doubt that rules of public international law are hierarchically situated above States and operate downward in respect of them. Instead, it devoted its attention to the provenance of those rules, concentrating on the independence of States. In international jurisprudence and doctrine, States are commonly characterized by means of the concept of sovereignty and/or the concept of independence.[23] These concepts, moreover, imply each other.[24] In view of the sovereignty and independence of

---

[22] *Case of the S.S. "Lotus"*, Judgment No. 9 of 7 September 1927, Series A.—No. 10, 18.

[23] *Island of Palmas Case*, 875; *Competence of the General Assembly for the Admission of a State to the United Nations*, Advisory Opinion of 3 March 1950, Dissenting Opinion Judge Alvarez, ICJ Reports 1950, 4, 13; Dissenting Opinion Judge Azevedo, 26; *Interpretation of Peace Treaties with Bulgaria, Hungary and Romania (First Phase)*, Advisory Opinion of 30 March 1950, Dissenting Opinion Judge Zoričić, ICJ Reports 1950, 65, 99–100; Dissenting Opinion Judge Krylov, 109.

States and the concomitant absence of authority above States, the structure of public international law is commonly described as 'horizontal' or in synonymous terms ('co-ordinate'; 'decentralized').[25] As a consequence of the horizontal structure of public international law, the PCIJ considered that rules of public international law binding States must—'therefore'—emanate from the free will of those States. In this way, States are commonly described as both 'subjects' and 'legislators' of public international law.[26] This characterization of the structure of public international law as horizontal, derived from the concepts of sovereignty and independence, is precisely what Lauterpacht rejected as the so-called special character of public international law.

In light of the above, the similarity and difference between the Lauterpacht view and the Lotus view may be summarized as follows. Both the Lauterpacht view and the Lotus view regard the concept of public international law as hierarchically situated above States and consisting of rules which operate downwards in respect of States. The Lauterpacht view and the Lotus view differ as regards the origin of those rules. Whereas the Lauterpacht view locates the origin of those rules in the concept of community, the Lotus view derives the origin of those rules from the sovereignty and independence of States. It is submitted, however, that both the vertical Lauterpacht view and the horizontal Lotus view about the origin of rules of public international law actually inscribe themselves within the vertical structure of the concept of law underlying the concept of public international law. This may be demonstrated as follows.

Doctrinally, the horizontal structure of public international law is commonly contrasted with the vertical structure of the internal law of the State. Whereas, by virtue of its vertical structure, the internal law of the State emanates from an established authority, rules of public international law, because of the absence of authority above States, must emanate from the free will of States. The fact that the formation of rules of public international law is dependent on the free will of States, is said, from this perspective, to be simply inherent in the horizontal structure of public international law.[27] In other words, even if there might be a

---

(Footnote 23 continued)

Strupp 1934, pp. 491–497; Fitzmaurice 1957a, para 3; Gilson 1984, pp. 53–58; Onuf 1994, p. 17; Carillo Salcedo 1997, pp. 583–584; Zemanek 1997, para 38; Dupuy 2002, pp. 95–96.

[24] Mahiou 2008, pp. 118–119.

[25] Weil 1992, pp. 33–39; Zemanek 1997, paras 29–31; Tomuschat 1999, Chap. I, para 23; Kolb 2006, para 52.

[26] Strupp 1934, pp. 418–421; Carillo Salcedo 1997, p. 584; Zemanek 1997, para 41; Tomuschat 1999, Chap. I, para 25; Kolb 2000, p. 106.

[27] Weil 1992, pp. 53–58, 203–225; Carillo Salcedo 1997, pp. 583–585: 'As international law is required to govern a fundamentally different society from that within the state, it therefore has specific functions adapted to the needs of that society. Indeed, alleged imperfections so often complained of in international law are for the most part only structural features inherent to the system, since they correspond to the needs of international society. (…) [T]he development and application of law depend on the nature of the social group to which it refers, and it is clear in this connection that the features of international society sharply contrast with those of the political

tension, as identified by critical theory of public international law, between the proposition that the concept of public international law governs or regulates relations between States and the proposition that rules of public international law emanate from the free will of States, such a tension is deemed to be inherent in the horizontal structure of public international law.

It is submitted, however, that this view of the horizontal structure of public international law—which reflects the Lotus view—actually involves relying on an inherent vertical structure of the concept of law underlying the concept of public international law. From the perspective of this vertical structure, elements are derived from the absence of authority above States. From this perspective, the function of public international law is characterized as governing or regulating relations between States. From this perspective, the absence of authority above State transforms itself into the requirement of consent of States to rules of public international law. Finally, from this perspective, States are regarded as having a freedom to act in the absence of a rule of public international law restricting that freedom to act. In this way, the vertical structure of the concept of law underlying the concept of public international law makes itself felt by its simultaneous presence and absence. It is present in the definition of public international law in terms of governing relations between States. It is present in the residual rule of a freedom to act in the absence of a restrictive rule of public international law. It is simultaneously present and absent in the view that binding rules of public international law must emanate, in view of the absence of authority above States, from their consent.

It would thus appear that the concept of law underlying the concept of public international law may be formulated as follows. In principle, rules of law must emanate from an authority, hierarchically situated above the subjects of the law and operating downwards in respect of the subjects of the law. Because the concept of public international law must take account of the absence of authority

(Footnote 27 continued)
community at the state level. While the latter comprises, if only in principle, centralized and hierarchically organized social groups, international society is essentially a society of sovereign, independent states.' Kolb 1998, p. 667; Kolb 2000, pp. 104–113: 'Tout droit s'inscrit dans l'une des branches d'une alternative. *Primo*, il peut s'agir d'un droit reposant sur des structures centralisées où les pouvoirs procèdent d'un pôle de pouvoir unique. C'est une forme de droit <étatique>. Il s'agit d'un droit <non-primitif>. *Secundo*, il peut s'agir d'un droit décentralisé où les pouvoirs restent répartis sur des centres autonomes. C'est une forme de droit de <sociétés-non-étatiques>. Il s'agit dès lors d'un droit <primitif>. Le terme primitif n'est donc qu'un descripteur de toutes les conséquences qui découlent du caractère coordinatif du droit international, du fait que le sujet *uti singuli* et non la communauté juridiquement organisée détient les pouvoirs constitutionnels, du fait que la souveraineté individuelle n'a pas été expropriée. (…) S'il y a donc primitivité du droit international, c'est par rapport à l'expérience des droits étatiques centralisés. (…) C'est sur ce point empirique, dépourvu de tout jugement de valeur, qu'on peut légitimement parler de <primitivité>, en entendant par là la structure décentralisée de la société internationale et les conséquences que ce fait imprime au droit qui régit cette société.'

above States, it delegates the authority to make rules of public international law to the subjects of public international law. At the same time, those subjects of public international law are regarded as having a freedom to act in the absence of rules of public international law. As a consequence and in this way, both the freedom of States to act and the authority to restrict the freedom of States to act are imputed to States.[28]

In consequence, the contrast between the horizontal structure of public international law and the vertical structure of the internal law of the State is subsumed by the vertical structure of the concept of law underlying the concept of public international law. This 'inherent' contrast is produced by the vertical structure of the concept of law underlying the concept of public international law and the attending differentiation according to the absence or presence of authority. The concept of public international law only apparently relinquishes this vertical structure by delegating the authority to make rules of law to States and transforming, to this extent, into a horizontal structure. At the same time, the concept of public international law retains this vertical structure by understanding itself in terms of governing or regulating relations between States. Similarly, this vertical structure is retained in the assumption that the absence of a rule of public international law is tantamount to a freedom of States to act.

If the absence of authority above States is to be taken seriously, however, nothing can be inferred from the vertical structure of the concept of law underlying the concept of public international law, which presupposes the presence of authority above States. In the absence of authority above States, the concept of public international law cannot be defined in terms of governing relations between States, because that definition assumes the presence of authority. Concomitantly, in an exclusively horizontal structure, States cannot be seen as legislators, because that qualification simultaneously presumes the presence and absence of authority. By the same token, in an exclusively horizontal structure, States cannot be seen as subjects, because that would presuppose defining the concept of public international law in terms of governing relations between States. Moreover, in an exclusively horizontal structure, a freedom to act cannot be imputed to States, because such a freedom to act would simultaneously presuppose the presence and the absence of authority and result, as Lauterpacht observed, in contradiction. It is interesting to note, furthermore, that such an exclusively horizontal structure can only be observed from the perspective of a vertical structure, which reinforces the point about the vertical structure of the concept of law underlying the concept of public international law. At the same time, such an exclusively horizontal structure only

[28] *Case of the S.S. "Wimbledon"*, Judgment No. 1 of 17 August 1923, Series A.—No. 1, 25: 'The Court declines to see in the conclusion of any Treaty by which a State undertakes to perform or refrain from performing a particular act an abandonment of its sovereignty. No doubt any convention creating an obligation of this kind places a restriction upon the exercise of the sovereign rights of the State, in the sense that it requires them to be exercised in a certain way. But the right of entering into international engagements is an attribute of State sovereignty.'

tells us negatively how the concept of public international law should not be seen. In order to arrive at a more positive notion, a vertical dimension is required. Accordingly, it might tentatively be inferred that the structure of a coherent concept of public international law must contain within itself, at least, a vertical dimension.

1.3 Function: Framework of Obligation and Framework of Authorization

If it is established that the structure of the concept of law underlying the concept of public international law is vertical and that the structure of a coherent concept of public international law must contain within itself, at least, a vertical dimension, where does this bring us? The definition of the concept of public international law in terms of governing relations between States projects the link between law and authority—law as emanating from an established authority—as axiomatic. Delegating the legislative function to States was just a partial concession to the absence of authority above States. This state of affairs implies, however, that States have not played any role in deciding whether the function of the international legal system should be cast in terms of governing relations between States and, if so, in what, limiting or conferring, form. As a matter of self-determination and in the absence of authority above States, should States not themselves determine this important constitutional matter? If that is accepted, it may tentatively be inferred that the structure of a coherent concept of public international law must also contain within itself, a horizontal dimension.

The view of the concept of public international law and the internal law of the State as inscribing themselves within a vertical structure, is consonant with the observation that the concept of public international law is built on a so-called domestic analogy.[29] According to the domestic analogy, relations between States may be compared to relations between individuals in the so-called state of nature. Just as those individuals have proceeded to build the institution of the State, States may proceed to develop the concept of public international law. In that way, States could be regarded as having created the vertical structure of the concept of law underlying the concept of public international law on the basis of the horizontal structure of public international law. It must be remarked, however, that the domestic analogy is only tenable if, in the internal sphere, it explains coherently the institution of the State and the internal law of the State as proceeding from the state of nature. If it does not, then we do not have a basis for assuming that such a movement from a horizontal structure to a vertical structure is possible and then we do not have an explanation for the vertical structure of the concept of law underlying the concept of public international law. Moreover, in social contract theory, the horizontal structure of public international law is commonly put

[29] Koskenniemi 2005, pp. 17–23, 89–94.

forward as the prime example of a permanent state of nature, which may suggest that, at the international plane, such a movement is not possible.

The view that both the concept of public international law and the internal law of the State inscribe themselves within a vertical structure also seems consonant with the concept of Global Administrative Law. Global Administrative Law has been defined as comprising the mechanisms, principles, practices, and supporting social understandings that promote or otherwise affect the accountability of global administrative bodies, in particular by ensuring they meet adequate standards of transparency, participation, reasoned decision, and legality, and by providing effective review of the rules and decisions they make.[30] The purpose of Global Administrative Law is to achieve accountability of the institutions of global governance. The concept of law in Global Administrative Law has been characterized in terms of the theory of law developed by Hart, complemented by general principles of public law: (i) the principle of legality; (ii) the principle of rationality; (iii) the principle of proportionality; (iv) the rule of law; and (v) human rights.[31] Global Administrative Law involves relying on a domestic analogy, which may operate both bottom-up and top-down.[32] On the basis of this description, it may be observed that the concept of Global Administrative Law appears to take as a starting point that global administrative bodies are in a position of authority above States as well as individuals; the point of Global Administrative Law is to achieve accountability of those bodies, which implies a limitation of their authority. In so far as Global Administrative Law takes a vertical structure as a starting point, it coincides with the approach adopted here. Global Administrative Law does not, however, seek to explain that vertical structure; it works within that vertical structure by reversing the hierarchy between law and authority, subjecting authority to law. In contrast, the argument developed here addresses that vertical structure itself, by focusing on the function of public international law and the concomitant function of international institutions, with a view to transforming them in terms of the constituting of international society. So in contrast to the approach of Global Administrative Law, which takes the position of authority of international administrative organs as given and subsequently seeks to limit that authority by resorting to law, the approach taken here is to problematize and reformulate the relationship between the members of international society and international institutions in terms of the constituting of international society. (For the purpose of this analysis, it is not insignificant to note that the concept of law in Global Administrative Law is oriented towards the Lauterpacht view[33] and that both Global Administrative Law and critical theory of public international law problematize the authority of international institutions.[34])

[30] Kingsbury et al. 2005, p. 17.

[31] Kingsbury 2009, Sections 2, 3.

[32] Kingsbury 2005, pp. 53–59; Dyzenhaus 2005, p. 155.

[33] Dyzenhaus 2005, pp. 153–165.

[34] Koskenniemi 2009, pp. 7–12, 14–18.

How, then, could an analysis of the function of public international law result in a reformulation of the relationship between the members of international society and international institutions in terms of the constituting of international society? If it is accepted that the structure of both the concept of public international law and the structure of the internal law of the State should be characterized as vertical, the next step is to divide this vertical structure into two mutually exclusive functions, along the lines of the distinction between rights and obligations: the framework of obligation (previously referred to as the limiting form) and the framework of authorization (previously referred to as the conferring form). Historically, these frameworks were presented to the PCIJ by France and Turkey in the *Case of the S.S. "Lotus"*. In *Legality of the Threat or Use of Nuclear Weapons*, these frameworks were presented to the ICJ by the Nuclear Weapon States and the Non-Nuclear Weapon States. The contrast between those frameworks is also reflected in doctrine. Reacting to the framework of obligation adhered to by the PCIJ in the *Case of the S.S. "Lotus"*, Bruns argued that the concept of public international law should conform to the framework of authorization.[35] As remarked at the end of Sect. 1.1, social idealism, as formulated by Allott, may be analyzed as a reaction, in the form of the framework of authorization, to the international unsociety propelled by the framework of obligation.

In analytical terms, the framework of obligation may be described as follows: (i) According to the framework of obligation, the function of rules of public international law is to restrict the freedom of States to act. (ii) According to the framework of obligation, rules of public international law contain obligations which restrict the freedom of States to act. (iii) The framework of obligation is based on the assumption that in the absence of rules of public international law, States have a freedom to act. Within this framework, the concept of right is equated with the freedom of States to act. In terms of the differentiation between weak and strong permissions, the concept of right as used within the framework of obligation corresponds to a weak permission.[36]

Analytically, the framework of authorization may be described as follows: (i) According to the framework of authorization, the function of rules of public international law is to confer on States a power to act. (ii) According to the framework of authorization, rules of public international law contain rights by virtue of which States can act. (iii) The framework of authorization is based on the assumption that in the absence of rules of public international law, States do not have a power to act. Within this framework, the concept of right is equated with the concept of power. In terms of the differentiation between weak and strong permissions, the concept of power as used within the framework of authorization corresponds to a strong permission.[37]

[35] Bruns 1929, pp. 9–12; Bruns 1933, pp. 459–465.

[36] Dekker and Werner 2003, pp. 14–23.

[37] Dekker and Werner 2003, pp. 14–23.

It must be observed at this point that the framework of obligation and the framework of authorization are mutually exclusive. It cannot be asserted simultaneously that the function of rules of public international law is to restrict the freedom of States to act and that the function of rules of public international law is to confer on States a power to act. Metaphorically speaking, the former have a 'narrowing' function and the latter have a 'broadening' function. Similarly, the assumption on which the framework of obligation is based and the assumption on which the framework of authorization is based cannot simultaneously be adhered to. It cannot be asserted simultaneously that, in the absence of rules of public international law, States have a freedom to act and that States do not have a power to act.

It is, furthermore, submitted that, because both the framework of obligation and the framework of authorization are situated within the vertical structure of the concept of law underlying the concept of public international law, both are incoherent. As regards the framework of obligation, it cannot be explained coherently why and how rules of public international law are binding on States. This always involves relying on an elusive assumption (such as *voluntas civitatis maximae est servanda*), within or without the concept of law. At the same time, the assumption of a freedom of a State to act is inconsistent with the equal freedom of another State to act. Although within the framework of obligation this furnishes an explanation as to the social necessity of binding rules of law (cf. the requirement of normativity in critical theory of public international law), if this assumption is inconsistent, it cannot support the necessity of that character of rules of law.

Located within the vertical structure of the concept of law underlying the concept of public international law, the framework of authorization is also incoherent. If, in the absence of rules of public international law, States do not have a power to act, States cannot be relied on to explain the formation of rules of public international law. If States are seen as the principal members of international society, it follows that there is no other basis to explain the formation of rules of public international law. Accordingly, within the framework of authorization, the formation and existence of rules of public international law remain a matter of assumption. At the same time, from the perspective of the concept of public international law and in the absence of rules of public international law, States must be regarded as not having a power to act. That perspective leaves States incapable of constituting international society by means of international politics and fails to explain the social necessity of rules of law.

Some remarks may be made at this point about the notions of incoherence and coherence that are used here. The notion of incoherence constitutes an integral part of critical theory of public international law and it is used there to denote contradiction, inconsistency. Thus, as the descending strand and the ascending strand exclude each other, they cannot both be adhered to at the same time; they pull the system in different directions. That notion of incoherence is also used here. Accordingly, it may be observed that the framework of obligation contains two assumptions, which cannot be adhered to at the same time: that rules of public international law are binding and that States have a freedom to act; these assumptions are inconsistent. The absence of inconsistency, however, does not necessarily entail coherence. The use of the term coherence that is sought here denotes the requirement that the elements of a system must have some connection to each other, in the sense that they explain each other's existence, that they constitute each other. This may be illustrated with respect to the framework of authorization. The non-power of a member of society and the non-power of another member of society may coexist, they are consistent. But, that being so, this does not explain the need for rules of law. Furthermore, if rules of law cannot emanate from acts of the members of society, rules of law cannot be explained at all; they depend on the presumed existence of some authority. In a similar way, this notion of coherence also reflects on the framework of obligation. It remains a perennial assumption that rules of law are binding. This is not an auxiliary assumption; it is the principal assumption that permeates the whole system. On the other hand, the framework of obligation involves the members of international society in the formation of rules limiting their freedom to act but, according to critical theory of public international law, in an incoherent way. Subjacent to the argument developed here is the assumption that the members of society must have some role in the formation of the rules of their society. Otherwise, we will simply have to assume the pre-existence of some institution vested with authority. Social contract theory has attempted to do this. Social contract theory, however, presupposes what it tries to explain—the State. By explaining the institution of the State on the basis of the state of nature existing at the international plane, social contract theory already assumes the existence of the State. All the same, the argument developed here concords with social contract theory to the extent that it seeks to explain the connections between the members of society and their rules and institutions.

1.4 Reformulated Framework

The third step of the argument developed here is that the incoherence of both the framework of obligation and the framework of authorization may be turned into a reformulated framework, which comprises both. This is a paradox. How, it may be asked, can two frameworks that are both analyzed as incoherent be combined into a reformulated framework which is deemed to be coherent? The answer is that the incoherence of both frameworks results precisely from the fact that they exclude each other. Both the framework of obligation and the framework of authorization claim to occupy for themselves the whole field of public international law. That is how it has been said that rules of public international law cannot at the same time be both restrictive and permissive. That is how it has been said that the assumption that, in the absence of rules of public international law, States have a freedom to act, is not consistent with the assumption that, in the absence of rules of public international law, States do not have a power to act. Seen in this light, the framework of obligation and the framework of authorization form a dichotomy.

If, however, both frameworks are incoherent, their mutual exclusivity cannot be maintained as coherent either. If their mutual exclusivity cannot be maintained, it follows that the field of public international law may comprise both frameworks. This leads to a complex constellation. It follows that the field of public international law then contains, within itself, opposites. It includes within itself the assumption that rules of public international law must be restrictive and the assumption that rules of public international law must be permissive. It includes within itself the assumption that, in the absence of rules of public international law, the members of international society have a freedom to act, and the assumption that, in the absence of rules of public international law, the members of international society do not have a power to act.

Finally, it must be seen that these elements constitute extremities of a resulting, reformulated, framework. Rules of public international law cannot be only restrictive or permissive, but must always be both at the same time. In the absence of rules of public international law, the members of international society cannot be characterized as having a freedom to act or as having no power to act, but must be characterized as having a power to act which is not an unlimited freedom to act. This reformulated framework consists, in other words, of opposites which encompass the field of public international law. The field of public international law where the constituting of international society actually takes place, is where these opposites interact with each other. This may seem similar to the pattern of descending and ascending strands identified by critical theory of public international law, but it is dissimilar in two respects. First, the structure of the reformulated framework is not exclusively vertical or horizontal; vertical, horizontal, and diagonal movements are possible. Second, the function of public international law has been transformed; it is no longer a question of limiting the freedom of States to act; it has become a question of the constituting of international society by the members of international society by means of restrictive/permissive rules of public international law, on the basis of their dilemma situation of having a power, but not an unlimited freedom to act.

In overview, this reformulated framework may be described as follows. Within the reformulated framework, the function of rules of public international law is neither exclusively to limit the freedoms of the members of international society to act, nor exclusively to confer on the members of international society powers to act; instead, the function of rules of public international law is to be both restrictive and permissive at the same time. Accordingly, rules of public international law must simultaneously be both enabling and disabling. Concurrently, those rules of public international law must be regarded neither as exclusively containing obligations nor as exclusively containing rights; instead, those rules must be regarded as containing rights/obligations in respect of each member of international society at the same time. Concomitantly, in the absence of rules of public international law, States can neither be regarded as having a freedom to act nor as having no power to act. Instead, in the absence of rules of public international law, States must be regarded as having a power to act which is not an unlimited freedom to act. These three layers, the function of public international law, the content of rules of public international law, and the situation of the members of international society in the absence of rules of public international law, are directed at each other. The function of rules of public international law corresponds to the dilemma situation of the members of international society of having a power, but not a freedom to act. By virtue of those rules, the members of international society can move so as to exit that dilemma situation (enabling aspect); at the same time, those rules canalize those movements (disabling aspect). From the perspective of their dilemma situation, the members of international society must resort to these rules of public international law, because they allow them to move so as to exit their dilemma situation and guide those movements.

Described metaphorically, the power of States to act, which is not a freedom of States to act, may be characterized as the power of States to constitute international society. The members of international society constitute international society in the form of rules of public international law, which are both enabling and disabling at the same time. The enabling aspect consists in the movement out of the dilemma situation of the members of international society of having a power to act which is not a freedom to act. The disabling aspect consists in the crystallization of these movements of the members of international society into a particular pattern. That crystallization is disabling in so far as the members of international society do not have an unlimited freedom to act so as to circumvent the rules of international society. Outside the rules, the dilemma situation persists. On the other hand, those crystallized patterns remain susceptible to change; change, however, must likewise be approached from the dilemma situation of the members of international society. In this way, the reconstituting of international society is indistinguishable from the constituting of international society. The reformulated framework incorporates, in this manner, both stability and change.

The process whereby the members of international society constitute international society is, it is submitted, practical reasoning. In order to move out of the dilemma situation of having a power, but not a freedom to act, the members of international society must have recourse to practical reasoning. They are compelled to do so because all members of international society have such a power to act and because all these powers to act must be regarded as equivalent. The purpose of the process of practical reasoning is to allow the members of international society to turn their powers to act into a workable international society. It cannot be assumed that those powers are complementary; there may be friction. Nor can it be assumed that those powers conflict; there may be cooperation. The point of the process of practical reasoning is to turn those elements of cooperation and friction into a common good of international society, consisting of fruitful relationships between the members of international society. That process is propelled toward the common good of international society by the initial and recurrent dilemma situation of the members of international society of having a power, but not a freedom to act. On the basis of pluralism, the process of practical reasoning about the common good of international society may give rise to diverging approaches to that common good. Against the background of the dilemma situation, those diverging approaches must be directed at turning the common good into a coherent whole, defined by elements of cooperation and friction.

The process of practical reasoning, directed at the common good of international society and forming the vehicle whereby the members of international society constitute international society, may appropriately be characterized by reference to the work of Kratochwil. Kratochwil has described the process of practical reasoning as differing in five respects from our ordinary scientific discourse: (i) while natural phenomena are analyzed in terms of necessity, human action is understood in terms of free will; (ii) the finding of the relevant premises, or starting points, is of decisive importance; (iii) the process is informed by assent to practical judgments (for example, 'more is better than less' or 'quality is better than quantity'); (iv) the process is also informed by procedural requirements, which aim at the equitable participation of all members of international society; and (v) specialized techniques justify exclusions and therewith lend persuasive force to a final decision.[38]

Within the reformulated framework, the requirement that the process of practical reasoning be directed at the common good of international society also informs international politics. As thus situated, the concept of public international law and the concept of international politics converge on the common good of international society and may be characterized as two perspectives on that common good: while the concept of public international law must be directed at the coherence of the common good of international society, the concept of international politics must be directed at the formation of that common good. Within the reformulated framework, the field of public international law and the field of international politics may thus be seen to constitute each other. In contrast, critical theory of public international law saw mainstream public international law as eclipsed by the concept of international politics. The notion of international politics relied on by critical theory was undifferentiated and undirected, consisting of freedoms of States to act which presupposed the applicability of the framework of obligation. Within the reformulated framework, as developed here, the concept of public international law and the concept of international politics both inform, from different angles, the constituting of international society.

In the light of this description of the reformulated framework, it may be explained how incoherence can be turned into the common good of international society. As analyzed by critical theory of public international law, incoherence is a matter of contradiction between opposites. It has been seen that the reformulated framework contains within itself the opposite elements of the framework of obligation and the framework of authorization. These opposites do not, however, necessarily lead to contradiction. Coherence may be understood as a middle ground between those opposites, just as, for example, different shades of gray are constituted by black and white. It may perhaps be said that these different shades of gray reflect different proportions in which white is superior to black and black is

[38] Kratochwil 1989, pp. 34–43.

superior to white; in other words, this singular relationship is composed of a double relationship. This form of coherence also contains within itself incoherence, because the proportion may be taken apart and be substituted by a different proportion. Along these lines, incoherence does not entail arbitrariness, but provides starting points for the reconstituting of international society. The reason why incoherence is transformed in this manner, is that the reformulated framework transforms the function of public international law. It is no longer a matter of having to impose obligations so as to limit freedoms of States to act. The process of practical reasoning does not operate top-down, from the institution of the State, via the internal law of the State, to the members of society. The process of practical reasoning forms the vehicle by which the members of (international) society constitute (international) society. It is directed, in the form of international politics, at the formation of the common good and, in the form of the concept of public international law, at the coherence of that common good. That coherence may be any shade of gray. The important thing is that the process of practical reasoning is guided by the black and the white that the reformulated framework contains. Since coherence also contains within itself incoherence, the process of practical reasoning may likewise be directed at the reconstituting of international society.

Since the argument developed here focuses on the function of public international law and therewith on the vertical structure of the concept of law underlying the concept of public international law, it seems appropriate to indicate its position in respect of other works which have dealt with the structure of public international law. In 1964, Friedmann identified, in *The Changing Structure of International law*, a developing law of cooperation grafting itself onto a law of coexistence. In 1987, Kennedy identified, in *International Legal Structures*, objective and subjective elements of international legal discourse, analyzing international legal discourse as informed by elements taken from justice and elements taken from consent. Two years later Koskenniemi, in *From Apology to Utopia – The Structure of International Legal Argument*, from within, deconstructed those elements into contradiction and incoherence. In 1990, Allott, in *Eunomia – New Order for a New World*, from without, criticized the concept of public international law as the law of international unsociety and transformed it into the law of international society. In the age of globalization and global governance, the concept of Global Administrative Law takes a vertical structure of the concept of public international law as a starting point and aims to limit authority by means of concepts taken from administrative law. At about the same time, Spiermann, in *International Legal Argument in the Permanent Court of International Justice – The Rise of the International Judiciary*, took up the distinction between a law of cooperation and a law of coexistence and argued that international legal argument contains a double structure, consisting of a law of cooperation and a law of coexistence.

The difference between the argument developed here and in the work of Spiermann is that Spiermann's work sees the two substructures, the law of cooperation and the law of coexistence, as existing separately, the law of cooperation superposed on the law of coexistence. The law of cooperation, as Spiermann sees it, coincides with mainstream public international law as analyzed by critical theory of public international law. The law of coexistence, which arises from the coexistence of States, is endowed by that coexistence with a degree of binding force. It might thus be said that there is some similarity between Spiermann's work and the argument developed here, because the dilemma situation of the members of international society, as having a power to act which is not a freedom to act, is inferred from their coexistence. In the approach developed here, this aspect is not associated with a separate structure, but as indicating, so to speak, that the law of cooperation, which approximates the framework of obligation, and the law of coexistence, which approximates the framework of authorization, should be joined within the reformulated framework. In this way, the law of cooperation and the law of coexistence to which the PCIJ referred when it propounded the Lotus view, are drawn onto each other. Out of the coexistence, the dilemma situation of the members of international society, arises not merely the faculty of cooperation, but the practical necessity of constituting international society.

The reformulated structure has been derived from the incoherence of two vertical structures. Proceeding in this manner reveals the complex problem of the relationship between a structure and the acts done pursuant to that structure. The reformulated structure, as identified here, indicates that a structure cannot be explained solely on the basis of the acts of the members of international society; it is in part given. On the other hand, it cannot be regarded entirely as given, because that would leave the members of international society no role in the constituting of international society and imply seeing the concept of public international law purely in terms of natural law. Accordingly, the solution which imposes itself is that both, structure and acts, imply each other. An act directed at the constituting of international society implies the existence of a structure; at the same time, that structure is not immutable and susceptible to change pursuant to the acts of the members of international society. In other words, the acts of the members of international society inscribe themselves into and, at the same time, constitute the structure of international society. The constituting of international society is thereby always both about the constituting of the structure of international society and about the constituting of international society within that structure. In this way, the two ways of knowing and demonstrating identified by Artistotle—by means of archai/axioma or by means of topoi[39]—may ultimately be regarded as interdependent.

Finally, as a methodological point, the argument put forward here aims to provide, as a matter of practical reasoning, a perspective on the concept of public international law. It is not intended here to refute the concept of public international law in the sense that critical theory of public international law has taken mainstream public international law apart. It has not been so difficult for proponents of mainstream public international law to point out incoherence in critical

[39] Kolb 2006, para 18, footnote 67.

theory of public international law.[40] Critical theory of public international law has by and large acknowledged its ineffectiveness in respect of mainstream public international law.[41] For critical theory of public international law to achieve its objective, its spears would have had to be stronger than its object—and, if everything is relative, it could never have been so. Does it follow that mainstream public international law is immutable? That would mean that the mainstream concept of public international law has a kind of self-explanatory existence, whether in the form of the framework of obligation or in the form of the framework of authorization. By the approach taken, the perspective sought to be provided here is simultaneously both descriptive and prescriptive of the framework surrounding the concept of public international law. It is descriptive, because it seeks to describe the incoherence of the framework of obligation and the framework of authorization and to show how a reformulated framework can be derived from suppressing their mutual exclusivity. It is prescriptive, because, thereby—and to that extent, it seeks to prescribe the inferred transformation of the function of public international law. In this way, the approach adopted here is simultaneously both deductive and inductive.[42] It is deductive, because the reformulated framework is derived from two metaphysical models. It is inductive, because the reformulated framework is inferred from how these models operate 'on the ground'.

1.5 Outline

This is the short of the argument. The long of the argument is contained in the succeeding eight chapters, which are organized into three parts. Part I contains Chaps. 3–5. Chapter 3 is, firstly, intended to describe the provenance of the idea that the vertical structure of the concept of law underlying the concept of public international law can be subdivided into the framework of obligation and the framework of authorization. Both frameworks were considered by the PCIJ in the *Case of the S.S. "Lotus"* and by the ICJ in *Legality of the Threat or Use of Nuclear Weapons*. Secondly, it will be argued that the objective structural framework described by Judge Shahabuddeen in his Dissenting Opinion in *Legality of the Threat or Use of Nuclear Weapons* approximates the reformulated framework described in Sect. 1.4. Subsequently, Chap. 4 will deal with two aspects of theory of law. Firstly, it will be argued that the institution of the State and the internal law of the State cannot be explained by social contract theory. This is important because, at the international plane, it then follows that the vertical structure of the concept of law underlying the concept of public international law presupposes the

[40] Scobbie 1990, pp. 339–352.

[41] Koskenniemi 2009, p. 8.

[42] Kratochwil 1989, pp. 40–43.

existence of a super-State. Secondly, important theories of law coincide with the internal law of the State, which make them unsuitable in principle for transposition to the international plane. It will also be argued, however, that elements of those theories are transposable to the reformulated framework. Chapter 5 will, on the one hand, identify the framework of obligation and the framework of authorization in theories of public international law. On the other hand, it will identify elements of those theories that are transposable to the reformulated framework. Part II contains Chaps. 8–10. These chapters will situate the traditional sources of public international law-general principles of law, conventional international law, and customary international law-within the framework of obligation and the framework of authorization. As a whole, it will be argued that those sources may fruitfully be transposed to the reformulated framework, where they may be regarded as informing the process of practical reasoning about the constituting of international society. Part III contains Chaps. 13 and 14, which are differentiated according to the distinction between organized international society and unorganized international society. Accordingly, Chap. 13 will analyze the concept of international institution from the perspectives of the framework of obligation and the framework of authorization. Secondly, it will be argued that the concept of international institution may fruitfully be transposed to the reformulated framework. Similarly, Chap. 14 will analyze the concept of international community, underlying the concepts of *jus cogens* and obligation *erga omnes*, from the perspectives of the framework of obligation and the framework of authorization. Secondly, it will be argued that the concept of international community, transformed into the concept of international society, may fruitfully be transposed to the reformulated framework. Chapter 16 is intended to draw the threads of the preceding chapters together and to describe corollaries and implications of the reformulated framework.

Part I
Mutual Exclusivity in Jurisprudence and Theory

Chapter 2
Introduction to Part I

Part I is intended to unfold and develop the principal issues that have been raised in Sects. 1.2–1.4. Chapter 3 returns to the moment when the PCIJ, in the *Case of the S.S. "Lotus"*, was asked by the parties, France and Turkey, to choose between the framework of authorization and the framework of obligation described in Sect. 1.3. In order to illustrate the actuality of this question, the chapter then turns to *Legality of the Threat or Use of Nuclear Weapons*, where the issue was revisited by the Nuclear Weapon States and Non-Nuclear Weapon States. Both Courts, spanning the transition from the League of Nations to the United Nations, opted for the framework of obligation. In its tail, the chapter then describes how the question was extensively pondered by Judge Shahbuddeen in his Dissenting Opinion in *Legality of the Threat or Use of Nuclear Weapons*. The objective structural framework which he derived from the work of Prosper Weil approximates the reformulated framework identified in Sect. 1.4. The analysis contained in this chapter is located at the international plane.

Chapter 4 zooms in on the claim in Sect. 1.2 that the structure of public international law, while commonly regarded as, in principle, horizontal, must actually be characterized as vertical. To this end, the chapter will, metaphorically, descend into the internal sphere of States by turning to general theory of law. This move is intended to demonstrate the claim that general theory of law and the internal law of the State coincide. To make this claim, it is first argued that the institution of the State and the internal law of the State cannot be explained by social contract theory. If that assertion is sustainable, it follows that the internal law of the State presupposes the existence of the institution of the State and, likewise, that the concept of public international law presupposes the existence of a super-State. It then follows that there is no basis for the so-called domestic analogy, by virtue of which, just like individuals exiting the state of nature have constituted the State, so States may have constituted the concept of public international law. Rather, the vertical structure of the concept of law underlying the concept of public international law is presupposed. This vertical structure

J. A. Vos, *The Function of Public International Law*,
DOI: 10.1007/978-90-6704-861-3_2,

predetermines the choice between the framework of obligation and the framework of authorization. The transposition of domestic legal concepts to the international plane may, in this light, be evaluated in two ways. This transposition may be seen as inappropriate in view of the contrast between the horizontal structure of public international law and the vertical structure of the internal law of the State. Alternatively, this transposition may be seen as appropriate in view of the similarity between the vertical structure of the concept of law underlying the concept of public international law and the vertical structure of the internal law of the State. In so far as social contract theory is rejected as an explanation of the institution of the State and the internal law of the State, however, the explanation of that vertical structure remains absent.

Chapter 5 will then return to the international plane and identify the vertical structure of the concept of law underlying the concept of public international law, in the form of the framework of obligation and the framework of authorization, in theory of public international law. The dominance of the framework of obligation, which the ICJ inferred from the practice of States in *Legality of the Threat or Use of Nuclear Weapons*, corresponds to the main current in theory of public international law prescribed by Grotius and Vattel. Nevertheless, the adequacy and the justification of the framework of obligation continue to be questioned. While critical theory of public international law had done so from the inside, theory of public international law, from Bruns to Allott, has also reverted to the framework of authorization.

Chapters 4 and 5 will also deal with elements in theories of law and theories of public international law which, while developed within the context of a vertical structure of law, can be transposed to the reformulated framework developed in Sect. 1.4. These elements may be fitted to the objective structural framework identified by Judge Shahabuddeen. In this way, the reformulated framework identified deductively in Sect. 1.4, may also be arrived at inductively, by joining the elements provided by theory of law (MacCormick; Finnis) and theory of public international law (Kratochwil; Allott) to the objective structural framework.

Chapter 3
The Framework of Obligation and the Framework of Authorization in the *Case of the S.S. "Lotus"* and in *Legality of the Threat or Use of Nuclear Weapons*

3.1 Introduction

In Sect. 1.2, it was submitted that the structure of the concept of law underlying the concept of public international law can be said to be vertical. In Sect. 1.3, it was subsequently submitted that, from the perspective of the function of public international law, this vertical structure of the concept of law underlying the concept of public international law can be analyzed in terms of two mutually exclusive frameworks, the framework of obligation and the framework of authorization.

According to the framework of obligation, the function of rules of public international law is to restrict the freedom of States to act. Within the context of the framework of obligation, rules of public international law contain obligations which restrict the freedom of States to act. The framework of obligation is based on the assumption that in the absence of rules of public international law, States have a freedom to act. According to the framework of authorization, the function of rules of public international law is to confer on States a power to act. Within the context of the framework of authorization, rules of public international law contain rights by virtue of which States can act. The framework of authorization is based on the assumption that in the absence of rules of public international law, States do not have a power to act.

The framework of obligation and the framework of authorization are mutually exclusive. It cannot be asserted simultaneously that rules of public international law restrict the freedom of States to act and that rules of public international law confer on States a power to act. Similarly, the assumption on which the framework of obligation is based and the assumption on which the framework of authorization is based cannot simultaneously be adhered to. It cannot be asserted simultaneously that, in the absence of rules of public international law, States have a freedom to act and States do not have a power to act.

J. A. Vos, *The Function of Public International Law*,
DOI: 10.1007/978-90-6704-861-3_3,

This chapter returns to the moments when the PCIJ and the ICJ were confronted with the question of whether the concept of public international law conforms to the framework of obligation or the framework of authorization. In the *Case of the S.S. "Lotus"*, the PCIJ addressed this question of principle raised by the positions adopted by France and Turkey and opted for the framework of obligation. In *Legality of the Threat or Use of Nuclear Weapons*, when the point was revisited by the Nuclear Weapon States and the Non-Nuclear Weapon States, the ICJ followed in the footsteps of its predecessor. This chapter is intended to trace in detail the pertinent reasoning of both Courts and to illustrate the incoherence attaching to reasoning within either of those frameworks.

It is also submitted, however, that, if both frameworks are incoherent in the sense of internally inconsistent, their postulated mutual exclusivity also falls away. This, in turn, opens the door to the formulation of an alternative framework which combines their perspectives; this would be a framework which would have both a restricting and a broadening function and which would situate the members of international society as having an inherent power, but not an unlimited freedom, to act. By virtue of such power, members of international society constitute international society in the form of rules of public international law. The analysis in this chapter culminates in a discussion of the framework considered by Judge Shahabuddeen in his Dissenting Opinion in *Legality of the Threat or Use of Nuclear Weapons*, which approximates the reformulated framework outlined in Sect. 1.4 with a view to transcending the incoherence of the mutual exclusivity of the framework of obligation and the framework of authorization.

3.2 The Framework of Obligation and the Framework of Authorization Considered in the *Case of the S.S. "Lotus"*

On 2 August 1926, a collision occurred on the high seas between a steamship of French nationality, the *Lotus*, and a steamship of Turkish nationality, the *Boz-Kourt*. As a result of this collision, the *Boz-Kourt*, bisected, sank; eight Turkish nationals perished. After having done everything possible to save the shipwrecked persons, the *Lotus* proceeded to Constantinople, where it arrived on 3 August 1926. On 5 August 1926, the Turkish authorities instituted criminal proceedings against both Lieutenant Demons, officer of the watch of the *Lotus*, and Hassan Bey, captain of the *Boz-Kourt*, on a charge of involuntary manslaughter.

The French government challenged the criminal jurisdiction assumed by Turkey, asserting exclusive criminal jurisdiction with respect to Lieutenant Demons. In this manner, a dispute arose between France and Turkey concerning the question whether France could assume exclusive criminal jurisdiction with respect to Lieutenant Demons or whether Turkey could assume concurrent criminal jurisdiction with respect to Lieutenant Demons.

By means of a special agreement, the two States subsequently referred this issue of jurisdiction to the PCIJ in the form of the following question:

> Has Turkey, contrary to Article 15 of the Convention of Lausanne of July 24th, 1923, respecting conditions of residence and business and jurisdiction, acted in conflict with the principles of international law – and if so, what principles – by instituting, following the collision which occurred on August 2nd, 1926, on the high seas between the French steamer *Lotus* and the Turkish steamer *Boz-Kourt* and upon the arrival of the French steamer at Constantinople – as well as against the captain of the Turkish steamship – joint criminal proceedings in pursuance of Turkish law against M. Demons, officer of the watch onboard the *Lotus* at the time of the collision, in consequence of the loss of the *Boz-Kourt* having involved the death of eight Turkish sailors and passengers?[1]

After it established in Part I of Judgment No. 9 the position resulting from the special agreement, the PCIJ determined, in Part II of Judgment No. 9, the principles of international law to which Article 15 of the Convention of Lausanne of July 24th, 1923, respecting conditions of residence and business and jurisdiction, referred. Article 15 provided, in relevant part:

> (...) all questions of jurisdiction shall, as between Turkey and the other contracting Powers, be decided in accordance with the principles of international law.

The Court considered that the meaning of the words 'principles of international law' was clear and could only mean international law as it is applied between all nations belonging to the community of States. The Court also said that the expression 'principles of international law' had to be construed as meaning the principles which are in force between all independent nations and which therefore apply equally to all the Contracting Parties of the Convention respecting conditions of residence and business and jurisdiction.[2] The PCIJ thus attributed a comprehensive character to the principles of international law.

Subsequently, in Part III of Judgment No. 9, the PCIJ arrived at what it characterized as a question of principle: what was the function of the principles of international law it had identified previously? The French government had relied on the framework of authorization and argued that Turkey should identify a rule of public international law authorizing it to assume criminal jurisdiction with respect to Lieutenant Demons. The French government considered that in the absence of such a rule of public international law, the Court should conclude that Turkey could not assume criminal jurisdiction with respect to Lieutenant Demons. The Turkish government had relied on the framework of obligation and argued that France should identify a rule of public international law prohibiting it from assuming criminal jurisdiction with respect to Lieutenant Demons. The Turkish government considered that in the absence of such a rule of public international

---

[1] *Case of the S.S. "Lotus"*, Judgment No. 9 of 7 September 1927, Series A.—No. 10, 5.

[2] *Case of the S.S. "Lotus"*, Judgment No. 9 of 7 September 1927, Series A.—No. 10, 16–17.

law, the Court should conclude that Turkey could assume criminal jurisdiction with respect to Lieutenant Demons. As has been noted by commentators, this was a crucial moment in the Judgment.[3]

Resolving this problem, the PCIJ adopted the approach advocated by Turkey, considering that it was both in conformity with the special agreement and dictated by the very nature and existing conditions of international law, which it described as follows:

> International law governs relations between independent States. The rules of law binding upon States therefore emanate from their own free will as expressed in conventions or by usages generally accepted as expressing principles of law and established in order to regulate the relations between these co-existing independent communities or with a view to the achievement of common aims. Restrictions upon the independence of States cannot therefore be presumed.[4]

Thereby, the PCIJ adhered to the framework of obligation. Accordingly, the Court considered that the function of rules of public international law is to restrict the freedom of States to act and that in the absence of rules of public international law States have a freedom to act. Furthermore, it considered that the formation of rules of public international law restricting the freedom of States to act is dependent on the exercise of the freedom of States to act. Incidentally, it may be remarked that in this passage the PCIJ did not actually address the framework of authorization. The presumption of restrictions on the independence of States does not correspond directly to the framework of authorization. In fact, it may be said that, by focusing on the independence of States, the Court was already working within the context of the framework of obligation.

After establishing this position, the PCIJ proceeded to the question of jurisdiction. It started by drawing a distinction between the exercise of jurisdiction by a State within the territory of another State and the assumption of jurisdiction by a State within its own territory with respect to persons, property and acts outside its territory. With respect to the exercise of jurisdiction by a State within the territory of another State, the Court identified as a restriction imposed by public international law the rule that, in the absence of a permissive rule of public international law, a State may not exercise power in any form within the territory of another State.[5]

However, as regards the assumption of jurisdiction by a State within its own territory with respect to persons, property and acts outside its territory, the Court considered that States may extend the application of their laws and the jurisdiction

[3] Siorat 1958, paras 446–470; Haggenmacher 1986, para 51; Dekker and Werner 2003, pp. 14–23.

[4] *Case of the S.S. "Lotus"*, Judgment No. 9 of 7 September 1927, Series A.—No. 10, 18.

[5] *Case of the S.S. "Lotus"*, Judgment No. 9 of 7 September 1927, Series A.—No. 10, 18–19.

of their courts to persons, property and acts outside their territory, unless public international law contains a prohibitive rule applying to that particular case.[6]

Notwithstanding this conclusion, the PCIJ further examined whether these general considerations applied specifically to the question of criminal jurisdiction. Thus, the Court went on to consider whether the question of criminal jurisdiction must be situated within the framework of obligation or within the framework of authorization. The Court then observed that the framework of authorization would only come into play if a principle of international law restricting the discretion of States in regard to criminal jurisdiction existed. In other words, the Court located the framework of authorization within the framework of obligation, understanding a permissive rule as an exception to a prohibitive rule. Therefore, the Court arrived at the conclusion that it had to ascertain in any event whether or not a rule of public international law, limiting the freedom of States to extend the criminal jurisdiction of their courts to a collision on the high seas between ships of different nationalities, existed.[7]

Conducting this examination, the PCIJ considered the following three arguments which had been advanced by the French government pursuant to the framework of authorization: (1) that public international law does not allow a State to initiate proceedings with regard to offences committed by foreigners abroad simply by reason of the nationality of the victim and that the offence must be regarded as having been committed on board the *Lotus*; (2) that international law recognizes the exclusive jurisdiction of the State whose flag is flown as regards everything which occurs on board a ship on the high seas; and (3) that this principle is especially applicable in collision cases.[8]

The Court did not find it necessary to consider the first argument, because, according to the Court, if the collision was localized on board the *Boz-Kourt*, the assumption of criminal jurisdiction by Turkey could be based on the principle of territoriality and a rule of public international law forbidding Turkey to localize

---

[6] *Case of the S.S. "Lotus"*, Judgment No. 9 of 7 September 1927, Series A.—No. 10, 19: 'It does not, however, follow that international law prohibits a State from exercising jurisdiction in its own territory, in respect of any case which relates to acts which have taken place abroad, and in which it cannot rely on some permissive rule of international law. Such a view would only be tenable if international law contained a general prohibition to States to extend the application of their laws and the jurisdiction of their courts to persons, property and acts outside their territory and if, as an exception to this general prohibition, it allowed States to do so in certain specific cases. But this is certainly not the case under international law as it stands at present. Far from laying down a general prohibition to the effect that States may not extend the application of their laws and the jurisdiction of their courts to persons, property and acts outside their territory, it leaves them in this respect a wide measure of discretion which is only limited in certain cases by prohibitive rules; as regards other cases, every State remains free to adopt the principles which it regards as best and most suitable. (…) In these circumstances, all that can be required of a State is that it should not overstep the limits which international law places upon its jurisdiction; within these limits, its title to exercise jurisdiction rests in its sovereignty.'

[7] *Case of the S.S. "Lotus"*, Judgment No. 9 of 7 September 1927, Series A.—No. 10, 20–21.

[8] *Case of the S.S. "Lotus"*, Judgment No. 9 of 7 September 1927, Series A.—No. 10, 22.

the collision on board the *Boz-Kourt*, did not exist.[9] On a similar ground, the Court rejected the second argument, considering that a ship may be assimilated to national territory and that there is no rule of international law prohibiting a State from regarding an offence producing effects in its territory as having been committed in its territory.[10] The Court also rejected the third argument, finding it impossible to identify, on the basis of an inconsistent practice of collision cases before national courts, a rule of international law according to which the State whose flag is flown has exclusive jurisdiction in collision cases.[11]

Observing that a rule of public international law limiting the freedom of Turkey to assume concurrent criminal jurisdiction with respect to Lieutenant Demons could not be identified, the PCIJ concluded, consistent with its adherence to the framework of obligation, that Turkey was free to assume concurrent criminal jurisdiction with respect to Lieutenant Demons.[12] The PCIJ further observed that this conclusion was also in accordance with the requirements of justice. According to the Court, limiting the jurisdiction of either State to those parts of the collision which happened on board the respective ships, or recognizing the exclusive jurisdiction of either flag State with respect to the collision as a whole would not be in accordance with the requirements of justice and protect effectively the interests of the two States involved. Therefore, Turkey could assume concurrent

---

[9] *Case of the S.S. "Lotus"*, Judgment No. 9 of 7 September 1927, Series A.—No. 10, 22–23: '[T]he Court does not think it necessary to consider the contention that a State cannot punish offences committed abroad by a foreigner simply by reason of the nationality of the victim. For this contention only relates to the case where the nationality of the victim is the only criterion on which the criminal jurisdiction of the State is based. Even if that argument were correct generally speaking—and in regard to this the Court reserves its opinion—it could only be used in the present case if international law forbade Turkey to take into consideration the fact that the offence produced its effects on the Turkish vessel and consequently in a place assimilated to Turkish territory in which the application of Turkish criminal law cannot be challenged, even in regard to offences committed there by foreigners. But no such rule of international law exists.'

[10] *Case of the S.S. "Lotus"*, Judgment No. 9 of 7 September 1927, Series A.—No. 10, 25: 'If, therefore, a guilty act committed on the high seas produces its effects on a vessel flying another flag or in foreign territory, the same principles must be applied as if the territories of two different States were concerned, and the conclusion must therefore be drawn that there is no rule of international law prohibiting the State to which the ship on which the effects of the offence have taken place belongs, from regarding the offence as having been committed in its territory and prosecuting, accordingly, the delinquent.'

[11] *Case of the S.S. "Lotus"*, Judgment No. 9 of 7 September 1927, Series A.—No. 10, 29: 'It will suffice to observe that, as municipal jurisprudence is thus divided, it is hardly possible to see in it an indication of the existence of the restrictive rule of international law which alone could serve as a basis of the contention of the French Government.'

[12] *Case of the S.S. "Lotus"*, Judgment No. 9 of 7 September 1927, Series A.—No. 10, 31: 'It must therefore be held that there is no principle of international law, within the meaning of Article 15 of the Convention of Lausanne of July 24th, 1923, which precludes the institution of the criminal proceedings under consideration. Consequently, Turkey, by instituting, in virtue of the discretion which international law leaves to every sovereign State, the criminal proceedings in question, has not, in the absence of such principles, acted in a manner contrary to the principles of international law within the meaning of the special agreement.'

criminal jurisdiction with respect to the collision as a whole.[13] The PCIJ thus added a justification to the result it had arrived at on the basis of the assumption of a freedom of States to act.[14]

According to Castberg, this justification demonstrated that in the process of deduction of a special norm (the right of a State to exercise its jurisdiction with respect to a collision on the high seas between ships of different nationalities) from a general principle of international law (the general faculty of States to exercise jurisdiction whenever this was not prohibited by rules of international law) the appreciation of what serves best the legitimate interests of the international community is decisive.[15] Leaving aside the question whether the legitimate interests of the international community corresponded to the requirements of justice and the effective protection of the interests of the States involved, it may be observed that such a justification is inconsistent with the framework of obligation. Within this framework, the establishment of a right does not depend on justification; the right of a State to act is assumed in the absence of a rule of public international law limiting that right to act. Invoking the justification would seem to involve relying, to that extent, on the framework of authorization previously, and more or less implicitly, rejected by the Court.

The Judgment of the Court was adopted on the basis of the votes of President Huber and Judges De Bustamante, Oda, Anzilotti, Pessôa, and Feïzi-Daïm Bey. Former President Loder, Vice-President Weiss, Lord Finlay and Judges Nyholm, Moore, and Altamira voted against the Judgment. The votes thus being equally divided, the casting vote of President Huber was decisive. It must be remarked, however, that Judge Moore concurred in adhering to the framework of obligation. Referring to Article 15 of the Convention respecting conditions of residence and business and jurisdiction, Judge Moore considered that the relevant question was whether an independent State is forbidden by public international law to institute criminal proceedings against the officer of a ship of another nationality in respect of a collision on the high seas by which one of its own ships was sunk and lives of

---

[13] *Case of the S.S. "Lotus"*, Judgment No. 9 of 7 September 1927, Series A.—No. 10, 30–31: 'The conclusion at which the Court has therefore arrived is that there is no rule of international law in regard to collision cases to the effect that criminal proceedings are exclusively within the jurisdiction of the State whose flag is flown. This conclusion moreover is easily explained if the manner in which the collision brings the jurisdiction of two different countries into play be considered. The offence for which Lieutenant Demons appears to have been prosecuted was an act—of negligence or imprudence—having its origin on board the *Lotus*, while its effects made themselves felt on board the *Boz-Kourt*. These two elements are, legally, entirely inseparable, so much so that their separation renders the offence non-existent. Neither the exclusive jurisdiction of either State, nor the limitations of the jurisdiction of each to the occurrences which took place on the respective ships would appear calculated to satisfy the requirements of justice and effectively to protect the interests of the two States. It is only natural that each should be able to exercise jurisdiction and to do so in respect of the incident as a whole. It is therefore a case of concurrent jurisdiction.'

[14] Lauterpacht 1933, Chap. IV, para 18; Siorat 1958, paras 475–477.

[15] Castberg 1933, p. 358.

persons on board were lost.[16] There were thus five judges who rejected the framework of obligation: Former President Loder, Vice-President Weiss, Lord Finlay, Judge Nyholm, and Judge Altamira.

Supporting the exclusive criminal jurisdiction of France, Lord Finlay adhered to the framework of authorization. Lord Finlay considered that it would be unfair to require France to produce a rule of public international law forbidding the assumption of criminal jurisdiction by Turkey. According to Lord Finlay, in the absence of a principle of international law, consisting of the consent of other States, conferring such power, Turkey could not assume criminal jurisdiction with respect to Lieutenant Demons.[17]

Judges Loder, Weiss, Nyholm, and Altamira supported the exclusive criminal jurisdiction of France on the basis of the principle of territorial sovereignty[18] and the freedom of the seas.[19] In support of this position, Judges Loder, Weiss, and

---

[16] *Case of the S.S. "Lotus"*, Judgment No. 9 of 7 September 1927, Dissenting Opinion Judge Moore, Series A.—No. 10, 67: 'When Article 15 speaks of 'the principles of international law', it means the principles of international law as they exist between independent and sovereign States. It evidently was intended to recognize the right of Turkey to exercise her judicial jurisdiction as an independent and sovereign State, except so far as the exercise of national jurisdiction is limited by the mutual obligations of States under the Law of Nations. (...) I will next consider the broad question submitted under the *compromis* as to whether Turkey violated the principles of international law by instituting criminal proceedings in the present case, and it is obvious that, under the interpretation I have given to Article 15 of the Lausanne Convention, this question in effect is, whether an independent State is forbidden by international law to institute criminal proceedings against the officer of a ship of another nationality in respect of a collision on the high seas, by which one of its own ships was sunk and lives of persons on board were lost.'

[17] *Case of the S.S. "Lotus"*, Judgment No. 9 of 7 September 1927, Dissenting Opinion Lord Finlay, Series A.—No. 10, 52: 'The first point with which the Court has to deal is this: What is the exact meaning of the question put in the *compromis: La Turquie a-t-elle agi en contradiction des principes du droit international?* It has been argued for Turkey that this question implies that France, in order to succeed, must point to some definite rule of international law forbidding what Turkey did. I am unable to read the *compromis* in this sense. What it asks is simply whether the Turkish Courts had jurisdiction to try and punish Demons; if international law authorizes this, the question would be answered in the affirmative, otherwise in the negative. The *compromis* cannot, with any fairness, be read so as to require France to produce some definite rule forbidding what was done by Turkey. If the Turkish proceedings were not authorized by international law, Turkey acted *en contradiction des principes du droit international.* (...) The question is put in the *compromis* with perfect fairness as between the two countries and the attempt to torture it into meaning that France must produce a rule forbidding what Turkey did arises from a misconception. The question is whether the principles of international law authorize what Turkey did in this matter.'

[18] *Case of the S.S. "Lotus"*, Judgment No. 9 of 7 September 1927, Dissenting Opinion Judge Loder, Series A.—No. 10, 35–36; Dissenting Opinion Judge Weiss, 44–45, 49; Dissenting Opinion Judge Nyholm, 59–63; Dissenting Opinion Judge Altamira, 95–104.

[19] *Case of the S.S. "Lotus"*, Judgment No. 9 of 7 September 1927, Dissenting Opinion Judge Weiss, Series A.—No. 10, 45–46, 49.

Nyholm considered that the offence which might have caused the collision should be localized on board the *Lotus*.[20]

On the basis of the reasoning in the Judgment and the Dissenting Opinions, as described above, a number of observations may be made with respect to the incoherence of the framework of obligation and the framework of authorization.

As regards the framework of obligation, although the principles of international law referred to in Article 15 of the Convention respecting conditions of residence, business, and jurisdiction were applicable to Turkey, the identification by the Court of a rule of public international law restricting the freedom of Turkey to assume concurrent jurisdiction would have met the obstacle that—even if State practice had not been divided—it would have been inconsistent with the exercise of the free will of Turkey manifested in the assumption of concurrent jurisdiction. In so far, it would seem that the examination conducted by the Court could not have been fruitful. The assumption underlying the Court's examination—that such a principle would have been binding—resulted from its adherence to the framework of obligation.

On the other hand, as the Court observed, adherence to the framework of authorization has a paralyzing effect in the absence of an identifiable rule of public international law.[21] Moreover, if the relevant rules of public international law are seen as emanating from the consent of other States, as suggested by Lord Finlay,[22] this would amount to subjecting the power of a State to act to the free will of other States and would be inconsistent with the mutual exclusivity of the framework of obligation and the framework of authorization. Similarly, the position adopted by Judge Altamira, that a freedom of States to assume criminal jurisdiction must be limited by the consent of other States,[23] seems to subject the freedom of that State to the freedom to act of those other States. Moreover, within the framework of obligation, the limitation of a freedom of a State to act can only emanate from an exercise of the freedom to act of that State.

As noted, the Court arrived at the result of concurrent jurisdiction in respect of the incident as a whole on the basis of the assumption of a freedom to act of Turkey in the absence of a restrictive rule of public international law, supported by the requirements of justice, which rule out the exclusive jurisdiction of either State

---

[20] *Case of the S.S. "Lotus"*, Judgment No. 9 of 7 September 1927, Dissenting Opinion Judge Loder, Series A.—No. 10, 36–37; Dissenting Opinion Judge Weiss, 47–48; Dissenting Opinion Judge Nyholm, 61.

[21] *Case of the S.S. "Lotus"*, Judgment No. 9 of 7 September 1927, Series A.—No. 10, 19–20.

[22] *Case of the S.S. "Lotus"*, Judgment No. 9 of 7 September 1927, Dissenting Opinion Lord Finlay, Series A.—No. 10, 56–58.

[23] *Case of the S.S. "Lotus"*, Judgment No. 9 of 7 September 1927, Dissenting Opinion Judge Altamira, Series A.—No. 10, 103: 'In my opinion, the freedom which, according to the argument put forward, every State enjoys to impose its own laws relating to jurisdiction upon foreigners is and must be subject to limitations. In the case of competing claims to jurisdiction such as those in question (according to those who recognize the existence of such competition), this freedom is conditioned by the existence of the express or tacit consent of other States and particularly of the foreign State directly interested.'

in respect of the collision as a whole or the restriction of the jurisdiction of the States involved to those parts of the incident that happened on board of the respective vessels. In the Court's view, upholding the exclusive jurisdiction of France in respect of the incident as a whole would unfairly have precluded Turkey from exercising its jurisdiction in respect of an incident affecting its interests.

This conclusion assumes that the result of concurrent jurisdiction in respect of the incident as a whole reconciles the interests of the States involved. It may be observed, however, that the solution of concurrent jurisdiction is too comprehensive as it comprises both the concurrent jurisdiction of France and the concurrent jurisdiction of Turkey in respect of the incident as a whole, without coordinating them. Furthermore, the contention of France that it had exclusive jurisdiction in respect of the incident as a whole contradicted the conclusion of the Court that concurrent jurisdiction in respect of the incident as a whole effectively protected the interests of both States. In effect, the freedom of France to act and exercise exclusive jurisdiction in respect of the incident as a whole was limited, not by a rule of public international law restricting that freedom to act, but by the recognition of concurrent jurisdiction in respect of the incident as a whole as inherent in the freedom to act of Turkey and as justified by the requirements of justice. The Court in fact inferred, in other words, a freedom to assume concurrent jurisdiction in respect of maritime incidents from the freedom of the seas.

The main point that may be retained is that, while the PCIJ fully endorsed the framework of obligation, it based the result arrived at both on the concepts of sovereignty and independence and on the requirements of justice. In this way, it attempted, in the words of Kennedy, 'to make the soft (justice) lie down with the hard (freedom to act)'.[24] Thus, while adhering to the framework of obligation, the PCIJ in the same judgment transcended that framework and adopted a form of practical reasoning, adjoining considerations of justice to the concepts of sovereignty and independence.

It may be added that, although in the *Case of the S.S. "Lotus"* the PCIJ was clearly presented by the parties with the choice between the framework of obligation and the framework of authorization, it had in fact in its jurisprudence already adhered to the framework of obligation.[25] In *Nationality Decrees Issued in Tunis and Morocco (French Zone)*, the Court gave its opinion to the Council of the League of Nations as to whether a dispute between Great Britain and France concerning nationality decrees issued in Tunis and Morocco fell, as contended by France, outside the competence of the Council by virtue of Article 15, para 8, of the Covenant of the League of Nations, which read:

> If the dispute between the parties is claimed by one of them, and is found by the Council, to arise out of a matter which by international law is solely within the domestic jurisdiction of that party, the Council shall so report, and shall make no recommendation as to its settlement.

---

[24] Kennedy 1987, p. 86.

[25] Klabbers 1998, pp. 349–351.

In the course of its reasoning, the PCIJ famously remarked:

> The words "solely within the domestic jurisdiction" seem (…) to contemplate certain matters which, though they may very closely concern the interests of more than one State, are not, in principle, regulated by international law. As regards such matters, each State is sole judge.
>
> The question whether a certain matter is or is not solely within the jurisdiction of a State is an essentially relative question; it depends upon the development of international relations. Thus, in the present state of international law, questions of nationality are, in the opinion of the Court, in principle within this reserved domain.
>
> For the purpose of the present opinion, it is enough to observe that it may well happen that, in a matter which, like that of nationality, is not, in principle, regulated by international law, the right of a State to use its discretion is nevertheless restricted by obligations which it may have undertaken towards other States. In such a case, jurisdiction which, in principle, belongs solely to the State, is limited by rules of international law. Article 15, paragraph 8, then ceases to apply as regards those States which are entitled to invoke such rules, and the dispute as to the question whether a State has or has not the right to take certain measures becomes in these circumstances a dispute of an international character and falls outside the scope of the exception contained in this paragraph. To hold that a State has not exclusive jurisdiction does not in any way prejudice the final decision as to whether that State has a right to adopt such measures.[26]

The Court had thereby already adhered to the framework of obligation, transforming the domestic jurisdiction of a State into a freedom to act by the absence of regulation by public international law and transforming the freedoms to act of other States into interests. From this perspective, as long as States had not created public international law, international relations did not exist; the conflict of freedoms to act inherent in a structure of sovereign equality could only be accounted for by differentiating between interests and domestic jurisdiction. The establishment of international relations in the form of public international law was, from this perspective, in fact, a harmonization of the conflicting freedoms to act inherent in the structure of sovereign equality, which, however, would always be insufficient, because it would always be based upon an exercise of that same freedom to act.

The next section is intended to show, first, that the problematique formed by the dichotomy between the framework of obligation and the framework of authorization is not something peculiar to the interbellum, but equally pervasive in the jurisprudence of the ICJ and, second, that in a structure of sovereign equality, no freedoms to act can be imputed to States so that, rather than envisaging a transition from domestic jurisdiction to public international law and international relations, both public international law and international politics must be regarded as inherent in a structure of sovereign equality.

---

[26] *Nationality Decrees Issued in Tunis and Morocco (French Zone)*, Advisory Opinion of 7 February 1923, Series B.—No. 4, 23–24.

3.3 The Framework of Obligation and the Framework of Authorization Considered in *Legality of the Threat or Use of Nuclear Weapons*

In resolution 49/75 K, adopted on 15 December 1994, the UN General Assembly requested the ICJ to give an advisory opinion on the following question:

> Is the threat or use of nuclear weapons in any circumstance permitted under international law?[27]

In its Advisory Opinion delivered in response to this question, *Legality of the Threat or Use of Nuclear Weapons*, the ICJ observed that the interpretation of the word 'permitted' in the question put by the General Assembly had been disputed between the States appearing before the Court. The Nuclear Weapon States (NWS) had argued that States have a freedom to act, including the use or threat of use of nuclear weapons, in the absence of a rule of public international law limiting that freedom to act. Accordingly, the relevant question was whether a prohibition of the use or threat of use of nuclear weapons could be identified in conventional international law or customary international law. In the absence of such a prohibition, it would have to be concluded that the use or threat of use of nuclear weapons is permitted under public international law. The Non-Nuclear Weapon States (NNWS) had argued that States do not have a power to use or threaten the use of nuclear weapons in the absence of a rule of public international law conferring such power. Accordingly, the relevant question was whether an authorization of the use or threat of use of nuclear weapons could be identified in conventional international law or customary international law. In the absence of such an authorization, it would have to be concluded that the use or threat of use of nuclear weapons is not permitted under public international law.[28] Thereby, the NWS adhered to the framework of obligation and the NNWS adhered to the framework of authorization. An exact parallel may be drawn between these positions and the positions adopted by Turkey and France, respectively, in the *Case of the S.S. "Lotus"*. Put differently, the NWS argued that the word 'permitted' should be understood in the weak sense, which means that an act is permitted if a rule prohibiting that act cannot be identified. In contrast, the NNWS argued that the word 'permitted' should be understood in the strong sense, which means that an act is permitted if a rule permitting that act can be identified.

With respect to this question, the ICJ noted that both the NWS and the NNWS appearing before the Court recognized that their freedom to act was restricted by the principles and rules of international law, in particular the principles and rules of international humanitarian law. Therefore, according to the Court, the argument concerning the use of the word 'permitted', as well as the related question of the

[27] General Assembly resolution 49/75 K.

[28] *Legality of the Threat or Use of Nuclear Weapons*, Advisory Opinion of 8 July 1996, ICJ Reports 1996, 226, para 21.

burden of proof, was irrelevant.[29] At this point, it may be observed, however, that this response did not really answer the contention of the NNWS. Whether the NWS recognized that their freedom to act was restricted by the principles and rules of international law was irrelevant if the question whether the use or threat of use of nuclear weapons was permitted under international law had to be answered within the framework of authorization. Within the framework of authorization, it would have been incumbent on the NWS to prove the existence of a rule of public international law permitting the use or threat of use of nuclear weapons. Within the framework of obligation, it was for the NNWS to prove the existence of a rule of public international law restricting the freedom to use or threaten the use of nuclear weapons. The question of the burden of proof was thus intimately connected to the choice between the framework of obligation and the framework of authorization.

Subsequently, the Court examined the question put to it in the light of what it considered to be the most directly relevant applicable law: the law relating to the use of force contained in the Charter of the United Nations and the law applicable in armed conflict as well as conventional international law relating specifically to nuclear weapons.[30] At the beginning of its examination of the law applicable in situations of armed conflict, the Court returned to the function of rules of public international law, noting that conventional international law and customary international law do not contain a prescription authorizing the use or threat of use of nuclear weapons. At the same time, it noted the absence of a principle or rule of international law making the legality of the use or threat of use of nuclear weapons dependent on an authorization. The Court observed that the practice of States showed that the illegality of the use of nuclear weapons would not be dependent on the absence of authorization, but would be dependent on a prohibition.[31] It would seem that the Court did not take into consideration the relevance of a principle or

[29] *Legality of the Threat or Use of Nuclear Weapons*, Advisory Opinion of 8 July 1996, ICJ Reports 1996, 226, para 22: 'The Court notes that the nuclear-weapon States appearing before it either accepted, or did not dispute, that their independence to act was indeed restricted by the principles and rules of international law, more particularly humanitarian law, as did the other States which took part in the proceedings. Hence, the argument concerning the legal conclusions to be drawn from the use of the word "permitted", and the conclusions of burden of proof to which it was said to give rise, are without particular significance for the disposition of the issues before the Court.'

[30] *Legality of the Threat or Use of Nuclear Weapons*, Advisory Opinion of 8 July 1996, ICJ Reports 1996, 226, para 34.

[31] *Legality of the Threat or Use of Nuclear Weapons*, Advisory Opinion of 8 July 1996, ICJ Reports 1996, 226, para 52: 'The Court notes (...) that international customary and treaty law does not contain any specific prescription authorizing the threat or use of nuclear weapons or any other weapon in general or in certain circumstances, in particular those of the exercise of legitimate self-defence. Nor, however, is there any principle or rule of international law which would make the legality of the threat or use of nuclear weapons or of any other weapons dependent on a specific authorization. State practice shows that the illegality of the use of certain weapons as such does not result from an absence of authorization but, on the contrary, is formulated in terms of prohibition.'

rule of international law making the legality of the use or threat of use of nuclear weapons dependent on the absence of prohibition. The practice of States as such was apparently the determining factor in identifying the appropriate framework.

In its examination of the principles and rules of international humanitarian law, the Court identified two cardinal principles: (i) the principle which prohibits making civilians the object of attack and the use of weapons which cannot discriminate between civilian and military targets; and (ii) the principle which prohibits causing unnecessary suffering to combatants. With respect to these principles, the Court considered that it could not determine whether the use or threat of use of nuclear weapons would necessarily be prohibited.[32]

In its examination of the law relating to the use of force, the Court referred to the prohibition of the use or threat of use of force contained in Article 2, para 4, of the Charter of the United Nations and the exception in the form of the right of self-defence contained in Article 51 of the Charter of the United Nations.[33] With respect to the right of self-defence, the Court identified the requirements of necessity and proportionality as emanating from a rule of customary international law.[34] The Court concluded that the principle of proportionality does not in itself exclude the use or threat of use of nuclear weapons in self-defence in all circumstances.[35]

The results of the examination whether the law relating to the use of force, the law applicable in armed conflict, and conventional international law relating specifically to nuclear weapons contained a prohibition of the use or threat of use of nuclear weapons were set out by the Court as follows:

A. There is in neither customary nor conventional international law any specific authorization of the threat or use of nuclear weapons;
B. There is in neither customary nor conventional international law any comprehensive and universal prohibition of the threat or use of nuclear weapons as such;
C. A threat or use of force by means of nuclear weapons that is contrary to Article 2, paragraph 4, of the United Nations Charter and that fails to meet all the requirements of Article 51, is unlawful;
D. A threat or use of nuclear weapons should also be compatible with the requirements of the international law applicable in armed conflict, particularly those of the principles and rules of international humanitarian law, as well as with specific obligations under treaties and other undertakings which expressly deal with nuclear weapons;
E. It follows from the above-mentioned requirements that the threat or use of nuclear weapons would generally be contrary to the rules of international law applicable in armed conflict, and in particular the principles and rules of humanitarian law;

---

[32] *Legality of the Threat or Use of Nuclear Weapons*, Advisory Opinion of 8 July 1996, ICJ Reports 1996, 226, paras 78, 95–97.

[33] *Case Concerning Military and Paramilitary Activities in and against Nicaragua (Merits)*, Judgment of 27 June 1986, ICJ Reports 1986, 14, para 193.

[34] *Case Concerning Military and Paramilitary Activities in and against Nicaragua (Merits)*, Judgment of 27 June 1986, ICJ Reports 1986, 14, para 194; *Case Concerning Oil Platforms (Merits)*, Judgment of 6 November 2003, ICJ Reports 2003, 161, paras 74, 76.

[35] *Legality of the Threat or Use of Nuclear Weapons*, Advisory Opinion of 8 July 1996, ICJ Reports 1996, 226, paras 37–42.

> However, in view of the current state of international law, and of the elements of fact at its disposal, the Court cannot conclude definitively whether the threat or use of nuclear weapons would be lawful or unlawful in an extreme circumstance of self-defence, in which the very survival of a State would be at stake; (…)[36]

The Declarations, Separate Opinions, and Dissenting Opinions appended to the Advisory Opinion reveal that the Judges of the Court had radically diverging views as regards the meaning and implications of this *dispositif.*

Judges Herczegh, Ferrari Bravo, Weeramantry, and Koroma considered that public international law prohibits the use or threat of use of nuclear weapons. According to their Declarations, Judge Herczegh, and Judge Ferrari Bravo were satisfied that this could be deduced from para E.[37] In contrast, the Dissenting Opinions of Judge Weeramantry and Judge Koroma are based on the view that this did not necessarily follow from para E.[38] Judge Shahabuddeen was of the view that the Court could have held that the use or threat of use of nuclear weapons is illegal under public international law.[39]

In view of the fact that the *jus ad bellum* consists of both a rule prohibiting the use or threat of use of force and a right of self-defence, and that the *jus in bello* consists of both principles and rules of humanity and considerations of military necessity, Vice-President Schwebel and Judges Higgins and Fleischhauer considered that the legality of the use or threat of use of nuclear weapons would be dependent on proportionality or balancing between the different elements involved. On that basis, the legality of the use or threat of use of nuclear weapons would have to be admitted in certain circumstances.[40]

In this respect, President Bedjaoui considered that a freedom to act could not be deduced from subpara E, emphasizing that, in view of the uncertainties surrounding the law and the facts, the Court did not find the use or threat of use of nuclear weapons to be either legal or illegal.[41] In contrast, Judge Guillaume

---

[36] *Legality of the Threat or Use of Nuclear Weapons*, Advisory Opinion of 8 July 1996, ICJ Reports 1996, 226, para 105.

[37] *Legality of the Threat or Use of Nuclear Weapons*, Advisory Opinion of 8 July 1996, Declaration Judge Herczegh, ICJ Reports 1996, 226, Declaration Judge Ferrari Bravo.

[38] *Legality of the Threat or Use of Nuclear Weapons*, Advisory Opinion of 8 July 1996, Dissenting Opinion Judge Weeramantry, ICJ Reports 1996, 226, 476–477, 497–500, 513; Dissenting Opinion Judge Koroma, 556, 562–563, 570–571, 580–581.

[39] *Legality of the Threat or Use of Nuclear Weapons*, Advisory Opinion of 8 July 1996, Dissenting Opinion Judge Shahabuddeen, ICJ Reports 1996, 226, 402–403, 411.

[40] *Legality of the Threat or Use of Nuclear Weapons*, Advisory Opinion of 8 July 1996, Separate Opinion Judge Fleischhauer, ICJ Reports 1996, 226, para 5; Dissenting Opinion Vice-President Schwebel, 320–323; Dissenting Opinion Judge Higgins, 12–18, 19–24.

[41] *Legality of the Threat or Use of Nuclear Weapons*, Advisory Opinion of 8 July 1996, Declaration President Bedjaoui, ICJ Reports 1996, 226, paras 11–15, 14: 'In the present Opinion (…) the Court does not find the threat or use of nuclear weapons to be either legal or illegal; from the uncertainties surrounding the law and the facts it does not infer any freedom to take a position. Nor does it suggest that such license could in any way be deduced therefrom. Whereas the Permanent Court gave the green light of authorization, having found in international law no

deduced that the Court should have concluded that States have a freedom to act if the law is silent. If the Court could not identify a comprehensive and universal prohibition of the use or threat of use of nuclear weapons, it should, according to Judge Guillaume, have deferred to the freedom of States to act.[42] Judges Shahabudeen and Koroma adopted a similar interpretation of para E.[43]

Concerning the relation between the right of a State to survival and international humanitarian law, President Bedjaoui observed that self-defence may not produce a situation in which a State would exonerate itself from complying with intransgressible norms of international humanitarian law. Therefore, according to President Bedjaoui, in certain circumstances, a collision may arise between fundamental principles, neither of which can take precedence over the other. Because the use or threat of use of nuclear weapons by a State, in circumstances in which the survival of that State is in question, may endanger the survival of humanity, the survival of that State cannot take precedence over the survival of humanity.[44]

Judge Shahabuddeen, considering it unacceptable to arrive at a right which would result in the extinction of humanity, dealt extensively with the question how such a result, which seemed to flow from the reasoning of the PCIJ in the *Case of the S.S. "Lotus"*, could be avoided. Judge Shahabuddeen examined four solutions that the Court could have adopted.[45]

A first solution, proceeding on the basis of the reasoning in the *Case of the S.S. "Lotus"*, would involve an interpretation of Articles 2, para 4, and 51 of the Charter of the United Nations, according to which an act leading to the extinction of humanity cannot be considered as an act of self-defence, so that it would be prohibited by Article 2, para 4, of the Charter of the United Nations.[46] Similarly, according to a second solution, proceeding on the basis of the reasoning in the *Case of the S.S. "Lotus"*, a right of a State inconsistent with the assumption that

(Footnote 41 continued)
reason for giving the red light of prohibition, the present Court does not feel able to give a signal either way.'

[42] *Legality of the Threat or Use of Nuclear Weapons*, Advisory Opinion of 8 July 1996, Separate Opinion Judge Guillaume, ICJ Reports 1996, 226, paras 5, 9: 'In operative para 2 E the Court decided in fact that it could not in those extreme circumstances conclude definitely whether the threat or use of nuclear weapons would be lawful or unlawful. In other words, it concluded that in such circumstances the law provided no guidance for States. But if the law is silent in this case, States remain free to act as they intend.'

[43] *Legality of the Threat or Use of Nuclear Weapons*, Advisory Opinion of 8 July 1996, Dissenting Opinion Judge Shahabuddeen, ICJ Reports 1996, 226, 426; Dissenting Opinion Judge Koroma, 559–560.

[44] *Legality of the Threat or Use of Nuclear Weapons*, Advisory Opinion of 8 July 1996, Declaration President Bedjaoui, ICJ Reports 1996, 226, paras 19–22.

[45] *Legality of the Threat or Use of Nuclear Weapons*, Advisory Opinion of 8 July 1996, Dissenting Opinion Judge Shahabuddeen, ICJ Reports 1996, 226, 391–392.

[46] *Legality of the Threat or Use of Nuclear Weapons*, Advisory Opinion of 8 July 1996, Dissenting Opinion Judge Shahabuddeen, ICJ Reports 1996, 226, 392.

humanity would continue would be inconsistent with the Charter of the United Nations.[47]

According to a fourth solution, which Judge Shahabuddeen retained and which, for purposes of exposition, will be dealt with before the third solution, a right to use or threaten with the use of nuclear weapons would be dependent on an authorization from public international law, which Judge Shahabuddeen considered to be absent.[48] Judge Shahabuddeen thus ultimately adhered to the framework of authorization propounded by the NNWS. Judge Shahabuddeen thereby took the position that had been taken by Lord Finlay in the *Case of the S.S. "Lotus"*. Significantly, however, Judge Shahabuddeen also considered a framework that went beyond the dichotomy between the framework of obligation and the framework of authorization.

In a third solution, proceeding on the basis of the reasoning in the *Case of the S.S. "Lotus"*, Judge Shahabuddeen regarded a freedom of States to act, including a freedom to use or threaten with the use of nuclear weapons, as not extending to acts which cannot form the subject of a right, such as an act which could destroy humanity and thus the basis on which States exist and, consequently, the basis on which rights and obligations exist within the international community. In particular, Judge Shahabuddeen considered that such a freedom would be inconsistent with the sovereignty of other States. Developing this argument, Judge Shahabuddeen situated the concept of sovereignty within an objective structural framework, itself defined by the concept of sovereignty, which places limits on the rights of States.[49]

---

[47] *Legality of the Threat or Use of Nuclear Weapons*, Advisory Opinion of 8 July 1996, Dissenting Opinion Judge Shahabuddeen, ICJ Reports 1996, 226, 392.

[48] *Legality of the Threat or Use of Nuclear Weapons*, Advisory Opinion of 8 July 1996, Dissenting Opinion Judge Shahabuddeen, ICJ Reports 1996, 226, 394–397.

[49] *Legality of the Threat or Use of Nuclear Weapons*, Advisory Opinion of 8 July 1996, Dissenting Opinion Judge Shahabuddeen, ICJ Reports 1996, 226, 392–394: 'The existence of a number of sovereignties side by side places limits on the freedom of each State to act as if the others did not exist. These limits define an objective structural framework within which sovereignty must necessarily exist; the framework, and its defining limits, are implicit in the reference in "*Lotus*" to "co-existing independent communities" (…) Thus, however far-reaching may be the rights conferred by sovereignty, those rights cannot extend beyond the framework within which sovereignty itself exists; in particular, they cannot violate the framework. The framework shuts out the right of a State to embark on a course of action which would dismantle the basis of the framework by putting an end to civilization and annihilating mankind. It is not that a State is prohibited from exercising a right which, but for the prohibition, it would have; a State can have no such right to begin with. So a prior question in this case is this: even if there is no prohibition, is there anything in the sovereignty of a State which would entitle it to embark on a course of action which could effectively wipe out the existence of all States by ending civilisation and annihilating mankind? An affirmative answer is not reasonable; that sovereignty could not include such a right is suggested by the fact that the acting State would be one of the (…) "co-existing independent communities", with a consequential duty to respect the sovereignty of other States. It is difficult for the Court to uphold a proposition that, absent a prohibition, a State has a right in law to act in ways which could deprive the sovereignty of all other States of meaning.'

Judges Weeramantry and Koroma developed a similar argument, arguing that inferring a freedom to act from the concept of sovereignty, including a freedom to use or threaten with the use of nuclear weapons, would be incoherent with the concept of sovereignty itself.[50]

On the basis of the reasoning in the Advisory Opinion, Declarations, Separate Opinions, and Dissenting Opinions, several observations with respect to the incoherence of the framework of obligation and the framework of authorization may be made.

According to the framework of obligation, the question of the illegality or legality of the use or threat of use of nuclear weapons was dependent on the presence of a rule of public international law containing a prohibition. In view of the balancing nature of international humanitarian law (humanitarian considerations/military necessity) and of the rule/exception structure that the Court identified in the law relating to the use of force (prohibition/self-defence), the Court could not *in abstracto* have identified a prohibition. In this respect, it can indeed be said, with President Bedjaoui, that the Court gave neither a red nor a green light. It was not that a relevant rule of public international law could not be identified. There was applicable law, but the question of the illegality or legality of the use or threat of use of nuclear weapons would turn on the interpretation and application of that law in a particular case.

Nevertheless, as Vice-President Schwebel and Judges Fleischhauer and Higgins seem to have suggested, in view of that same structure of public international law, it would necessarily follow that in certain extreme circumstances the use or threat of use of nuclear weapons would neither be unnecessary or indiscriminate nor be incompatible with the principle of proportionality.[51] In the two subparagraphs of para E the Court expressed this more reluctantly, stating, on the one hand, the view that the use or threat of use of nuclear weapons would 'generally' be contrary to the rules of international law applicable in armed conflict and in particular with the principles and rules of humanitarian law, and adding, on the other hand, the qualification that, in view of the current state of international law, and of the elements of fact at its disposal, it could not conclude definitively whether the use or threat of use of nuclear weapons would be unlawful or lawful in ultimate self-defence. If, however, in the presence of those extreme facts, the only remaining ambiguity related to the 'current state of international law', then there would indeed be silence of the law. Within the context of the framework of obligation, such silence must be understood as the absence of prohibition. Consequently, the

---

[50] *Legality of the Threat or Use of Nuclear Weapons*, Advisory Opinion of 8 July 1996, Dissenting Opinion Judge Weeramantry, ICJ Reports 1996, 226, 494–496: 'It is implicit in "*Lotus*" that the sovereignty of other States should be respected. One of the characteristics of nuclear weapons is that they violate the sovereignty of other countries who have in no way consented to the intrusion upon their fundamental sovereign rights, which is implicit in the use of the nuclear weapon.'; Dissenting Opinion Judge Koroma, 576.

[51] McDougal and Feliciano 1987, pp. 269–274, 309–317; Akande 1997, pp. 212–215.

position of the Court would have to result, as Judge Guillaume observed, in a freedom to act, a weak permission.

Thus, whether the law was regarded as clear or whether the law was regarded as silent, the resulting conclusion would have to be that in certain extreme circumstances the use or threat of use of nuclear weapons could not be regarded as prohibited by rules of public international law. Whether the freedom to act was restricted by rules of public international law would turn on 'balancing' and on the interpretation of the requirements of necessity and proportionality.

From a wider perspective, it may be observed that pursuant to the analysis conducted within the framework of obligation, the question of the legality or illegality of the use or threat of use of nuclear weapons is essentially regarded as a bilateral issue between an attacking State and a defending State. From the perspective of the framework of obligation, a State attacked by nuclear weapons or threatened with attack by nuclear weapons cannot be denied the right to defend itself by the use of nuclear weapons or the threat of use of nuclear weapons. Yet, admitting such a right at the same time endangers the interests or existence of the other members of the international community. The analyses of President Bejaoui and Judges Koroma, Weeramantry and Shahabuddeen therefore focused on humanity or international society.

A curious point in this respect is that the Court, while referring to the law of neutrality when outlining the applicable law of armed conflict,[52] did not apply it to the use or threat of use of nuclear weapons.[53] Judge Shahabuddeen, who did examine the question, considered that the use or threat of use of nuclear weapons would violate Article 1 of Hague Convention V, Respecting the Rights and Duties of Neutral Powers and Persons in Case of War on Land, which provides that the territory of neutral Powers is inviolable.[54]

As stated, President Bedjaoui found that the use or threat of use of nuclear weapons by a State may endanger the survival of humanity and cannot, therefore, take precedence over the survival of humanity. This view takes account of the possible effects of the use or threat of use of nuclear weapons by a State for the international community as a whole. It entails the difficulty, however, that, even if this use or threat of use cannot take precedence over the survival of humanity, the converse viewpoint also seems unacceptable. If the survival of humanity does take precedence over the use or threat of use of nuclear weapons by a State, this would mean that such a State would have to abstain from the use or threat of use of nuclear weapons, in view of the superior interests of the international community, even if it thereby ceases to be a member of that community. Nevertheless, even though a restriction of a freedom to use or threaten with the use of nuclear

52 *Legality of the Threat or Use of Nuclear Weapons*, Advisory Opinion of 8 July 1996, ICJ Reports 1996, 226, paras 51, 88–89.

53 Akande 1997, pp. 202–203.

54 *Legality of the Threat or Use of Nuclear Weapons*, Advisory Opinion of 8 July 1996, Dissenting Opinion Judge Shahabuddeen, ICJ Reports 1996, 226, 387–389.

weapons cannot be derived from this consideration, it does indicate that the fundamental interests of international society may be diametrically opposed to inferring a right from the concept of sovereignty.

The considerations developed by Judges Weeramantry and Koroma, observing that a freedom to use or threaten with the use of nuclear weapons would be inconsistent with the sovereignty of other States,[55] point in the same direction. These considerations no longer envisage the function of public international law in terms of restrictions, prohibitions, or limitations, but directly consider to what extent a freedom to act of a State infringes a freedom to act of another State and infer a limitation of that freedom to act from those other freedoms to act.

The furthest in this direction goes the third solution envisaged by Judge Shahabuddeen, which seeks the protection of the interests of international society in what approaches a reformulation of the function of public international law:

> The existence of a number of sovereignties side by side places limits on the freedom of each State to act as if the others did not exist. These limits define an objective structural framework within which sovereignty must necessarily exist (…)[56]

It is submitted that it is fruitful to go yet one step further. The formulation as presented by Judge Shahabuddeen seems to distinguish between an objective structural framework which is formed by the coexistence of sovereignties and which limits the freedom of States to act derived from the concept of sovereignty, on the one hand, and the freedom of States to act derived from the concept of sovereignty, on the other hand. To go that step further, it is submitted that, if the coexistence of sovereignties inherently limits a freedom to act derived from the concept of sovereignty, then there cannot be an inherent freedom to act in the concept of sovereignty at all.[57] Elsewhere in the same passage, Judge Shahabuddeen also notes:

---

[55] *Legality of the Threat or Use of Nuclear Weapons*, Advisory Opinion of 8 July 1996, Dissenting Opinion Judge Weeramantry, ICJ Reports 1996, 226, 494–496; Dissenting Opinion Judge Koroma, 576.

[56] *Legality of the Threat or Use of Nuclear Weapons*, Advisory Opinion of 8 July 1996, Dissenting Opinion Judge Shahabuddeen, ICJ Reports 1996, 226, 393.

[57] D'Amato 1971, pp. 179–185: 'A second line of argument [in the *Fisheries Case*] looked to the substantive question involved; Norway contended that the littoral state had the sovereign freedom of action to delimit its coastline, but the United Kingdom countered this by arguing that the principle of freedom of the seas put the onus of proof on Norway in any attempt to extend its internal waters beyond generally accepted limits. In light of the way the case progressed, and in view of the ultimate opinion by the Court, this second line of argument was a stalemate. Generally it illustrates a basic fact of international law that whenever any state claims a freedom to act, its act is impinging in some way upon the freedom of another state or of the general body of states. If this were not so—if, for instance, the issue was one arising solely within the domestic jurisdiction of a state—then by definition international law would not be involved. Thus any state's claim of freedom to act will, in some manner, restrict the freedom of action of another state, even though the other state is entitled to claim the same degree of freedom of action. There is no *a priori* freedom of action.'; Tomuschat 1999, Chap. V, paras 10, 43; Dupuy 2002, pp. 98–99.

> It is not that a State is prohibited from exercising a right which, but for the prohibition, it would have; a State can have no such right to begin with.[58]

The third solution envisaged by Judge Shahabuddeen thus goes beyond the framework of obligation. While Judge Shahabuddeen opted for the framework of authorization, it is here submitted that the mutual exclusivity of the framework of obligation and the framework of authorization may be rejected in favor of a transformation into a reformulated framework. Within that reformulated framework, States cannot have an unlimited freedom to act, because the coexistence of such unlimited freedoms would be incoherent. On the other hand, States must have a power to act, because otherwise they could not be regarded as political members of international society and the concept of public international law could not be explained by virtue of their acts. Consequently, States may be regarded as situated in a dilemma situation; they must have a power to act, which is not an unlimited freedom to act.

To this fundamental dilemma situation corresponds a reformulated function of public international law. Within the reformulated framework, the function of public international law is neither exclusively to restrict the freedom of States to act nor exclusively to confer on States powers to act, but both. Within the reformulated framework, rules of public international law must have both an enabling aspect and a limiting aspect. The enabling aspect corresponds to the dilemma situation; rules of public international law enable the members of international society to overcome their dilemma situation. Moreover, those rules of public international law are created by the members of international society themselves. At the same time, those rules of public international law contain a limiting aspect, because the members of international society cannot circumvent them by virtue of an unlimited freedom to act, which they do not have.

In light of these considerations, it may be said that the power to act of the members of international society must be directed at the constituting of international society and thereby at the common good of international society. The main point of this transformation is the removal of the mutual exclusivity of the framework of obligation and the framework of authorization. This entails that both public international law and international politics must be directed at the constituting of international society and of the common good of international society. In a way, the PCIJ also saw public international law and international politics go hand in hand when it linked the development of public international law to the establishment of international relations, but the PCIJ saw that stage as sequential to a pre-societal stage, characterized by the coexistence of domestic jurisdictions, 'harmonized' by their transformation into interests. In the reformulated framework, the members of international society constitute international society by public international law and international politics, but there is no pre-stage, no international un-society.

[58] *Legality of the Threat or Use of Nuclear Weapons*, Advisory Opinion of 8 July 1996, Dissenting Opinion Judge Shahabuddeen, ICJ Reports 1996, 226, 393.

This view entails the consequence that there is no room, within the reformulated framework, for the classical distinction between a law of peace and a law of war. On the basis of their dilemma situation, the power to act of the members of international society must be directed at the constituting of international society and at the common good of international society. This does not mean, of course, that there may not be conflicts between the members of international society. Diverging interests of the members of international society inform the constituting of international society and provide coherence to the constituting of international society. Finally, as regards the *Case of the S.S. "Lotus"*, the reformulated framework would mean that the question of jurisdiction vis-à-vis a collision on the high seas between ships of different nationalities has an inherently international character and must, as such, be addressed by both States involved. As regards *Legality of the Threat or Use of Nuclear Weapons*, the reformulated framework would mean that the question of the legality or illegality of the use or threat of use of nuclear weapons inherently affects the interests of all members of international society and must be addressed from all those angles.

3.4 Comparative Analysis and Conclusion

Both the PCIJ, in the *Case of the S.S. "Lotus"*, and the ICJ, in *Legality of the Threat or Use of Nuclear Weapons*, were confronted by States with the question whether the function of public international law conforms to the framework of obligation or the framework of authorization. Both decided that the function of public international law conforms to the framework of obligation.[59] In fact, both Courts seem to have situated their reasoning already within the framework of obligation. In determining whether the concept of public international law conforms to the framework of authorization or the framework of obligation, the PCIJ responded by saying that international law governs relations between independent States and continued to stress that binding rules must emanate from that independence. That reasoning only tangentially addressed the choice between the framework of obligation and the framework of authorization and seemed more directed at explaining the provenance of rules of public international law within the framework of obligation.

A similar observation may be made in respect of its reasoning in respect of the question whether the framework of obligation also applied to criminal jurisdiction. Observing that the identification of a permission was only relevant if public international law contained a comprehensive prohibition, the Court was already reasoning within the framework of obligation. The same applies to the reasoning

[59] The ICJ has confirmed this approach in *Accordance with International Law of the Unilateral Declaration of Independence in respect of Kosovo*, Advisory Opinion of 22 July 2010, not yet reported, paras 49–56.

of the ICJ, where it observed that it could not identify a rule of public international law which would make the legality of the use or threat of nuclear weapons dependent on the identification of a permission.

Nevertheless, it seems fair to say that the Judgment of the PCIJ reflects a much higher awareness of the importance of the issue than the Advisory Opinion of the ICJ. While the PCIJ was aware of the crucial importance of the issue, and gave serious consideration to it, the ICJ simply observed that the NWS had recognized that they were bound by the rules and principles of international humanitarian law. This was not an answer to the contention of the NNWS at all, which had argued that unless an authorization could be identified in public international law, the use or threat of use of nuclear weapons would be illegal. The observation by President Bedjaoui that the ICJ was more circumspect than the PCIJ in this regard is not borne out by the texts of the Judgment and the Advisory Opinion. The inconclusive outcome at which the ICJ arrived, in fact underlines the importance of the issue. Within the framework of obligation, the uncertainty of the law would resolve itself in the freedom of States to act. Within the framework of authorization, the uncertainty of the law would have implied the absence of a specific authorization, which the Court, in fact, established.

It is interesting to note that, in *Legality of the Threat or Use of Nuclear Weapons*, several Judges sought to avoid the consequences of the reasoning followed by the PCIJ in the *Case of the S.S. "Lotus"*. For example, President Bedjaoui distinguished that case on the basis of the nature of the problem posed, the implications of the Court's pronouncement and the underlying philosophy of the submissions upheld.[60] Judge Weeramantry emphasized that the reasoning in the *Case of the S.S. "Lotus"*, was confined to the law of peace.[61]

It is not so easy, however, to dispose of the *Case of the S.S. "Lotus"* by restricting its scope of application *ratione materiae* or *ratione temporis*. The *Case of the S.S. "Lotus"* is, for example, commonly associated in a similar manner with a law of coexistence.[62] In the work which inspired Judge Shahabuddeen to formulate his objective structural framework, it is pointed out, however, that the Lotus view, rendered after such Advisory Opinions as *Nationality Decrees Issued in Tunis and Morocco (French Zone)* and *Article 3, paragraph 2, of the Treaty of Lausanne (Frontier between Iraq and Turkey)*, in which the PCIJ emphasized the wide competence of the League of Nations, already differentiated between a law of coexistence and a law of cooperation.[63]

Moreover, in the *Case of the S.S. "Lotus"* the PCIJ adhered to the framework of obligation in view of the very nature and existing conditions of public international

---

[60] *Legality of the Threat or Use of Nuclear Weapons*, Advisory Opinion of 8 July 1996, Declaration President Bedjaoui, ICJ Reports 1996, 226, para 14.

[61] *Legality of the Threat or Use of Nuclear Weapons*, Advisory Opinion of 8 July 1996, Dissenting Opinion Judge Weeramantry, ICJ Reports 1996, 226, 494–496.

[62] Dupuy 2002, pp. 34–35, 53–56.

[63] Weil 1992, pp. 33–39.

law. This does not suggest that the PCIJ confined its endorsement of the framework of obligation to the case of a collision on the high seas between ships of different nationalities. Judges Loder, Nyholm and Altamira understood and rejected the framework of obligation in general terms. Judge Loder considered the contention that what is not prohibited is permitted as incompatible with the spirit of international law.[64] Judge Nyholm observed that it confuses international facts with international law.[65] Judge Altamira observed that, although the Judgment was confined to the case of a collision on the high seas between ships of different nationalities, it endorsed a general system of unrestricted freedom, which might lead to unforeseen and dangerous consequences.[66]

It is those consequences that many of the Judges of the ICJ sought to evade in *Legality of the Use or Threat of Use of Nuclear Weapons*. Judge Shahabuddeen rejected the framework of obligation in favor of the framework of authorization, taking up the position adopted by Lord Finlay in the *Case of the S.S. "Lotus"*. However, Judge Shahabuddeen also formulated an objective structural framework which approximated the reformulated framework developed here. It has been

---

[64] *Case of the S.S. "Lotus"*, Judgment No. 9 of 7 September 1927, Dissenting Opinion Judge Loder, Series A.—No. 10, 34: 'Turkey, having arrested, tried and convicted a foreigner for an offence which he is alleged to have committed outside her territory, claims to have been authorized to do so by reason of the absence of a prohibitive rule of international law. Her defence is based on the contention that under international law everything which is not prohibited is permitted. In other words, on the contention that, under international law, every door is open unless it is closed by treaty or by established custom. The Court in its judgment holds that this view is correct, well founded, and in accordance with the facts. (…) It seems to me that the contention is at variance with the spirit of international law.'

[65] *Case of the S.S. "Lotus*, Judgment No. 9 of 7 September 1927, Dissenting Opinion Judge Nyholm, Series A.—No. 10, 60–61: 'Thenceforward, it cannot be maintained—as the judgment sets out—that, failing a positive restrictive rule, States leave other States free to edict their legislations as they think fit and to act accordingly, even when, in contravention of the principle of territoriality, they assume rights over foreign subjects for acts which the latter have committed abroad. The reasoning of the judgment appears to be that, failing a rule of positive law, the relations between States in the matter under consideration are governed by an absolute freedom. If this reasoning be followed out, a principle of public international law is set up that where there is no special rule, absolute freedom must exist. The basis of this reasoning appears to be that it is vaguely felt that, even outside the domain of positive public international law, the situation of fact as regards relations between nations in itself embodies a principle of public law. But that is a confusion of ideas. In considering the existing situation of fact, a distinction should be drawn between that which is merely an international situation of *fact* and that which constitutes a rule of international *law*. The latter can only be created by a special process and cannot be deduced from a situation which is merely one of fact.'

[66] *Case of the S.S. "Lotus"*, Judgment No. 9 of 7 September 1927, Dissenting Opinion Judge Altamira, Series A.—No. 10, 104: 'Any decision leading to the establishment of a system of unrestricted freedom in States (…) would (…) be very serious. Even where a very circumscribed and particular case was concerned, there would, in such a conclusion, be a risk of giving rise almost inevitably to dangerous constructions and applications. In spite of all the provisos that might be added, it would be very difficult, I think, in view of the shifting ground upon which the case rests, to prevent the decision being construed in a manner going beyond its underlying intention.'

suggested that, within that reformulated framework, the members of international society are situated in terms of a dilemma, as having a power to act which is not an unlimited freedom to act. To that dilemma situation corresponds a reformulated function of public international law. Within the reformulated framework, the function of public international law is neither exclusively to restrict the freedom to act of the members of international society, nor exclusively to confer powers to act on the members of international society, but both. Accordingly, rules of public international law must have both an enabling and a disabling aspect. On the basis of these parameters, the reformulated framework associates the concept of public international law with the constituting of (the common good of) international society, as informed by international politics.

Chapter 4
The Framework of Obligation and the Framework of Authorization in General Theory of Law

4.1 Introduction

In Sect. 1.3, it has been argued in a preliminary way that the vertical structure of the concept of law underlying the concept of public international law consists of the framework of obligation and the framework of authorization. In a converse way, the identification of the framework of obligation and the framework of authorization illustrates and confirms the vertical structure of the concept of law underlying the concept of public international law, described in Sect. 1.2.

The identification of the framework of obligation and the framework of authorization in the jurisprudence of the PCIJ and the ICJ, in Chap. 3, foregrounding the argument put forward in Sect. 1.3, related to the international plane. A parallel can be drawn between the vertical structure of the concept of law underlying the concept of public international law, on the one hand, and the vertical structure of the internal law of the State, on the other hand. In view of the fact that general theory of law and the internal law of the State seem to coincide, in the sense that general theory of law inscribes itself within the vertical structure of the internal law of the State, this chapter now turns to general theory of law.

As briefly alluded to in Sect. 1.3, there is, of course, a standard explanation for the vertical structure of the internal law of the State. That is the idea of the social contract: finding themselves within a so-called state of nature, individuals perceive the requirement to transcend it and proceed to establish the institution of the State by means of a social contract. If that explanation were tenable, there would—notwithstanding the claims made so far about the vertical structure of the concept of law underlying the concept of public international law and the incoherence of the framework of obligation and the framework of authorization—be a coherent explanation of that vertical structure. Just as individuals have proceeded, in the internal sphere of the State, to establish the institution of the State and the internal law of the State by means of a social contract, so States may have proceeded to constitute the vertical structure of the concept of law underlying the concept of public international law. Such a perception may be found, for example, in the

J. A. Vos, *The Function of Public International Law*,
DOI: 10.1007/978-90-6704-861-3_4,

theory of public international law developed by Vattel.[1] At work, in other words, is a domestic analogy, pursuant to which concepts or institutions that work in the internal sphere of States may fruitfully be transposed to the international plane. It would follow that the vertical structure of the concept of law underlying the concept of public international law could be derived from the horizontal structure of public international law.

The view that the vertical structure of the concept of law underlying the concept of public international law may be derived from the horizontal structure of public international law, is only tenable, however, if the institution of the State and the internal law of the State constitute a coherent whole in the sense that both the institution of the State and the internal law of the State may be explained coherently on the basis of the notion of a state of nature. Consequently, in order to prove the axiomatic nature of the vertical structure of the concept of law underlying the concept of public international law, we must 'descend' from the international plane to the internal sphere of States, so as to examine the relationship between the institution of the State and the internal law of the State.

Therefore, the intention of the first part of this chapter, including the theory of law developed by Rawls, is to demonstrate that the institution of the State and the internal law of the State do not form a coherent whole in the sense that both can be explained on the basis of the notion of a state of nature. Because its main proponents have adopted diverging approaches to the idea of the social contract, it has been thought useful to describe these approaches side by side. The main point of the analysis is that social contract theory presupposes what it seeks to explain: that the 'state' of nature has characteristics which resemble the institution of the State, in which case it is superfluous to proceed to its establishment. In this analysis, it is assumed to be indifferent whether the notion of the social contract is portrayed as an actual historical process, as a hypothesis, or as a matter of practical reasoning. What matters is that, even considered as a hypothesis or as a matter of practical reasoning, the idea of the social contract relies on elements which are incompatible with what it seeks to explain. This criticism is formulated in the awareness that the solution offered here, the reformulated framework, is, in some respects, not so different from the idea of the social contract. It is different, however, to the extent that the reformulated framework does not rely on the notion of a transfer of power; instead, it seeks to mobilize the social power of the members of society towards the common good of society.

Turning to the second part of this chapter, which describes the general theories of law developed by Hart, Dworkin, MacCormick, and Finnis, if the point about social contract theory is sustainable, it follows that general theory of law does not explain the institution of the State and that it inscribes itself within, or aligns itself with, the vertical structure of the internal law of the State. In a sense, these theories of law are descriptive; they describe how the internal law of the State works or should work. Briefly, it is submitted, both the internal law of the State and general

[1] Vattel 1916, introduction, para 4.

theory of law inscribe themselves within, and presuppose the existence of, the institution of the State. If social contract theory does not provide a coherent explanation of the institution of the State, and in particular for the authority ascribed to it, it remains axiomatic.

Directing then, from the internal sphere of States, our attention again toward the international plane, and applying the preceding analysis thereto, it follows that we do not possess a coherent explanation for the vertical structure of the concept of law underlying the concept of public international law. If we look at the total picture combining the international plane and the internal sphere of States, we see, at the international plane, the vertical structure of the concept of law underlying the concept of public international law and, in the internal sphere of States, the vertical structure of the internal law of the State. The vertical structure of the concept of law underlying the concept of public international law reflects the assumed presence, it may be said, of a super-State. At the same time, the horizontal structure of public international law is inferred from the absence of authority above States. Subtracting, metaphorically, the horizontal structure of public international law from the vertical structure of the concept of law underlying the concept of public international law, what remains is the unexplained coexistence of sovereign and independent States, which project both externally and internally their absolute authority in terms of legislative, executive, and judicial powers.

This chapter, then, is about the internal sphere of States, but at the same time adopts a perspective on the vertical structure of the concept of law underlying the concept of public international law, that is, on the international plane. This is already apparent from the social contract theory developed by Hobbes, which starts, in a way, at the international plane and then transposes the state of nature to the internal sphere of the State to be established. Kant works from the internal sphere of States to the international plane and, in view of the irreconcilability of a super-State and the sovereignty and independence of States, settles for a voluntary federation or association. This domestic analogy, in the form of the movement from the first original position to the second original position, is especially prevalent in the social contract theory developed by Rawls.

As theories of law which inscribe themselves within, or align themselves with, the vertical structure of the internal law of the State, consideration will be given to those developed by Hart, Dworkin, MacCormick, and Finnis. The influence that the theory of law developed by Hart has had on the concept of public international law is especially pervasive. It may be recalled, for example, as mentioned in Sect. 1.3, that it informs the concept of law underlying Global Administrative Law. For our present purposes, it is most significant how the concept of law developed by Hart is projected onto the international plane and how it is considered deficient in terms of the union of primary and secondary rules. The inscription in or alignment with the internal law of the State is particularly conspicuous in the theory of law developed by Dworkin. Dworkin focuses on principles, community, and associative obligations, but at the same time governmental power is presupposed. The theory of law developed by MacCormick has built on the theory of law developed by Hart, by bringing principles and rules into relationship. Although situated within a vertical structure, the notion that it propels-legal reasoning as a form of practical reasoning, which must satisfy requirements of coherence and consistency-is transposable to the reformulated framework. In a similar way, the theory of law developed by Finnis inscribes itself within or aligns itself with the vertical structure of the internal law of the State. For example, Finnis remarks that the common good ensures that the basic values of the members of the community can be coordinated; the common good may be relied on to limit the rights, understood as freedoms to act, of the members of the community. On the other hand, where Finnis considers that coordination may be achieved by authority or unanimity, he seems to navigate between a vertical and a horizontal structure. Significantly, as regards the international plane, Finnis associates the notion of unanimity with the concept of customary international law. While these aspects remain within the framework of obligation, the theory of law developed by Finnis may also be seen as approaching the reformulated framework, in particular where the relationship between rules and institutions is characterized in a circular manner.

Synoptically, the reformulated framework has been derived, in Sect. 1.4, from the mutual incoherence of the framework of obligation and the framework of authorization, by suppressing their mutual exclusivity. The framework of obligation and the framework of authorization have been located at the international plane within the vertical structure of the concept of law underlying the concept of public international law. This chapter traces the provenance of that vertical structure in the internal sphere of the State along the lines of the distinction between the framework of obligation and the framework of authorization.

4.2 Transition I: Hobbes

The first general theory of law and/or politics to be considered is the concept of law developed by Hobbes. In *Leviathan*, Hobbes explains the institution of the State as emanating from a 'condition of nature'. In this condition of nature, individuals are considered to have unlimited rights and liberties and to be subject only to the laws of nature, which they may disregard if they should be regarded by them as incompatible with the exercise of those rights and liberties.[2]

Hobbes argues that those unlimited rights and liberties negate each other, because they cannot coexist, concluding on this basis that individuals must give up those unlimited rights and liberties.[3] According to Hobbes, they can do so by concluding a contract constituting a commonwealth, represented by a sovereign exercising power in respect of them.[4] By means of this contract the individuals are

[2] Hobbes 1996, Chaps. XIII–XV.

[3] Hüning 1998, pp. 115–116.

[4] Hobbes 1996, Chaps. XVII–XVIII.

deemed to have authorized the sovereign to exercise power in respect of them.[5] In this manner, Hobbes derives the concept of obligation from the contradictory nature of absolute rights.[6]

Importantly, Hobbes derives the hypothesis of the condition of nature from the condition of nature that exists between commonwealths.[7] Hobbes imputes unlimited rights and liberties to commonwealths and considers that, although the law of nations applies to relations between commonwealths, sovereigns may disregard the law of nations if it should be regarded by them as incompatible with the exercise of those rights and liberties or the safety of the commonwealth.[8]

This transition from the condition of nature to the commonwealth, as described by Hobbes, is, it is submitted, incoherent. First, the suggestion that this transition may be effected by means of a contract presupposes the existence of a legal framework. Hobbes acknowledges this by distinguishing three laws of nature which would also be binding in the condition of nature: to seek peace; to relinquish the unlimited rights and liberties and *pacta sunt servanda*.[9] This distinction, however, implicitly relies on a legal framework which puts these three laws of nature in a separate category and provides for their purposive and binding character. At the same time, the coexistence of unlimited rights and freedoms of individuals in the condition of nature presupposes the presence of a legal framework by virtue of which individuals have those inconsistent rights and freedoms.

Another problem is related to the function that law should have in the commonwealth. One of the rights of the sovereign, according to Hobbes, is the right to determine the Civil Law, which is the law of the commonwealth, consisting of commands of the sovereign. According to Hobbes, the function of the Civil Law is to limit the liberty of the subjects. Therefore, according to Hobbes, if the sovereign does not prescribe a rule of law, it must be assumed that the subjects have retained

---

5 Hüning 1998, pp. 213–218.

6 Hüning 1998, pp. 39–40, 44, 76–80.

7 Hobbes 1996, Chap. XIII: 'But though there had never been any time, wherein particular men were in a condition of warre one against another; yet in all times, Kings, and Persons of Soveraigne authority, because of their Independency, are in continual jealousies, and in the state and posture of Gladiators; having their weapons pointing, and their eyes fixed on one another; that is, their Forts, Garrisons, and Guns upon the Frontiers of their Kingdomes; and continuall Spyes upon their neighbors, which is a posture of War.'

8 Hobbes 1996, Chap. XXX: 'Concerning the Offices of one Soveraign to another, which are comprehended in that Law, which is commonly called the *Law of Nations*, I need not say any thing in this place; because the Law of Nations, and the Law of Nature, is the same thing. And every Soveraign hath the same Right, in procuring the safety of his People, that any particular man can have, in procuring his own safety. And the same Law, that dictateth to men that have no Civil Government, what they ought to do, and what to avoyd in regard of another, dictateth the same to Common-wealths, that is, to the Consciences of Soveraign Princes, and Soveraign Assemblies; there being no Court of Naturall Justice, but in the Conscience only; where not Man, but God raigneth; whose Lawes, (such of them as oblige all Mankind,) in respect of God, as he is the Author of Nature, are *Naturall*; and in respect of the same God, as he is King of Kings, are *Laws*.'

9 Hüning 1998, pp. 213–218.

a freedom to act.[10] If, however, by means of the contract, individuals have authorized the sovereign to exercise power in respect of them, they must be deemed to have transferred power to the sovereign. If power was transferred to the sovereign, individuals cannot, at the same time, be considered as having retained the corresponding rights and liberties. As a result of the authorization, the law of the commonwealth should, it is submitted, conform to the framework of authorization. Moreover, if the silence of the law may be interpreted as a freedom to act of the subjects, the condition of nature has not, to that extent, been transcended.

Hüning has explained the binding nature of the contract by arguing that the fact that unlimited rights and liberties negate each other, produces a rational will to institute a legal order which delimits those rights and liberties from each other. He considers that the fact that individuals must will this order, constitutes a requirement ('Zwang') sufficient to explain the binding force of the contract.[11] This transforms the question of the binding character of the contract into a form of practical reasoning. It is submitted, however, that, if the assumption of unlimited freedoms and liberties is inconsistent in itself, it is this assumption which should be rejected, rather than building on this inconsistent assumption the hypothesis that the subjects of the law should recognize the necessity of a law delimiting their rights and liberties. This would mean that the function of law does not reside solely in imposing obligations, pursuant to a transition from rights to obligations, and that, in an exclusively horizontal structure, rights cannot exist as such.

It is crucial to note that Hobbes derived his hypothesis of a condition of nature from the international plane. Furthermore, it is precisely at the international plane that the condition of nature did not lead to, or require, the establishment of an 'international commonwealth'. To the contrary, in the way Judge Nyholm described in his Dissenting Opinion in the *Case of the S.S. "Lotus"*, Hobbes inferred from an international situation of fact a normative proposition which could always override the Law of Nature and the Law of Nations, which, according to Hobbes, were one and the same thing. The general theory of law and/or politics developed by Hobbes does not, therefore, provide support for a domestic analogy pursuant to which the vertical structure of the concept of law underlying the concept of public international law can be derived from the horizontal structure of public international law. Quite the reverse: the notion of a condition of nature was derived by Hobbes from the international plane. This implies at the same time that the notion of an international state of nature cannot be relied on to explain the institution of the State. This international state of nature is based on the coexistence of sovereign and independent States and therefore assumes that the institution of the State has already been established.

---

[10] Hobbes 1996, Chap. XXI: 'As for other Lyberties, they depend on the Silence of the Law. In cases where the Soveraign has prescribed no rule, there the Subject hath the Liberty to do, or to forbeare, according to his own discretion'; See also Chap. XXVI.

[11] Hüning 1998, pp. 154–156.

4.3 Transition II: Locke

Locke starts his reasoning from a state of nature, characterized by freedom and equality, which is governed by a law of nature.[12] Like Hobbes, Locke points to the international plane as the best example of a state of nature. This state of nature is characterized by Locke in a dual way.

On the one hand, it is regarded as having many imperfections. First, the law of nature cannot be regarded as an established, settled, known law, received and allowed by common consent to be the standard of right and wrong and the common measure for all controversies between the members of society.[13] Secondly, the state of nature is characterized by the absence of a known and indifferent judge, with authority to determine all differences according to the established law.[14] Locke also formulated this point thus, that in the state of nature, the execution of the law of nature, in the forms of punishment and reparation, is in the hands of individuals.[15] Thirdly, in the state of nature, a power of execution is often absent.[16]

On the other hand, the state of nature is characterized by the existence of property, understood in the comprehensive sense of the lives, liberties, and estates of individuals.[17] Locke argues that individuals enter into political society for the preservation of their property, in this comprehensive sense, so as to evade the inconveniences of the state of nature.[18]

Whereas, in the state of nature, each individual may judge whether a breach of the law of nature has occurred, political society is characterized by the existence of an authority which decides controversies between the members of society and as to breaches of the law, according to such rules as the community determines; these Locke calls, inversely, the legislative and executive powers.[19] Locke adds that the power of the society, or the legislative power constituted by them, cannot extend further than the common good. This means that the legislative power of a society is bound to govern by established standing laws, by indifferent and upright judges and to employ the force of the community at home only in the execution of those laws or abroad to prevent or redress foreign injuries and secure the community from inroads and invasion.[20]

In conjunction with the foregoing, Locke locates the legislative power in the consent of the members of society.[21] Locke then formulates four limitations of the

---

[12] Locke 1988, paras 4–6.

[13] Locke 1988, para 124.

[14] Locke 1988, para 125.

[15] Locke 1988, paras 7–8, 10–12.

[16] Locke 1988, para 126.

[17] Locke 1988, para 123.

[18] Locke 1988, paras 124, 127.

[19] Locke 1988, paras 87–89, 127–130, 143–144.

[20] Locke 1988, para 131.

[21] Locke 1988, paras 134, 212.

legislative power: (i) the legislative power must be conformable to the law of nature and can only extend to the preservation of the property of the members of society[22]; (ii) the legislative power must be exercised in the form of standing, settled, and declared laws[23]; (iii) the legislative power cannot take away the property of the members of society without their consent[24]; and (iv) because the legislative power depends on delegation and authorization, it cannot be transferred.[25]

Crucial in Locke's system is the notion of trust and the view that the legislative power emanates from authorization and delegation.[26] Locke deduces from this that the government is dissolved: (i) when the legislative power is altered[27]; and (ii) when the executive power is disfunct.[28] More generally, and crucially, Locke argues that the government is also dissolved when the legislative power or the executive power act contrary to their trust.[29] This brings Locke to the ultimate question *Who shall be Judge* whether the legislative power or executive power act contrary to their trust? According to Locke, this must be the People, which entrusted those powers and must, accordingly, also have a power to revoke them.[30]

From the perspective of the dichotomy between the framework of obligation and the framework of authorization, Locke's general theory of law and/or politics invites a number of observations. Most fundamental is the tension residing, on the one hand, in the crucial role played by the legislative power, which has the function of delimiting the properties of the members of society, and, on the other hand, in the position that the legislative power emanates from authorization and consent. The former position relies on the legislative power to order the properties of the members of society, whereas the latter position presupposes that the members of society are in a position to determine whether or not the legislative power is exercised according to their trust, which in turn implies that the members of society have a superior way of measuring whether their properties are well-ordered. Locke in fact acknowledges that the relationship between the legislative power and the people is similar to the state of nature, because there is no judge that can be appealed to in this matter. The principal reasons for the transition from the state of nature to the commonwealth—the absence of legislative, judicial, and executive powers—are thus only partially overcome, because no judicial power is available to determine whether the legislative power and the executive power diverge from the interests of the members of society.

---

22 Locke 1988, paras 135, 142.

23 Locke 1988, paras 136–137, 142.

24 Locke 1988, paras 138–140, 142.

25 Locke 1988, paras 141–142.

26 Locke 1988, paras 134, 136, 142, 212.

27 Locke 1988, paras 212–218.

28 Locke 1988, para 219.

29 Locke 1988, paras 209–219, 221–222.

30 Locke 1988, para 240.

Locke's treatment of the state of nature is also ambiguous in other respects. Insisting, on the one hand, on the inconveniences of the state of nature—the absence of the legislative, judicial, and executive powers—Locke proceeds nevertheless on the basis that, in essence, the status of property is clear, because the execution of the law of nature, in the form of punishment or reparation, is aimed at the preservation of the property of individuals. This presupposes that the law of nature must be clearer than Locke suggests and affects the rationale for the transition to the commonwealth. Moreover, Locke suggests that the executive power (which comprises the judicial power) is conferred on individuals in the state of nature. Here also, the presence of a legal framework which, moreover, confers inconsistent, because too wide, powers on individuals, is presupposed.

Just like Hobbes, Locke derives the plausibility of the existence of the state of nature from the existence of the state of nature at the international plane. Thus, rather than providing support for the domestic analogy, according to which, just like individuals transcended a state of nature by establishing the institution of the State and the internal law of the State, so States may constitute the vertical structure of the concept of law underlying the concept of public international law, the general theory of law and/or politics formulated by Locke undermines such a domestic analogy. In the general theory of law and/or politics formulated by Locke, the necessity of the transition resides in the assumption that the properties of the members of society are not clearly delineated and that the executive power resides in the members of society. These assumptions are a reflection of the presence of a legislative power and an executive power in the state of nature. Coupled with the observation that in political society the state of nature is not really overcome, Locke does not really provide a rationale for the transition from the state of nature to political society. To a significant extent, Locke suggests that the people as a whole are organized, either in the state of nature or as the principals delegating power to the organs of society. This fails to explain, however, how in such an exclusively horizontal structure, the organization of society comes about and what the proper role of such organs should be.

4.4 Transition III: Rousseau

The principles of political law ('droit politique') developed by Rousseau in *Du Contrat Social* also postulate a transition from a state of nature ('état de nature') to a civil state ('état civil'). In the state of nature, individuals are deemed to have unlimited rights and freedoms. In the civil state, individuals have rights and freedoms limited by the general will, which is regarded as sovereign. The transition from the state of nature to the civil state is effected by means of a social contract (or pact). Rousseau argues that, according to its terms, each individual thereby alienates its rights to the community or political body ('corps politique').[31]

[31] Rousseau 2001, Book I, Chaps. VI–VIII.

Rousseau thus envisages a transition from a situation in which individuals have unlimited rights and freedoms, via a social contract, to a situation in which individuals, as members of a political body, have rights and freedoms which are limited by the general will of that political body. The state of nature conforms to the framework of obligation in so far as reliance is placed on the concept of the social contract. The contradictory nature of the unlimited rights and freedoms necessitates the transition to the civil state. The civil state also conforms to the framework of obligation, the function of law being regarded as the limitation of the freedoms and rights of the members of the political body. The relationship between the political body and its members is regarded as having two aspects: as citizens, those members contribute to the formation of the general will; as subjects they are subject to the general will.

From the perspective of the dichotomy between the framework of obligation and the framework of authorization, it is submitted that the transition from the state of nature to the civil state as postulated by Rousseau is incoherent for the following reasons. First, the assumption that the social contract is binding presupposes the presence of a legal framework which determines this quality. At the same time, the assumption that the state of nature is characterized by unlimited rights and freedoms of individuals also presupposes the presence of a legal framework by virtue of which individuals have those unlimited rights and freedoms. Furthermore, this legal framework is deemed to provide for inconsistent rights and freedoms.

Second, if all individuals alienate their rights and freedoms to the political body, in the civil state, the rights of members should be conferred by the political body. In other words, in the civil state, the function of law should conform to the framework of authorization. If the function of law in the civil state conforms to the framework of obligation, this suggests that the state of nature has not been transformed into a civil state, because it is still necessary to limit the rights and freedoms of members of the political body.

Third, the two aspects of the relationship between the political body and its members are problematic in so far as the general will is seen at the same time as formed by the particular wills of its members, as citizens, and as limiting the wills of its members, as subjects. It does not seem coherent to see the relationship between the political body and a member at the same time as an exercise and as a limitation of the freedom of that member; these movements exclude each other. To the extent that, in the civil state, the function of the general will as a limitation of the freedom of the members takes precedence, the significance of the particular will of those members for the formation of the general will is relinquished. Rousseau continues to uphold the importance of the freedom of members of the political body, as citizens, in the civil state. On the basis of these freedoms, the particular wills of the members of the political body (as citizens) converge into the general will.[32] The necessity of seeing that convergence in terms of limitations of particular wills arises from the presumed applicability of the framework of

[32] Rousseau 2001, Book II, Chap. III.

obligation. To the extent that the aggregate level of the political body is capable of transforming the exercise of a freedom into a limitation of that freedom, this would be feasible only on the basis of a presupposed sovereignty, not explained by the notion of a social contract.

In *Du Contrat Social*, Rousseau was not able to address the concept of public international law. He intended to deal with this subject in another work, *Institutions Politiques*, which did not materialize. It may be observed, however, that the pattern according to which the general will is regarded at the same time as formed by and as limiting the particular wills, is strikingly similar to the pattern described in Sect. 1.2, according to which a rule of public international law constitutes at the same time a restriction and an exercise of the will of States. (States as both legislators and subjects of public international law) Nevertheless, the difference is that, whereas Rousseau gave precedence to the regulative aspect of the general will, the pattern as described with respect to the concept of public international law does not succeed in effectively establishing rules delimiting the freedom of States to act, because those rules must always remain an emanation from that same will.

Therefore, the characterization of the general will as sovereign and the characterization of the function of law as the limitation of the rights and freedoms of the members of the political body are situated within a legal framework by virtue of which the general will is sovereign and the function of law is the limitation of the rights and freedoms of the members of the political body. The general theory of law and/or politics developed by Rousseau presupposes this framework as necessary because of the assumption of the existence of unlimited rights and freedoms. That very assumption, however, is projected by the general theory of law and/or politics developed by Rousseau.

4.5 Transition IV: Kant

A fourth transitional process from a state of nature to a civil state has been described by Kant in several of his writings. Kant defined the concept of right (i.e. law) as the restriction of the external freedom of each individual so that it harmonizes with the external freedom of every other individual, in so far as this is possible within the framework of a general law.[33]

In order to explain the institution of the State, Kant postulated the concept of a state of nature, in which individuals have unlimited rights and freedoms. Kant considered that, in view of the contradictory nature of these rights and freedoms, practical reason produces a duty to leave this state of nature and move into a civil state by means of a contract. Kant made it clear that this is a hypothesis, intended to ensure that the constitution of the State is based on the principles of freedom, equality, and independence. He defined the principle of freedom elliptically as the

[33] Kant 1991a, pp. 73–74.

happiness which each may seek in whatever way he sees fit, provided that he does not infringe upon the freedom of others to pursue a similar end, which can be reconciled with the freedom of everyone else, within the framework of a general law.[34] The principle of equality was defined by Kant as the equal right of individuals to bind each other.[35]

In another definition of the concept of freedom, which applies to the situation after the constitution of the State, Kant described it as the right to obey no external laws other than those to which one had consented.[36] However, Kant made it clear that this did not mean that the consent of a subject was required in order to apply an external law to it. In fact, the consent that an individual was deemed to have given to the contract facilitating the movement from the state of nature to the civil state was considered sufficient. After the constitution of the State, this consent is deemed to extend to whatever legislation is adopted pursuant to the general will.

By analogy with the internal law of the State, Kant regarded States as having unlimited and conflicting freedoms and as having an obligation to leave their state of nature by forming an association or federation on the basis of a contract.[37] Kant considered, however, that such a contract could not constitute a super-State, because this would be incoherent with the sovereignty and independence of States.[38] Therefore, Kant argued that the federation or association formed by the contract should be voluntary.[39]

From the perspective of the dichotomy between the framework of obligation and the framework of authorization, it is submitted that the transition from the state of nature to the civil state postulated by Kant is incoherent for the following reasons. First, the elliptic definition of the principle of freedom before the constitution of the State presupposes that a general law exists. Likewise, the definition of the principle of equality before the constitution of the State presupposes that the rights of individuals have the characteristic of binding each other. Both definitions imply that in the state of nature a legal framework already exists. Furthermore, it is suggested that this legal framework provides for inconsistent rights.

Second, the concept of law and the definitions of the principles of freedom and equality are circular. The freedom of an individual is dependent on the freedoms of other individuals as harmonized by a general law; this leads into an infinite regress, defining the concept of freedom by reference to the concept of freedom. Moreover, if any freedom conflicts with another freedom in so far as it is not harmonized, nothing of this initial freedom remains. The right to bind each other cannot in the

[34] Kant 1991a, p. 74.

[35] Kant 1991a, pp. 74–75; Kant 1991b, p. 99; Kant 1996, p. 91.

[36] Kant 1991b, p. 99; Kant 1996, p. 91.

[37] Kant 1996, pp. 114–115; Hackel 2000, pp. 64–76.

[38] Kant 1991b, p. 102; Kant 1996, pp. 114–115; Hackel 2000, pp. 76–82.

[39] Kant 1991a, p. 90; Kant 1991b, p. 102; Kant 1996, pp. 114–115, 119–120; Hackel 2000, pp. 82–91.

end lead to any result, because the right of A to bind B is counteracted by the right of B to bind A. There is thus neither initial freedom nor binding law.

Third, the constitution of the State should transform the function of law from the framework of obligation into the framework of authorization. Otherwise, the state of nature has not been abandoned, notwithstanding the duty, derived from practical reason, to do so. Nevertheless, Kant continues to understand the function of law, after the constitution of the State, in terms of the framework of obligation.

Fourth, as regards relations between States, the solution of a voluntary association or federation, put forward by Kant as an intermediate solution because of the impossibility of the super-State, implies that a general law emanating from that association/federation requires the consent of States and cannot succeed in surpassing the state of nature subsisting between States. Whereas consent to an external law which forms part of the internal law of the State is presupposed, consent to an external law from a federation/association requires the consent of States. Accordingly, an external law is necessary to restrict the freedom of States, but must emanate from the consent of States. This is problematic, because it cannot be explained how an external freedom of a State which is already regarded as inconsistent with the freedom of another State, can nevertheless produce an external law which succeeds in harmonizing the external freedoms of States. We may note, at this point, a perfect parallel between Kant's voluntary association or federation and the view of the PCIJ in *Nationality Decrees Issued in Tunis and Morocco (French Zone)* that the development of public international law and, thereby, of international relations depends on the extent to which States have restricted their freedoms to act by means of an exercise of those freedoms to act.

4.6 Interlocutory Conclusion

From the preceding analysis it is submitted that the international plane plays a distorting role in social contract theory. Both Hobbes and Locke actually seem to have derived the idea of a state of nature from the international plane. Social contract theory suggests that it is possible to move from an exclusively horizontal structure to an exclusively vertical structure. But it must be observed that the state of nature which was deemed to be exclusively horizontal, already contained vertical elements. This may in particular be seen from the general theory of law and/or politics developed by Locke which inferred, in the state of nature, certain consequences from the absence of a legislative power and of an executive power. To the extent of drawing such consequences from those absences, the presence of a vertical structure was at the same time assumed.

In sum, the transition from a state of nature to the institution of the State and the internal law of the State cannot be explained coherently. If this position is tenable, this means that we do not have a coherent explanation for the institution of the State and the internal law of the State and in particular for the vertical structure of the concept of law, identified previously, in either of its forms, the framework of obligation or the framework of authorization. Moreover, this also means that we have no basis for transposing to the international plane, pursuant to a domestic analogy, concepts related to the institution of the State or to the internal law of the State. Precisely such an extension, however, is at the heart of the Law of Peoples as formulated by Rawls. To round off this part of the analysis, it is therefore appropriate to turn presently to that theory of law, presented by Rawls as a development of the social contract tradition.

4.7 Law of Peoples: Rawls

The argument of the Law of Peoples is that the general social contract idea can be extended to a Society of Peoples consisting of so-called well-ordered peoples, which term embraces both liberal and decent peoples. This extension takes place in two steps; first to the society of liberal democratic peoples and subsequently to the society of decent peoples.[40]

In what is comprised in the First Part of Ideal Theory, Rawls formulates six conditions for a liberal conception of justice of a reasonably just constitutional democracy and argues that these are parallel conditions for a reasonably just Society of Peoples: (i) it is realistic, taking people as they are and laws as they might be; (ii) it is utopian by endorsing basic rights and liberties, assigning them a special priority and assuring primary goods; (iii) the category of the political contains within itself all essential elements for a political conception of justice; (iv) political and social institutions foster a sense of justice; (v) the unity of society resides in public reason; and (vi) toleration.[41]

The Law of Peoples as formulated by Rawls conceives of liberal peoples and decent peoples as the actors in the Society of Peoples. Liberal peoples, according to Rawls, have three basic features: (i) a reasonably just constitutional democratic government that serves their fundamental interests; (ii) citizens united by common sympathies; and (iii) a moral nature. The first feature is institutional and means that the government is effectively under the political and electoral control of citizens. The second feature is cultural and refers to a common language and shared historical memories. The third feature means that liberal peoples are both reasonable and rational; (reasonable) liberal (or decent) peoples will offer fair terms of cooperation to other peoples and the people will honor these terms when assured that other peoples will do so as well.[42]

Rawls derives the Law of Peoples by distinguishing between two original positions. The first original position models fair and reasonable conditions for the parties, who are rational representatives of free and equal, reasonable and rational

[40] Rawls 1999b, introduction, paras 1, 4; Rawls 2005, Chap. VII, *passim*.

[41] Rawls 1999b, paras 1.2–1.3.

[42] Rawls 1999b, para 2.1.

citizens, to specify fair terms of cooperation for regulating the basic structure of society. This entails five essential features: (1) the original position models the parties as representing citizens fairly; (2) it models them as rational; (3) it models them as selecting from available principles of justice those that apply to the basic structure; (4) the parties are modeled as making these selections for appropriate reasons; and (5) as selecting for reasons related to the fundamental interests of reasonable and rational citizens.[43]

The second original position models fair conditions under which the parties, the rational representatives of liberal peoples, are to specify the Law of Peoples. It is stipulated that both the parties as representatives and the peoples they represent are situated fairly. Peoples are modeled as rational, since the parties select from among available principles for the Law of Peoples guided by the fundamental interests of democratic societies, expressed by the liberal principles of justice for a democratic society. Finally, the parties are guided by appropriate reasons. Thus: (1) people's representatives are reasonably and fairly situated as free and equal; (2) peoples are modeled as rational; (3) their representatives are deliberating about the Law of Peoples; (4) their deliberations proceed in terms of the right reasons; and (5) the selection of principles of the Law of Peoples is based on a peoples's fundamental interests, given by a liberal conception of justice.[44]

According to Rawls, deliberation in the second original position results in the selection of the following eight principles of the Law of Peoples:

(i) Peoples are free and independent, and their freedom and independence are to be respected by other peoples;
(ii) Peoples are to observe treaties and undertakings;
(iii) Peoples are equal and are parties to the agreements that bind them;
(iv) Peoples are to observe a duty of non-intervention;
(v) Peoples have the right of self-defense, but no right to instigate war for other reasons than self-defense;
(vi) Peoples are to honor human rights;
(vii) Peoples are to observe certain specified restrictions in the conduct of war; and
(viii) Peoples have a duty to assist other peoples living under unfavourable conditions that prevent their having a just or decent political and social regime.

Rawls stresses that with respect to the Law of Peoples, the parties select different interpretations of these principles rather than—as in the first original position—the principles themselves.[45]

Rawls argues that the Law of Peoples as thus formulated would also be adopted in a second step, proceeding from a second original position similar to the second original position of liberal peoples, by decent hierarchical peoples.[46] A decent

---

[43] Rawls 1999b, paras 3.1, 12.1; Rawls 2005, Chap. VIII, para 4.

[44] Rawls 1999b, paras 3.2, 12.1.

[45] Rawls 1999b, paras 4.1, 12.1.

[46] Rawls 1999b, paras 8.1, 8.4.

hierarchical people, according to Rawls, must satisfy two conditions so as to be a member in good standing in a reasonable Society of Peoples. First, it does not have aggressive aims and respects the political and social order of other societies. The second criterion has three parts: (a) its system of law, in accordance with its common good idea of justice, secures human rights for all members of the people; (b) its system of law imposes moral duties and obligations on all members of the people; (c) the officials of the system of law believe that it is guided by a common good idea of justice.[47] Central to these criteria is the idea of a common good idea of justice, which is manifested in the idea of a consultation hierarchy; accordingly, the groups into which the society is organized must be represented by a body which forms part of the consultation hierarchy.[48]

The third part of the Law of Peoples is formed by nonideal theory, which deals, on the one hand, with conditions of noncompliance and, on the other hand, with unfavorable conditions.[49] As regards conditions of noncompliance, the Law of Peoples accords both liberal peoples and decent peoples the right to war in self-defense against so-called outlaw states.[50] In addition, the Law of Peoples prescribes six principles restricting the conduct of war.[51] As regards unfavorable conditions, the Law of Peoples prescribes a duty for well-ordered peoples to assist burdened societies.[52] It formulates three guidelines for this duty of assistance: (i) its aim is to realize and preserve just or decent basic institutions[53]; (ii) it should be accompanied by insistence on human rights[54]; and (iii) it should result in burdened societies becoming free and equal members of the Society of Well-ordered Peoples.[55]

In light of the interlocutory conclusion, drawn previously, let us now zoom in on the relationship between the international plane and the several stages of development of the Law of Peoples. The first original position only applies to liberal peoples—but, it may be asked, how do liberal peoples know that they are such a people? This clearly presupposes the existence, at the international plane, of a framework which delimits peoples from one another. The same applies to the second original position, in which peoples deliberate about the Law of Peoples. This presupposes the pre-existence of a Law of Peoples which determines the peoples that take part in this deliberation. Both liberal and decent peoples are, moreover, in part qualified by their adherence to human rights. This is at the same time a principle of the Law of Peoples and a criterion which determines which

---

47 Rawls 1999b, paras 8.2, 10.2.

48 Rawls 1999b, para 9.1.

49 Rawls 1999b, para 13.1.

50 Rawls 1999b, para 13.2.

51 Rawls 1999b, para 14.1.

52 Rawls 1999b, para 15.1.

53 Rawls 1999b, para 15.2.

54 Rawls 1999b, para 15.3.

55 Rawls 1999b, para 15.4.

peoples are part of the second original position in which they deliberate about the principles of the Law of Peoples. The reasoning here is, in other words, circular.

Further, the function of the principles of the Law of Peoples seems to conform to the framework of obligation. This seems to follow most clearly from the fact that those principles limit two traditional freedoms of sovereignty—the right to go to war and the right to treat the population as one pleases. This presupposes the pre-existence of a legal framework which is not, however, explained in theoretical terms. Both at the international plane and in the internal sphere, the general theory of law and/or politics formulated by Rawls focuses on the liberty of citizens and peoples and, to a certain extent, on their equality. It assumes that the principles of justice apply to, or are part of, a concept of law with a vertical structure. With respect to the internal sphere, this can be derived from the fact that Rawls distinguishes two kinds of constitutional essentials to which the idea of public reason applies: (a) fundamental principles that specify the general structure of government and the political process: the powers of the legislature, executive, and the judiciary; the scope of majority rule; and (b) equal basic rights and liberties of citizenship that legislative majorities are to respect: such as the right to vote and to participate in politics, liberty of conscience, freedom of thought and of association, as well as the protections of the rule of law.[56] The principles of justice that are deemed to result from the original position are directed primarily at category (b) and do not pertain to category (a). This means that the institution of the State and the internal law of the State are presupposed; the main task of the principles of justice is to supplement them by means of the constitutional essentials contained in category (b).

It is concluded, therefore, that the vertical structure of the concept of law remains without a theoretical foundation and that there is no basis for applying to the international plane a domestic analogy which ultimately derives, as Hobbes and Locke made clear, from the international plane itself. It also follows that, in so far as general theory of law conforms to the vertical structure of the concept of law, it situates itself within and assumes the presence of the institution of the State, without, however, explaining that existence and, concomitantly, the existence of the internal law of the State. This may be seen in particular from an analysis of the general theories of law formulated by Hart and Dworkin.

4.8 Union of Primary and Secondary Rules: Hart

The concept of law as developed by Hart consists of a union of primary and secondary rules. Primary rules are rules of obligation.[57] The function of obligations is to restrict human conduct.[58] According to Hart, although a legal system

[56] Rawls 2005, Chap. VI, para 5.

[57] Hart 1994, pp. 89–91.

[58] Hart 1994, pp. 79–80.

could consist of only primary rules, such a legal system would exhibit a number of weaknesses. First, there would be uncertainty as to whether primary rules were legal or other rules. Second, it would not be possible to change primary rules; primary rules would accordingly be static. Third, primary rules would be inefficient, because there would not be an authoritative determination of the law in a particular case.[59] The function of secondary rules is to remedy those weaknesses.[60] Hart thus identifies three corresponding types of secondary rules: (1) a rule of recognition, which enables the identification of the rules of a legal system; (2) rules of change, in accordance with which primary rules may be changed; and (3) rules of adjudication, which permit an authoritative determination whether a primary rule has been infringed.[61] The rule of recognition may be seen as the basis of the legal system, which gives validity to its other rules. According to Hart, the validity of the rule of recognition itself is primarily a matter of its acceptance by the officials of the legal system.[62] The *Postscript* makes clear that what Hart has in mind are primarily the judicial officials of the legal system.

With respect to public international law, Hart considers that it does not form a legal system containing a rule of recognition, but that it consists of several rules accepted by States as binding.[63] However, according to Hart, public international law may be in a stage of transition and developing into a legal system that resembles the internal law of the State.[64]

In view of the stated function of primary rules, the general theory of law developed by Hart clearly conforms to the framework of obligation.[65] A problematic point resides in the question of the identification and location of the rule of recognition, which gives validity to the legal system. With respect to the internal law of the State, Hart locates the validity of the rule of recognition in its acceptance by the officials of the system. This, however, presupposes a legal framework providing that

---

[59] Hart 1994, pp. 89–91.

[60] Hart 1994, pp. 91–92.

[61] Hart 1994, pp. 92–95; Dupuy 2002, pp. 74–77.

[62] Hart 1994, pp. 97–107.

[63] Hart 1994, pp. 230–231: '(...) it is submitted that there is no basic rule providing general criteria of validity for the rules of international law, and that the rules which are in fact operative constitute not a system but a set of rules, among which are the rules providing for the binding force of treaties.'; Paulus 2001, pp. 80–81.

[64] Hart 1994, p. 231.

[65] Hart 1994, p. 218: 'For if in fact we find that there exists among states a given form of international authority, the sovereignty of states is to that extent limited, and it has just that extent which the rules allow. Hence we can only know which states are sovereign, and what the extent of their sovereignty is, when we know what the rules are; just as we can only know whether an Englishman or an American is free and the extent of his freedom when we know what English or American law is. The rules of international law are indeed vague and conflicting on many points, so that doubt about the area of independence left to states is far greater than that concerning the extent of a citizen's freedom under municipal law. (...) The question for municipal law is: what is the extent of the supreme legislative authority recognized in this system? For international law it is: what is the maximum area of autonomy which the rules allow to states?'

this acceptance gives validity to the rule of recognition. Moreover, the clarification in the *Postscript* that these are primarily the judicial officials of the legal system seems to pose a problem in terms of the separation of powers, for if the rule of recognition is a rule accepted by the judicial officials, it is the judicial function which ultimately determines the rules which belong to the legal system.

The view that primary rules are rules of obligation and that the function of obligations is to restrict human conduct is related to the rule of recognition in so far as the role of the rule of recognition is to facilitate the identification of the rules containing obligations. It does not follow from the rule of recognition, however, that those rules are rules of obligation. While remaining legal rules, these rules could, in principle, also contain rights. The fact that primary rules, according to Hart, are rules of obligation relies on the presumption that the union of primary and secondary rules is situated within the framework of obligation which, in turn, presupposes the institution of the State.

As for public international law, the view that the rules which are in fact operative, including the rules providing for the binding force of treaties, constitute a set of rules which have been accepted by States, gives rise to the problem that, in the absence of a rule of recognition, there is no explanation as to why the acceptance of those rules by States would render them operative as a set of rules. But the most pervasive problem is Hart's view that the concept of public international law may be in a state of transition and develop into a legal system resembling the internal law of the State. That view seems to be based on the assumption that the internal law of the State embodies a development from an exclusively horizontal structure to an exclusively vertical structure. If the union of primary and secondary rules is situated within and explained by the pre-existence of the institution of the State, as argued previously, it cannot account for such a transition from an exclusively horizontal structure to an exclusively vertical structure. Rather, it is the centrality of the institution of the State which radiates, externally, the concept of public international law and, internally, the internal law of the State. Concomitantly, it is submitted that the development of the concept of public international law should not be located in its approximation to the internal law of the State. Rather, it should be located in the reformulation of the function of primary rules which, pursuant to the reformulated framework, must contain simultaneously within themselves both rights and obligations.

4.9 Integrity: Dworkin

The general theory of law developed by Dworkin is based on the assumption of the factual existence of governmental power. The function of the internal law of the State, according to Dworkin, is both to guide and constrain that power. The law of a community is described by Dworkin as a scheme, enclosed in past political decision, of rights and responsibilities determining when the use of collective power is permitted or obligatory.[66]

On the basis of this (general) concept of law, Dworkin develops a conception of law as integrity, which means that the members of a political community regard as law not only the rules of a community, but also the principles presupposed by these rules.[67] Law as integrity, according to Dworkin, aims at a kind of equality among citizens that makes their community more genuine and improves the moral justification for the exercise of its collective political power.[68]

Dworkin relates the conception of law as integrity to the concept of a community of principle through the intermediate concept of a true community. Distinguishing between a bare community and a true community, Dworkin argues that relations between members of a true community must satisfy four conditions: (i) they must regard their obligations as special; (ii) they must view these responsibilities as personal, relating member to member; (iii) they must view these responsibilities as flowing from a more general responsibility of concern for the well-being of others; and (iv) members must suppose that the practices of the group show an equal concern for all members.[69] Dworkin refers to such responsibilities as associative obligations, which attach to the membership of a community.[70]

Subsequently, Dworkin transposes these requirements to the concept of a political community, classifying a political community that satisfies the requirements of a true community as a community of principle.[71] Such a community of principle, according to Dworkin, accepts law as integrity.[72] In this way, the principles presupposed by the rules are linked indirectly to associative obligations.

Although the definition of the concept of law as a scheme of rights and responsibilities—as well as the description of the role of law as both guiding and constraining (licensing or requiring) governmental power—seem ambiguous, Dworkin's conception of law as integrity clearly conforms to the framework of

---

[66] Dworkin 1998, p. 93: 'Governments have goals: they aim to make the nations they govern prosperous or powerful or religious or eminent; they also aim to remain in power. They use the collective force they monopolize to these and other ends. Our discussions about law assume by and large, I suggest, that the most abstract and fundamental point of legal practice is to guide and constrain the power of government in the following way. Law insists that force not be used or withheld, no matter how useful that would be to ends in view, no matter how beneficial or noble these ends, except as licensed or required by individual rights and responsibilities flowing from past political decisions about when collective force is justified. The law of a community on this account is the scheme of rights and responsibilities that meet that complex standard: they license coercion because they flow from past political decision of the right sort. They are therefore 'legal' rights and responsibilities.'

[67] Dworkin 1998, pp. 96, 176–275.

[68] Dworkin 1998, pp. 95–96, 176–275.

[69] Dworkin 1998, pp. 199–201.

[70] Dworkin 1998, pp. 195–202, 211–214.

[71] Paulus 2001, pp. 23–26.

[72] Dworkin 1998, pp. 206–211.

obligation. This may be inferred in particular from the link between principles and associative obligations.

Dworkin's general theory of law does not attempt to explain the phenomenon of governmental power as such. While a community of principle imposes, on the one hand, associative obligations on its members and, on the other hand, is characterized by law as integrity, which comports the principles presupposed by the rules, it would seem that these viewpoints do not make it possible for a community of principle to 'accept' law as integrity. It would rather seem that this entity inscribes itself into a vertical structure emanating from governmental power. The fact that the concept of community should be described in terms of the concept of obligation thus remains a matter of assumption. Locating the role of governmental power within the context of the scheme of rights and responsibilities, stated both to guide and constrain (license or require) governmental power, would seem to suggest that governmental power itself is subject to legal requirements. However, the description of a community of principle in terms of associative obligations does not seem to leave room for a simultaneous mechanism whereby those members can control the exercise of governmental power. That view is informed rather by the description that the scheme of rights and responsibilities determines when the exercise of governmental power is licensed or required. This ambiguous description bridges the dichotomy formed by the mutual exclusivity of the framework of obligation and the framework of authorization. At the same time, it does not cohere with the exclusive adherence to the framework of obligation inferred from the link between principles and associative obligations.

4.10 Legal Reasoning: MacCormick

The general theory of law as legal reasoning developed by MacCormick may be seen as building a bridge between the general theories of law developed by Hart and Dworkin, in the sense that MacCormick inserts the category of principles into the framework of primary and secondary rules developed by Hart. It is understood by MacCormick as situated within the broader framework of practical reasoning, which involves applying principles and rules to action by means of reasoning.[73]

The main concern of MacCormick's general theory of law as legal reasoning is the justification of legal decisions. Its basis is formed by what MacCormick describes as deductive justification. This legal reasoning is based on premised rules and involves bringing operative facts within their fields of application so as to draw a logical conclusion on that basis.[74] However, although this type of reasoning is regarded as useful, it has, according to MacCormick, three main shortcomings. There may be disputes as regards the interpretation of the rules (problem of

73 MacCormick 1994, Chap. X.

74 MacCormick 1994, p. 100 and Chap. II.

interpretation), disputes as regards the classification of the facts (problem of classification), or disputes as regards the existence of the rules (problem of relevancy).[75]

MacCormick then first makes the point that legal decisions in such cases must satisfy the requirement of formal justice, which means that they can be brought within the ambit of a universal or general 'ruling'.[76] Subsequently, MacCormick's main point is how a non-arbitrary choice can be made between divergent rulings. This involves what he refers to as 'second-order justification'.[77]

Second-order justification, as formulated by MacCormick, may be regarded as comprising three elements:

(i) Consequentialist arguments;
(ii) The requirement of coherence (principles and analogies);
(iii) The requirement of consistency.[78]

Consequentialist reasoning involves examining what consequences a ruling which might justify the legal decision in the instant case would have for other cases which are more or less similar; the key word in this connection is the acceptability of those consequences. As MacCormick stresses, this may involve diverse considerations, such as justice, common sense, public interest, and convenience. As this also makes clear, consequentialist reasoning is, more or less, evaluative and subjective. It is in order to situate consequentialist reasoning within certain limits that recourse must be had to the requirements of coherence and consistency.[79]

The requirement of coherence is formulated by MacCormick in terms of principles, which are described by MacCormick as general norms having positive value, which both justify and explain rules. By this quality, principles are considered to make sense of the numerous rules of a legal system and thus to ensure their coherence. At the same time, principles are regarded as a legal warrant on the basis of which the legal decision justified by means of consequentialist reasoning can also be regarded as justifiable. In this manner, principles ensure the separation between the legislative and the judicial functions. Principles may both be identified directly and be derived by analogy from rules of law. As a prominent example of a principle, MacCormick mentions the 'neighbour principle' famously identified by Lord Atkin in *Donoghue v. Stevenson* [1932] A.C. 562; 1932 S.C. (H.L.) 31 as a general duty to take reasonable care to avoid causing foreseeable harm by one's acts or omissions to those whose relationship to one is such that their suffering harm as a result of a lack of care in carrying out the act or omission in question is a foreseeable risk. MacCormick stresses that, unlike mandatory rules, principles are

---

75 MacCormick 1994, pp. 65–72, 100.

76 MacCormick 1994, p. 100 and Chap. IV.

77 MacCormick 1994, pp. 100–101.

78 MacCormick 1994, pp. 103–108.

79 MacCormick 1994, pp. 108–119 and Chap. VI.

not compelling and merely provide legal support for a judicial decision. Further, MacCormick acknowledges that in a given case there may be competing principles or that competing conclusions may be drawn from a principle.[80]

The requirement of consistency is formulated by MacCormick as a boundary and means that a ruling arrived at by consequentialist reasoning and supported by reasons of principle may not be contradicted by a rule which forms part of the legal system. This applies to both statute and precedent. Here, the problem of interpretation resurfaces. As regards statutory interpretation, an envisaged ruling must be reconcilable with the ordinary meaning of the words of the statute. As regards the interpretation of precedents, avoiding conflict between an envisaged ruling and a rule entails distinguishing a precedent. Although MacCormick insists that the requirement of consistency does form a limitation of legal reasoning, it seems clear that it does not constitute a rigid boundary.[81]

From the perspective of the dichotomy between the framework of obligation and the framework of authorization, it may be observed that this general theory of law as legal reasoning is situated within the framework of obligation. There is, however, also an element of the framework of authorization in so far as, pursuant to the requirement of coherence, consequentialist reasoning is dependent on the presence of a principle. In view of the admitted possibility of competing principles or of inferring competing conclusions from a principle, however, the influence of the framework of authorization seems minimal.

Nevertheless, it is submitted that this description by MacCormick of a legal system need not necessarily be situated within the exclusively vertical structure of the framework of obligation or the framework of authorization. The elements of this system are formed by principles and rules, which both are neither totally fixed nor totally flexible, as well as consequentialist reasoning which comprises considerations of justice and policy. The transposition of these elements to the reformulated framework, which transcends the dichotomy between the framework of obligation and the framework of authorization, and which has both restricting and enabling components, would, it is submitted, change the relationship between consequentialist reasoning and the requirement of coherence, by increasing the steering role of principles and thereby canalizing the space for consequentialist, political, arguments.

4.11 Coordination: Finnis

In the general theory of law developed by Finnis, the concept of law is derived from basic values and basic requirements of practical reasonableness. As basic values, Finnis identifies seven values of fundamental importance to human life: life

[80] MacCormick 1994, pp. 119–128 and Chap. VII.

[81] MacCormick 1994, pp. 119–128 and Chap. VIII.

itself; knowledge; play; aesthetic experience; sociability; practical reasonableness; and religion.[82] As basic requirements of practical reasonableness, Finnis identifies the following requirements for moral reasoning and well-being: (i) a coherent plan of life; (ii) no arbitrary preferences amongst values; (iii) no arbitrary preferences amongst persons; (iv) detachment; (v) commitment; (vi) efficiency; (vii) respect for every basic value in every act; (viii) the requirements of the common good; (ix) and following one's conscience.[83]

Finnis subsequently defines the concepts of community and common good. A complete community is described by Finnis as an all-round association which co-ordinates the initiatives and activities of individuals, families, and intermediate associations. The aim of this all-round association is to ensure the whole ensemble of material and other conditions, including forms of collaboration, that tend to favour, facilitate, and foster the realization by each individual of his or her personal development.[84] The common good, according to Finnis, ensures that the basic values of the members of the community can be coordinated.[85] The concept of right is understood by Finnis in terms of freedoms to act of persons, which may conflict. The common good may be relied on to delimit those freedoms to act.[86] In order to achieve this objective, the common good relies mainly on the concepts of authority and law.[87]

The concept of authority is relied on by Finnis in order to co-ordinate the acts of the members of a community. According to Finnis, the coordination of the acts of the members of a community requires either unanimity or authority.[88] If a body can achieve coordination between the members of a community, those members should, as a matter of practical reasonableness, accept its authority.[89]

The concept of law is defined by Finnis as rules made, in accordance with regulative legal rules, by a determinate and effective authority (itself identified and, standardly, constituted as an institution by legal rules) for a complete community, and buttressed by sanctions in accordance with the rule-guided stipulations of adjudicative institutions, this ensemble of rules and institutions being directed to reasonably resolving any of the community's coordination problems (and so ratifying, tolerating, regulating, or overriding coordination solutions from any other institutions or sources of norms) for the common good of that community, according to a manner and form itself adapted to that common good by features of specificity, minimization of arbitrariness, and maintenance of a quality of reciprocity between the subjects of the law both amongst themselves and in their

82 Finnis 1980, Section IV.2.
83 Finnis 1980, Sections V.2–V.9.
84 Finnis 1980, Section VI.6.
85 Finnis 1980, Section VI.8.
86 Finnis 1980, Sections VIII.3–4.
87 Finnis 1980, Section VI.8.
88 Finnis 1980, Section IX.1.
89 Finnis 1980, Section IX.4.

relations with the lawful authorities.[90] According to Finnis, rules and institutions are interrelated in the sense that rules define, constitute, and regulate institutions and that institutions create and administer rules and settle questions about their existence, scope, applicability, and operation.[91]

With respect to the concept of public international law, Finnis considers that an international community may be developing.[92] Pointing to the formation of rules of customary international law, Finnis considers that a rule of law can develop in a situation of coordination on the basis of unanimity.[93]

This general theory of law clearly conforms to the framework of obligation, as may be inferred from Finnis' definition of the concept of right in terms of freedoms of persons which may conflict. Finnis sees the interrelated concepts of common good, authority, rules, and institutions as a matter of resolving coordination problems resulting from the exercise of those freedoms.

Nevertheless, from the perspective of the function of law, it may be seen that this general theory of law is adaptable to a framework which combines vertical and horizontal dimensions. As noted, the common good is defined in terms of coordination requirements of the members of a complete community. Within a vertical structure, it would be problematic that Finnis, as noted, situates institutions and rules in a circular relationship, rules determining institutions and institutions determining rules, because the step from rules to institutions cannot be accounted for. Both the framework of authorization and the framework of obligation pertain to the step from institutions to rules and presuppose the existence of the institution.

Furthermore, the steps from authority to coordination and from unanimity to coordination require clarification. Finnis adopts the position that, where authority achieves coordination, it should be accepted as a matter of practical reasonableness. However, the fact that coordination has been achieved would seem either to be the result of authority or not to have required authority. The notion that authority, in so far as it has achieved coordination, should be accepted as a matter of practical reasonableness, renders it conditional. Moreover, in so far as coordination can be achieved in several ways, the notion of authority does not afford substantive criteria to choose between them. From the opposite perspective, seeing unanimity as achieving coordination would seem to downplay the coordination problems, since unanimity might also be regarded as reflecting coordination. Furthermore, it gives every member of the community a veto. While put forward as equal coordination mechanisms, authority and unanimity actually seem mutually exclusive. Where authority is decisive, it overrides unanimity; conversely, where unanimity must be attained, authority cannot step in.

---

[90] Finnis 1980, Section X.6.

[91] Finnis 1980, Section X.3: '(...) law brings definition, specificity, clarity, and thus predictability into human interactions, by way of a system of rules and institutions so interrelated that rules define, constitute and regulate the institutions, while institutions create and administer the rules, and settle questions about their existence, scope, applicability and operation.'

[92] Finnis 1980, Section VI.8.

[93] Finnis 1980, Section IX.3.

Nevertheless, the vertical and horizontal dimensions outlined in this general theory of law seem to go well into the direction of a general theory of law which exceeds the mutual exclusivity of the frameworks of obligation and authorization. If the 'rights' which Finnis identifies are reformulated as powers to constitute the common good, the concept of law may be reformulated as a process of practical reasoning about the common good of a community. This process cannot exclusively be cast in terms either of authority or of unanimity; the former would result in unaccountability of its institutions, the latter would result in irresponsibility of the members. In this way, a concept of law must always, at least, be both vertical and horizontal, located at the transition between authority and unanimity. If seen from this perspective, the circular relationship between institutions and rules described by Finnis is not problematic but unavoidable. Pursuant to their power to act, rules are formed by the members of society, which sustain the formation of institutions; in turn, these institutions give rise to rules which inform the constituting of society by its members. As a comprehensive concept, the common good is no longer seen as something constraining, but as embodying the totality of the constituting of society, including its rules and institutions.

4.12 Conclusion

The conclusions that are drawn here from the discussion of the preceding general theories of law are the following. The first four general theories of law, developed by Hobbes, Locke, Rousseau, and Kant, attempted to explain the institution of the State and the internal law of the State on the basis of an internal movement from a state of nature; a movement from an exclusively horizontal structure to an exclusively vertical structure. It has been argued that this movement cannot be explained coherently and does not adequately explain the institution of the State and the internal law of the State. If that argument is tenable, it follows that the vertical structure of the concept of law underlying the concept of public international law cannot be based on the domestic analogy. Indeed, in respect of the general theories of law developed by Hobbes and Locke, it was observed that the notion of a state of nature was actually derived from the horizontal structure of public international law itself. Reliance on a domestic analogy therefore involves circular reasoning between the international plane and the internal sphere of States. It follows that we do not possess a coherent explanation of the vertical structure of the concept of law underlying the concept of public international law and that the ensuing mutual exclusivity of the framework of obligation and the framework of authorization must be rejected as incoherent.

This means that, rather than the institution of the State and the internal law of the State being explicable from the hypothesis of a state of nature and the concept of public international law being explicable on the basis of a domestic analogy—which implies a double upward movement, first from the state of nature to the institution of the State and then to the concept of public international law, as described by Rawls in the Law of Peoples in terms of the two consecutive original positions—what remains unexplained, and this is the most essential point, is actually the existing plurality of sovereign and independent States, which gives rise, internally, to the internal law of the State and, externally, to the concept of public international law. If the coherence of social contract theory cannot be demonstrated, this existing plurality of sovereign and independent States gives rise, externally, to the unexplained vertical structure of the concept of law underlying the concept of public international law and, internally, to the unexplained vertical structure of the internal law of the State. Both emanate from the unexplained institution of the State. As regards the concept of public international law, it may be said that the image of the institution of the State is, so to speak, superposed on the existing plurality of sovereign and independent States; from the perspective of this superposed image of the institution of the State, combined with the simultaneous absence of authority above States, the existing plurality of sovereign and independent States is seen in terms of the horizontal structure of public international law.

With respect to the general theories of law developed by Hart and Dworkin, it was remarked that they conform to the framework of obligation and inscribe themselves within the vertical structure predetermined by the institution of the State. Seeing the concept of law in terms of obligation, those general theories of law make it impossible to separate the exercise of authority from the identification, interpretation, and application of principles or rules of law. It simply depends on the views of the judicial officials of the legal system or on what law as integrity licenses or requires.

On the basis of the general theories of law developed by MacCormick and Finnis, an attempt was made to initiate the development of a general theory of law which is neither vertical nor horizontal but, at least, both. Such a general theory of law sees the concept of law as a process of practical reasoning directed at the common good of a community within a legal framework which is neither exclusively oriented towards obligations nor exclusively oriented towards rights. In any situation of practical reasoning about the common good of a community, the starting point cannot be formed by initial rights or obligations.

That legal framework may be regarded as a structure which, paradoxically, both incorporates and gives rise to the formation of the common good of a community. This common good may be regarded as consisting of institutions and rules which are interrelated thus, as Finnis says, that rules constitute institutions and that institutions produce rules. Moreover, this legal framework is also informed by principles which must be both enabling and disabling along the lines of the requirements of coherence and consistency identified by MacCormick. Within MacCormick's general theory of law, the enabling aspect was derived from the need to maintain the separation between the legislative power and the judicial power. Within the reformulated framework, the enabling element corresponds to the situating of the members of international society by virtue of the reformulated framework itself; within the reformulated framework, the members of international society must be deemed to have a power to act, but not an unlimited freedom to act. Because all members of international society must have such a power to act, the acting of the members of international society must be directed at the constituting of international society and, thereby, at the common good of international society. The fundamental basis of international society is thus a dilemma situation, which requires the members of international society to cooperate by constituting international society and, thereby, the common good of international society.

Chapter 5
The Framework of Obligation and the Framework of Authorization in Theory of Public International Law

5.1 Introduction

Chapter 3 returned to the two instances in which the PCIJ and the ICJ, respectively in the *Case of the S.S. "Lotus"* and *Legality of the Threat or Use of Nuclear Weapons*, addressed the question of whether the vertical structure of the concept of law underlying the concept of public international law conforms to the framework of obligation or the framework of authorization. Subsequently, Chap. 4 followed the parallel between the vertical structure of the concept of law underlying the concept of public international law, on the one hand, and the vertical structure of the internal law of the State and general theory of law, on the other hand. It was suggested that if the vertical structure of the internal law of the State and general theory of law could explain, conjointly, the vertical structure of the concept of law underlying the concept of public international law, the transition from the horizontal structure of public international law to the vertical structure of the concept of law underlying the concept of public international law would seem coherent. Chapter 4 therefore descended into the internal sphere of States with a view to arguing that the institution of the State and the internal law of the State do not form a coherent whole in the sense that both can be explained as emanating from a state of nature. It was accordingly concluded that there is no basis for the idea of a domestic analogy in the concept of public international law. Chapter 4 subsequently analyzed the general theories of law developed by Dworkin and Hart to situate these general theories of law within the legal framework formed by the institution of the State. Finally, consideration was given to the way in which the general theories of law developed by MacCormick and Finnis, which are built within a vertical structure, can be transposed to the reformulated framework identified in Sect. 1.4.

This chapter reascends, so to speak, to the international plane and gives consideration to theories of public international law. It will be argued that the theories of public international law developed by Grotius, Vattel, Kelsen, McDougal,

J. A. Vos, *The Function of Public International Law*,
DOI: 10.1007/978-90-6704-861-3_5, © J. A. Vos, The Netherlands 2013

Kratochwil, and Allott all inscribe themselves within the vertical structure of the concept of law underlying the concept of public international law, identified in Sect. 1.2. These theories of public international law conform to the dichotomy between the framework of obligation and the framework of authorization, described in Sect. 1.3. It will be argued that the vertical structure of the concept of law underlying those frameworks renders these theories of public international law incoherent. It will, however, also be argued that this incoherence indicates the fruitfulness of developing a concept of public international law which transcends the mutual exclusivity of those frameworks and which, accordingly, is neither exclusively vertical nor exclusively horizontal, but, at least, both. It will be argued that the theories of public international law developed by Kratochwil and Allott may be transposed to the reformulated framework so as to arrive at a coherent concept of public international law.

The selection of those six theories of public international law may be accounted for as follows. Together, the theories of public international law developed by Grotius and Vattel may be seen as having given shape to the mainstream concept of public international law and as providing, therefore, appropriate starting points. In addition, from the perspective of the function of public international law, both theories are interesting because both arrive, in a different way, at the identification of coexisting rights of States.

The theory of public international law developed by Kelsen is subsequently discussed as providing a vivid illustration of the parallel between the vertical structure of the concept of law underlying the concept of public international law and the vertical structure of the internal law of the State. In the pure theory of law, these vertical structures coincide. The point of view adopted by Kelsen is completely at odds with the conclusion arrived at in Chap. 4 that, if social contract theory does not hold, the structure of sovereign and independent States remains unexplained, projecting externally the concept of public international law and projecting internally the internal law of the State. This monist perspective of a vertical structure comprising both the concept of public international law and the internal law of the State has informed the layered structure of superordinate and subordinate societies put forward in the theory of public international law developed by Allott. The theory of public international law formulated by Lasswell/McDougal, also conceived as an alternative approach to mainstream public international law, is interesting because, although its appearance aligns with the horizontal structure of public international law, it actually follows the domestic analogy. The idea that the concept of public international law should be seen in terms of process rather than rules is another influence on the theory of public international law developed by Allott.

Finally, two theories of public international law deemed susceptible of transposition to the reformulated framework are discussed. These are the theories of public international law developed by Kratochwil and Allott. The theory of public international law developed by Kratochwil is important because it revolves, like the reformulated framework, around the notion of practical reasoning. In fact, the notion of practical reasoning described by Kratochwil significantly informs the argument developed here. As described in Sect. 1.4, its fifth component element consists of special techniques which operate to justify exclusions so as to justify final decisions. Its aim is to provide a degree of rigidity to a process that would otherwise be too flexible. If transposed to the reformulated framework, as propounded here, that degree of rigidity is provided by the reformulated framework itself. There, the process of practical reasoning, described by Kratochwil in terms of starting points, practical judgments, and procedural requirements, propels the members of international society out of their dilemma situation.

The theory of public international law developed by Allott revolves around the self-constituting of international society by the members of international society. Simultaneously, it defines the concept of public international law as inherent in international society, in the sense that international society delegates power-rights to the members of international society. The notion of international society as the society of all societies, identified by Allott, seeks, in a way, to circumvent the institution of the State which here, in its multiplicity of sovereign and independent States, is regarded as unexplained, projecting the concept of public international law externally and the internal law of the State internally. It must be observed, however, that social idealism also dissociates public international law from international society, in so far as it sees the function of public international law as subordinate to international society. The reformulated framework developed here sees, like social idealism, the concept of public international law and international society as intertwined. In the reformulated framework, however, the relationship between public international law and international society may be seen as mutually constitutive. On the basis of their dilemma situation, the members of international society constitute simultaneously the principles and rules of international society and international society itself. In this sense, the concept of public international law may be seen as inherent in international society. As the members of international society constitute international society, they form at the same time the principles and rules of public international law. Conversely, as the members of international society form the principles and rules of public international law, they constitute at the same time international society.

5.2 Permission Inferred from the Absence of Obligation: Grotius

In *De Jure Belli ac Pacis*, Grotius defined the concept of law as a rule of moral action imposing obligation to what is right. Permission was regarded by Grotius as the result of the absence of a rule of law. However, Grotius added that a permission inferred from the absence of an obligation simultaneously implied an obligation imposed on another person not to impede the permitted act.[1] Thus,

[1] Grotius 1964, Book I, Chap. I, Section IX.

according to Grotius, permission could not be inferred solely from the absence of an obligation, but presupposed an obligation imposed on another person. On the basis of this definition, Grotius divided the concept of law into two categories, the law of nature and volitional law.[2]

Grotius defined the law of nature as a dictate of right reason according to which an act is forbidden or enjoined.[3] As described by Grotius, the function of the law of nature is to balance the rights or interests of a member of society and of society as a whole, or of different members of society, by imposing obligations on members of society.[4] This conception of the law of nature, as described by Grotius, clearly conforms to the framework of obligation. Members of society are assumed to have a freedom to act, which gives rise to rights or interests. The function of the law of nature is to limit these freedoms of the members of society.[5] Grotius asserted that an act is permitted, or that members of society have a right to act, in the absence of an obligation inferred from the law of nature.[6] At the same time, however, Grotius maintained that an act is not permitted, if it conflicts with the right of another member of society.[7]

Volitional law, according to Grotius, emanates from either human or divine will.[8] Human law is subdivided by Grotius into municipal law and the law of nations.[9] Grotius defined the State as a complete association of free men, joined together for the enjoyment of rights and for their common interest.[10] Sovereignty, according to Grotius, signifies a power whose actions are not subject to the legal control of another, so that they cannot be rendered void by another human will.[11] By virtue of its sovereignty, the State determines municipal law; consequently, the State is not bound by municipal law.[12] The law of nations, according to Grotius, emanates from the will of nations and consists of custom, agreement or tacit

[2] Grotius 1964, Book I, Chap. I, Section IX.

[3] Grotius 1964, Book I, Chap. I, Section X.

[4] Grotius 1964, Book I, Chap. I, Section X, Book II, Chap. XX, Section V, Book III, Chaps. I, IV, Sections III, XV.

[5] Grotius 1964, Book II, Chap. XX, Sections VIII, IX.

[6] Grotius 1964, Book III, Chap. I, Sections II, XI.

[7] Grotius 1964, Book III, Chap. I, Section XI.

[8] Grotius 1964, Book I, Chap. I, Section XIII.

[9] Grotius 1964, Book I, Chap. I, Section XIV.

[10] Grotius 1964, Book I, Chap. I, Section XIV.

[11] Grotius 1964, Book I, Chap. III, Section VII.

[12] Grotius 1964, Book II, Chap. IV, Section XII: 'For in order that any one may be bound by a law, both power and intent, at least presumed, are requisite in the maker of the law. No one can bind himself after the manner of a law, that is after the manner of a superior. Hence it is that the makers of laws have the right to change their own laws. Still, one can be bound by his own law, not directly, but by implication; inasmuch as he is a member of the community, he is under an obligation imposed by natural fairness, which desires that the parts be adjusted in relation to the whole (...) But here this is not in point, because we are considering the maker of laws not as a part of the community but as the one in whom the power of the entire body resides. We are in fact treating of sovereignty as such.'; Chap. XX, Section XXIV.

consent.[13] Both municipal law and the law of nations conform to the framework of obligation.

From the perspective of the dichotomy between the framework of obligation and the framework of authorization, the following observations may be made with respect to these different forms of law perceived by Grotius: the concept of law, the law of nature, and the law of nations.

First, as regards the concept of law, Grotius recognizes that inferring permission from the absence of obligation can only give rise to a coherent relationship between the members of society in so far as obligations, corresponding to this permission, are imposed on other persons. Thus, all law would necessarily consist of obligations. Grotius applies this concept of law to his conception of the law of nature, inferring permission or right from the absence of obligation. At the same time, however, Grotius observes that an act is not permitted if it conflicts with the right of another member of society. If permission or right is inferred from the absence of obligation, this would, however, always be the case. Unless that permission correlates with an obligation imposed on another member of society, permissions inferred from the absence of obligation and translated into rights or interests are inherently conflicting, because all members of society are deemed to have, in the absence of obligations, equal rights and interests. It would also follow that, in order to fully balance the rights or interests of the members of society, all rights or interests would need to correspond to obligations. But in that case, no rights or interests would remain.

In Grotius' system, rights must be matched by obligations, because only an obligation imposed on a member of society can give rise to a right of another member of society which does not conflict with rights of other members of society. Nevertheless, Grotius also seems to presuppose the prior existence of rights in so far as he locates the function of law in the balancing of the rights or interests of the members of society by means of obligations. This involves, however, relying on an assumption that incoherent rights or interests of the members of society can be derived from their freedom to act. Grotius observed that such an act is not permitted if it conflicts with the right of another member of society. Yet, he also relied on the coexistence of such inconsistent rights when locating the function of the law of nature in the balancing of the rights or interests of the members of society. Grotius' system thus gives rise to the following circular sequence: in principle, permission can be inferred from the absence of obligation; this permission translates into a right if an obligation is imposed on another person; however, this permission may also not conflict with a right of another person; such a right entails an obligation imposed on the first person; to this extent, permission cannot be inferred from the absence of obligation. It follows that obligations must be omnipresent in Grotius' system. Incidentally, this result concords with the turn to

[13] Grotius 1964, Book I, Chap. I, Section XIV, Book II, Chap. XVIII, Section IV, Chap. XIX, Section I, Book III, Chap. II, Section II, Chap. IV, Section XV.

the passive form in his definition of the State as a complete association of free men, joined together for the enjoyment of rights and for their common interest.

This tension in the law of nature between inferring permission from the absence of obligation and observing that an act is not permitted if it conflicts with the right of another member of society, disappears when Grotius moves to the law of nations. When dealing with the law of nations, Grotius' analysis, overall, is descriptive and limited to the question whether the law of nations prohibits an act. If the law of nations does not prohibit an act, Grotius concludes that such an act is permitted, without considering the question whether such an act might conflict with the right of another member of international society.[14]

It may thus be observed that Grotius has great difficulty in accounting in a coherent manner for the coexistence of rights. If not balanced by obligations, rights are both regarded as self-existent and as inconsistent. If balanced by obligations, rights do not in fact exist as such but are a reflection of obligations. This whole scheme is crucially dependent on the existence of an authority above the members of society which is capable to perform the balancing function required to harmonize the rights or interests of the members of society. On the other hand, the location of the function of law in the balancing of the rights or interests of the members of society would seem to indicate their a priori character. The step from the interests of the members of society to the establishment of authority is too big to be accommodated within this scheme. Hence the twist in the definition of the State. Since this authority is by definition absent in the society of States, Grotius, not surprisingly, recedes to the view that permission results from the absence of obligation.

It may be noted at this point that the tension in the law of nature which Grotius tried to reconcile, between inferring permission from the absence of obligation and observing that an act is not permitted if it conflicts with the right of another member of society, points to the view that there can be no inherent freedoms to act, rights, or interests of the members of (international) society. Any such inherent right would necessarily conflict with a similar inherent right of another member of (international) society. It would also follow that the function of public international law does not reside exclusively in imposing obligations on the members of international society. This matches well with the view put forward here that a rejection of the mutual exclusivity of the framework of obligation and the framework of obligation leads to the conclusion that a coherent concept of law does not admit the a priori existence of either rights or obligations. In comparison to the scheme developed by Grotius, the reformulated framework sees the basic position of the members of society in terms of a dilemma, as having a power, but not a freedom to act. It sees the function of public international law in terms of the constituting of international society by means of rules of public international law. That view comprises an element of balancing, but, other than Grotius' approach, that balancing is informed by both an obligation aspect and a right aspect.

---

[14] Grotius 1964, Book III, Chap. IV, Sections II–IV, XV.

5.3 Voluntary Law: Vattel

Vattel defined the Law of Nations as the science of the rights which exist between Nations or States, and of the obligations corresponding to these rights. As regards the relationship between rights and obligations, Vattel considered that rights result from obligations.[15] Vattel situated States in a state of nature and characterized them, on this basis, as free and independent.[16] At the same time, Vattel situated States in a society of nations with the stipulated purpose of mutual assistance.[17]

According to Vattel, the Law of Nations consists primarily of the Law of Nature, which is also termed the necessary Law of Nations.[18] Within this framework, Vattel identifies as a first general law that each Nation should contribute as far as it can to the happiness and advancement of other Nations. Vattel stipulated, however, that a nation must give priority to its own happiness and advancement.[19] Moreover, Vattel identifies as a second general law the liberty and independence of States and deduces from that general law the proposition that it is for each State to decide what the Law of Nature requires of it.[20] Vattel supported this reasoning by a distinction between imperfect rights and obligations and perfect rights and obligations, claiming that obligations produced by the Law of Nature merely give rise to imperfect rights.[21] Vattel concluded that a nation is free to act, in so far as its acts do not affect the perfect rights of another nation or, in other words, unless it is under a perfect external obligation.[22]

Vattel continued that, in the case of a dispute between States, it must be assumed that they have equal rights and that their claims are equally just.[23] Vattel subsequently distinguished three further branches of the Law of Nations: (a) the voluntary Law of Nations[24]; (b) the conventional Law of Nations or law of treaties[25]; and (c) the customary Law of Nations,[26] which, together, form the positive Law of Nations.[27]

The most important of these branches, in Vattel's work, is the voluntary Law of Nations, because it gives rise to perfect rights. Thus, in the crucial Chap. V in Book II, dedicated to justice, Vattel writes that every State has the right to resist

[15] Vattel 1916, introduction, para 3.
[16] Vattel 1916, introduction, para 4.
[17] Vattel 1916, introduction, para 12.
[18] Vattel 1916, introduction, paras 5–7.
[19] Vattel 1916, introduction, paras 13–14.
[20] Vattel 1916, introduction, paras 15–16.
[21] Vattel 1916, introduction, para 17.
[22] Vattel 1916, introduction, para 20.
[23] Vattel 1916, introduction, para 21.
[24] Vattel 1916, introduction, paras 21–23.
[25] Vattel 1916, introduction, para 24.
[26] Vattel 1916, introduction, paras 25–26.
[27] Vattel 1916, introduction, para 27.

any attempt to deprive it of its rights or of anything which lawfully belongs to it. This right is derived from the duty and right of self-preservation.[28] It gives rise to: (i) the right of lawful self-defence; (ii) the right to obtain justice by force; and (iii) the right to inflict punishment. As an extension of the right to inflict punishment, Vattel admits the right of all nations to suppress a Nation that systematically violates the rights of other States.[29] Vattel essentially derives these rights from the welfare of the State and of the society of States.

When dealing with the voluntary Law of Nations as regards the effects of regular (declared) war, in Chap. XII of Book III, Vattel argues that, because of the absence of a common judge in the state of nature, the following three rules should be adopted: First, as regards its effects, regular war must be regarded as just on both sides; second, in a regular war, both sides have the same rights; third, the voluntary Law of Nations does not confer true rights, but merely impunity on the unjust side.[30] Vattel explained this step by arguing that in this way, while each side would naturally dress up its acts in clothes of justice, a worsening of the consequences of the war could be avoided and the return to peace could be facilitated.[31]

Within his central concept of the voluntary Law of Nations, Vattel thus made an essential distinction along the lines of the *jus ad bellum* and the *jus in bello*. While arguing with respect to the *jus in bello* that, in the absence of a common judge above nations, it could not be determined which side was acting in accordance with justice, Vattel maintained at the same time that with respect to an injury, a nation had a perfect right of defensive war, of offensive war, and of punishment.

Thus, in the domain of *jus ad bellum*, Vattel assumed the existence of perfect rights and obligations. The crucial question, then, is whence those perfect rights and obligations could be derived. Vattel maintains that treaties could give rise to such perfect rights and obligations.[32] His treatment is ambiguous, however. With regard to the interpretation of treaties, Vattel stipulates as the third general principle of interpretation that neither of the parties who have an interest in the contract or treaty may interpret it after his own mind.[33] It is remarkable that in the domain of *jus ad bellum* Vattel did not admit the relativity of the concept of justice as well. This is, however, easily explained if it is realized that Vattel did not derive those perfect rights from the existence of perfect obligations, but from the duty and right of self-preservation and from the right to the welfare of nations. Those rights being the same for all nations, Vattel thereby set up a system of mutually incoherent rights to self-preservation and welfare. The difficulty that then arises is that this system is difficult to square with Vattel's starting point that rights result from

[28] Vattel 1916, Book II, paras 65–66.

[29] Vattel 1916, Book II, paras 67–70.

[30] Vattel 1916, Book III, paras 190–192.

[31] Vattel 1916, Book III, paras 188–189.

[32] Vattel 1916, Book II, para 164.

[33] Vattel 1916, Book II, para 265.

obligations. In so far as the system is inferred from imperfect obligations, it could not, it would seem, give rise to perfect rights.

5.4 Legal Order: Kelsen

In the pure theory of law ('Reine Rechtslehre'), developed by Kelsen, the concept of law is regarded as a legal order ('Rechtsordnung'), in which norms are connected to each other in a relation of super- and sub-ordination ('Stufenbau'). Validity ('Geltung') signifies the existence of a norm in this legal order; a super-ordinate norm validates a sub-ordinate norm. The apex of this legal order is formed by a basic norm ('Grundnorm') that itself is not validated by a super-ordinate norm; the existence of this norm is pre-supposed ('vorausgesetzt'). The institution of the State itself, Kelsen argues, may be seen as a legal order.[34]

In the pure theory of law, a norm is defined as the connection ('Verknüpfung') between an act and a sanction. The human conduct is the condition ('Bedingung') of the norm; the sanction is the consequence ('Folge') of the norm. Kelsen considered that a norm may also have the function of permitting acts ('erlauben/ermächtigen'). In this respect, Kelsen distinguished between a negative permission, which results from the absence of a norm, and a positive permission, issued pursuant to a norm limiting the scope of a norm containing an obligation.[35] Like Grotius, Kelsen considered that, if a coherent relation is to be arrived at, a negative permission should correspond to an obligation imposed on another subject of the norm. However, according to Kelsen, in practice, a legal order cannot achieve this completeness and must therefore necessarily leave a minimum of freedom ('Freiheitsminimum'). These considerations clearly indicate that the legal order as a whole, as conceived by Kelsen, conforms to the framework of obligation. Permissions are either inferred from the absence of an obligation or are the result of an exception to an obligation.

---

[34] Kelsen 1960, paras 4(a)–(d), 6, 34–35, 41.

[35] Kelsen 1960, para 4(a)–(d): 'In einem weitesten Sinne, kann jedes menschliche Verhalten, das in einer normativen Ordnung als Bedingung oder Folge bestimmt ist, als durch diese Ordnung ermächtigt und in diesem Sinne als positiv geregelt gelten. In einer negativen Weise ist menschliches Verhalten durch eine normative Ordnung geregelt, wenn dieses Verhalten durch die Ordnung nicht verboten ist, ohne durch eine den Geltungsbereich einer verbietenden Norm einschränkende Norm positiv erlaubt zu sein, und daher in einem nur negativen Sinne erlaubt ist. Diese bloss negative Funktion des Erlaubens muss von der positiven, weil in einem positiven Akt bestehenden, Funktion des Erlaubens unterschieden werden. Der positive Charakter einer Erlaubnis tritt dann besonders hervor, wenn die Einschränkung einer ein bestimmtes Verhalten verbietenden Norm durch eine Norm erfolgt die das sonst verbotene Verhalten unter der Bedingung erlaubt, dass diese Erlaubnis von einem hiezu ermächtigten Gemeinschaftsorgan erteilt wird. Die – negative wie positive – Funktion des Erlaubens ist somit wesentlich mit der des Gebietens verbunden. Nur innerhalb einer normativen Ordnung, die bestimmtes menschliches Verhalten gebietet, kann ein bestimmtes menschlichen Verhalten erlaubt sein.'; 6 (b), (e).

Like the concept of law in general, the concept of public international law is regarded by Kelsen as a legal order, consisting of norms connected to each other in a relation of super- and sub-ordination ('Stufenbau').[36] The apex of the international legal order is formed by a basic norm ('Grundnorm'), which is pre-supposed ('vorausgesetzt').[37] The basic norm validates the concept of general international law ('allgemeines Völkerrecht'), which consists of customary international law and which, in turn, validates the concept of conventional international law. According to Kelsen, the relation between the basic norm and customary international law is such that the basic norm authorizes States to form norms of customary international law. Similarly, Kelsen considered that the relation between customary international law and conventional international law is such that customary international law authorizes States to form norms of conventional international law.[38]

From the perspective of the dichotomy between the framework of obligation and the framework of authorization, it may be remarked that Kelsen situates the relations between the basic norm, customary international law, and conventional international law within the framework of authorization. At the same time, however, Kelsen described the function of both customary international law and conventional international law in terms of limiting ('Einschränken') the sovereignty of States by means of obligations ('Verpflichtungen').[39] This situates the function of customary international law and conventional international law within the framework of obligation. Thus, in the transitions from the basic norm to customary international law and from customary international law to conventional international law, the framework of authorization transforms into the framework of obligation.

This transformation of the framework of authorization into the framework of obligation is problematic in the light of their mutual exclusivity. If the relationship between the basic norm and customary international law is situated within the framework of authorization, States can only form customary international law in so far as they are authorized to do so by the basic norm. This presupposes that States do not have a general freedom to form norms of customary international law. Within the framework of authorization, the function of the basic norm is to confer on States a power to make norms of customary international law. If, however, the function of norms of customary international law consists of limiting the sovereignty of States by means of obligations, this presupposes that States have a general freedom to act, including a general freedom to form norms of customary international law. Those perspectives are mutually exclusive.

Similarly, if the relationship between customary international law and conventional international law is situated within the framework of authorization,

---

36 Paulus 2001, pp. 170–173.

37 Dupuy 2002, pp. 67–69.

38 Kelsen 1960, paras 34(h), 42(c).

39 Kelsen 1960, para 43(c), (d).

States can only form conventional international law in so far as they are authorized to do so by customary international law. This presupposes that States do not have a general freedom to form norms of conventional international law. Within the framework of authorization, the function of norms of customary international law is to confer on States a power to make norms of conventional international law. If, however, the function of norms of conventional international law consists of limiting the sovereignty of States by means of obligations, this presupposes that States have a general freedom to act, including a general freedom to form norms of conventional international law. Those perspectives are mutually exclusive.

It is also interesting to note the difference between the vertical structure described by Kelsen—consisting of the international legal order and the national legal orders—and the existing plurality of States, to which reference was made in Sect. 4.12. As conceived by Kelsen, the vertical structure—consisting of the international legal order and the national legal orders—is a monist system, the basic norm of which may be indifferentially located either in the international legal order or in a national legal order. In contrast, the existing plurality of States gives rise, externally, to the vertical structure of the concept of law underlying the concept of public international law and, internally, to the internal law of the State. At the point of transition from the external to the internal and from the internal to the external, the institution of the State remains unexplained. Both the vertical structure described by Kelsen and the existing plurality of States are situated in an exclusively vertical framework. For Kelsen, the difficulty remains how to explain the basic norm itself which, although it gives validity to all other norms of the legal order, cannot itself be explained by virtue of the legal order.[40] It is perhaps not accidental that the basic norm, while functionally located at the apex of the legal order, is metaphorically located at the basis of the legal order, which suggests a circular element in a hierarchical structure. For the existing plurality of States, the difficulty remains that, in the absence of a plausible explanation on the basis of social contract theory, it remains entirely unexplained. If, however, the mutual exclusivity of the framework of obligation and the framework of authorization must be discarded, the transition to a reformulated framework, which is both enabling and disabling, renders the identification of a basic norm unnecessary and provides a structure which gives rise to the constituting of international society by the members of international society. Internally, the members of international society may themselves be regarded as a structure which gives rise to the constituting of society.

---

[40] Mahiou 2008, pp. 102–108.

5.5 Process: McDougal/Lasswell

The policy approach, developed by McDougal and Lasswell, sees itself as an alternative to the mainstream approach to public international law, which focuses on process rather than rules. In terms of process, the (world) legal process is seen as embedded in a (world) power process comprised by a (world) social process, so that in the policy approach the legal element, although apparently centrally described by means of concentric circles, is not decisive. Its role is circumscribed by the political element.

The policy approach revolves around the concept of a public order system. According to McDougal and Lasswell, a public order system consists of the social process of a community. This social process comprehends a power process which, in turn, comprises a legal process.[41] This legal process is defined by McDougal and Lasswell as the making of authoritative and controlling decisions. Authority, in this connection, is understood as the structure of expectation concerning who, with what qualifications and mode of selection, is competent to make which decisions by what criteria and what procedures. Control refers to an effective voice in decision, whether authorized or not. The concept of law, then, is defined by McDougal/Lasswell as the conjunction of common expectations concerning authority with a high degree of corroboration in actual operation.[42]

According to McDougal/Lasswell, the objective of the policy approach is the realization of human dignity in public order systems, which entails a social process in which values (power, wealth, respect, well-being, skill, enlightenment, recti-tude, and affection) are widely and not narrowly shared, and in which private choice, rather than coercion, is emphasized as the predominant modality of power.[43]

Similarly, a world public order system, according to the policy approach, is a public order system consisting of a world social process, which comprehends a world power process, which, in turn, comprises a world legal process.[44] Drawing these threads together, McDougal and Laswell stipulate as the overall objective of the policy approach the attainment of universal human dignity in a world public order system.[45] McDougal and Lasswell argue that the achievement of this objective requires the development of a jurisprudence enabling one to evaluate public order systems on the basis of the criterion of human dignity and the development of authority structures and functions (principles and procedures) for a world public order system that realizes human dignity.[46]

[41] McDougal and Lasswell 1987, p. 15.

[42] McDougal and Lasswell 1987, pp. 13–14.

[43] McDougal and Lasswell 1987, pp. 16–19.

[44] McDougal and Lasswell 1987, pp. 10–13.

[45] McDougal and Lasswell 1987, p. 21.

[46] McDougal and Lasswell 1987, p. 39; Paulus 2001, pp. 194–198.

Against this background, McDougal and Lasswell appraise public order systems according to the degree to which specialized organs have developed to conduct the decision process within an inclusive territory (positive appraisal criterion) and the degree to which the organs employed by each inclusive territory carry on the decision process for the whole (negative appraisal criterion).[47] Observing that a public order system in which the organs employed by each inclusive territory carry on the decision process for the whole is not a complete public order system—this is the heart of their criticism of mainstream public international law—McDougal and Lasswell recommend that specialized organs should be developed in the world public order system.

In view of these statements, it would seem that the policy approach must be situated within the framework of obligation. It would also seem that the policy approach constitutes a conspicuous example of the domestic analogy. The positive appraisal criterion, the degree to which specialized organs have developed to conduct the decision process within an inclusive territory seems to correspond to the public order system embodied by the institution of the State. The negative appraisal criterion, the degree to which the organs employed by each inclusive territory carry on the decision process for the whole, seems to correspond to the horizontal structure of international society, which admits the coexistence of inconsistent decisions. While observing that the world public order system is not a complete public order system, because it satisfies the negative appraisal criterion, and recommending that, therefore, specialized organs should be developed in the world public order system, McDougal and Lasswell appear to rely on the assumption that such a world public order system which, moreover, achieves universal human dignity, is attainable when proceeding from a world public order system that satisfies the negative appraisal criterion. This movement implies that a world public order system satisfying the negative appraisal criterion is both different from and similar to a public order system satisfying the positive appraisal criterion.

More generally, there is a perfect parallel between the world public order system and the various public order systems which it comprises, on the one hand, and the existing plurality of States described in Sect. 4.12. Each public order system is aligned to a vertical structure and the world public order system is also aligned to a vertical structure to the extent that specialized organs must be developed. Similar to Hart's view that the concept of public international law should develop into a union of primary and secondary rules, McDougal and Lasswells's view that the world public order system should develop specialized organs assumes that public order systems have been established on the basis of a transition from a horizontal structure to a vertical structure. The envisaged development of specialized organs for the world public order system seems calculated to extend, at the international plane, this development in the direction of a super-State, similar to the formulation of the principles of the Law of Peoples, in

[47] McDougal and Lasswell 1987, p. 16.

Rawls' work, pursuant to a second original position. From the perspective of the dichotomy between the framework of obligation and the framework of authorization, the question of the interrelationship between such a world public order system and the realization of human dignity is intriguing.

5.6 Practical Reasoning: Kratochwil

Practical reasoning, as defined by Kratochwil, is reasoning about practical situations on the basis of rules or norms. In practical reasoning, topoi (commonplaces) are both starting-points for arguments and common understandings providing structure to an argument. Practical reasoning does not necessarily provide one good solution to a practical situation, but is a communicative process about such situations based on rules/norms. Kratochwil considers legal reasoning to be a specialized form of practical reasoning, which uses legal topoi. Such legal topoi play an important role, for example, when a legal issue is characterized, when the relevant facts and norms of a case are determined, when the pleadings of the parties are formulated, when interpretation takes place, and when reasons for an authoritative decision are given.[48]

Kratochwil makes a distinction between regulative and institutional rules/norms, defining regulative rules/norms as constraining rules/norms, and institutional rules/norms as enabling rules/norms. As an example of an institutional rule/norm, Kratochwil refers to rules/norms allowing the use of the institutions of promising or contracting.[49] Within this context, it may be noted that both regulative and institutional rules/norms conform to the framework of obligation. Although the characterization of institutional rules as enabling rules might indicate reliance on the framework of authorization, the description of the function of institutional rules, as rules which enable regulative rules to function, for example by providing that a promise or contract is binding,[50] clearly suggest conformity with the framework of obligation.

According to Kratochwil, practical reasoning is not dependent on the existence of formal institutions. However, because the process of practical reasoning does not in itself lead to determinate outcomes, only authoritative decision-making can provide determinate outcomes, by fixing the choice, out of a plurality of solutions, of a particular solution. In the absence of formal institutions, the resolution of a practical problem requires an accepted normative practice.[51] This contrast between formal institutions and accepted normative practices bears a striking resemblance, it may be noted, with the two modes for achieving coordination distinguished by

---

[48] Kratochwil 1989, pp. 34–39, 205–248.

[49] Kratochwil 1989, pp. 26, 61, 90–92.

[50] Kratochwil 1989, pp. 117, 122, 123, 144, 146.

[51] Kratochwil 1989, pp. 34, 62–63, 79, 125, 142, 189.

Finnis: authority and unanimity. Continuing in this horizontal direction, Kratochwil understands the concept of public international law, like the concept of law in general, as a form of practical reasoning. Mirroring the contrast between the horizontal structure of public international law and the vertical structure of the internal law of the State, Kratochwil sees public international law as consisting of the acceptance of normative practices and the recognition of mutual rights, informed by analogies with private law.[52]

To the extent that Kratochwil's theory of public international law as a form of practical reasoning remains situated within the framework of obligation, it remains problematic in so far as the framework of obligation requires the identification of clear, precise rules of law so as to delimit the freedoms to act of legal persons. Practical reasoning is neither capable nor intended to deliver one good solution to a practical situation. If several solutions are possible, there does not seem to be a basis for imposing a particular solution on legal persons. In the presence of formal institutions, although authoritative decision-making can provide determinate outcomes, practical reasoning does not furnish criteria for the exercise of authority if several good solutions to a practical situation exist. In the absence of formal institutions, this plurality of outcomes in combination with the dependence of any solution on its acceptance by the members of international society seem to render it incapable of rendering definitive normative outcomes to a practical situation.[53]

However, if the mutual exclusivity of the framework of obligation and the framework of authorization is rejected as incoherent, seeing the concept of public international law as a form of practical reasoning may acquire a crucial place. Within the framework of a concept of public international law which transcends the dichotomy between the framework of obligation and the framework of authorization, the members of international society are situated as having a power to act. Within the parameters of this reformulated framework, the concept of public international law as a form of practical reasoning may be regarded as the process through which the members of international society constitute international society, in the form of principles and rules of public international law which are simultaneously enabling and disabling, containing rights/obligations. This process of practical reasoning takes place on the basis of the ground structure of international society and gives rise to the constituting of international society. Within the reformulated framework, the flexibility of practical reasoning is thus paired to the rigidity of the ground structure. As situated within the reformulated framework, this combination straddles the opposition between stability and change. As constituted, international society simultaneously provides a new structure for the reconstituting of international society. Embedded within and shaping the reformulated framework, the flexibility characterizing the process of practical reasoning must accordingly be dynamic.

---

[52] Kratochwil 1989, 161, pp. 250–256.

[53] Scobbie 1990, pp. 352–362.

5.7 International Law as Intrinsic to International Society: Allott

In social idealism, developed by Allott, the concept of society is defined as a sharing of willing and acting of the members of society.[54] This process of self-creating of society is described by Allott as the socializing of society, which involves the continuous struggle of society with five dilemmas inherent in social relations: the dilemma of identity (the self and the other), the dilemma of power (the one and the many), the dilemma of will (unity of nature, plurality of value), the dilemma of order (justice and social justice), and the dilemma of becoming (new citizens, old laws).[55]

Allott describes the constitution of society as the structure-system of society and distinguishes three, interrelated, forms of the constitution of society, the legal constitution, the real constitution, and the ideal constitution. According to Allott, the legal constitution is the constitution as law, as a structure-system of retained acts of will, which are concerned with the distribution and use of social power. The real constitution is the constitution as it is actualized in the social process, a structure-system of power. The ideal constitution is the constitution that presents to society an idea of what society might become.[56]

Allott puts forward seven generic principles of a constitution, which are proposed as common to the constitution of any society: (1) the principle of integration (law is part of the total social process); (2) the principle of transformation (law is dynamic); (3) the principle of delegation (legal power is delegated power); (4) the principle of the intrinsic limitation of power (legal power is limited); (5) the principle of the supremacy of law (social power is under the law); (6) the principle of the supremacy of the social interest (legal power is power in the social interest); (7) the principle of social responsibility (social power is accountable).[57]

Within this framework, the concept of a social exchange plays a central role. The result of the social exchange is social power, which is power produced by the systematic activity of society. According to Allott, social power may be delegated by society to the members of society in the form of legal power. Social power results from a process of communication between society and its members.[58]

According to Allott, like the relation between society and its members, societies are also connected to each other in a relation of super- and sub-ordination. International society is defined by Allott as the society of all societies and situated above all other societies.[59] Within this context, Allott defines the function of

---

[54] Allott 1990, paras 1.1, 3.1, 9.2, 19.27.

[55] Allott 1990, paras 4.13, 4.14, 4.24, 5.1, 5.32, 6.1.

[56] Allott 1990, paras 9.2, 9.7, 9.8, 9.10.

[57] Allott 1990, paras 11.5, 11.11, 11.14, 11.17, 11.20, 11.23, 11.27, 11.31.

[58] Allott 1990, paras 10.18–10.20, 10.32.

[59] Allott 1990, paras 1.1, 19.27.

international law, characterized as the law of international society, as delegating social power in the form of legal power to the sub-ordinate societies.[60]

From the perspective of the dichotomy between the framework of obligation and the framework of authorization, the theory of society and law developed by Allott may be situated within the framework of authorization. As a result of the social exchange, social power, produced by the systematic activity of society, is delegated to the members of society in the form of legal power. Concordantly, the function of international law is located in the delegation of social power in the form of legal power to sub-ordinate societies.[61] It would seem, however, that, since social power is regarded as the result of a social exchange, this presupposes that the members of society already have a measure of social power and thus legal power. Similarly, if the social power of international society is the result of the systematic activity of international society, this presupposes that the members of international society already have a measure of social power and thus legal power.

To a certain extent, therefore, the theory of public international law formulated by Allott presupposes the existence of (international) society and, to that, extent, does not account for the constituting of (international) society by the members of (international) society. While characterizing public international law as inherent in international society, it also separates public international law from the members of international society, in so far as it does not involve the members of international society in the production of social power. It is submitted, however, that this theory of public international law may be transposed to the reformulated framework developed here, by seeing the members of (international) society as having power-rights which cannot, however, extend so far as to be inconsistent with the power-rights of other members of (international) society and, therefore, cannot be unlimited freedoms to act. Like the theory of public international law developed by Allott, the reformulated framework therefore sees the members of international society in terms of a dilemma. Joining social power and legal power, the ground structure of the reformulated framework directs the members of international society to the constituting of international society in the form of principles and rules of public international law. Within the reformulated framework, therefore, the concept of public international law is seen as inherent in the constituting of international society in the sense that the constituting of international society takes the form of principles and rules of public international law and that the formation of principles and rules of public international law incorporates the constituting of international society.

---

60 Allott 1990, paras 16.39–16.41, 16.100: 'The function of international law is to organize the distribution of legal relations, and especially power-rights, throughout the world in the social interest of the whole of international society – and to control the implementation of those relations, including especially the exercise of power-rights.'

61 Paulus 2001, pp. 145–148.

5.8 Conclusion

When considered from the perspective of the dichotomy between the framework of obligation and the framework of authorization, the theories of public international law considered in this chapter may be analyzed as incoherent. There is always an assumption about the origin and character of rules, which presupposes a legal framework which cannot be explained coherently. Similarly, there is always an assumption about the normative relations between the members of society, which presupposes a legal framework which situates the members of society inconsistently in respect of each other.

The analysis of the theories of public international law developed by Grotius and Vattel brought to the fore that, within a horizontal structure, rights cannot coherently coexist. Both Grotius and Vattel seem to have been aware of this aspect. Grotius observed that a permission could only be inferred from the absence of obligation, when combined with an obligation imposed on another member of society. Nevertheless, with respect to the law of nations, he proceeded to infer permission from the absence of obligation. Similarly, Vattel attached special importance to the voluntary law of nations, because it could give rise to perfect rights. In fact, those rights were not derived from the sources of public international law, but from the welfare and self-preservation of nations.

The theories of public international law developed by Kelsen and McDougal/Lasswell may also be compared. Both Kelsen's legal order and McDougal/Lasswell's public order system are aligned along a vertical axis. Kelsen had to assume the pre-existence of the basic norm; it does not seem coincidental that Kelsen treated the institution of the State as a legal order. Within the parameters of the argument developed here, it may be said that it is precisely the institution of the State that provides the basic norm. Similarly, McDougal/Lasswell appraised public order systems according to whether specialized organs had been developed along the lines drawn, it is submitted, by the institution of the State.

On the other hand, the theories of public international law developed by Kratochwil and Allott were put forward as transposable to the reformulated framework. While situated within the framework of obligation, the theory of public international law as practical reasoning seemed insufficiently precise to delimit the freedoms to act of the members of international society. Similarly, while situated within the framework of authorization, the theory of public international law as inherent in international society seemed to presuppose a hierarchical relationship between international society and public international law.

In this connection, it might be said that the history of public international law exhibits a distinctive pattern, according to which the formulation of an alternative to the framework of obligation takes the form of the framework of authorization. There is a distinctive similarity between the theory of public international law developed by Allott and the writings of Bruns, which also reacted to the framework of obligation—endorsed in the *Case of the S.S. "Lotus"*—in the form of the framework of authorization.[62] It must be stressed that this choice is forced by the postulated mutual exclusivity between the framework of obligation and the framework of authorization. The reformulated framework developed here seeks to suppress that mutual exclusivity by analyzing both the framework of obligation and the framework of authorization as incoherent. In turn, suppressing this mutual exclusivity paves the way to the formulation of the reformulated framework, to which theory of public international law as practical reasoning and the theory of public international law as inherent in international society may be transposed. It sees the concept of public international law as inherent in international society, not by delegation from international society, but because the members of international society constitute international society in the form of rules and institutions on the basis of their power to act. The process of practical reasoning enables the members of international society to do so. At the same time, it canalizes the exercise of their power to act in the direction of the common good of international society.

[62] Bruns 1929, pp. 9–12; Bruns 1933, pp. 459–465.

Chapter 6
Conclusion to Part I

Overlooking the ground covered by Chaps. 3–5, it may be observed that both Chaps. 3 and 5 reflected the alternation between the framework of obligation and the framework of authorization. In Chap. 3, this reflection was projected by international judicial practice. The identification of the framework of obligation and the framework of authorization in both the *Case of the S.S. "Lotus"* and *Legality of the Threat or Use of Nuclear Weapons* highlights that the problem of the structure and function of public international law is not something peculiar to the *Case of the S.S. "Lotus"*, superseded after the blossoming of the law of co-operation post WW II. Rather, its neglected prominence in *Legality of the Threat or Use of Nuclear Weapons* demonstrates that it is an issue which pre-structures and pre-determines the solutions to the problems of the twenty-first century.[1] Chapter 3 culminated in the identification of a reformulated framework, consisting, so to speak, of a merger of the framework of obligation and the framework of authorization. That merger was made possible by relinquishing the mutual exclusivity of these frameworks. At the same time, this implied that the structure of the reformulated framework is not exclusively vertical, because there is no entity which precedes and explains the concept of (public international) law.

Similarly, in Chap. 5 the alternation between the framework of obligation and the framework of authorization was projected by theory of public international law. Most of these conformed to the framework of obligation, but there was a conspicuous counterpoint in the form of the theory of public international law as inherent in international society, formulated by Allott, which corresponded to the framework of authorization. It was remarked that this pattern in a way repeated the observations which had been formulated by Bruns in opposition to the Lotus view. That similarity should not detract, however, from the crucial insight formulated in *Eunomia* that the concept of public international law may be seen as inherent in

[1] The ICJ has confirmed this approach in *Accordance with International Law of the Unilateral Declaration of Independence in respect of Kosovo*, Advisory Opinion of 22 July 2010, not yet reported, paras 49–56.

J. A. Vos, *The Function of Public International Law*,
DOI: 10.1007/978-90-6704-861-3_6, © J. A. Vos, The Netherlands 2013

international society. While in *Eunomia* the concept of public international law was treated as subordinate to international society, if transposed to the reformulated framework, it may be said that the concept of public international law and international society are coterminous; the members of international society constitute international society in the form of rules of public international law. As thus conceived, the reformulated framework constituted an appropriate structure in which to embed the theory of public international law as practical reasoning, formulated by Kratochwil. That theory of public international law remained problematic while situated within the framework of obligation, because the plurality of outcomes to which it gives rise could not accommodate the need for clear and precise rules of public international law delineating the freedoms to act of the members of international society. Transposed to the reformulated framework, however, the theory of public international law as practical reasoning provides an indispensable element. The reformulated framework requires the members of international society to resort to practical reasoning about the constituting of international society. In that context, the plurality of outcomes reflects the richness to which that process may give rise.

Between Chaps. 3 and 5, an excursion was made, in Chap. 4, to the internal sphere of the institution of the State. Part of that excursion was to discard the domestic analogy, so as to reinforce the view that as hitherto constituted, the concept of (public international) law has an exclusively vertical structure. That means that both the concept of public international law and the internal law of the State derive their ultimate explanation from the—unexplained—existing plurality of States. The reformulated framework shows, however, that the concept of (public international) law can be detached from the pre-existence of an entity. That line was pursued by focusing on the theories of law developed by MacCormick and Finnis. The theory of law as practical reasoning provides from the internal sphere the same element as the theory of public international law as practical reasoning provides on the international plane. Transposed to the reformulated framework, the theory of law as practical reasoning retains its flexibility; at the same time, it becomes more rigorous, because the requirement of coherence must be satisfied not only in terms of principles, but also in terms of the constituting of international society. The theory of law as coordination, developed by Finnis, furnishes a final element, in the sense that it explains that the constituting of international society by the members of international society is about the common good of international society. But the relationship between the common good and the concept of law is, to some extent, reversed. While within the theory of law as coordination it was the common good which preceded and shaped the concept of law, in the reformulated framework the constituting of international society takes the form of the concept of (public international) law; at the same time, this constitutes the common good of international society.[2] The circular relationship between rules and institutions, while problematic if situated within the framework of obligation, inscribes itself

[2] Rawls 2005, Chap. V, para 7.

coherently within the reformulated framework. In the reformulated framework, rules and institutions are mutually constitutive; rules may be regarded as giving rise to institutions and institutions may be regarded as giving rise to rules. In view of the relationships, on the one hand, between law and the common good, and, on the other hand, between rules and institutions, it follows that, within the reformulated framework, institutions form part of the common good.

Part II
Mutual Exclusivity in Sources

Chapter 7
Introduction to Part II

Part I has been directed at identifying the vertical structure of the concept of law underlying the concept of public international law. That vertical structure has been broken down into a framework of obligation and a framework of authorization, the relationship between which has been characterized in terms of mutual exclusivity. Both frameworks have been analyzed as incoherent in so far as they do not result in obligations or rights which situate the members of international society coherently in respect of each other and can be explained, in part, as created by those members. Because, in the light of that incoherence, the mutual exclusivity of both frameworks cannot be maintained, it has become possible to identify a reformulated framework which, in a way, combines the framework of obligation and the framework of authorization.

Simply put, the reformulated framework is composed of both the framework of obligation and the framework of authorization by using their elements as extremes which create a tension between them. Thus, the basic situation of the members of international society can neither be characterized in terms of a freedom to act nor in terms of the absence of a power to act. Their middle ground, it may be said, is formed by the power to act of the members of international society. Similarly, the function of rules of public international law consists neither exclusively in imposing obligations nor exclusively in conferring rights, but both. In this way, the reformulated framework provides a basic structure for the constituting of international society by the members of international society. The constituting of international society by the members of international society on the basis of that ground structure takes the form of rules of public international law, which are the products of the power to act of the members of international society and, in turn, define that power to act. Within the reformulated framework, the concept of public international law is seen as inherent in international society.

Within the vertical structure of the concept of law underlying the concept of public international law, rules of public international law are not seen as inherent in international society. Mainly through the prism of the framework of obligation,

J. A. Vos, *The Function of Public International Law*,
DOI: 10.1007/978-90-6704-861-3_7,

rules of public international law are regarded as emanating from a political process in the form of the sources of public international law. By implication from its subpara (d), Article 38, para 1, subparas (a)–(c), of the Statute of the International Court of Justice lists as primary sources: conventional international law, customary international law, and general principles of law.

When situated within the mutual exclusivity of the framework of obligation and the framework of authorization, however, those sources of public international law do not, it is submitted, produce coherent rules of public international law. Even though conventional international law or customary international law may stipulate both rights and obligations, the mutual exclusivity of both frameworks only allows one or the other to be operative. The present part situates these traditional sources of public international law within the mutual exclusivity formed by the framework of obligation and the framework of authorization and describes how general principles of law, conventional international law, and customary international law may be resituated within the reformulated framework. This does not require transposing these sources to the reformulated framework, but delineating a transition from the incoherence of the mutual exclusivity of both frameworks to the reformulated framework. As a consequence of this transition, the function of rules of public international law produced by the sources of public international law would be transformed. Within the reformulated framework, general principles of law may be seen as transiting the reformulated framework and the constituting of international society. Customary international law may be regarded as involving the direct constituting of international society on the basis of the ground structure. Conventional international law may be regarded as transiting general principles of law and customary international law, incorporating both principles and rules.

Chapter 8
The Concept of General Principles of Law Situated Within the Framework of Obligation and the Framework of Authorization

8.1 Introduction

The concept of general principles of law is traditionally conceived as a supplementary source of public international law, enabling the PCIJ and the ICJ to settle a dispute between States in the eventuality of the absence of an applicable rule of conventional international law or customary international law. The category of general principles of law was included in the Statute of the PCIJ and retained in the Statute of the ICJ, in other words, so as to enable the Court to avoid having to pronounce *non liquet*. Because it was also deemed desirable to limit the discretion of the Court in this respect, it was suggested that the Court should draw these general principles of law from the internal law of the members of international society. This historical background will be described in Sect. 8.2. Section 8.3 will then outline how this link between the concept of general principles of law and the internal law of States turned the question of the use of general principles of law into the question of the appropriateness of the transposition of a general principle of the internal law of the members of international society to the international plane. In this way, the domestic analogy became central to the concept of general principles of law.

These connections and movements, it will be argued in Sect. 8.4, locate the concept of general principles of law within the framework of obligation. Accordingly, the incoherence of the framework of obligation, it is submitted, distorts our understanding of the concept of general principles of law. On the one hand, as will be elaborated in Sect. 8.4, as a supplementary source of public international law, the concept of general principles of law conforms to the framework of obligation, because it is intended to avoid the outcome of *non liquet* and the consequent result, from the perspective of the judicial function, of the parties to the dispute retaining their freedom to act. On the other hand, to reach this result, the judicial function must rely on analogies from the internal law of the members of international society so as to limit their external freedom to act. Furthermore, it is by virtue of the framework of obligation, in the form of the assumption of a freedom of States to act, that the

J. A. Vos, *The Function of Public International Law*,
DOI: 10.1007/978-90-6704-861-3_8, © J. A. Vos, The Netherlands 2013

residual 'rule' of State freedom of action is envisaged as a possible result. Operating within the framework of obligation, the concept of general principles of law is directed both at limiting the freedom of States to act and at respecting it. From within the framework of obligation, it is not possible to resolve this dilemma. Adopting the perspective of the function of public international law impels, it is submitted, a transition from the mutual exclusivity of the framework of obligation and the framework of authorization to the reformulated framework developed in Part I.

Subsequently, Sect. 8.5 briefly describes the concept of (general) principles of international law, which may alternatively be seen as a second branch of the concept of general principles of law, not envisaged by the drafters but developed in doctrine and practice, or as a separate notion. In Sect. 8.6, the concept of (general) principles of international law will be situated within the mutual exclusivity formed by the framework of obligation and the framework of authorization, so as to argue in favor of the reformulated framework developed in Part I. Section 8.7 contains the conclusions of this chapter.

To begin this discussion of the sources of public international law with the concept of general principles of law diverges from more traditional presentations, converging around the concepts of conventional international law and customary international law and their interrelationship. The enumeration of the sources of public international law in Article 38, para 1, of the Statute of the ICJ, in fact, reflects a somewhat hybrid status of the category of general principles of law, classifying them *a contrario*, on the one hand, as non-subsidiary, but, on the other hand, reflecting their supplementary nature vis-à-vis conventional international law and customary international law. The function which general principles of law perform within the framework of obligation, however, steers the argument of its incoherence-when affected by the mutual exclusivity of the framework of obligation and the framework of authorization-towards the consideration of the reformulated framework itself. Resituated within the reformulated framework, the concept of general principles of law is, to some extent, assimilated by it. However, because, from this perspective, it also embodies the transition from the reformulated framework to the concept of conventional international law, it also retains, to this extent, its separate character. Thus, resituating the concept of general principles of law in this way provides a framework for the subsequent consideration of the concepts of conventional international law and customary international law. Part of the argument in respect of these two 'main' sources of public international consists precisely in the point that neither can be self-standing and depends on assumptions *dehors* those categories. If the reformulated framework is capable of constituting such a framework, it seems appropriate to start with the category of general principles of law.

8.2 The Concept of General Principles of Law

Article 38, para 1(c), of the Statute of the ICJ directs the Court to apply 'the general principles of law recognized by civilized nations'. The reference in para 1(d) to judicial decisions and the teachings of the most highly qualified publicists of the various nations as 'subsidiary' means for the determination of rules of law suggests, *a contrario*, that the general principles of law form a 'main' source of public international law. Yet, the drafting history of this provision suggests that this source does not stand on the same footing as customary international law and conventional international law and reveals its intended supplementary character. As part of its work, the Advisory Committee of Jurists appointed by the Council of the League of Nations to draft the Statute of the PCIJ, took up the question what the envisaged Court should do in case it could not identify a rule of customary international law or conventional international law applicable to an international dispute submitted to it.

This discussion was initiated by the President of the Advisory Committee of Jurists, Baron Descamps, who introduced a text specifying the categories of public international law to be applied by the Court. In order to avoid a situation in which the Court would be compelled to declare *non liquet*, because of the absence of a rule of customary international law or conventional international law applicable to an international dispute submitted to it, Baron Descamps proposed that the 'rules of international law as recognised by the legal conscience of civilised nations' be included as a category of the law to be applied by the Court.[1]

Several members of the Advisory Committee of Jurists objected to this proposal, questioning whether a situation such as depicted by Baron Descamps was undesirable or even possible. As a matter of principle, Mr. Root and Lord Phillimore considered that the Statute should not circumscribe the law to be applied by the PCIJ. If, however, the Committee proceeded in this direction, it should not, according to Mr. Root, adopt the broad formulation proposed by Baron Descamps.[2] Adopting a practical perspective, Lord Phillimore took the view, shared by Mr. De Lapradelle, that a situation such as described by Baron Descamps would not be undesirable. In those circumstances, the case should be transferred to the Council or the Assembly—the political organs—of the League of Nations,[3] or to another international judicial institution.[4]

From a theoretical perspective, Mr. Ricci-Busatti remarked that a situation such as described by Baron Descamps would not be possible. According to Mr. Ricci-Busatti, in the absence of an applicable rule of public international law, the PCIJ would declare the absence of an international legal limitation on the freedom of the parties and thereby establish a legal situation. Consequently, the Court should

[1] Advisory Committee of Jurists 1920, pp. 293, 306–307, 310–311, 318–319, 322–325, 332, 336.

[2] Advisory Committee of Jurists 1920, p. 293 (Mr. Root), 315 (Lord Phillimore).

[3] Advisory Committee of Jurists 1920, p. 316, 320 (Lord Phillimore).

[4] Advisory Committee of Jurists 1920, pp. 312–314 (Mr. De Lapradelle).

simply declare that one party had no rights against the other and that the conduct of the accused State was not contrary to any admitted rule of public international law. In other words, the Court should follow the principle that what is not forbidden is allowed, which, incidentally and paradoxically, constituted at the same time an example of a general principle of law.[5]

Nevertheless, the necessity of providing for a situation in which an applicable rule of customary international law or conventional international law did not exist was recognized by several other members of the Advisory Committee of Jurists, including Mr. Loder,[6] Mr. De Lapradelle,[7] and Mr. Hagerup.[8] As a compromise, based on a joint proposal of Mr. Root and Lord Phillimore, the Advisory Committee of Jurists defined the envisaged supplementary source of public international law more narrowly in terms of 'the general principles of law recognised by civilised nations'.

It was suggested that this circumscription connected the supplementary source of public international law to the internal law of the State and limited in this manner the discretion of the envisaged Court. Lord Phillimore referred in this respect to the principles of common law, which were applicable to international affairs and formed part of public international law, maxims of law, and the general principles accepted by nations *in foro domestico*, such as certain principles of procedure, the principle of good faith and the principle of *res judicata*.[9] In a similar manner, Mr. De Lapradelle stated that the principles which formed the bases of national law were also sources of public international law.[10]

In the Advisory Committee of Jurists there were, therefore, divergent views as to the undesirability or possibility of the Court having to pronounce *non liquet* in the absence of an applicable rule of customary international law or conventional international law. The mainstream view, which resulted in the formulation adopted, considered that the result of *non liquet* was undesirable. According to the view taken by Lord Philimore and Mr. de Lapradelle, the result of *non liquet* was not undesirable and simply meant that the Court should defer to the political organs of the League of Nations or another international judicial institution. Finally, the view of Mr. Ricci-Busatti was that the result of *non liquet* was not possible, because the concept of public international law contained a general principle of

[5] Advisory Committee of Jurists 1920, p. 314 (Mr. Ricci-Busatti): 'By declaring the absence of a positive rule of international law, in other words an international limitation on the freedom of the parties, nevertheless a legal situation is established. That which is not forbidden is allowed; that is one of the general principles of law which the Court shall have to apply. If a case is brought before the Court and if the latter finds that no rules exist concerning it, the Court shall declare that one party has no right against the other, that the conduct of the accused State was not contrary to any admitted rule.'

[6] Advisory Committee of Jurists 1920, pp. 311–312 (Mr. Loder).

[7] Advisory Committee of Jurists 1920, pp. 312–313, 335–336 (Mr. De Lapradelle).

[8] Advisory Committee of Jurists 1920, pp. 296–297, 307–308, 317, 319 (Mr. Hagerup).

[9] Advisory Committee of Jurists 1920, p. 316, 335 (Lord Phillimore).

[10] Advisory Committee of Jurists 1920, p. 335 (Mr. De Lapradelle).

law according to which what is not forbidden is allowed. The mainstream view prevailed and led to the inclusion of a supplementary source of public international law in the Statute of the Court in the form of the general principles of law recognized by civilized nations.[11] That formulation was intended to restrict the discretion of the envisaged Court by linking the general principles of law to the internal law of the State.[12] Section 8.3 will describe how this link between the general principles of law and the internal law of the State involves reliance on the domestic analogy.

8.3 The Relationship Between General Principles of Law and General Principles of the Internal Law of the State; The Domestic Analogy Reappears

As described in Sect. 8.2, the Advisory Committee of Jurists suggested that, in order to limit the discretion of the envisaged Court, the general principles of law should be linked to the internal law of the State. Another reason for this linkage between general principles of law and the internal law of the State has been seen in the fact of the more developed or mature nature of the internal law of the State. Against this background, it would appear that, analytically, two approaches to explaining the relationship between the concept of general principles of law and the internal law of the State may be distinguished. Both approaches take as a starting point the existence of general principles of the internal law of the State.

According to a first approach, the concept of general principles of law must be regarded as consisting of principles of law common to both public international law and the internal law of the State. It is based on the proposition that general principles of the internal law of the State reflect general principles of law which also radiate as part of public international law. The principal inference comprised by this approach is that a general principle of the internal law of the State forms part of a wider category of general principle of law which has, as another subcategory, a general principle of public international law. It, therefore, involves extrapolating from the category of general principles of the internal law of the State to the category of general principles of law, and thence to the category of general principles of

[11] Tomuschat 1999, Chap. IX, para 42; Dupuy 2002, pp. 180–182.

[12] Weil 1992, pp. 144–149.

public international law, on the basis of analogy between relations or situations which are deemed comparable.[13]

In a second approach to explaining the relationship between the concept of general principles of law and the internal law of the State, the concept of general principles of law is regarded as simply meaning general principles of the internal law of the State. It is based on the proposition that general principles of law may be derived directly, by analogy, from general principles of the internal law of the State. This second approach involves directly transposing a general principle of the internal law of the State to the international plane, but also relies on analogical reasoning.[14] In the context of this approach, it is, moreover, usually thought that the transposition of general principles of the internal law of the State to the international plane not only involves analogical reasoning, but may also require adaption of the general principles of the internal law of the State to the circumstances of international relations.[15] This more flexible view of the relationship between general principles of law and general principles of the internal law of the State was described and relied on, perhaps most famously and eloquently, by Sir Arnold McNair in his Separate Opinion in *International Status of South-West Africa*, in which he advocated that the Mandate for South-West Africa should be

---

[13] Spiropoulos 1928, pp. 9, 26–27, 32; Charles de Visscher 1933, pp. 406–411; Cheng 1953, p. 390: 'Law having been applied between individuals ever since men began to form into societies, and having been developed and elaborated in the course of time into highly technical and rigorous systems in the municipal sphere, it is natural that, in seeking the general principles of this universal concept in order to apply them to relations between States, we should look to the municipal sphere. Assuming a basic analogy between individuals and nations, between international relations and relations between individuals, international courts and tribunals apply to international relations those principles underlying municipal rules of law which have been found to work substantial justice between individuals, whenever circumstances similar to those justifying their application in the municipal sphere exist.'; Quadri 1964, pp. 350–351: 'La conscience juridique internationale (…) a tendance à se constituer dans une large mesure parallèlement à la conscience juridique interne; l'inverse est aussi vrai. Les principes généraux ne sont que des principes soutenus par l'autorité de l'opinion publique universelle qui se sont manifestés plus souvent in *foro domestico*, car l'expérience juridique interne est plus ancienne, plus intense et plus riche que l'expérience internationale; le droit interne ne doit cependant pas être considéré comme une source, mais comme un simple *indice* du *status conscientiae* des Etats, *status conscientiae* qui, lorsqu'il y a ressemblance entre les situations, est également décisif pour l'ordre interétatique.'

[14] Lauterpacht 1927, para 34; Waldock 1962, pp. 57, 64–65; Akehurst 1976, p. 814, 816; Elias and Lim 1997, p. 23.

[15] Ripert 1933, paras 11–13; Blondel 1968, p. 213.

understood from the perspective of the concept of trust rather than from the perspective of the concept of mandate.[16]

Both approaches to perceiving the relationship between the concept of general principles of law and the concept of general principles of the internal law of the State, it may be observed, entail significant interpretative discretion. In the first approach, the concept of general principles of law is regarded as comprising the overlap between general principles of the internal law of the State and general principles of public international law. However, to conclude that a general principle of the internal law of the State is a general principle of law and, as such, a general principle of public international law, only the concept of general principles of the internal law of the State available. The category of general principles of international law is treated, in fact, simultaneously as a constituent and as a result of the concept of general principles of law. As a source of public international law, however, the category of general principles of law cannot be regarded as informed by the category of general principles of public international law. In the second approach, the concept of general principles of law is understood as meaning general principles of the internal law of the State. Here, analogy between relations under the internal law of the State and relations between States is relied on directly and the need to adapt general principles of the internal law of the State to the circumstances of international relations is explicitly acknowledged. For both approaches, the maturity of the internal law of the State constitutes the rationale for deriving general principles of law from the internal law of the State and transposing them to the concept of public international law. In the light of these considerations, it may be noted at this point that the objective pursued by the Advisory Committee of Jurists—to limit the discretion of the Court by linking the concept of general principles of law to the internal law of the State—does not seem to be facilitated by the flexibility involved in analogical transposition.

Whatever approach is adopted with respect to perceiving the relationship between general principles of law and general principles of the internal law of the State, whether through recourse through an intermediate concept or through direct analogical reasoning, it is clear, in sum, that analogical reasoning is at the heart of this relationship,[17] taking the similarity of relations between States and relations

[16] *International Status of South-West Africa*, Advisory Opinion of 11 July 1950, Separate Opinion Sir Arnold McNair, ICJ Reports 1950, 128, 148: 'International law has recruited and continues to recruit many of its rules and institutions from private systems of law. Article 38 (I) (c) of the Statute of the Court bears witness that this process is still active, and it will be noted that this article authorizes the Court to 'apply … (c) the general principles of law recognised by civilised nations'. The way in which international law borrows from this source is not by means of importing private law institutions 'lock, stock and barrel', ready-made and fully equipped with a set of rules. It would be difficult to reconcile such a process with the application of 'the general principles of law'. In my opinion, the true view of the duty of international tribunals in this matter is to regard any features or terminology which are reminiscent of the rules and institutions of private law as an indication of policy and principles rather than as directly importing these rules and institutions.'

[17] Siorat 1958, paras 341–348, 419–426.

between individuals as its point of departure.[18] On this basis, the similarity of the horizontal structure of relations between States and the horizontal structure of relations between individuals is usually considered to give rise to the transposition of general principles of private law to public international law.[19] Accordingly, as general principles of private law, the concept of contract[20] and the concept of responsibility[21] are commonly transposed to public international law.

However, doctrine also supports the transposition of general principles of public law to public international law. For example, Cheng considered that both general principles of private law and general principles of public law may be transposed to public international law and mentioned the principle of self-preservation (*salus populi suprema lex*) as an example of a general principle of public law that forms part of public international law.[22] In his Dissenting Opinion in the *South West Africa Cases (Second Phase)*, Judge Tanaka regarded it possible to transpose general principles of public law comprehensively to public international law, including general principles of administrative law and general principles of constitutional law.[23] In general, doctrine commonly connects the transposition of general principles of public law to the development of international institutions.[24]

It is submitted, however, that the transposition of both general principles of private law and general principles of public law is based on an analogy which, from the perspective of the function of public international law, is incoherent. Horizontal relations between States may seem similar to horizontal relations between individuals under general principles of private law. Nevertheless, although general principles of private law apply to relations between individuals,

---

[18] Lauterpacht 1927, para 34; Cheng 1953, p. 390.

[19] Lauterpacht 1927, paras 29–34: 'This means that although the Court may apply, for the purpose of a particular case, a rule of criminal or administrative law of sufficient generality, it is of general rules of private law that, on the whole, we must needs think in this connection. For it is, as a rule, private law which gives shape and definite form to those general sources. Here lies the organising and ordering part played by it. Those 'general principles' threaten otherwise to degenerate into altogether subjective natural law or legal philosophy.'; Spiropoulos 1928, p. 9, 31; Ripert 1933, para 13; Charles de Visscher 1933, p. 410; Grapin 1934, pp. 53–54; Küntzel 1935, pp. 47–48, 50.

[20] Lauterpacht 1927, paras 69–79a; Ripert 1933, paras 17–36; Grapin 1934, pp. 67–89; Blondel 1968, pp. 214–220.

[21] Lauterpacht 1927, paras 58–66; Spiropoulos 1928, pp. 37–41; Ripert 1933, paras 37–56; Grapin 1934, pp. 89–134; Küntzel 1935, p. 50; Cheng 1953, pp. 161–253; Blondel 1968, pp. 221–222; Verdross 1968, pp. 521–530.

[22] Cheng 1953, pp. 29–31, 49–51, 390, 392.

[23] *South West Africa Cases (Second Phase)*, Judgment of 18 July 1966, Dissenting Opinion Judge Tanaka, ICJ Reports 1966, 6, 294.

[24] Lauterpacht 1927, para 34: 'However, it is probable that with the legal development of international organisation and the creation of central authoritative institutions, a body of rules will evolve which, as regulating the relations between individual States and the authoritative organs of the international community, will closely correspond to public law within the municipal sphere, for instance, to constitutional and administrative law. In fact, there are already now rudiments of international rules of this kind.'; Quadri 1964, pp. 352–353.

general principles of private law are at the same time a branch of the internal law of the State and, therefore, a form of public law. In this sense, the transposition of general principles of private law and the transposition of general principles of public law both involve relying on the internal law of the State and, therewith, on the institution of the State. Incidentally, it may be noted that the principle of self-preservation, identified by Cheng as a principle of public law, transposed to the international plane transforms itself into the assumption of a freedom of States to act and seems antithetical to the existence, at the international plane, of general principles of public law applying to the society of States as a whole.

Now, on the one hand, it may be remarked that the transposition of both general principles of private law and general principles of public law to the international plane is inconsistent with the horizontal structure of public international law. While the internal law of the State presupposes the institution of the State, the concept of public international law is characterized by the absence of authority above States. In this respect, any transposition of a general principle of private law or a general principle of public law would be incoherent. On the other hand, the point has precisely been made that the horizontal structure of public international law is itself a reflection of the vertical structure of the concept of law underlying the concept of public international law. So from that perspective, neither the transposition of general principles of private law nor the transposition of general principles of public law would be incoherent. Nevertheless, if the institution of the State and the internal law of the State cannot be explained coherently on the basis of social contract theory, it remains that the vertical structure itself, both of the internal law of the State and of the concept of public international law, cannot be explained.

8.4 The Concept of General Principles of Law Situated Within the Framework of Obligation

The previous section dealt with the process of analogical reasoning involved in deriving general principles of law from general principles of the internal law of the State. Incoherence arises either by virtue of the fact that general principles of the internal law of the State, which presuppose the institution of the State, are transposed to the horizontal structure of public international law, which is characterized by the absence of authority above States, or by virtue of the fact that if the horizontal structure of public international law itself is seen as a reflection of the vertical structure of the concept of law underlying the concept of public international law, a coherent explanation for the vertical structure of both the concept of public international law and the internal law of the State is lacking.

The mainstream view which prevailed in the Advisory Committee of Jurists and which led to the inclusion of the category of general principles of law as a supplementary source of public international law, clearly indicates that the concept of general principles of law must be situated within the framework of obligation. Accordingly, in the absence of a rule of customary international law or conventional international law applicable to an international dispute and in order to avoid the result of *non liquet*, general principles of law could be relied on so as to restrict the freedom of States to act.[25] The underlying assumption is that in the absence of general principles of law, States would have a freedom to act.

It would seem, however, that international jurisprudence has not succeeded in identifying general principles of law which are sufficiently clear and precise to delimit the freedom of States to act. While principles of procedure are frequently mentioned as examples of general principles of law, the identification of substantive general principles of law does not seem to have extended beyond the principle of good faith (and the related principle of abuse of right).[26] The principle of good faith, however, while straddling the boundary between the concept of justice and the concept of law, would seem insufficiently clear and precise to delimit the freedom of States to act.[27] Furthermore, it may be noted that, whereas the category of general principles of law was linked to the internal law of the State in order to minimize the discretion of the Court, its manifestation in the form of the flexible principle of good faith would seem to maximize the discretion of the Court.

The assumption underlying the view of the mainstream that States have a freedom to act unless a general principle of law is identified which restricts that freedom, was regarded by Mr. Ricci-Busatti as itself forming a general principle of law: what is not forbidden is allowed.[28] Thus, both the mainstream in the Advisory Committee of Jurists and Mr. Ricci-Busatti recognized the validity of the assumption of a freedom of States to act. The mainstream sought to counteract the consequences of this assumption by relying on general principles of law. Mr. Ricci-Bussatti saw this assumption as itself a general principle of law. These approaches, it may be observed, are mutually exclusive: if one relies on the identification of general principles of law in order to avoid *non liquet*, one cannot,

---

25 *Case Concerning Military and Paramilitary Activities in and against Nicaragua (Merits)*, Judgment of 27 June 1986, Dissenting Opinion Judge Oda, ICJ Reports 1986, 14, para 52.

26 Report of the Appellate Body, *United States – Import Prohibition of Certain Shrimp and Shrimp Products*, WT/DS58/AB/R, para 158.

Lauterpacht 1927, para 50; Spiropoulos 1928, pp. 32–35, 35–37, 41–43; Ripert 1933, paras 57–75; Grapin 1934, pp. 136–143; Verdross 1935, p. 204; Cheng 1953, pp. 103–160; Blondel 1968, pp. 229–233.

27 *Corfu Channel Case (Merits)*, Judgment of 9 April 1949, Dissenting Opinion Judge Azevedo, ICJ Reports 1949, 4, 83.

28 Advisory Committee of Jurists 1920, p. 314: 'By declaring the absence of a positive rule of international law, in other words an international limitation on the freedom of the parties, nevertheless a legal situation is established. That which is not forbidden is allowed; that is one of the general principles of law which the Court shall have to apply. If a case is brought before the Court and if the latter finds that no rules exist concerning it, the Court shall declare that one party has no right against the other, that the conduct of the accused State was not contrary to any admitted rule.'

at the same time adhere to the principle that what is not forbidden is allowed; conversely, if one adheres to the principle that what is not forbidden is allowed, there is no need to have recourse to (other) general principles of law in order to avoid *non liquet*.

The pattern of this discussion in the Advisory Committee of Jurists between the mainstream view and the view espoused by Ricci-Busatti is reflected with exact precision in the distinction drawn by Lauterpacht between the formal and the material completeness of the law. According to Lauterpacht, the formal completeness of the law consists of the residual freedom of action (what is not forbidden is allowed); the material completeness of the law resides in the possibility of deriving a material solution to a dispute from principles of justice or rules of law.[29] Lauterpacht saw the judicial function as essentially revolving around the competence and ability to determine when the formal completeness of the law could be resorted to and when to have recourse to the material completeness of the law with a view to achieving a just result.[30] For Lauterpacht, judicial discretion, within the limits of the law, was unavoidable and entirely acceptable.[31] From a rather different angle, Weil has suggested a similar complementarity between the supplementary role of general principles of law/equity and a residual rule of freedom.[32]

These views are proximate to the position adhered to by Siorat, according to which it falls within the judicial function to interpret the law and to supplement it; to deal, in other words, with obscurities, logical insufficiencies and gaps.[33] On the other hand, an international judge would not be competent to deal with social insufficiencies or regulatory defaults.[34] The competence to supplement the law, according to Siorat, is twofold: systematization of particular provisions[35] and individualization of its abstract notions, in particular, the notion of abuse of right.[36] The surfacing problem with both the Lauterpacht view and the Siorat view is that, even though the processes of systematization and individualization seem indicative of a structure, the judicial function is not circumscribed by the law; to the contrary, it is the judicial function which determines what the law, what that structure, is. This tendency is inherent in the framework of obligation, where the focus is on the restriction of the freedom of States to act.

---

29 Lauterpacht 1933, Chap. V, para 14.

30 Lauterpacht 1933, Chap. V, paras 15–20.

31 Lauterpacht 1933, Chap. V, para 21.

32 Weil 1992, pp. 204–212.

33 Siorat 1958, paras 279–282, 287–288.

34 Siorat 1958, paras 276–278, 283–288.

35 Siorat 1958, paras 349–352.

36 Siorat 1958, paras 385–389.

It may be observed, however, although the existence of a residual rule of freedom continues to find the support of prominent authors (Friedmann[37]; Kolb[38]), that other authors are more reluctant to support it. Fastenrath has argued that in the case of gaps in public international law, relations between States should be regarded as situated in a so-called non-legal area ('rechtsfreier Raum').[39] According to Fastenrath, this means that in the case of a gap in public international law, public international law does not positively endorse, but is indifferent to a freedom of States to act. Fastenrath acknowledged, however, that ultimately both approaches result in a freedom of States to act.[40] In respect of the notion of a non-legal area, it might be remarked that this area can be described as non-legal in so far as an applicable rule of public international law does not exist. From the perspective of the function of public international law, however, such an area cannot be regarded as non-legal because it obtains this character by virtue of the framework of obligation. It is by virtue of the assumption that States have a freedom to act in the absence of an applicable rule of public international law, that such an area is characterized as non-legal—that is, not regulated—and that assumption is a reflection of a legal framework which locates the function of law in the limitation of the freedom to act of the members of society.

Castberg has gone even further, pointing out that a rule according to which everything which is not prohibited is permitted would be contradictory, granting, for example, a right to a State to forbid aerial navigation above its territory and, simultaneously, rights to other States to overflight by their aircraft of the territory of that State.[41] Castberg denounced such a rule as derived from an inappropriate

[37] Friedmann 1964, p. 118: 'The relative scarcity of positive norms of conduct stemming from international law is not to be confused with the entirely different principle of *non liquet*, *i.e.*, the inability of international law to answer a given question because of absence of a definitive rule. That latter principle has been overwhelmingly rejected by writers as well as by the practice of international courts.'; 189: 'the *Lotus Case* (...) is not, of course, a proposition for the application of *non liquet* in international law, but for the very different theory that international law grants to states the liberty to invoke national jurisdiction over foreigners where there is no positive international norm to the contrary.'

[38] Kolb 1998, p. 668: 'Le droit international n'a peut-être pas de lacunes formelles, car dans tout ordre juridique on peut faire application de la règle résiduelle de liberté ou repousser une demande insufissament fondée en droit.'; Kolb 2001, *passim*.

[39] Fastenrath 1991, p. 246: 'Aus dem Souveränitätsprinzip folgt also nicht so sehr die Gewährung rechtlicher Handlungsfreiheit als die Regel, dass Völkerrecht nur insoweit besteht, als die Staaten Rechtssätze aufgestellt haben; ausserhalb dieses Bereichs liegt ein rechtsfreier Raum.'

[40] Fastenrath 1991, p. 251: 'Unabhängig davon, ob nun der negative Freiheitssatz Bestandteil der Völkerrechtsordnung ist oder nicht, könnte man meinen, im Ergebnis ändere sich - oweit der Satz auf der Handlungsebene überhaupt anwendbar ist – nichts: In beiden Fällen seien die Völkerrechtssubjekte nicht gehindert, sich nach Belieben zu verhalten. Es sei letztlich gleichgültig, ob dies aufgrund eines Rechtssatzes oder in einem rechtsfreien Raum geschehe.'

[41] Castberg 1933, pp. 342–351.

analogy with criminal law,[42] followed by Siorat,[43] inferring that restrictions of the freedom of States may not only result from positive rules of customary international law and conventional international law, but also from interpretation by analogy,[44] the deduction of a principle of international law[45] and the application of considerations of equity.[46] Having thus established, on the one hand, the incoherence of an assumption of a freedom of States to act, Castberg reverted, on the other hand, to the approach adopted by the mainstream in the Advisory Committee of Jurists. The categories Castberg identified as appropriate to fill the gap (analogy; principle of international law; equity) seem different from but also approximate an extensive interpretation of the concept of general principles of law.

The preceding discussion thus reveals two competing lines in the concept of general principles of law: on the one hand the notion that general principles of law exist and can be relied on so as to limit the freedom of States to act; on the other hand the notion of the freedom of States to act itself. This contrast is present in the difference between the majority position in the Advisory Committee of Jurists and the position of Mr. Ricci-Busatti. It is reflected in Lauterpacht's distinction between the material and the formal completeness of the law. Castberg and, in his tracks, Siorat recognized the incoherence of the assumption of a freedom of States to act, but simultaneously relied on it so as to expand the arsenal to fight it to analogy, the deduction of a principle of international law and equity. But as previously observed, these two kinds of general principles of law are inherently contradictory and exclude one another. If one relies on the assumption of a freedom of States to act, there is no residual need to resort to a general principle of law. Conversely, a general principle of law does not admit the simultaneous existence of the assumption of a freedom to act. These diverging movements can be transformed into converging movements, it is submitted, by relying on the incoherence of the mutual exclusivity of the framework of obligation and the framework of authorization, in transit to the reformulated framework.

As situated within the framework of obligation, the concept of general principles of law locates law both at the level of the judicial function and at the level of the members of international society. But it does so in an incoherent way. It requires the judicial function to produce law so as to avoid *non liquet*; but as it restricts more and more the freedom of States to act, its basis in international society becomes more and more tenuous. To the extent that it leaves the freedom of States to act intact, it leaves the members of international society in an incoherent situation. If, however, the freedom of States to act is incoherent as a basic assumption, it cannot sustain the function of public international law as projected by the framework of obligation. To the extent that this assumption is rejected, the

[42] Castberg 1933, pp. 343–344.

[43] Siorat 1958, paras 358–360.

[44] Castberg 1933, pp. 351–354.

[45] Castberg 1933, pp. 354–362.

[46] Castberg 1933, pp. 362–366.

function of general principles of law turns away from limiting the freedom of States to act. If, in view of the incoherence of their mutual exclusivity, the framework of obligation and the framework of authorization are combined into the reformulated framework, the basis position of States must be described in terms of a power to act, which is not an unlimited freedom to act. That power to act directs the members of international society to the constituting of international society. The transition to the reformulated framework entails a transformation of the function of public international law, projecting rules of public international law which simultaneously contain both enabling and disabling aspects vis-à-vis the members of international society. Metaphorically, these rules of public international law may be seen as occupying the middle ground of international society, located between the judicial function and the members of international society, where the constituting of the common good of international society takes place. In that light, general principles of law may inform practical reasoning about the common good of international society.

8.5 The Concept of (General) Principles of International Law

As described in the previous section, Castberg identified principles of international law as one of the categories to which the judicial function may resort in order to fill a gap. The Advisory Committee of Jurists, however, envisaged the category of general principles of law as connected to the internal law of the State; in that constellation, general principles of public international law flow from general principles of law and do not form a separate category. Overlooking international legal discourse, it seems clear that the category of general principles of law and the category of (general) principles of international law tend to be seen as complementary,[47] regardless of the question whether the latter constitutes an, unintended, additional branch of the former[48] or a separate category.[49]

Analytically, the category of (general) principles of international law may be subdivided into: (i) (general) principles of international law derived from

[47] *Mavrommatis Palestine Concessions*, Judgment No. 2 of 30 August 1924, Series A. – No. 2, 28.

[48] Castberg 1933, pp. 369–373; Favre 1968, pp. 373–374; Mosler 1974, pp. 136–157; Lammers 1980, pp. 66–69; Mosler 1992, pp. 513; Zemanek 1997, para 242.

[49] Charles de Visscher 1933, p. 406; Basdevant 1936, p. 498; Waldock 1962, pp. 68–69; Blondel 1968, pp. 204–211; Weil 1992, pp. 149–151; Tomuschat 1999, Chap. IX, para 49; Dupuy 2002, pp. 179–187.

customary international law or conventional international law[50] and (ii) (general) principles of international law recognized or accepted by States..[51] This distinction is not, however, clear cut in so far as the recognition or acceptance by States of a (general) principle of international law may be inferred from rules of customary international law or conventional international law.

The jurisprudence of the ICJ contains several conspicuous examples of (general) principles of international law derived from customary international law or conventional international law and/or (general) principles of international law recognized or accepted by States. In the *Corfu Channel Case (Merits)*, the ICJ famously based obligations to notify the existence of a minefield in Albanian territorial waters and to warn the approaching British warships of the imminent danger to which the minefield exposed them, 'on certain general and well-recognized principles, namely: elementary considerations of humanity, even more exacting in peace than in war; the principle of the freedom of maritime communication; and every State's obligation not to allow knowingly its territory to be used for acts contrary to the rights of other States'.[52] Two years later, in *Reservations to the Convention on the Prevention and Punishment of the Crime of Genocide*, the ICJ referred to the principles 'underlying' the Convention on the Prevention and Punishment of the Crime of Genocide as 'principles which are recognised by civilised nations as binding on States'.[53] Combining, in a way, these two previous instances, the ICJ identified, in the *Case Concerning Military and Paramilitary Activities in and against Nicaragua (Merits)*, principles of humanitarian law 'underlying' Hague Convention VIII relative to the Laying of Automatic Submarine Contract Mines.[54] Elsewhere in the *Case Concerning Military and Paramilitary Activities in and against Nicaragua (Merits)*, the Court adopted the view

---

[50] Charles de Visscher 1933, pp. 406–407: 'Par là nous n'entendons pas établir entre les principes généraux *de droit* et les principes généraux *du droit des gens* une opposition *de nature*, mais bien plutôt marquer une différenciation dans l'évolution historique de ces principes envisagés dans leur ensemble. Tout en répondant à la conviction juridique des nations civilisées, les principes généraux de droit, visés à l'article 38, 3° du Statut de la Cour, ne se sont pas encore affirmés dans la sphère des relations internationales, tandis que les principes généraux du droit des gens se dégagent de normes déja sanctionnées par le droit international conventionnel ou coutumier; 406: Les principes généraux du droit international (...) procèdent directement de la pratique internationale elle-même, des traités ou des coutumes (...)'; Lammers 1980, pp. 57–59; Weil 1992, pp. 149–151, 179–186; Zemanek 1997, para 242; Tomuschat 1999, Chap. IX, para 49.

[51] *Case Concerning Military and Paramilitary Activities in and against Nicaragua (Merits)*, Judgment of 27 June 1986, Separate Opinion President Nagendra Singh, ICJ Reports 1986, 14, 153.
Lammers 1980, pp. 57–59; Mosler 1992, p. 523.

[52] *Corfu Channel Case (Merits)*, Judgment of 9 April 1949, ICJ Reports 1949, 4, 22.
Mosler 1974, pp. 85–90; Weil 1992, pp. 149–151; Tomuschat 1999, Chap. IX, para 71; Dupuy 2002, pp. 182–187.

[53] *Reservations to the Convention on the Prevention and Punishment of the Crime of Genocide*, Advisory Opinion of 28 May 1951, ICJ Reports 1951, 15, 23.
Mosler 1974, pp. 85–90; Tomuschat 1999, Chap. IX, para 71.

[54] *Case concerning Military and Paramilitary Activities in and against Nicaragua (Merits)*, Judgment of 27 June 1986, ICJ Reports 1986, 14, para 215.

that Common Articles 1 and 3 of the 1949 Geneva Conventions expressed fundamental general principles of humanitarian law and elementary considerations of humanity.[55]

Separate mention may be made of the principle of good faith, stipulated in Article 2, para 2, of the Charter of the United Nations and developed in General Assembly resolution 2625 (XXV), to which the ICJ referred in the *Case Concerning the Land and Maritime Boundary between Cameroun and Nigeria (Preliminary Objections)* as a well-established principle of international law.[56] Likewise, separate mention may be made of the principle of sovereign equality, stipulated in Article 2, para 1, of the Charter of the United Nations and also developed in General Assembly resolution 2625 (XXV), which is alternatively characterized as a (general) principle of international law or as a principle inherent in international society.[57]

8.6 The Concept of (General) Principles of International Law Situated Within the Framework of Obligation

Like the concept of general principles of law, the concept of (general) principles of international law should be seen, it is submitted, as conforming to the vertical structure of the concept of law underlying the concept of public international law. As a consequence of the mutual exclusivity of the framework of obligation and the framework of authorization, the concept of general principles of international law cannot be perceived in a coherent manner. In this context, it is submitted that the sub-categories of (general) principles of international law derived from customary international law or conventional international law and (general) principles of international law recognized or accepted by States, are both situated within the framework of obligation. Accordingly, it is the function of those (general) principles of international law to restrict the freedom of States to act. It is assumed that in the absence of those (general) principles of international law, States have a freedom to act. Moreover, (general) principles of international law restricting the freedom of States to act are simultaneously regarded as reflecting the exercise of those freedoms to act.

---

[55] *Case concerning Military and Paramilitary Activities in and against Nicaragua (Merits)*, Judgment of 27 June 1986, ICJ Reports 1986, 14, paras 218, 220. Weil 1992, pp. 149–151; Tomuschat 1999, Chap. IX, para 49; Dupuy 2002, pp. 182–187.

[56] *Case Concerning the Land and Maritime Boundary between Cameroon and Nigeria (Preliminary Objections)*, Judgment of 11 June 1998, ICJ Reports 1998, 275, para 38. Zemanek 1997, paras 49–80.

[57] Favre 1968, pp. 373–374; Mosler 1992, pp. 513, 522–524; Elias and Lim 1997, pp. 28–30; Zemanek 1997, paras 49–80; Tomuschat 1999, Chap. V, para 1.

But, if a freedom of a State to act interferes with a freedom of another State to act, it seems incoherent to assume that in the absence of a (general) principle of international law, such a freedom of States to act exists. At the same time, it does not seem possible to delimit coherently a freedom of a State to act from a freedom of another State to act by means of (general) principles of international law derived from customary international law or conventional international law and/or (general) principles of international law accepted or recognized by States. Those (general) principles of international law delimiting these freedoms must at the same time be regarded as exercises of these freedoms. Moreover, the view that (general) principles of international law are binding remains a matter of assumption. The examples of (general) principles of international law derived from customary international law or conventional international law and/or (general) principles of international law accepted or recognized by States, briefly described in the previous section, will now be analyzed from the perspective of the framework of obligation.

As described in the preceding section, in the *Corfu Channel Case (Merits)*, the ICJ identified obligations incumbent on Albania to notify the presence of a minefield in its territorial waters to other States, for the benefit of shipping in general, and, specifically, to warn the approaching British warships. The Court based these obligations on the 'general and well-recognised principles' it had identified: 'elementary considerations of humanity, even more exacting in peace than in war; the principle of the freedom of maritime communication; and every State's obligation not to allow knowingly its territory to be used for acts contrary to the rights of other States'.[58] As thus formulated, the second and the third principle remain abstract and do not lead directly to the obligations identified by the Court. The connection becomes clear, however, in the light of the Court's determinations elsewhere that the North Corfu Channel was an international highway through which, by virtue of general recognition and customary international law, other States had a right of innocent passage and that the passage of the British warships was innocent.[59] The position of Albania would appear not to have been entirely consistent, acknowledging, on the one hand, its obligations to warn the British vessels and shipping in general if it had had knowledge of the minefield (p. 22) and denying, on the other hand, that the North Corfu Channel was an international highway (pp. 28–29). In any case, the second and the third principle identified by the Court are informed to a significant extent by the Court's position

[58] *Corfu Channel Case (Merits)*, Judgment of 9 April 1949, ICJ Reports 1949, 4, 22.

[59] *Corfu Channel Case (Merits)*, Judgment of 9 April 1949, ICJ Reports 1949, 4, 28–29: 'It is, in the opinion of the Court, generally recognized and in accordance with international custom that States in time of peace have a right to send their warships through straits used for international navigation between two parts of the high seas without the previous authorization of a coastal State, provided that the passage is *innocent*. (...) the Court has arrived at the conclusion that the North Corfu Channel should be considered as belonging to the class of international highways through which passage cannot be prohibited by a coastal State in time of peace.'

with respect to customary international law, which it did not, however, further explain.

In contrast, the first principle, relating to elementary considerations of humanity, would appear to be entirely of a moral nature. Apparently, whether or not the British warships would have been entitled to a right of passage, lack of notification or warning in respect of the presence of a minefield in its territorial waters was in any case inconsistent with Albania's obligations deriving from elementary considerations of humanity. To this effect, the Court may have relied on an analogy derived from Hague Convention VIII relative to the Laying of Automatic Submarine Contact Mines, extending its scope to the law of peace. It would seem that, in this way, the Court performed an implicit balance between considerations of humanity and 'military' considerations, regarding the omissions imputed to Albania as disproportionate to the considerations of humanity.

In *Reservations to the Convention on the Prevention and Punishment of the Crime of Genocide*, the ICJ considered that the principles 'underlying' the Convention on the Prevention and Punishment of the Crime of Genocide were 'principles recognised by civilised nations as binding on States'.[60] These principles might be seen both as principles of international law derived from conventional international law and as principles of international law recognized or accepted by States. In view of the fact that the Genocide Convention is silent on State responsibility for acts of genocide, except in Article IX, the dispute settlement clause, it might be that the Court was in effect saying that States, in the form of civilized nations, had in fact recognized an obligation not to commit acts of genocide. It might also be that, according to the Court, the fact that States committed themselves to preventing and punishing acts of genocide by individuals must have implied that they understood themselves as not having a freedom to commit acts of genocide themselves. This latter interpretation would seem plausible in so far as, under the constellation envisaged in the Convention, the prevention and punishment of acts of genocide by individuals was entrusted to them. That act of entrustment would seem incomprehensible in so far as these entities originally themselves had a freedom to commit acts of genocide, which was only restricted by the recognition, by civilized nations, of the principles underlying the Convention as binding on States.

This second interpretation would imply a movement away from the framework of obligation because, viewing States in the role of trustees in respect of the prevention and punishment of acts of genocide by individuals, implies that the assumption of a freedom of States to act is not operative. It also gives rise to the question by whom States have been entrusted with this role—where the cestui que trust must be located—a question to which the answer, it would seem, must be the States themselves, in the form of conventional international law. In view of the

[60] *Reservations to the Convention on the Prevention and Punishment of the Crime of Genocide*, Advisory Opinion of 28 May 1951, ICJ Reports 1951, 15, 23; *Case Concerning Armed Activities on the Territory of the Congo (New Application: 2002; Jurisdiction of the Court and Admissibility of the Application)*, Judgment of 3 February 2006, ICJ Reports 2006, 3, para 64.

emphasis on the 'recognition by civilized nations as binding on States', the reference point formed by conventional international law in the form of the Convention on the Prevention and Punishment of the Crime of Genocide, as well as the reference to State responsibility in Article IX, the former interpretation seems more plausible. This position has, in fact, been endorsed by the ICJ in its Judgment in the *Case Concerning Application of the Convention on the Prevention and Punishment of the Crime of Genocide*, relying on Article I of the Convention, while maintaining that the responsibility incurred is not of a criminal nature. Thus, in the view of the Court, States would have a freedom to commit acts of genocide, even if they created conventional international law relating to the prevention and punishment of acts of genocide by individuals, unless that gap is closed by underlying principles recognized by civilized nations in the form of logical or implicit obligations.[61] Situated within the framework of obligation, the Court's approach to the role of States with respect to the Convention on the Prevention and Punishment of the Crime of Genocide seems reassuring. At the same time, it seems highly unsettling, because it admits the possibility that, while turning to the common good of international society in the form of the Convention on the Prevention and Punishment of the Crime of Genocide, States would have had a freedom not do so in so far as they had not recognized, as civilized nations, the underlying principles.

In the *Case concerning Military and Paramilitary Activities in and against Nicaragua (Merits)*, the ICJ relied on principles of humanitarian law to identify an obligation incumbent on the United States not to lay mines off the coast of Nicaragua and not to interfere indirectly in the internal conflict in Nicaragua. The Court based the obligation not to lay mines off the coast of Nicaragua both on the freedoms of navigation, communication, and commerce,[62] and on the principles of humanitarian law 'underlying' Hague Convention VIII relative to the Laying of Automatic Submarine Contact Mines, to which it referred as elementary considerations of humanity.[63] This aspect of the dispute more or less resembled the situation at issue in the *Corfu Channel Case (Merits)*.[64] The same applies to the Court's appraisal, performing an implicit balance between considerations of humanity and military exigencies, regarding the acts of the United States as disproportional.

The Court based the obligation not to interfere indirectly in the internal conflict in Nicaragua on an extensive conception of fundamental general principles of

[61] *Case Concerning Application of the Convention on the Prevention and Punishment of the Crime of Genocide*, Judgment of 26 February 2007, ICJ Reports 2007, 43, paras 161–167.

[62] *Case Concerning Military and Paramilitary Activities in and against Nicaragua (Merits)*, Judgment of 27 June 1986, ICJ Reports 1986, 14, para 214.

[63] *Case Concerning Military and Paramilitary Activities in and against Nicaragua (Merits)*, Judgment of 27 June 1986, ICJ Reports 1986, 14, para 215.

[64] *Case Concerning Military and Paramilitary Activities in and against Nicaragua (Merits)*, Judgment of 27 June 1986, Dissenting Opinion Judge Oda, ICJ Reports 1986, 14, para 89; Dissenting Opinion Judge Sir Robert Jennings, 536–537.

humanitarian law, as expressed in Common Articles 1 and 3 of the 1949 Geneva Conventions and reflecting elementary considerations of humanity. The Court identified an obligation, pursuant to Article 1, to ensure respect of the provisions of Article 3, effectively interpreting Article 1 in the sense of a prohibition of participation in breaches of international humanitarian law in the context of an internal conflict. This interpretation presupposes that Article 1 can be interpreted in the context of internal conflicts as requiring the States Parties not to participate in breaches of international humanitarian law. This gives a criminal law coloring to Article 1, which is reminiscent of the approach of the Court in *Reservations to the Convention on the Prevention and Punishment of the Crime of Genocide*. In this way, judicial discretion and (general) principles of international law are both directed at restricting the freedom of States to act. Inversely, this degree of verticalization makes it more difficult to continue to see these (general) principles of international law as derived from customary international law or conventional international law and/or as accepted or recognized by States.[65]

When the principle of good faith, contained in Article 2, para 2, of the UN Charter, and the principle of sovereign equality, contained in Article 2, para 1, of the UN Charter, are seen from the perspectives of the framework of obligation and the framework of authorization, the following observations may be made. With respect to the principle of good faith as a principle of international law, the ICJ has remarked that, although well-established, it does not constitute an independent source of obligations.[66] This would appear to mean that, within the framework of obligation, the principle of good faith as a principle of international law does not have a gap-filling function, unless it can be tied to a rule of conventional international law or a rule of customary international law.

The principle of sovereign equality is alternatively situated within the framework of obligation or within the framework of authorization. According to the framework of obligation, the function of rules of public international law is to restrict the freedom of States to act. The framework of obligation is based on the assumption that, in the absence of a rule of public international law, States have a freedom to act. If situated within the framework of obligation, the principle of sovereign equality coincides with the assumption of a freedom of States to act. It cannot, within that context, be seen as a principle of international law, because it does not operate so as to restrict the freedom of States to act. It follows that the principle of sovereign equality cannot meaningfully be situated within the framework of obligation. Furthermore, if a freedom of a State to act in itself interferes with a freedom of another State to act, a freedom to act, in the absence of a restrictive rule of public international law, cannot be inferred from the principle of sovereign equality.

[65] *Case Concerning Military and Paramilitary Activities in and against Nicaragua (Merits)*, Judgment of 27 June 1986, Separate Opinion Judge Ago, ICJ Reports 1986, 14, para. 6.

[66] *Case Concerning the Land and Maritime Boundary between Cameroon and Nigeria (Preliminary Objections)*, Judgment of 11 June 1998, ICJ Reports 1998, 275, para 39.

In doctrine, the principle of sovereign equality is commonly explained as deriving from a source of public international law, for example, conventional international law,[67] customary international law,[68] general principles of law,[69] (general) principles of international law accepted or recognized by States[70] or *jus cogens.*[71] It may be observed, however, that, within the framework of obligation, the function of rules of public international law emanating from those sources is to restrict the freedom of States to act, while simultaneously reflecting the exercise of that freedom of States to act. It follows that the principle of sovereign equality cannot be derived from those sources and is presupposed.[72]

Explaining the principle of sovereign equality as dependent on those sources would imply relying on the framework of authorization. Within the framework of authorization, the power of States to act is dependent on a permissive rule of public international law. This would simultaneously mean, however, that the sources of public international law cannot themselves be explained by reference to the principle of sovereign equality, as that would involve circular reasoning, which is incapable of explaining unilateral causality. From this perspective, then, the sources of public international law would not have any basis in international society. If the sources of public international law could be explained by reference to the principle of sovereign equality, this would mean that the principle of sovereign equality is not dependent on those sources, which would be inconsistent with the framework of authorization. Inconsistency with the framework of authorization therefore implies that the principle of sovereign equality must already have, to a degree, a legal character.

It is concluded, therefore, that the principle of sovereign equality cannot be situated coherently and exclusively either within the framework of obligation or within the framework of authorization. In so far as both frameworks are incoherent, their mutual exclusivity must be rejected. Consequently, it is submitted, the principle of sovereign equality may coherently be resituated within the reformulated framework identified in Part I. Within the reformulated framework, the concept of sovereignty may be understood as a power to act, which is not an unlimited freedom to act. This power to act situates the members of international society in a dilemma in the sense that in order to exercise their power to act they must turn to the constituting of international society. (General) principles of international law may form and inform the constituting of (the common good of) international society. Operating within the reformulated framework, (general) principles of international law do not play a limiting role, such as elementary considerations of humanity within the framework of obligation, but may be seen as

67 Elias and Lim 1997, pp. 28–30; Graf Vitzthum 1997, para 72; De Wet 2000, p. 190.

68 Elias and Lim 1997, pp. 28–30.

69 Elias and Lim 1997, pp. 28–30.

70 Touret 1973, pp. 172–184.

71 Touret 1973, pp. 172–184; De Wet 2000, p. 191.

72 Tomuschat 1999, Chap. V, para 3, Chap. IX, para 40.

the interface between the reformulated framework, on the one hand, and conventional international law and customary international law, on the other hand.

How the previous considerations may be brought together in an analysis proceeding from the reformulated framework, may be illustrated by returning to the reasoning of the ICJ in the Judgment in the *Corfu Channel Case (Merits)*. In this Judgment, the ICJ considered the following two questions submitted by the United Kingdom and Albania by virtue of a Special Agreement of 25 March 1948:

(1) Is Albania responsible under international law for the explosions which occurred on the 22nd October 1946 in Albanian waters and for the damage and loss of human life which resulted from them and is there any duty to pay compensation?
(2) Has the United Kingdom under international law violated the sovereignty of the Albanian People's Republic by reason of the acts of the Royal Navy in Albanian waters on the 22nd October and on the 12th and 13th November 1946 and is there any duty to give satisfaction?

From two series of facts, Albania's attitude before and after the incident of 22 October 1946 and the feasibility of observing minelaying from the Albanian coast, the Court inferred that Albania had had knowledge of the laying of the minefield which had been struck, on 22 October 1946, by the destroyers Saumarez and Volage, which were making their way, together with the cruisers Mauritius and Leander, through the North Corfu Channel.[73] Thereupon, the Court identified the obligations incumbent upon Albania as consisting in notifying, for the benefit of shipping in general, the existence of a minefield in Albanian territorial waters and in warning the approaching British warships of the imminent danger to which the minefield exposed them. As the Court said, these obligations were based on certain general and well-recognized principles, namely: elementary considerations of humanity, even more exacting in peace than in war; the principle of the freedom of maritime communication; and every State's obligation not to allow knowingly its territory to be used for acts contrary to the rights of other States.[74] The Court then proceeded to establish that Albania had violated the obligation to warn the British warships, because there would have been enough time to warn them.[75]

With regard to the first part of the second question, whether the United Kingdom had violated, under international law, the sovereignty of Albania by reason of the passage of the squadron through the North Corfu Channel on 22 October 1946, the Court established that the North Corfu Channel should be considered as belonging to the class of international highways through which passage cannot be prohibited by a coastal State in time of peace.[76] The Court was

[73] *Corfu Channel Case (Merits)*, Judgment of 9 April 1949, ICJ Reports 1949, 4, 17–22.
[74] *Corfu Channel Case (Merits)*, Judgment of 9 April 1949, ICJ Reports 1949, 4, 22.
[75] *Corfu Channel Case (Merits)*, Judgment of 9 April 1949, ICJ Reports 1949, 4, 22–23.
[76] *Corfu Channel Case (Merits)*, Judgment of 9 April 1949, ICJ Reports 1949, 4, 28–30.

also of the opinion that the passage that had been effected by the British warships had been innocent.[77] Finally, in respect of the second part of the second question, whether the United Kingdom had violated, under international law, the sovereignty of Albania by Operation Retail, on 12 and 13 November 1946, which had removed, without the consent of Albania, the minefield in the North Corfu Channel, the Court found that this had indeed been a violation of the sovereignty of Albania.[78]

The individual opinions appended to the Judgment focused mainly on the question whether Albania had had knowledge of the laying of the minefield or should have had knowledge thereof. The Dissenting Opinions of Judge Badawi Pasha, Judge Krylov and Dr. Ečer examined the question whether Albania had had knowledge of the minefield and concluded that there was insufficient evidence that that had indeed been so.[79] As regards the question whether Albania should have had knowledge of the existence of the minefield, i.e. whether it had exercised due diligence in respect of its territory, the dissenting opinions diverged, Judge Winiarski considering that Albania had failed to exercise due diligence and Judge Krylov finding that Albania had exercised due diligence.[80]

The identification by the Court of the general and well-recognized principles on which the obligations to notify and to warn, incumbent upon Albania, were based, is not explained in the reasoning of the Court. It is preceded and followed by factual observations and deductions; the third principle is informed by the view taken by the Court in respect of the first part of the second question, i.e. that the North Corfu Channel belonged to the class of international highways through which passage cannot be prohibited by the coastal State. The Court's answer to the first question was clearly situated within the framework of obligation. However, the Court's answer to the first part of the second question was situated within the framework of authorization. At the beginning of the Court's examination of that question, it remarked:

> It is, in the opinion of the Court, generally recognized and in accordance with international custom that States in time of peace have a right to send their warships through straits used for international navigation between two parts of the high seas without the previous authorization of a coastal State, provided the passage is *innocent*.[81]

The Court thus identified on a compound basis—general recognition and international custom—a right of States. It would appear that the Court was establishing a right-obligation relationship between States and Albania through the

---

[77] *Corfu Channel Case (Merits)*, Judgment of 9 April 1949, ICJ Reports 1949, 4, 28–32.

[78] *Corfu Channel Case (Merits)*, Judgment of 9 April 1949, ICJ Reports 1949, 4, 33–35.

[79] *Corfu Channel Case (Merits)*, Judgment of 9 April 1949, Dissenting Opinion Judge Badawi Pasha, ICJ Reports 1949, 4, 60–64; Dissenting Opinion Judge Krylov, 69–71; Dissenting Opinion Dr. Ečer, 118–127.

[80] *Corfu Channel Case (Merits)*, Judgment of 9 April 1949, Dissenting Opinion Judge Winiarski, ICJ Reports 1949, 4, 51–56; Dissenting Opinion Judge Krylov, 71–72.

[81] *Corfu Channel Case (Merits)*, Judgment of 9 April 1949, ICJ Reports 1949, 4, 28.

interconnection between these different parts of its Judgment. However, the rights of States and the obligations of Albania cannot coexist within the mutual exclusivity of the framework of authorization and framework of obligation. The right of States would presuppose the existence of the framework of authorization, but within that framework, rights cannot be explained as emanating from general recognition or international custom, because that would presuppose that States already have a power to act. The obligations incumbent upon Albania would presuppose the existence of the framework of obligation, but the Court only referred to characteristics of the North Corfu Channel that brought it within the class of international highways, without establishing a connection between that status and the corresponding restriction of the freedom of Albania to act. Moreover, the framework of obligation cannot account for the right of States, just as the framework of authorization cannot account for the obligations incumbent upon Albania.

The background reasoning of the Court, it may be said, was focused on establishing a relationship between the general interest and an individual member of the international community. It did so, however, in an authoritarian and unbalanced manner, which imposed obligations on the coastal State and allowed a State to enforce a right which, in view of the mutual exclusivity of the framework of obligation and the framework of authorization, could not have existed. Moreover, as emerges from the remarks of Judge Krylov, Judge Azevedo and Judge ad hoc Ečer, whether a right of passage through straits could be derived from the practice of States and whether the passage effected by the squadron had been innocent, was controversial.[82] Within the reformulated framework, both States would have been found not to have acted so as to constitute international society. The reformulated framework does not accord rights to States, so the United Kingdom could not have insisted to have a right to enforce a right of innocent passage. On the other hand, Albania could not have derived a right from its sovereignty not to warn approaching warships of the existence of a minefield, even if the intended passage were not innocent. The absence of such a right would not be a reflection of elementary considerations of humanity, but of the reformulated framework. Within the reformulated framework, States are situated as having a power to act, but not an unlimited freedom to act. This means that their mutual relationship can only be given form by the constituting of international society on the basis of practical reasoning directed at the common good.

---

[82] *Corfu Channel Case (Merits)*, Judgment of 9 April 1949, Dissenting Opinion Judge Krylov, ICJ Reports 1949, 4, 73–75; Dissenting Opinion Judge Azevedo, paras 27–39; Dissenting Opinion Dr. Ečer, 128–130.

8.7 Conclusion

In light of the above, it is concluded that the concept of general principles of law conforms to the framework of obligation. According to the framework of obligation, the function of general principles of law is to restrict the freedom of States to act. It is assumed that in the absence of general principles of law, States have a freedom to act. It is likewise concluded that, if situated within the framework of obligation, the concept of general principles of law gives rise to incoherence. If a freedom of a State to act interferes in itself with a freedom of another State to act, if follows that the residual rule according to which States have a freedom to act in the absence of a general principle of law restricting that freedom, must be rejected. It then follows that the function of general principles of law does not reside in restricting the freedom of States to act. This conclusion is supported by the difficulty which arises if it is sought to explain coherently the transposition of general principles of private law or general principles of public law to the concept of public international law, so as to restrict the freedom of States to act. The problem arising is that such general principles of the internal law of the State emanate, internally, from the institution of the State which, externally, radiates its absence.

(General) principles of international law derived from customary international law or conventional international law and (general) principles of international law recognized or accepted by States are generally situated within the framework of obligation. The difficulty arising with regard to those sub-categories is that it does not seem possible to arrive at a restriction of the freedom of States to act which can coherently be based on the exercise of the freedom of those States to act.

The principle of sovereign equality is situated either within the framework of obligation or within the framework of authorization. Neither framework situates the concept of sovereignty coherently. If situated within the framework of obligation, the principle appears as the inconsistent assumption of a freedom of States to act. If regarded as emanating from the sources of public international law, the principle is effectively situated within the framework of authorization and is excluded as an explanation of those sources.

When situated within the framework of obligation, the concept of general principles of law seeks to combine within itself the competition between general principles of law and the assumption of a freedom of States to act. These principles are mutually exclusive, in the sense that if recourse is had to the assumption of a freedom of States to act, no room remains for reliance on a general principle of law. Conversely, a general principle of law may leave no ground of the assumption of a freedom of States to act uncovered, without undermining its own justification.

Transposed to the concept of (general) principles of international law, this divergence translates into a competition between moral principles, such as elementary considerations of humanity or general principles of international humanitarian law, on the one hand, and the sovereignty and independence of States, on the other hand. When a plausible case for the existence of such principles can be made, as with the principles underlying the Convention on the

Prevention and Punishment of the Crime of Genocide, this raises in turn doubts as to whether, in respect of conventional international law prescribing rules with regard to acts of genocide by individuals, States could hypothetically, but for the existence of a prohibitive principle, be considered as disposing of a freedom to commit acts of genocide.

It is submitted, therefore, that these considerations taken together require that the vertical structure of the concept of law underlying the concept of public international law be taken into consideration, involving the contrast between the framework of obligation and the framework of authorization. This, in turn, impels, it is submitted, the transition to a reformulated framework which combines elements of both frameworks by suppressing their mutual exclusivity. When combined, this leads to a transformation of the function of public international law which is neither exclusively enabling nor exclusively disabling, but both at the same time. Correspondingly, the members of international society are situated as having a power to act, but not an unlimited freedom to act, by virtue of which they act so as to constitute (the common good of) international society pursuant to practical reasoning. The important consequence for the relationship between the sources of public international law and the sovereignty and independence of the members of international society is that it becomes circular: the sources of public international law—conventional international law and customary international law—and the sovereignty and independence of the members of international society become mutually constitutive. By forming rules of public international law, the members of international society constitute international society; at the same time, these rules of public international law constitute the members of international society as members of international society.

This transition from the incoherence of the framework of obligation and the framework of authorization to the reformulated framework impels a reversal of the traditional sources of public international law. Whereas the concept of general principles of law was, initially, supplementary to customary international law and conventional international law, the transition to the reformulated framework approximates the concept of general principles of law to the reformulated framework. At the same time, the concept of general principles of law and the concept of (general) principles of international law may be seen as forming and informing the constituting of international society by the members of international society, on the basis of considerations taken from the structure of international society or inferred from principles or rules of conventional international law or customary international law.

Chapter 9
The Concept of Conventional International Law Situated Within the Framework of Obligation and the Framework of Authorization

9.1 Introduction

The present chapter analyzes the concept of conventional international law from the perspectives of the framework of obligation and the framework of authorization. In comparison with the concepts of general principles of law and customary international law—unwritten public international law, the concept of conventional international law may be seen as relatively unproblematic, because it consists of textually formulated rules to which States have, or have not, given their consent. Moreover, in contrast with the concepts of general principles of law and customary international law, the concept of conventional international law, in the form of the Vienna Convention on the Law of Treaties, contains within itself a body of 'secondary' rules, rules about conventional international law. Nevertheless, when analyzed from the perspectives of the framework of obligation and the framework of authorization, the concept of conventional international law is incoherent, relying on inconsistent assumptions relating to the origin of rules of public international law and to the way in which the members of international society are situated in respect of each other.

Section 9.2 presents several definitions of the concept of treaty, which suggest that the concept of conventional international law is commonly situated within the framework of obligation. Section 9.3 presents several classifications of treaties which rely on concepts of the internal law of the State, contract and legislation. These comparisons confirm the view that the concept of conventional international law is commonly situated within the framework of obligation and reveal the operation of the domestic analogy underlying the concept of conventional international law. Subsequently, Sect. 9.4 analyzes the concept of treaty as situated within the framework of obligation and the framework of authorization. Section 9.5 seeks to illustrate the incoherence arising from these frameworks with respect to the position of third States.

J. A. Vos, *The Function of Public International Law*,
DOI: 10.1007/978-90-6704-861-3_9,

It will be concluded from these analyses that the concept of conventional international law should be resituated within a reformulated framework, resulting from a transition emanating from the incoherence of the mutual exclusivity of the framework of obligation and the framework of authorization. Resituated within this reformulated framework, the concept of conventional international law has both an enabling and a disabling aspect. Thus, the members of international society may be regarded as constituting the common good of international society in the form of conventional international law, which consists of both principles and rules. The members of international society must adhere to the common good of international society as thus constituted in the form of conventional international law or reconstitute the common good of international society by restarting the cycle of practical reasoning. Simultaneously, the concept of conventional international law understood as the common good of international society constitutes the members of international society as members of international society. Within the reformulated framework, the relationship between conventional international law and the members of international society is circular.

9.2 The Concept of Conventional International Law

The concept of conventional international law revolves around the notions of 'treaty' and 'convention'. These notions have been defined in doctrine and in the practice of States as follows.

A first definition that may be considered was formulated in the Draft Convention on the Law of Treaties, prepared by the Research in International Law of the Harvard Law School. Article 1 (a) of the Draft Convention on the Law of Treaties defined a 'treaty' as 'a formal instrument of agreement by which two or more States establish or seek to establish a relation under international law between themselves'.[1] The Comment to Article 1 (a) clarified that this definition was based on a distinction between 'agreement' as such, described as an accord of wills, and a formal instrument incorporating such agreement. Only the latter was to be regarded as a treaty, susceptible of interpretation.[2]

Under the heading 'Pacta Sunt Servanda' Article 20 of the Draft Convention on the Law of Treaties stipulated that a State is bound to carry out in good faith the obligations which it has assumed by a treaty (*pacta sunt servanda*).[3] This would suggest that the relation which two or more States establish or seek to establish consists of binding obligations. Nevertheless, the Comment to Article 1 (a) further

---

1 Harvard Research in International Law 1935, Article 1 (a), p. 657.

2 Harvard Research in International Law 1935, Comment to Article 1 (a), pp. 690–691.

3 Harvard Research in International Law 1935, Article 20, p. 661.

specified that the term relation comprehended both rights and obligations as well as relations that did not consist of rights or obligations.[4]

Similarly, Article 2, para 1 (a), of the Vienna Convention on the Law of Treaties defines the concept of treaty as an international agreement concluded between States in written form and governed by international law, whether embodied in a single instrument or in two or more related instruments and whatever its particular designation. Under the heading "Pacta sunt servanda", Article 26 of the Vienna Convention on the Law of Treaties provides that every treaty in force is binding upon the parties to it and must be performed by them in good faith.

In doctrine, McNair defined the concept of treaty as a written agreement by which two or more States create a relation between themselves operating within the sphere of international law.[5] Reuter defined the concept of treaty as an expression of concurring wills attributable to two or more subjects of international law and intended to have legal effects under the rules of international law.[6]

These definitions of the concept of treaty describe or suggest in various ways and degrees the function of rules of conventional international law. When read together, Articles 1 (a) and 20 of the Draft Convention on the Law of Treaties suggest that the relation that two or more States establish or seek to establish consists of binding rules containing obligations. The clarification in the Comment to Article 1 (a) that the term relation might comprise both rights and obligations as well as relations that do not consist of rights and obligations actually renders matters rather unclear. While the term 'relation' used in Article 1 (a) might be regarded as comprehending both rights and obligations as well as relations that do not consist of rights and obligations, the formulation of the rule *pacta sunt servanda* suggests that the function of rules of conventional international law is limited to containing obligations. Metaphorically, the description 'under international law' situates the concept of treaty within the vertical structure of the concept of law underlying the concept of public international law. Similarly, the combined effect of Articles 2, para 1 (a), and 26 of the Vienna Convention on the Law of Treaties suggests that conventional international law consists of binding rules containing obligations. The expression 'governed by international law' clearly evokes the perspective of the vertical structure of the concept of law underlying the concept of public international law. The definition formulated by McNair is less clear in this respect, referring to a relation operating within the sphere of international law. The definition adhered to by Reuter focuses more on the composite nature of the concept of agreement as consisting of concurring wills. At the same time, these concurring wills are situated within the vertical structure of the concept of law underlying the concept of public international law by the legal effects which they may have 'under the rules of international law'.

---

4 Harvard Research in International Law 1935, Comment to Article 1 (a), p. 692.

5 McNair 1961, p. 4.

6 Reuter 1995, paras 63–75.

These perspectives locate the notion of agreement at the heart of the concept of treaty.[7] Simultaneously, these perspectives situate that notion of agreement within the concept of public international law, as follows. First, as described in the definition contained in Article 1 (a) of the Draft Convention on the Law of Treaties and the definition adhered to by McNair, the concept of agreement constitutes a structure consisting of a relation between States. Second, except as left open by the definition adhered to by McNair, the concept of agreement is situated 'under' or as 'governed by' the concept of public international law. While, as already remarked, these descriptions evoke the vertical structure of the concept of law underlying the concept of conventional international law, at the same time they suggest a separation between the concept of treaty and the concept of public international law. Third, concurrently, the provision that a treaty in force binds the States parties to it reintegrates the concept of conventional international law within the concept of public international law, because the relation established by the agreement under or governed by public international law consists of rules which bind States and contain obligations by virtue of the concept of public international law. These perspectives clearly situate the concept of conventional international law within the framework of obligation. Before addressing the incoherence arising from that framework, Sect. 8.2 will describe the link between the concept of treaty and the internal law of the State.

9.3 The Concept of Treaty and Analogy with the Internal Law of the State

The concept of treaty is commonly compared to one or more concepts of the internal law of the State. Thus, in doctrine, the concept of treaty is commonly compared to the concept of contract.[8] Both the Draft Convention on the Law of Treaties and the Vienna Convention on the Law of Treaties may be said to rely on an extensive analogy with the concept of contract.[9] Pursuant to this analogy, the Appellate Body of the Dispute Settlement Body of the WTO considered the Agreement Establishing the WTO in contractual terms.[10]

On the other hand, in doctrine, a broad analogy has also been drawn between the concept of treaty and the concept of legislation.[11] Raftopoulos has criticized

[7] Klabbers 1996, pp. 51–54.

[8] Lauterpacht 1927, para 70; Grotius 1964, Book II, Chap. XV, Section I; Dupuy 2002, pp. 26, 128–130.

[9] Raftopoulos 1990, pp. 207–214, 238–254.

[10] Report of the Appellate Body, *Japan – Taxes on Alcoholic Beverages*, WT/DS8/AB/R, WT/DS10/AB/R, WT/DS11/AB/R, 15: 'The *WTO Agreement* is a treaty—the international equivalent of a contract.'

[11] Friedmann 1964, p. 124; Zemanek 1997, paras 320–331.

the contractual analogy in the concept of treaty, arguing that such a framework prevents a treaty text from being seen in terms of the realization of a public, legislative purpose directed at the contextual, relational accommodation of competing interests on the basis of consensus rather than consent.[12]

According to the abovementioned views, the concept of treaty should be compared either to the concept of contract or to the concept of legislation. However, in doctrine, it is also common to identify categories of treaties on the basis of the distinction between the concept of contract and the concept of legislation. Thus, a broad distinction is commonly made between a treaty resembling legislation ('traité-loi') and a treaty resembling a contract ('traité-contrat'). This distinction has been developed, successively, in the doctrinal work of Bergbohm, Triepel, Roxburgh, and McNair.

Bergbohm distinguished treaties establishing 'Rechtsgeschäfte' and treaties establishing 'Rechtssätze'. According to Bergbohm, treaties establishing 'Rechtsgeschäfte' create or abrogate subjective rights of States and may be compared to contracts. As examples, Bergbohm mentioned treaties relating to peace, alliance, succession, servitude, territorial changes, and economic goods. In contrast, according to Bergbohm, treaties establishing 'Rechtssätze' create general rules. In this category, Bergbohm included conventions relating to *jus in bello*, the rights and duties of neutrals, extradition, the international protection of copyright, institutions for the promotion of trade, and diplomatic ceremonies.[13]

Triepel drew a similar distinction between the concept of 'Vertrag' and the concept of 'Vereinbarung'. Triepel defined the concept of 'Vertrag' as the unification of opposed declarations of will directed at the same purpose.[14] According to Triepel, a 'Vertrag' is always a 'Rechtsgeschäft', a reciprocal exchange. In contrast, the concept of 'Vereinbarung' referred to the unification of declarations of will directed at the realization of the same or common interests.[15] According to Triepel, a 'Vereinbarung' could be directed at the creation of one or more 'Rechtssätze', consisting of the common will of a community limiting the will of its members.[16]

Roxburgh drew a different distinction between treaties resembling contracts and treaties constituting authoritative settlements. Roxburgh regarded treaties as the contracts of international law, considering at the same time, however, that the applicability of the law of contract to treaties depended on the practice of States.[17] According to Roxburgh, the category of treaties resembling contracts was to be distinguished from the category of treaties constituting authoritative settlements. These were international settlements determined authoritatively by the great

[12] Raftopoulos 1990, *passim.*

[13] Bergbohm 1877, pp. 79–81.

[14] Triepel 1899, pp. 35–45.

[15] Triepel 1899, pp. 49–62.

[16] Triepel 1899, pp. 29–35; Dupuy 2002, pp. 123–127.

[17] Roxburgh 1917, para 3.

powers, for example, the Final Act of the Congress of Vienna (1815), the Treaty of Paris (1856), the Treaty of Berlin (1878), and the Treaty of Constantinople (1888).[18]

These three categories of treaties distinguished by Bergbohm, Triepel, and Roxburgh were subsequently incorporated in a comprehensive classification developed by McNair, which comprised the following four main categories of treaties: (i) treaties having the character of conveyances; (ii) treaties having the character of contracts; (iii) law-making treaties; and (iv) treaties akin to charters of incorporation.

(i) Treaties having the character of conveyances had to be regarded, according to McNair, as dispositive treaties, because they transfer territorial rights between States.[19]

(ii) As examples of treaties having the character of contracts, McNair mentioned treaties relating to peace, alliance, friendship, neutrality, guarantee, and commerce. Following Roxburgh in this respect, McNair considered that, although an analogy may be drawn between the concept of treaty and the concept of contract as regards form and the role of consent in the formation of obligations, rules regarding the formation, validity, interpretation, and discharge of contracts were not automatically applicable to treaties.[20]

(iii) (a) The category of law-making treaties was divided by McNair into (a) treaties creating constitutional international law (or international public law) and (b) treaties creating or declaring ordinary international law (law-making or legislative treaties). Treaties creating constitutional international law or international public law were further subdivided by McNair into (1) treaties creating international organs and general rules, such as the Covenant of the League of Nations, and (2) multilateral treaties which from time to time settle the political affairs of a group of countries in a particularly solemn and semi-dictatorial fashion which likens the arrangement to a governmental act imposed from above upon the parties affected, rather than to a voluntary bargain between them.[21] As examples McNair mentioned: (1) international settlements, such as the Final Act of the Congress of Vienna and the Treaty of Versailles and (2) treaties relating to waterways of interest to the international community, such as the Suez, Panama, and Kiel Canals. Although such settlements seemed incompatible with the requirement of consent, McNair considered that such treaties formed a substitute for the absence of a legislature in the society of States.[22]

---

[18] Roxburgh 1917, para 38.

[19] McNair 1930, pp. 101–102.

[20] McNair 1930, pp. 105–106.

[21] McNair 1930, pp. 112–114.

[22] McNair 1961, Chap. XIV.

(b) Treaties creating or declaring ordinary international law were regarded as such by McNair because they create rules of law which may be called ordinary or private law, not concerned with the constitutional relations of the members of the society of States. These included: (1) conventions relating to the laws of war; (2) labour conventions; (3) conventions relating to transit and communications.[23]

(iv) Finally, treaties akin to charters of incorporation formed a combination of ordinary law-making treaties and treaties creating international organs. McNair described such treaties as creating international unions for co-operation between States in non-political fields. According to McNair, the difference between those treaties and treaties creating international constitutional law or international public law in the form of international organs and general rules was that the rules administered by those unions should be considered as rules of private law.[24]

Category (ii) of the classification developed by McNair—treaties having the character of contracts—corresponds to the category characterized by Bergbohm as treaties establishing 'Rechtsgeschäfte' and to the category characterized by Triepel as 'Vertrag'. The category of treaties creating international constitutional law or international public law corresponds to the category identified by Roxburgh as international settlements. The category of ordinary law-making treaties corresponds to the category characterized by Bergbohm as treaties establishing 'Rechtssätze' and to the category characterized by Triepel as 'Vereinbarung'.

But while McNair incorporated these categories into his comprehensive classification, interesting transitions, along the axis formed by the public/private distinction, occur. First, it may be observed that the subdivision of constitutional international law or international public law into treaties creating international organs and general rules and international settlements is not clear-cut. In particular, the Covenant of the League of Nations is mentioned as an instance of international constitutional law or international public law, while the Treaty of Versailles is mentioned as an instance of an international settlement. Yet, the Covenant of the League of Nations formed Part I of the Treaty of Versailles.

Further, in the conjunct classifications adopted by Bergbohm and Triepel, the category of treaties establishing Rechtssätze, Vereinbarungen, as contrasted to the category of treaties establishing Rechtsgeschäfte, Verträge, was regarded as having a public character. However, when introduced into the comprehensive classification developed by McNair and contrasted with the category of constitutional international law or international public law, the same category, as ordinary law-making treaties, is regarded as having a private character. Along the vertical axis formed by the constitutional, at the top, and the contractual, at the bottom, the

---

23 McNair 1930, pp. 115–116.

24 McNair 1930, pp. 115, 116–118.

middle category of ordinary law-making treaties thus acquires a mixed character, seen from the contractual as public and seen from the constitutional as private.

Finally, we may note that international institutions and the rules of public international law to which they may give rise, are classified as public or private, depending on the question whether they form part of international constitutional law or international public law, on the one hand, or, akin to charters of incorporation, of ordinary public international law on the other hand. McNair located the criterion to differentiate between these two fields in their (non-)political nature.

More generally, the distinction between the notion of traité-loi and the notion of traité-contrat has been called into question.[25] It has been observed, for example, that in so far as a traité-contrat establishes rules for the States-parties, it seems indistinguishable from a traité-loi.[26] In the opposite direction, mention may be made of the view expounded by Fitzmaurice, according to which a treaty creates merely rights and obligations and should not be regarded as a source of law.[27] Moreover, we should not fail to mention that in respect of any category of treaties, in view of the absence of a legislature in international society, States are commonly regarded as their legislators.[28]

It is submitted that these different characterizations of constitutional, legislative, and private aspects within the concept of conventional international law defray a sense of the operation of the domestic analogy at work here. Broadly speaking, there is a sense of a structural difference between the notion of a multilateral treaty, which aims to establish rules for all members of the international community, and a bilateral treaty which aims to establish a relation between pairs of members of the international community. This distinction parallels the transition from the constitutional to the legislative to the private. But at the same time, these different characterizations all operate within the framework of a broader contractual analogy, so that even the constitutional and the legislative are based on the notion of consent and thus based on the assumption of a freedom to act of States.[29] The transposition of the constitutional, of the legislative, and of the private to the international plane equally must take account of the horizontal structure of the concept of public international law. As regards the internal sphere of the institution of the State, it may be noted that both the concept of legislation and the concept of contract partake of the internal law of the State. Transposing both concepts to the international plane thus simultaneously involves relying on the presence (legislation or contract is binding) and on the absence (this binding quality must be established by means of consent) of an authority above States.

---

25 Dupuy 2002, pp. 141–145.

26 Strupp 1934, pp. 324–329; Waldock 1962, pp. 74–76.

27 Fitzmaurice 1958a, pp. 157–160.

28 Lauterpacht 1936, p. 54.

29 Lauterpacht 1936, p. 54.

While the transition from the constitutional to the legislative to the private may be a matter of degree, the framework of obligation leaves these transitions unconstituted.

9.4 The Concept of Treaty Situated Within the Framework of Obligation

Whether the concept of treaty is compared to the concept of contract or to the concept of legislation, or to both, it already seemed to follow from the definitions of the concept of treaty, described in Sect. 9.2, that the concept of treaty conforms to the framework of obligation. Accordingly, it is the function of rules of conventional international law to restrict the freedom of States to act. In the absence of rules of conventional international law, it is assumed that States have a freedom to act. Moreover, as legislators of conventional international law, States create rules of conventional international law by means of an exercise of that freedom to act.

As regards the comparison with the concept of contract, the framework of obligation is clearly reflected in the combined effect of Articles 2, para 1 (a), and 26 of the Vienna Convention on the Law of Treaties. As reflected in those provisions, it is the function of rules of conventional international law to bind the States-parties. At the same time, those provisions of the Vienna Convention on the Law of Treaties presuppose that in the absence of rules of conventional international law, States have a freedom to act. Furthermore, those provisions of the Vienna Convention on the Law of Treaties are based on the assumption that the concept of treaty is based on the consent of States, which reflects the freedom of contract of States. This pattern may also be identified in the view adopted by the PCIJ in the *Case of the S.S. Wimbledon*, where it regarded conventional international law as giving rise to obligations restricting rights emanating from the sovereignty of a State and explaining these obligations in terms of the exercise of those rights.[30] A similar view has been adopted in WTO jurisprudence.[31]

---

[30] *Case of the S.S. Wimbledon*, Judgment No. 1 of 17 August 1923, Series A.—No. 1, 25: 'The Court declines to see in the conclusion of any Treaty by which a State undertakes to perform or refrain from performing a particular act an abandonment of its sovereignty. No doubt any convention creating an obligation of this kind places a restriction upon the exercise of the sovereign rights of the State, in the sense that it requires them to be exercised in a certain way. But the right of entering into international engagements is an attribute of State sovereignty.'

Klabbers 1998, pp. 359–364; Dupuy 2002, pp. 93–94.

[31] Report of the Appellate Body, *Japan – Taxes on Alcoholic Beverages*, WT/DS8/AB/R, WT/DS10/AB/R, WT/DS11/AB/R, 15: 'It is self-evident that in an exercise of their sovereignty, and in pursuit of their own respective national interests, the Members of the WTO have made a bargain. In exchange for the benefits they expect to derive as Members of the WTO, they have agreed to exercise their sovereignty according to the commitments they have made in the *WTO Agreement*.'

These assumptions presuppose that rules of conventional international law can be regarded at the same time as binding the States-parties and as emanating from the consent of the States-parties.[32] Within the framework of obligation, the assumption that rules of conventional international law bind the States-parties is axiomatic.[33] Without this assumption, the concept of conventional international law could not exist within the framework of obligation, because it could not give rise to binding rules limiting the freedom of States to act.[34] However, the view that the rule *pacta sunt servanda* forms part of public international law is ultimately a matter of assumption.[35] It may, of course, be pointed out that Article 26 of the Vienna Convention on the Law of Treaties formulates the rule *pacta sunt servanda*. This might perhaps explain why treaties concluded by States-parties to, and under, the Vienna Convention on the Law of Treaties, bind those States. But this simply relocates the problem to the question pursuant to what rule the Vienna Convention on the Law of Treaties itself is binding. While the answer to this question might be located in general principles of law or in customary international law or outside the concept of public international law, this involves relying on the assumption that those sources are indeed capable of producing and containing such a rule or that such a rule can coherently be situated outside of the concept of public international law. Illustrative of this infinite regress is that, as described in Sect. 5.4, in Kelsen's monist vertical structure, comprising both the international legal order and national legal orders, the basic norm cannot be explained by virtue of the legal order itself, but has to remain a matter of assumption. In a circular manner, while located at the apex of the legal order, it is characterized as a 'basic' norm. Similarly, locating, as suggested by Triepel, the binding character of the concept of public international law in the common will of the community (Gemeinwille), produced by a so-called 'Vereinbarung' informed by parallel interests, gives rise to the problem of explaining by virtue of what rule that Vereinbarung may be regarded as binding.[36] As regards, on the other hand, the principle of consent, rules of conventional international law must at the same time be regarded as restrictions of the freedom of States to act and as exercises of the freedom of States to act. However, if States are to be regarded as legislators of conventional international law, rules of conventional international law cannot be imposed on them. But if they cannot be imposed on States, rules of conventional international law cannot be regarded as restrictions of the free will of States and States cannot be regarded as subjects of conventional international law.

---

[32] Tomuschat 1999, Chap. IX, para 9.

[33] *Case Concerning the Gabčíkovo-Nagymaros Project*, Judgment of 25 September 1997, ICJ Reports 1997, 7, para 114.

Klabbers 1996, pp. 37–40; Dupuy 2002, pp. 123–127.

[34] Tomuschat 1999, Chap. IX, para 12.

[35] Basdevant 1936, pp. 640–643; Weil 1992, pp. 66–81.

[36] Triepel 1899, pp. 45–62.

Similarly, the framework of obligation may also be identified in the comparison of the concept of treaty with the concept of legislation. It seems to be presupposed that it is the function of general rules to bind the States-parties. In the absence of such general rules, the States-parties are regarded as having a freedom to act. As regards this comparison, it may be observed that the absence of a legislator situated above States is commonly regarded as inherent in the horizontal structure of public international law. It may be recalled in this respect that McNair justified the category of international settlements, which seems difficult to reconcile with the consent of States, by the absence of an international legislature. If so, those general rules should be regarded as emanating from the States-parties as co-legislators. But this contradicts the existence of general rules, because the existence and applicability of a rule vis-à-vis a State would be dependent on the legislative activity of that State. Disregarding the link between general rules and States as legislators in favor of a perspective of States as subjects of rules of conventional international law limiting their freedom to act, also involves relinquishing their basis in international society itself. In other words, if the perspective of States as subjects of conventional international law is favored, this results in imposable rules of conventional international law to the detriment of the perspective of States as legislators of conventional international law. If, on the other hand, the perspective of States as legislators of conventional international law is preferred, this results in unimposable rules of conventional international law. Both the absence and the presence of an international legislature are equally problematic; a middle ground is excluded.

Thus, regardless of whether the concept of treaty is compared to the concept of contract or to the concept of legislation, when situated within the framework of obligation, the concept of treaty gives rise to a dilemma: rules of conventional international law must be seen simultaneously as restrictions of the freedom of States to act and as exercises of the freedom of States to act. But as exercises of the freedom of States to act, rules of conventional international law cannot at the same time restrict that freedom. Conversely, as restrictions of the freedom of States to act, they cannot at the same time be exercises of that freedom. This dilemma also circumscribes what may be regarded as the heart of conventional international law, the field of interpretation. Article 31 of the Vienna Convention on the Law of Treaties formulates a general rule of interpretation, para 1 of which provides:

> A treaty shall be interpreted in good faith in accordance with the ordinary meaning to be given to the terms of the treaty in their context and in the light of its object and purpose.

This provision is usually regarded as a codification of customary international law.[37]

---

[37] *Case Concerning Kasikili/Sedudu Island*, Judgment of 13 December 1999, ICJ Reports 1999, 1045, para 18; *Legal Consequences of the Construction of a Wall in the Occupied Palestinian Territory*, Advisory Opinion of 9 July 2004, ICJ Reports 2004, 136, para 94; *Case Concerning Certain Questions of Mutual Assistance in Criminal Matters*, Judgment of 4 June 2008, ICJ Reports 2008, 177, paras 153–154; *Dispute Regarding Navigational and Related Rights*, Judgment of 13 July 2009, ICJ Reports 2009, 213, para 47.

Thus, interpretation must focus first of all on the text of a treaty, formed by its terms.[38] These terms may be articles or paragraphs of articles.

Second, when interpreting the text of a particular article, or paragraph of an article, the context must be taken into account.[39] According to Article 31, para 2, of the Vienna Convention on the Law of Treaties, the context consists, inter alia, of the text of the treaty as a whole, that is, of the other articles or paragraphs of articles. In this circular way, the context refers back to the terms of the treaty, evincing the mutually constitutive relationship between the text as a whole and the terms.

Third, the terms of the treaty must be considered, in their context, in the light of the object and purpose of the treaty.[40] At the same time, however, the object and purpose of the treaty must be inferred from the text of the treaty, in so far as it is therein expressed. We may thus also identify a circular relationship here, this time between the object and purpose of the treaty and the text as a whole. In WTO jurisprudence, it may be noted, it is deemed permissible to refer not only to the object and purpose of the treaty as a whole, but also to the object and purpose of articles of the treaty.[41]

(Footnote 37 continued)

Report of the Appellate Body, *United States – Standards for Reformulated and Conventional Gasoline*, WT/DS2/AB/R, 17; Report of the Appellate Body, *Japan – Taxes on Alcoholic Beverages*, WT/DS8/AB/R, WT/DS10/AB/R, WT/DS11/AB/R, 10.

[38] *Case of the S.S. "Wimbledon"*, Judgment No. 1 of 17 August 1923, Series A.—No. 1, 22; ICJ, *Case Concerning Kasikili/Sedudu Island*, Judgment of 13 December 1999, ICJ Reports 1999, 1045, para 20.

Report of the Appellate Body, *United States – Standards for Reformulated and Conventional Gasoline*, WT/DS2/AB/R, 17–18; Report of the Appellate Body, *Japan – Taxes on Alcoholic Beverages*, WT/DS8/AB/R, WT/DS10/AB/R, WT/DS11/AB/R, 11.

Vattel 1916, Book II, para 271; Yasseen 1976, pp. 25–26; Gardiner 2008, pp. 161–177.

[39] *Dispute Regarding Navigational and Related Rights*, Judgment of 13 July 2009, ICJ Reports 2009, 213, paras 51–56.

Case Concerning the Air Service Agreement of 27 March 1946 between the United States of America and France, Arbitral Award of 9 December 1978, XVIII Reports of International Arbitral Awards, 417–493, para 48.

Report of the Appellate Body, *United States – Standards for Reformulated and Conventional Gasoline*, WT/DS2/AB/R, 18; Report of the Appellate Body, *Japan – Taxes on Alcoholic Beverages*, WT/DS8/AB/R, WT/DS10/AB/R, WT/DS11/AB/R, 11–12.

Vattel 1916, Book II, para 285; Yasseen 1976, pp. 33–36; Gardiner 2008, pp. 177–189.

[40] *Case Concerning Kasikili/Sedudu Island*, Judgment of 13 December 1999, ICJ Reports 1999, 1045, paras 43–45; *Dispute Regarding Navigational and Related Rights*, Judgment of 13 July 2009, ICJ Reports 2009, 213, paras 68–69 (permanent settlement).

Report of the Appellate Body, *United States – Standards for Reformulated and Conventional Gasoline*, WT/DS2/AB/R, 18; Report of the Appellate Body, *Japan – Taxes on Alcoholic Beverages*, WT/DS8/AB/R, WT/DS10/AB/R, WT/DS11/AB/R, 12.

Vattel 1916, Book II, para 287; Yasseen 1976, pp. 55–59; Gardiner 2008, pp. 189–201.

[41] Report of the Appellate Body, *European Communities – Customs Classification of Frozen Boneless Chicken Cuts*, WT/DS269/AB/R, WT/DS286/AB/R, para 238.

Reference may further be made to the principle of effectiveness.[42] According to this principle, all articles and paragraphs of articles must be deemed to have some meaning and effect. When interpreting a treaty, it cannot be assumed that an article or paragraph of an article is redundant. This implies at the same time that giving an 'effet utile' to the text may not go beyond the text. Yet, the principle of effectiveness is sometimes understood and used with a view to giving effect to the perceived object and purpose of a treaty so as to go beyond its text.[43]

Finally, the text of a treaty as a whole, expressing its object and purpose and to which effect must be given, is understood as reflecting the common intentions of the States-parties.[44] Consequently, in the interpretation of the text of a treaty, the intention of one State-party cannot be decisive. Synoptically, then, interpretation may be said to involve a teleological and structural understanding of the text of a treaty, considered as a joint work of the States-parties.

When situated within the framework of obligation, these rules of interpretation do not seem, in fact, directed at identifying clear and precise limitations of the freedom to act of the States-parties. Within this context, the text of a treaty is deemed to bind the States-parties. Thus, rules contained in the text of a treaty, ascertained on the basis of the ordinary meaning of the terms, considered in their context and in the light of the object and purpose of the treaty, regarded as effective and as reflecting the common intentions of the Parties, should be capable of restricting the freedom to act of the States-parties. In order to be operative within the framework of obligation, an interpretation reflecting the intention of a State-party, viewed as a subject of conventional international law, cannot be

---

[42] *Corfu Channel Case (Merits)*, Judgment of 9 April 1949, ICJ Reports 1949, 4, 24; *Case Concerning Application of the International Convention on the Elimination of All Forms of Racial Discrimination (Preliminary Objections)*, Judgment of 1 April 2011, not yet reported, para 133.

Report of the Appellate Body, *United States – Standards for Reformulated and Conventional Gasoline*, WT/DS2/AB/R, 23; Report of the Appellate Body, *Japan – Taxes on Alcoholic Beverages*, WT/DS8/AB/R, WT/DS10/AB/R, WT/DS11/AB/R, 12.

Vattel 1916, Book II, para 283; Yasseen 1976, pp. 71–75; Gardiner 2008, pp. 159–161.

[43] *Case Concerning Application of the International Convention on the Elimination of All Forms of Racial Discrimination (Preliminary Objections)*, Judgment of 1 April 2011, Dissenting Opinion of Judge Cançado Trindade, not yet reported, paras 64–87.

Gardiner 2008, pp. 200–201.

[44] *Dispute Regarding Navigational and Related Rights*, Judgment of 13 July 2009, ICJ Reports 2009, 213, para 48: 'A treaty provision which has the purpose of limiting the sovereign powers of a State must be interpreted like any other provision of a treaty, i.e. in accordance with the intention of its authors as reflected by the text of the treaty and the other relevant factors in terms of interpretation.'; paras 63–66.

Report of the Appellate Body, *European Communities – Customs Classification of Certain Computer Equipment*, WT/DS62/AB/R, WT/DS67/AB/R, WT/DS68/AB/R, para 84: 'The purpose of treaty interpretation under Article 31 of the *Vienna Convention* is to ascertain the *common* intentions of the parties. These *common* intentions cannot be ascertained on the basis of the subjective and unilaterally determined "expectations" of *one* of the parties to a treaty.'

Vattel 1916, Book II, para 270; Yasseen 1976, pp. 16, 25–26, 57–59.

determinative.[45] However, attributing importance to the position of the same State-party as a co-legislator of conventional international law requires taking that intention into account at least to the extent that it cannot be contravened. Although the perspective of the State-party as subject of conventional international law requires the imposability of the obligation emanating from rules of conventional international law, adherence to the perspective of the State-party as co-legislator of the rules of conventional international law requires the unimposability of the obligation. In other words, even though the intention of one of the States-parties cannot be determinative, it does not follow that the text of the treaty, viewed as representing the common intentions of the States-parties, can therefore contain rules of conventional international law containing obligations imposable vis-à-vis the States-parties. Up to this point, this analysis accords with the analysis put forward by critical theory of public international law.[46]

It is submitted, however, that the perspective of the function of public international law affords the possibility of overcoming this dilemma by rejecting both the framework of obligation and the framework of authorization and transcending to the reformulated framework. It is submitted first that the difficulty of locating the rule *pacta sunt servanda* within the law of treaties or within the concept of public international law as a whole, the incoherence of assuming a freedom to act of States in the absence of a rule of conventional international law restricting that freedom and the incoherence of inferring a restriction of the freedom of States to act from a rule of conventional international law constituting an exercise of the freedom to act of that State, all militate against regarding the framework of obligation as the exclusive point of reference.

It is submitted, secondly, that the framework of authorization seems unsuitable to explain the concept of conventional international law. If the concept of treaty is situated within the context of the framework of authorization, there is no basis to explain the formation of rules of conventional international law. Since, according to the framework of authorization, in the absence of rules of conventional international law, States do not have a power to act, it is impossible to explain the existence of rules of conventional international law by reference to the common will of the States-parties. This means that the existence of rules of conventional international law must be presupposed. If it is attempted to explain the existence of rules of conventional international law by reference to acts of States, this requires a further rule of conventional international law by virtue of which States can act. Thus, ultimately, like the rule *pacta sunt servanda* within the framework of obligation, the framework of authorization relies on an unexplained assumption. If, notwithstanding this constellation, the function of rules of conventional international law would continue to consist of limiting the freedom of States to act, this would be inconsistent with the mutual exclusivity of the framework of authorization and the framework of obligation. Moreover, the framework of authorization

[45] Ost and Van de Kerchove 2002, pp. 391–411.

[46] Koskenniemi 2005, pp. 333–345.

situates the members of international society as non-political entities, uninvolved in the constituting of international society, and does not explain the rationale of its own authority.

It would thus seem that the function of rules of conventional international law must be regarded as consisting neither of restricting the freedom of the States-parties to act nor of authorizing the States-parties to act. It is therefore submitted, thirdly, that the function of rules of conventional international law should be seen as situated within the reformulated framework, which combines elements of both frameworks. Situated within this reformulated framework, rules of conventional international law should be seen as containing both an enabling element and a restrictive element. These elements correspond to the way in which the members of international society are situated in respect of each other within this reformulated framework, as having a power to act which, however, is not an unlimited freedom to act. On the basis of this initial situation, members of international society constitute international society by means of rules of conventional international law. These rules of conventional international law contain an enabling aspect in so far as they constitute international society. At the same time, they contain a restrictive aspect in so far as the members of international society do not have a freedom to ignore international society as thus constituted. This does not mean that international society cannot be reformed, but that in order to reform international society, the members of international society must engage in a process of practical reasoning about the reconstituting of international society. Conventional international law may be seen as embodying, in text, these constitutional acts, which at the same time contains the seeds for the reconstituting of international society. This reformulated framework would accord, it is submitted, much better with the general rule of interpretation, synoptically described in terms of the teleological and structural understanding of the text of a treaty, considered as the common work of the States-parties, which does not seem designed to identify clear, precise rules. Situated within the reformulated framework, this general rule seems suitable for containing the common good of the States-parties, understood as a purposive, coherent whole, which has a degree of rigidity, but which also has the requisite flexibility for the reconstituting of international society.

Such a reformulation of the function of conventional international law would, furthermore, accord with the common view that the text of a treaty contains both rights and obligations of States.[47] If, however, this conception is situated within the framework of obligation or the framework of authorization, this results in inconsistencies. Within the framework of obligation, rules of conventional

[47] See, for example, Article 3.2 of the DSU: ‘The dispute settlement system of the WTO is a central element in providing security and predictability to the multilateral trading system. The Members recognize that it serves to preserve the rights and obligations of Members under the covered agreements, and to clarify the existing provisions of those agreements in accordance with the customary rules of interpretation of public international law. Recommendations and rulings of the DSB cannot add to or diminish the rights and obligations in the covered agreements.’

international law are regarded as exclusively containing obligations restricting the freedom to act of the States-parties. The States-parties are deemed to have rights in so far as these are not limited by the text of the treaty. Within the framework of authorization, rules of conventional international law are regarded as exclusively containing rights conferring on the States-parties a power to act. The States-parties are deemed not to have a power to act in the absence of an authorization contained in the text of the treaty. Acceptance of the common view that the text of a treaty contains both rights and obligations accordingly requires rejection of the mutual exclusivity of the framework of obligation and the framework of authorization.

Mention may be made in this connection of the way in which the Appellate Body of the Dispute Settlement Body of the WTO dealt with the so-called trade/ environment nexus in *United States – Import Prohibition of Certain Shrimp and Shrimp Products*. This controversial case was brought by India, Pakistan Malaysia, and Thailand against the United States for having imposed an import ban on shrimp and shrimp products, originating in these countries, unless these were caught in a, so to speak, sea turtle-friendly way. When examining this import ban, the Appellate Body interpreted the so-called chapeau of Article XX of GATT 1994 as reflecting the need to maintain a balance of rights and obligations between the right of a Member to invoke one or another of the exceptions specified in paras (a)–(j) of Article XX (which includes under (b) the life and health of animals and under (g) the conservation of exhaustible natural resources) and the substantive rights of the other Members under the GATT 1994. The Appellate Body subsequently reformulated the same point by stating that a balance must be struck between the *right* of a Member to invoke an exception under Article XX and the *duty* of that same Member to respect the treaty rights of other Members.[48]

[48] Report of the Appellate Body, *United States – Import Prohibition of Certain Shrimp and Shrimp Products*, WT/DS58/AB/R, para 156: 'Turning to the chapeau of Article XX, we consider that it embodies the recognition on the part of the WTO Members of the need to maintain a balance of rights and obligations between the right of a Member to invoke one or another of the exceptions of Article XX, specified in paras (a) to (j), on the one hand, and the substantive rights of the other Members under the GATT 1994, on the other hand. Exercise by one Member of its right to invoke an exception, such as Article XX(g), if abused or misused, will, to that extent, erode or render naught the substantive treaty rights in, for example, Article XI:1, of other Members. Similarly, because the GATT 1994 itself makes available the exceptions of Article XX, in recognition of the legitimate nature of the policies and interests there embodied, the right to invoke one of those exceptions is not to be rendered illusory. The same concept may be expressed from a slightly different angle of vision, thus, a balance must be struck between the *right* of a Member to invoke an exception under Article XX and the *duty* of that same Member to respect the treaty rights of other Members. To permit one Member to abuse or misuse its right to invoke an exception would be effectively to allow that Member to degrade its own treaty obligations as well as to devalue the treaty rights of other Members. If the abuse or misuse is sufficiently grave or extensive, the Member, in effect, reduces its treaty obligation to a merely facultative one and dissolves its juridical character, and, in doing so, negates altogether the treaty rights of other Members. The chapeau was installed at the head of the list of "General Exceptions" in Article XX to prevent such far-reaching consequences.'

While thus reasoning in terms of both rights and obligations, consistently with Article 3.2 of the DSU, it may be observed that the Appellate Body derived the substantive rights of other WTO Members from provisions such as Article XI:1 (which contains the prohibition against quantitative restrictions), which formulates an obligation. The initial reasoning about balancing rights is, in fact, subsequently transformed by the Appellate Body into, the need to balance rights of Members to adopt measures in pursuance of the policies indicated in paras (a) to (j), and the obligation contained in the chapeau of Article XX. As the Appellate Body observed, both the obligation and the right must have their proper sphere of operation and neither may infringe upon the other.[49] In so far, however, as the Appellate Body was inferring these rights from the sovereignty and independence of the WTO Members, it was reasoning within the framework of obligation. To that same extent, it must have diverged from the conjunction of rights and obligations envisaged in Article 3.2 of the DSU.

To illustrate how the transition from the framework of obligation to the reformulated framework affects the concept of conventional international law, reference may be made to *Diversion of Water from the Meuse*. In this case, which was brought by The Netherlands against Belgium pursuant to the Optional Clause, The Netherlands alleged that Belgium had violated the Treaty concluded between The Netherlands and Belgium on 12 May 1863 and which concerned the regime governing diversions of water from the Meuse for the feeding of navigation canals and irrigation channels. This treaty dealt, on the one hand, with the navigability of the Meuse, and, on the other hand, with the use of the water of the Meuse for the feeding of the Zuid-Willemsvaart, which runs from Maastricht to Den Bosch, which are both in The Netherlands, but between them passes through Belgium. The Zuid-Willemsvaart had been extended from Maastricht to Liege. In Belgium, a branch, with further branches, had been added to the Zuid-Willemsvaart, so as to establish, through the Campine area, a connection with Antwerpen. In view of the difficulties to which the diversion of water from the Meuse for the feeding of this system of canals and channels had given rise, the Treaty of 12 May 1863 sought to establish a definitive and stable regime for this purpose.

To this effect, Article I of the Treaty of 12 May 1863 determined that there should henceforth be a single feeder for all canals situated below Maastricht, i.e., for the system of canals and channels previously described. Article IV of the Treaty of 12 May 1863 determined that when the level of the river was above normal level, an amount of 10 m^3/s was to pass through the feeder and that when

[49] Report of the Appellate Body, *United States – Import Prohibition of Certain Shrimp and Shrimp Products*, WT/DS58/AB/R, para 159: 'The task of interpreting and applying the chapeau is, hence, essentially the delicate one of locating and marking out a line of equilibrium between the right of a Member to invoke an exception under Article XX and the rights of the other Members under varying substantive provisions (e.g., Article XI) of the GATT 1994, so that neither of the competing rights will cancel out the other and thereby distort and nullify or impair the balance of rights and obligations constructed by the Members themselves in that Agreement. The location of the line of equilibrium, as expressed in the chapeau, is not fixed and unchanging; the line moves as the kind and the shape of the measures at stake vary and as the facts making up specific cases differ.'

the level of the river was at or below normal level an amount of 7.5 m^3/s from October to June and an amount of 6 m^3/s from June to October were to pass through the feeder. Out of this quantity, The Netherlands would have a share of 2 or 1.5 m^3/s, which was to re-enter The Netherlands at Loozen. This share could be increased up to the point that the speed of the current in the Zuid-Willemsvaart would not exceed the maximum stipulated in Article III of the Treaty of 12 May 1863. The point of these technical provisions was to maintain a balance between the uses of the Meuse and the uses of the Zuid-Willemsvaart.

The Netherlands essentially alleged that the construction of the Albert Canal, which runs from Liege to Antwerpen more or less in a straight line and is therefore located more southernly than the system of canals and channels which runs through the Campine, contravened the provisions of the Treaty of 12 May 1863. Specifically, The Netherlands alleged that a lock, the so-called Neerhaeren lock, in a junction canal between Briegden and Neerharen, which connected Liege through Briegden to the Zuid-Willemsvaart by a route alternative to the direct canal between Liege and Maastricht, allowed water from the Meuse to pass into the Zuid-Willemsvaart through another mechanism than the feeder located at Maastricht. The Netherlands also alleged that by connecting the Albert Canal to the system of canals and channels located in the Campine, Belgium allowed these canals and systems, located below Maastricht, to be fed by another mechanism, the Monsin barrage located at Liege, instead of the feeder located at Maastricht.

Belgium countered these allegations by submitting a counter-claim alleging that The Netherlands had itself violated the Treaty of 12 May 1863, first, by building the Borgharen barrage, second, by building the so-called Bosscheveld lock, which established a navigational connection between the Meuse and the Zuid-Willemsvaart, and third, by building the Juliana Canal, which established a connection between Maastricht and Maasbracht and constituted, within The Netherlands, a navigational alternative to the Meuse. The first and the third points formed the object of submissions. Belgium made the second point so as to argue that The Netherlands had forfeited its right to complain about the Neerhaeren lock, because, in so far as it infringed the Treaty of 12 May 1863, The Netherlands had committed a similar infringement.

These allegations and counter-allegations seemed by no means implausible. In its reasoning, the PCIJ remarked that the Treaty of 12 May 1863 should be interpreted in a systematic fashion.[50] That might have been taken as an indication that the Court would examine not only whether the acts of Belgium and The Netherlands were consistent with the provisions of the Treaty of 12 May 1863, taken individually, but also whether those acts were consistent with the Treaty of 12 May 1863 taken as a whole. However, in the end the PCIJ found that the Treaty of 12 May 1863 had not been violated, either by Belgium or by The Netherlands. The Court dealt rather swiftly with the contentions of The Netherlands that two

---

50 *Diversion of Water from the Meuse*, Judgment of 28 June 1937, Series A./B.—No. 70, 4, 21: 'The Treaty brought into existence a certain regime which results from all of its provisions in conjunction. It forms a complete whole, the different provisions of which cannot be dissociated from the other and considered apart by themselves.'

sections of the Albert Canal which had been connected to the system of canals and channels located in the Campine were in violation of the Treaty of 12 May 1863, stating, *inter alia*, that these sections were entirely situated in the territory of Belgium and that the Treaty of 12 May 1863 had not been intended to restrict Belgium in this respect.[51] As for the mirroring contention of Belgium relating to the Juliana Canal, the Court found that the Treaty of 12 May 1863 only applied to canals situated on the left bank of the Meuse, so that the Juliana Canal, which had been constructed on the right bank of the Meuse, fell outside its scope.[52] With respect to the Borgharen barrage, the effect of which was that the level of the river was raised so that the feeder would always transmit an amount of 10 m^3/s, the Court found that, notwithstanding the existence of Article IX, which provided for the joint improvement of navigability on the river, Belgium could not complain about the deterioration of the navigability of the river because it had already been poor. Moreover, an alternative route had meanwhile been constructed in the form of the Juliana Canal.[53] As Vice-President Hurst and Judge Anzilotti pointed out, however, it could very well have been held that the Borgharen barrage was inconsistent with the Treaty of 12 May 1863.[54]

The main point, however, relates to the Court's treatment of the Neerhaeren lock and the Bosscheveld lock. In the course of its reasoning, the PCIJ stated that it would have been prepared to consider the Neerhaeren lock as contrary to the Treaty of 12 May 1863, if it had contravened its object, i.e., if it had led to a deficiency of water in the Meuse or an excessive current in the Zuid-Willemsvaart. The Court continued, however, by comparing the Neerhaeren lock to the Bosscheveld lock, considering that if both locks were inconsistent with the treaty, The Netherlands could not complain about the Neerhaeren lock, having forfeited, so to speak, its right to do so by committing itself a violation of the Treaty of 12 May 1863.[55] This part of the judgment was also supported by the reasoning of Judges Anzilotti and Hudson.[56]

---

[51] *Diversion of Water from the Meuse*, Judgment of 28 June 1937, Series A./B.—No. 70, 4, 25–27.

[52] *Diversion of Water from the Meuse*, Judgment of 28 June 1937, Series A./B.—No. 70, 4, 31–32.

[53] *Diversion of Water from the Meuse*, Judgment of 28 June 1937, Series A./B.—No. 70, 4, 29–30.

[54] *Diversion of Water from the Meuse*, Judgment of 28 June 1937, Dissenting Opinion Vice-President Hurst, Series A./B. – No. 70, 4, 34–35; Dissenting Opinion Judge Anzilotti, para 4.

[55] *Diversion of Water from the Meuse*, Judgment of 28 June 1937, Series A./B.—No. 70, 4, 20–25: 'The Court cannot refrain from comparing the case of the Belgian lock with that of The Netherlands lock at Bosscheveld. Neither of these locks constitutes a feeder, yet both of them discharge their lock-water into the canal, and thus take part in feeding it with water otherwise than through the treaty feeder, though without producing an excessive current in the Zuid-Willemsvaart. In these circumstances, the Court finds it difficult to admit that The Netherlands are now warranted in complaining of the construction and operation of a lock of which they themselves set an example in the past.'

[56] *Diversion of Water from the Meuse*, Judgment of 28 June 1937, Dissenting Opinion Judge Anzilotti, Series A./B.—No. 70, 4, para 3; Separate Opinion Judge Hudson, 75–78.

From the perspective of the framework of obligation, the problem that arises here is that, on the hypothesis that a bilateral treaty has been violated by both parties, neither party can complain about the violation committed by the other party. In this manner, the regime in respect of which the Court insisted that it constituted a whole, is subjected by the parties to a process of erosion of its provisions, to the extent that acts of both parties that could very well have been considered to be inconsistent with the treaty, are deemed consistent with it. In this way, the common good, which consisted of the regime for the diversion of water from the Meuse, and which had been instituted by both parties, is minimized. Within the reformulated framework, the parties, if desirous to amend the regime as constituted so as to make room for the various works that were undertaken, would be required to examine and reconstitute this regime, taking into considerations the canals that would be wholly situated in either territory as well as the several navigational works. In this way, they would jointly have had to address the question of the relationship between the navigability of the Meuse and the interests on either side of it.

Diversion of Water from the Meuse may appropriately be contrasted with the *Case Concerning the Gabćikovo-Nagymaros Project*. Whereas the result of the former may be seen as minimizing the relevance of conventional international law, the latter maximizes, in an intermediate step, its significance. In the end, while the reasoning of the ICJ seeks to find a middle ground, it converges on the result of the *Diversion of Water from the Meuse*.

The *Case Concerning the Gabćikovo-Nagymaros Project* revolved around the construction and operation of a series of works on the Bratislava-Budapest section of the Danube. That series of works had been foreseen by the Treaty Concerning the Construction and Operation of the Gabćikovo-Nagymaros System of Locks, of 16 September 1977, concluded between Czechoslovakia and Hungary. Article 1, para 1, of the 1977 Treaty provided that these works were to be built partly at Gabćikovo and partly at Nagymaros, so as to constitute a single and indivisible operational system of locks.

The part to be built at Gabćikovo was to consist principally of a dam at Dunakiliti (in Hungarian territory), a reservoir upstream of that dam (in both Hungarian and Czechoslovak territory), and a bypass canal, containing the Gabćikovo system of locks and a hydroelectric power plant (in Czechoslovak territory). The part to be built at Nagymaros was to consist principally of the Nagymaros system of locks and a hydroelectric power plant. The project also foresaw the deepening of the bed of the Danube downstream of the junction of the bypass canal and the old bed of the Danube, as well as downstream of the Nagymaros system of locks. Upstream of the Nagymaros system of locks, flood-control works were to be reinforced. The connection between the two parts would have consisted primarily in the fact that the Nagymaros system of locks would have facilitated the operation of the Gabćikovo system of locks to operate in so-called peak-mode (dispersing the water at intervals), rather than according to the run of the river. In total, the project was expected to have beneficial effects in the fields of energy, navigation, and flood control.

In 1989, Hungary first suspended and then abandoned the works at Nagymaros, while, after suspending the works at Dunakiliti, deciding to maintain the status quo there, invoking environmental considerations. In 1991, Czechoslovakia proceeded to implementing the so-called 'Variant C', which consisted of replacing the dam that was to have been built at Dunakiliti by a dam at Čunovo (in Czechoslovak territory). Variant C was put into operation by Czechoslovakia in 1992, which was succeeded in 1993 by Slovakia.

On the basis of the special agreement pursuant to which the case was brought before it, the Court was essentially asked whether the suspension and abandonment of works at Nagymaros and Dunakiliti by Hungary, on the one hand, and the implementation and operation of Variant C by Czechoslovakia, taken over by Slovakia, were in conformity with the scheme foreseen by the 1977 Treaty. The Court found the suspension and abandonment of works at Nagymaros and Dunakiliti inconsistent with the 1977 Treaty and not justified by the state of ecological necessity invoked by Hungary.[57] As regards Variant C, the Court considered that Czechoslovakia was entitled to proceed, in 1991, to implementing it, but that it was not entitled to put it into operation in 1992.[58]

Like the PCIJ in *Diversion of Water from the Meuse*, the ICJ was confronted by inconsistent conduct of both parties to a bilateral treaty. But, instead of holding that in such a situation neither party could complain of the other's conduct, the ICJ took the view that both parties had acted unlawfully. In reply to the contention advanced by Hungary that both parties had repudiated the treaty, the Court firmly upheld the rule *pacta sunt servanda*.[59] When turning to the prescriptive part of the judgment, determining the rights and obligations of the parties—circumscribing their future conduct, the Court initially maintained this position of authority, insisting that the 1977 Treaty governs the relationship between the parties.[60]

But then, the Court started to descend from this high position, acknowledging that it could not disregard the fact that the 1977 Treaty had not been implemented by either party for years and that their acts of commission and omission had contributed to creating the resulting factual situation, which it could not overlook when deciding on the legal requirements for the future conduct of the parties. Still, this did not mean, the Court maintained, that facts determine the law, the principle *ex injuria jus non oritur* remaining intact. What was essential, according to the Court, was that this resulting factual situation was placed within the framework of

---

[57] *Case Concerning the Gabčikovo-Nagymaros Project*, Judgment of 25 September 1997, ICJ Reports 1997, 7, paras 27–59.

[58] *Case Concerning the Gabčikovo-Nagymaros Project*, Judgment of 25 September 1997, ICJ Reports 1997, 7, paras 60–88.

[59] *Case Concerning the Gabčikovo-Nagymaros Project*, Judgment of 25 September 1997, ICJ Reports 1997, 7, para 114.

[60] *Case Concerning the Gabčikovo-Nagymaros Project*, Judgment of 25 September 1997, ICJ Reports 1997, 7, para 132.

the 1977 Treaty, so as to achieve its object and purpose and remedy the existing irregular state of affairs.[61]

What this meant was that Variant C could be maintained and, in so far as it was operated in run-of-the-river mode, the Nagymaros part of the project could be discarded. Against this background, the rule *pacta sunt servanda* required, in the opinion of the Court that the parties find an agreed solution within the framework of the 1977 Treaty, so as to realize, in the light of the principle of good faith, its purpose.[62] Within this framework, the Court directed the parties to restore the joint character of the regime envisaged by the 1977 Treaty.[63] This entailed re-establishing the works at Čunovo as a jointly operated unit.[64] More generally, the Court directed that Variant C should be regularized, by including Hungary in the use, operation, and benefits of the regime.[65] Finally, re-establishment of the joint regime would reflect the concept of the common utilization of shared water resources, in line with Article 5, para 2, of the Convention on the Law of the Non-Navigational Uses of International Watercourses, which prescribes:

> Watercourse States shall participate in the use, development and protection of an international watercourse in an equitable and reasonable manner. Such participation includes both the right to utilize the watercourse and the duty to cooperate in the protection and development thereof (...).[66]

Although Variant C may have resembled the original conception of the Gabćikovo part of the project, as the Court pointed out, it was also radically different, because it transformed the joint character of the project into unilateral action. Czechoslovakia could thereby divert water from the old bed of the Danube, which downstream constitutes an international boundary, into the bypass canal. Because the construction and operation of Variant C shared this unilateral character, several Judges had taken the view that both proceeding to and putting into operation Variant C was inconsistent with the 1977 Treaty.[67]

---

[61] *Case Concerning the Gabćikovo-Nagymaros Project*, Judgment of 25 September 1997, ICJ Reports 1997, 7, para 133.

[62] *Case Concerning the Gabćikovo-Nagymaros Project*, Judgment of 25 September 1997, ICJ Reports 1997, 7, para 142.

[63] *Case Concerning the Gabćikovo-Nagymaros Project*, Judgment of 25 September 1997, ICJ Reports 1997, 7, para 144.

[64] *Case Concerning the Gabćikovo-Nagymaros Project*, Judgment of 25 September 1997, ICJ Reports 1997, 7, para 145.

[65] *Case Concerning the Gabćikovo-Nagymaros Project*, Judgment of 25 September 1997, ICJ Reports 1997, 7, para 146.

[66] *Case Concerning the Gabćikovo-Nagymaros Project*, Judgment of 25 September 1997, ICJ Reports 1997, 7, para 147.

[67] *Case Concerning the Gabćikovo-Nagymaros Project*, Judgment of 25 September 1997, Declaration President Schwebel, ICJ Reports 1997, 7; Separate Opinion Judge Bedjaoui, paras 28–52; Dissenting Opinion Judge Ranjeva, *passim*; Dissenting Opinion Judge Herczegh, 190–196; Dissenting Opinion Judge Fleischhauer, para 1.

The directions given by the Court were therefore aimed at associating Hungary with the point of control established at Čunovo, so that the parties could jointly determine the proportions of water that were to flow into the bypass canal and along the old bed of the Danube. These proportions should both ensure development (energy and navigation) and its sustainability (the protection of the Szigetköz area lying to the south of the old bed).[68]

Within the framework of obligation, however, both the agreement between the parties into which these directions were to be transformed, and the unilateral character of Variant C converge in the freedom to act of Slovakia. That is, the solution of transforming the unilateral character of Variant C into a joint regime is dependent on a unilateral act on the part of Slovakia. With the replacement of the original project by Variant C, the reciprocity that characterized the original project had also disappeared, so that the balance had tilted in favor of Slovakia.

It must not be forgotten, however, that Slovakia had been brought into this position by unilateral acts on the part of Hungary, both at Nagymaros and Dunakiliti, which, precisely, embodied that reciprocity. While Nagymaros was merely relevant for peak mode operation, Dunakiliti was indispensible for operating the Gabćikovo part of the project. It could, in fact, be said that, while building the dam at Čunovo took away the joint character of the project, not building the dam at Dunakiliti inhibited the operational character of the project. In view of this situation, many other judges saw both preceding to and putting Variant C into operation as not inconsistent with the 1977 Treaty, on the basis of reciprocal reasoning along the lines of the *Diversion of Water from the Meuse,*[69] or, similarly, in terms of lawful countermeasures.[70]

The equitable nature of this result may, however, not only be evaluated from the perspective of the acts of Hungary which brought it about, but also from the perspective of the situation into which it resulted. Along the lines of *Diversion of Water from the Meuse*, it would approve the trajectory from the original joint project to the unilateral *de facto* situation brought about by the upstream State. The resulting situation is stated clearly in the Dissenting Opinion of Judge ad hoc Skubiszewski, which relies on the right of the upstream State to carry out works in its own territory, provided that the downstream State receives an equitable share of the water resources. Along the lines of the *Lac Lanoux Arbitration*, that right is not

---

[68] *Case Concerning the Gabćikovo-Nagymaros Project*, Judgment of 25 September 1997, Separate Opinion Vice-President Weeramantry, ICJ Reports 1997, 7, Section A.

[69] *Case Concerning the Gabćikovo-Nagymaros Project*, Judgment of 25 September 1997, Separate Opinion Judge Koroma, ICJ Reports 1997, 7, 145–152; Dissenting Opinion Judge Oda, paras 21–24; Dissenting Opinion Judge Parra-Aranguren, paras 2–15; Dissenting Opinion Judge ad hoc Skubiszewski, Sections I and III.

[70] *Case Concerning the Gabćikovo-Nagymaros Project*, Judgment of 25 September 1997, Dissenting Opinion Judge Vereshchetin, ICJ Reports 1997, 7, 219–226; Dissenting Opinion Judge Parra-Araguren, paras 16–19.

dependent on the consent of the downstream State, which would effectively place the upstream State within the framework of authorization.[71]

Whether or not, therefore, Variant C is seen as inconsistent with the 1977 Treaty, both approaches show the problematic nature of seeing the situation of the upstream State in terms of a freedom to act. Even if the 1977 Treaty is seen as having been repudiated by both parties, the resulting situation between the parties remains the same.[72] Nevertheless, the approach followed by the Court seems preferable because it retains the 1977 Treaty as a framework, formulating the purposes to be achieved by the parties. Transposing the 1977 Treaty to the reformulated framework, would increase its significance as a structure guiding the parties, because it would take away the freedom to act of the upstream State and situate both parties in a dilemma situation of how best to deal with the international situation formed by their shared water resource. On the basis of practical reasoning, they would be required to jointly adopt a balanced approach, bringing together in a coherent manner the interests of navigation, energy production, and environmental protection. In this respect, the question on the territory of which State a work is located is of diminishing importance in so far as it affects the (re-)constituting of international society in the form of the shared water resource. The specific question of what proportion to divert into the bypass canal and what proportion flows through the old bed of the Danube admits of a plurality of answers. But, relating to a shared resource, practical reasoning would start, within the context of the parameters addressed, with a 50/50 division, requiring increasing justification for diverting from that middle ground. To the extent that the interests of other members of international society are involved,[73] this question becomes more complex.

9.5 The Concept of Conventional International Law and Third States

The incoherence which results if the concept of conventional international law is exclusively situated within the framework of obligation or the framework of authorization, may also be described with respect to the issue of treaties and third States.

Because a treaty relationship is deemed to be based on the consent of the States-parties, the position of third States is, in principle, considered thus that there exists no relationship between the States-parties and third States by virtue of the treaty.

---

[71] *Case Concerning the Gabčikovo-Nagymaros Project*, Judgment of 25 September 1997, Dissenting Opinion Judge ad hoc Skubiszewski, ICJ Reports 1997, 7, Section II.

[72] *Case Concerning the Gabčikovo-Nagymaros Project*, Judgment of 25 September 1997, Declaration Judge Rezek, ICJ Reports 1997, 7.

[73] *Case Concerning the Gabčikovo-Nagymaros Project*, Judgment of 25 September 1997, Separate Opinion Vice-President Weeramantry, ICJ Reports 1997, 7, Section C.

This is, in principle, entirely consistent with the notion of consent, because third States have, by definition, not consented to the rules contained in the text of the treaty. Thus, it is commonly considered that a treaty does not create either rights or obligations for third States. This principle, usually expressed in the maxim *pacta tertiis nec nocent nec prosunt*, was applied by the PCIJ in the *Case Concerning Certain German Interests in Polish Upper Silesia (Merits)*[74] and is widely recognized in doctrine.[75]

In concordance with this principle, Article 18 (a) of the Draft Convention on the Law of Treaties stipulated that a treaty may not impose obligations upon a State which is not a party thereto. Article 18 (b) provided that if a treaty contains a stipulation which is expressly for the benefit of a State which is not a party or a signatory to the treaty, such State is entitled to claim the benefit of that stipulation so long as the stipulation remains in force between the parties to the treaty.[76]

The provisions contained in Part III, Sect. 4, of the Vienna Convention on the Law of Treaties reflect similar considerations. Article 34 states the main rule, providing that a treaty does not create either rights or obligations for a third State without its consent. Subsequently, a distinction between obligations and rights is made. As regards obligations for third States, Article 35 provides that an obligation arises for a third State from a provision of a treaty if the parties to the treaty intend the provision to be the means of establishing the obligation and the third State expressly accepts that obligation in writing. As regards rights of third States, Article 36, para 1, first sentence, provides that a rights arises for a third State from a provision of a treaty if the parties to the treaty intend the provision to accord that right either to the third State, or to a group of States to which it belongs, or to all States, and the third State assents thereto. The second sentence adds that its assent shall be presumed so long as the contrary is not indicated, unless the treaty otherwise provides. Article 36, para 2, stipulates that a State exercising a right in accordance with para 1 shall comply with the conditions for its exercise provided for in the treaty or established in conformity with the treaty.[77]

The centrality of the concept of consent in those provisions of the Vienna Convention on the Law of Treaties blurs, to the extent of the obligation or of the right, the distinction between the States-parties and third parties.[78] In the case of an obligation arising for a third State from a provision of a treaty, the parties to the treaty must have intended the provision to be the means of establishing the obligation and the third State must expressly have accepted the obligation in writing. Thus, the consent of the States-parties and of the third State are required and must

---

[74] *Case Concerning Certain German Interests in Polish Upper Silesia (Merits)*, Judgment No. 7 of 25 May 1926, Series A.—No. 7, 29: 'A treaty only creates law as between the States which are parties to it (...)'.

[75] Roxburgh 1917, para 23; McNair 1961, Chap. XVI, pp. 309–321; Chinkin 1993, pp. 25–26; Reuter 1995, paras 153, 194.

[76] Harvard Research in International Law 1935, Article 18, p. 661.

[77] Chinkin 1993, pp. 32–34.

[78] Chinkin 1993, pp. 32–34, 39–44.

be reflected in the text of the provision and of the acceptance. In the case of a right arising for a third State from a provision of a treaty, the parties to the treaty must have intended the provision to accord that right and the third State must have assented to the accordance of the right. Thus, the consent of the States-parties is required and must be reflected in the text of the provision. The required assent of the third State is presumed and inferred from the actual exercise of the right.[79]

However, the centrality of the concept of consent in the formation of rights and obligations for third parties also conceals to some extent the problems that arise in the relation between the States-parties and third States within the framework of obligation. For the States-parties, the assumption of a freedom of States to act translates into a freedom of contract, implying a freedom of the States-parties to determine whether or not to provide in the text of the treaty for obligations or rights of third States. On the basis of the framework of obligation, those third States must be regarded as having a freedom to act. If a treaty does not expressly provide for rights for third States, it might nevertheless be regarded by them as infringing their freedom to act, because it should have provided for such rights. Similarly, if a treaty does not expressly provide for obligations of third States, it might nevertheless be regarded by them as infringing their freedom to act, because it implicitly imposes obligations on them. While pursuant to their freedom to act, third States could simply ignore the existence of a treaty, such disregard might be considered by the States-parties as infringing their freedom of contract.

Roxburgh argued that third States have a general duty not to interfere with a treaty if it does not contravene international law or their rights. According to Roxburgh, a treaty would infringe the rights of a third State if: (a) it contravenes a universally accepted rule of international law; (b) it is inconsistent with its safety; or (c) it violates rights previously acquired by that third State, on the basis of general rules of international law or on the basis of a convention.[80] Similarly, McNair considered that a third State must demonstrate the infringement of a rule of customary international law or conventional international law.[81] Within the framework of obligation, it would indeed be necessary to identify a rule of public international law restricting the freedom of contract of the States-parties. However, this would seem inconsistent with the freedom to act of the third State and render that freedom to act dependent on the identification of a rule of public international law, situating those third States in fact within the framework of authorization.

Thus, it would seem that with regard to the relation between the States-parties and third States, neither the text of a treaty, in so far as it determines rights or obligations for third States, nor the position adopted by third States with respect to that text can be conclusive. Furthermore, the idea that the text of a treaty provides only for an obligation or only for a right of a third State, seems insufficient to account for the complex relation between the States-parties and third States.

---

79 Harvard Research in International Law 1935, Comment to Article 18 (b), p. 936.

80 Roxburgh 1917, para 24.

81 McNair 1961, Chap. XII, pp. 213–224; Chap. XVI, p. 321.

Such problems may be identified, for example, in the *Report of the International Committee of Jurists Entrusted by the Council of the League of Nations with the Task of Giving an Advisory Opinion upon the Legal Aspects of the Åland Islands Question* of 5 September 1920. That Committee was asked to express its opinion on two points, the second of which concerned 'the present position with regard to international obligations concerning the demilitarization of the Åland Islands'. The Committee subdivided that question into two parts:

> (1) Firstly, it must be decided whether the Convention and Treaty of the 30th March, 1856, are still in force;
> (2) Secondly, the nature and legal consequences of these provisions, with reference to the present position, must be considered.[82]

The Convention to which the Committee referred was a Convention concluded between France, Great Britain, and Russia on 30 March 1856. The first Article thereof stated:

> His Majesty the Emperor of all the Russias, in compliance with the desire expressed to him by their Majesties the Queen of the United Kingdom of Great Britain and Ireland and the Emperor of the French, hereby declares that the Åland Islands shall not be fortified, and that no military or naval base shall be maintained or created there.

That Convention was attached to the General Treaty of Peace between Austria, France, Great Britain, Prussia, Russia, Sardinia, and the Ottoman Empire of 30 March 1856. Article 33 of that Treaty provided:

> The Convention, this day concluded between their Majesties the Emperor of the French and the Queen of the United Kingdom of Great Britain and Ireland on the one hand, and his Majesty the Emperor of all the Russias on the other, with reference to the Åland Islands, is and shall remain attached to the present Treaty and shall have the same force and effects as if it formed part of the said Treaty.[83]

After finding that the Treaty and the Convention were still in force,[84] the Committee turned to the nature and legal consequences of those provisions. After considering the possibility that they might be regarded as forming a servitude, to

---

[82] *Report of the International Committee of Jurists Entrusted by the Council of the League of Nations with the Task of Giving an Advisory Opinion upon the Legal Aspects of the Ålands Islands Question*, 5 September 1920, League of Nations Official Journal, Special Supplement No. 3, October 1920, 3, 14.

[83] *Report of the International Committee of Jurists Entrusted by the Council of the League of Nations with the Task of Giving an Advisory Opinion upon the Legal Aspects of the Ålands Islands Question*, 5 September 1920, League of Nations Official Journal, Special Supplement No. 3, October 1920, 15.

[84] *Report of the International Committee of Jurists Entrusted by the Council of the League of Nations with the Task of Giving an Advisory Opinion upon the Legal Aspects of the Ålands Islands Question*, 5 September 1920, League of Nations Official Journal, Special Supplement No. 3, October 1920, 15–16.

which it did not attach much significance,[85] the Committee examined the European character of the Convention. From that perspective, the Committee found that the Convention had created true objective law and constituted a settlement regulating European interests.[86] The Committee then proceeded to consider the positions of Russia, Finland, and Sweden.

As regards Russia, the Committee found that, as long as she retained possession of the Islands, she remained bound by the agreements of 1856, but that, since the Islands had passed into the possession of another State, she could henceforth, as an interested party, make use of the status created by those provisions.[87] As regards Finland, the Committee found that, both from the point of view of a servitude and from the point of view of a settlement, it was incumbent upon her to conform to the provisions of 1856.[88] Finally, the Committee considered the position of Sweden. The Committee first observed that, as a third State, Sweden could not derive a contractual right from the provisions of 1856. The Committee also considered it impossible to identify a right of Sweden by virtue of a *stipulation pour autrui*, because the agreements of 1856 did not mention such a possibility.[89] Nevertheless, according to the Committee, this did not mean that Sweden could not demand compliance with the obligations contained in those provisions; as a directly interested power, Sweden could insist on compliance with those provisions, because of

---

[85] *Report of the International Committee of Jurists Entrusted by the Council of the League of Nations with the Task of Giving an Advisory Opinion upon the Legal Aspects of the Ålands Islands Question*, 5 September 1920, League of Nations Official Journal, Special Supplement No. 3, October 1920, 16–17, 19.

[86] *Report of the International Committee of Jurists Entrusted by the Council of the League of Nations with the Task of Giving an Advisory Opinion upon the Legal Aspects of the Ålands Islands Question*, 5 September 1920, League of Nations Official Journal, Special Supplement No. 3, October 1920, 17–18.

[87] *Report of the International Committee of Jurists Entrusted by the Council of the League of Nations with the Task of Giving an Advisory Opinion upon the Legal Aspects of the Ålands Islands Question*, 5 September 1920, League of Nations Official Journal, Special Supplement No. 3, October 1920, 18.

[88] *Report of the International Committee of Jurists Entrusted by the Council of the League of Nations with the Task of Giving an Advisory Opinion upon the Legal Aspects of the Ålands Islands Question*, 5 September 1920, League of Nations Official Journal, Special Supplement No. 3, October 1920, 18.

[89] *Report of the International Committee of Jurists Entrusted by the Council of the League of Nations with the Task of Giving an Advisory Opinion upon the Legal Aspects of the Ålands Islands Question*, 5 September 1920, League of Nations Official Journal, Special Supplement No. 3, October 1920, 18: 'As concerns Sweden, no doubt she has no contractual rights under the provisions of 1856 as she was not a signatory Power. Neither can she make use of these provisions as a third party in whose favour the contracting parties had created a right under the Treaty, since – though it may, generally speaking, be possible to create a right in favour of a third party in an international convention – it is clear that this possibility is hardly admissible in the case in point, seeing that the Convention of 1856 does not mention Sweden, either as having any direct rights under its provisions, or even as being intended to profit indirectly by the provisions.'

the objective nature of the settlement of the question of the Åland Islands.[90] The Committee then made the further interesting point that if the Islands would pass into the possession of Sweden, the relationship between Finland and Sweden would be reversed; Sweden would 'still' be bound by the provisions of 1856 and Finland would acquire an interest in the demilitarization of the Islands. The Committee concluded that the provisions of 1856 had created a special international status relating to military considerations for the Islands. Any State in possession of the Islands would be bound by the corresponding obligations and every interested State had the right to insist upon compliance with them.[91]

From the perspective of the incoherence of the framework of obligation and the framework of authorization, a number of observations can be made with respect to the reasoning of the International Committee of Jurists. First, as regards the position of Finland, as the State possessing the Islands, the notions of status and settlement seem to obviate the need for any consent on the part of Finland. That would, in itself, be difficult to reconcile with the framework of obligation. But it may also be observed that, despite its insistence on those notions, the Committee also made reference to consensual notions. The Committee in effect linked the obligations imposed upon it by the settlement to its recognition as a State. That, however, seems inconsistent with the notions of status and settlement as truly objective law. Moreover, from that point of view, it seems to transform the issue into a matter of conditional recognition, leading into the tension between the constitutive and declarative views on recognition.

Secondly, as regards the position of Sweden, it may be observed that the States-parties to the agreements of 1856, if these were laid down in the general interest, thereby regulated a legal relation between a State-party and a third party, Sweden. The framework of obligation, however, only addresses the issue of the limitation of the freedoms of States to act by means of obligations. Thus, the agreements of 1856 may have restricted the freedom of Russia to act, but, pursuant to the framework of obligation, could not have conferred rights, not even to the actual States-parties, France and the United Kingdom. A fortiori, the reference to the notion of a settlement cannot confer a right on Sweden, or any third State. Furthermore, the Committee remarked that, in view of the objective nature of the settlement, Sweden could insist upon compliance with those provisions as long as the States-parties maintained them. This ultimate dependence of the existence of

---

90 *Report of the International Committee of Jurists Entrusted by the Council of the League of Nations with the Task of Giving an Advisory Opinion upon the Legal Aspects of the Ålands Islands Question*, 5 September 1920, League of Nations Official Journal, Special Supplement No. 3, October 1920, 18-19: 'Nevertheless by reason of the objective nature of the settlement of the Ålands Islands Question by the Treaty of 1856, Sweden may, as a Power directly interested, insist upon compliance with the provisions of this Treaty in so far as the contracting parties have not cancelled it.'

91 *Report of the International Committee of Jurists Entrusted by the Council of the League of Nations with the Task of Giving an Advisory Opinion upon the Legal Aspects of the Ålands Islands Question*, 5 September 1920, League of Nations Official Journal, Special Supplement No. 3, October 1920, 19.

the settlement or status upon the continuing will of the States-parties brings out the tension between the view that truly objective law had been created and the view that the basis of conventional international law resides in the consent of the States-parties. Even though the Committee interpreted the agreements of 1856 in the light of the general European interest, their ultimate existence remained dependent on the views of the two States-parties to which Russia had declared the demilitarization of the Islands. The general interest could therefore lapse into those private interests.

The *Case of the Free Zones of Upper Savoy and the District of Gex* offers another illustration of the incoherence of the concept of conventional international law when situated within the framework of obligation. With respect to the free zone of Gex, which had been formed by the withdrawal of the customs line of France from its political border with Switzerland, Article 435, second paragraph, of the Treaty of Versailles provided:

> The High Contracting Parties also agree that the stipulations of the Treaties of 1815 and of other supplementary Acts concerning the free zones of Upper Savoy and the Gex district are no longer consistent with the present conditions, and that it is for France and Switzerland to come to an agreement together with a view to settling between themselves the status of these territories under such conditions as shall be considered suitable by both countries.

On the basis of a special agreement, the PCIJ was asked by France and Switzerland to interpret this provision and to determine whether it had abrogated or was intended to lead to the abrogation of the Declaration of Paris of November 20th, 1815 and Article 1, para 3, of the Treaty of Paris of November 20th, 1815, by means of which the zone of Gex had been created.

The PCIJ found that these international instruments constituted an agreement to which Switzerland was a party[92] and from which it accordingly derived a contractual right.[93] The PCIJ further considered that a right of Switzerland to the maintenance of the zone could also have resulted from a *stipulation pour autrui* if it had been contained in the international instruments constituting the zone. According to the Court, this would have been dependent on the question of whether the States-parties

---

[92] *Case of the Free Zones of Upper Savoy and the District of Gex*, Judgment of 7 June 1932, Series A./B.—No. 46, 96, 147: 'It follows from all the foregoing that the creation of the Gex zone forms part of a territorial arrangement in favour of Switzerland, made as a result of an agreement between that country and the Powers, which agreement confers on this zone the character of a contract to which Switzerland is a Party.'

[93] *Case of the Free Zones of Upper Savoy and the District of Gex*, Judgment of 7 June 1932, Series A./B.—No. 46, 96, 148: 'All the instruments above mentioned and the circumstances in which they were drawn up establish, in the Court's opinion, that the intention of the Powers was, beside "rounding out" the territory of Geneva and ensuring direct communication between the Canton of Geneva and the rest of Switzerland, to create in favour of Switzerland a right, on which that country could rely, to the withdrawal of the French customs barrier behind the political frontier of the District of Gex, that is to say, of the Gex free zone.'

had intended to establish a right for a third State in the text of a treaty and whether that third State had accepted that right.[94]

In its Judgment, the PCIJ confirmed the position it had adopted in its Order of August 19th, 1929.[95] In the dissenting opinions appended to that Order, Judges Nyholm, Negulesco, and Dreyfus had interpreted the international instruments instituting the zone as not providing for a right of Switzerland to the maintenance of the zone.[96] Judge Nyholm considered that those international instruments only created legal relations between the States-parties and did not confer a right on Switzerland. Judge Nyholm held that, although the withdrawal of the customs line on French territory might affect Switzerland, a right of Switzerland to the maintenance of the zone could not be derived from the international instruments.[97] Similarly, Judge Negulesco examined whether Switzerland could derive a right to the maintenance of the zone from the international instruments as a party or from a *stipulation pour autrui*. Rejecting both possibilities, Judge Negulesco concluded that the international instruments only created legal relations between the States-parties, even though Switzerland might have a great interest in the maintenance of the zone.[98] Judge Dreyfus examined whether Switzerland could be regarded as a State-party to the international instruments or as having obtained a right by virtue

---

[94] *Case of the Free Zones of Upper Savoy and the District of Gex*, Judgment of 7 June 1932, Series A./B.—No. 46, 96, 147–148: 'The Court, having reached this conclusion simply on the basis of an examination of the situation of fact in regard to this case, need not consider the legal nature of the Gex zone from the point of view of whether it constitutes a stipulation in favour of a third Party. But were the matter also to be envisaged from this aspect, the following observations should be made: It cannot be lightly presumed that stipulations favourable to a third State have been adopted with the object of creating an actual right in its favour. There is however nothing to prevent the will of sovereign States from having this object and this effect. The question of the existence of a right acquired under an instrument drawn between other States is therefore one to be decided in each particular case: it must be ascertained whether the States which have stipulated in favour of a third State meant to create for that State an actual right which the latter has accepted as such.'

[95] *Case of the Free Zones of Upper Savoy and the District of Gex*, Order of 19 August 1929, Series A.—No. 22, 19–20, 20: 'Whereas all these instruments, taken together, as also the circumstances in which they were executed, establish, in the Court's opinion, that the intention of the Powers was, besides "rounding out" the territory of Geneva and assuring direct communication between the Canton of Geneva and the rest of Switzerland, to create in favour of Switzerland a right, on which she could rely, to the withdrawal of the French customs barrier from the political frontier of the District of Gex, that is to say, a right to the free zone of Gex; Whereas the Court, having reached this conclusion simply on the basis of an examination of the situation of fact in regard to this case, need not decide as to the extent to which international law takes cognizance of the principle of "stipulations in favour of third Parties".'

[96] Chinkin 1993, pp. 27–28.

[97] *Case of the Free Zones of Upper Savoy and the District of Gex*, Order of 19 August 1929, Dissenting Opinion Judge Nyholm, Series A.—No. 22, 26–27.

[98] *Case of the Free Zones of Upper Savoy and the District of Gex*, Order of 19 August 1929, Dissenting Opinion Judge Negulesco, Series A.—No. 22, 36-39, 38: 'As the Treaty says nothing, it is to be concluded that the Great Powers signatory of the Treaty of 1815 are the holders of the rights to be exercised against France. It is impossible, by reason of the silence of a treaty, to

of a *stipulation pour autrui*. He also concluded that those instruments had only created legal relations between the States-parties.[99]

In the light of the incoherence of the framework of obligation, the following observations may be made with respect to those diverging positions. First, the reasoning concerning the contractual relationship and the reasoning concerning the *stipulation pour autrui* are indistinguishable; in both cases the position of the Powers, including France, on the one hand, and Switzerland, on the other hand, is considered. In both cases, the position of France, as the State having assumed the obligation, in respect of the other Powers and in respect of Switzerland, is central. The main concern from the perspective of the framework of obligation is whether France can indeed be regarded as having assumed an obligation corresponding to a right conferred on Switzerland. That question does not depend on the participation of Switzerland; within the framework of obligation, it merely depends on the intention of France. Second, within the framework of obligation, a right could only be conferred on Switzerland if the obligation incumbent on France was regarded as fixed and dissociated from the intention of France. If the right could be revoked by France, no actual right of Switzerland would have come into existence.[100] Furthermore, within the framework of obligation, there is no place for the conferment of rights. Within that framework, States are already deemed to have unlimited, although conflicting, rights and the only function of rules of public international law is to restrict those rights by means of obligations. Third, if, notwithstanding these considerations, an actual right on the part of a third State is identified, this makes the subsequent reforming of the legal relationship entirely dependent on the consent of that State. This is illustrated by the *Case of the Free Zones of Upper Savoy and the District of Gex*. The PCIJ found that Article 435, para 2, of the Treaty of Versailles neither had abrogated nor was intended to abrogate the free zones. It also found that Article 435, para 2, of the Treaty of Versailles amounted to a declaration of disinterestedness on the part of the other Powers, so that it was for France and Switzerland to settle the regime of the zones. But this resulted in an unbalanced situation, locating the advantage on the side of Switzerland and the disadvantage on the side of France. Products could enter the zone from Switzerland, but products from the zone were caught between the customs barriers of France and Switzerland. In this way, the leverage of the obligation incumbent on France had shifted from the other Powers to Switzerland.[101]

Both the *Report of the International Committee of Jurists Entrusted by the Council of the League of Nations with the Task of Giving an Advisory Opinion*

(Footnote 98 continued)
create rights in favour of third States. It is clear that Switzerland has a great interest in the existence of this zone, but this interest does not justify the exercise of a right.'

99 *Case of the Free Zones of Upper Savoy and the District of Gex*, Order of 19 August 1929, Dissenting Opinion Judge Dreyfus, Series A.—No. 22, 42–43 (contractual relation), 43–45 (*stipulation pour autrui*).

100 Chinkin 1993, p. 32.

101 Chinkin 1993, p. 32.

upon the Legal Aspects of the Åland Islands Question and the *Case of the Free Zones of Upper Savoy and the District of Gex* are examples of the situation arising from an international settlement addressing a legal relation between a State-party and a third State by conferring a 'right' on that third State. Within the framework of obligation, the assumption of 'public' authority on the part of the States-parties as a whole, reflected in the establishment of a legal relation between a State-party and a third State, corresponds to a diminution of the importance of the freedom to act of those States. The analysis of the *Report of the International Committee of Jurists Entrusted by the Council of the League of Nations with the Task of Giving an Advisory Opinion upon the Legal Aspects of the Åland Islands Question* brings out that safeguarding a general interest, such as the demilitarization of islands situated in a strategic position, can only be brought about by disregarding the framework within which the concept of public international law is deemed to operate.

More generally, the idea that a treaty incorporating a public interest may be regarded as an international settlement or an objective regime, which binds not only the States-parties but also third States, irrespective of their consent, has been advocated in doctrine[102] and has found some recognition in international jurisprudence.[103] It has also been pointed out in doctrine that this idea is irreconcilable with the starting point that rules of conventional international law must emanate from the consent of States.[104] Within the framework of obligation, this irreconcilability is concealed under the concept of acquiescence.[105]

These considerations ultimately lead to the idea that, within the concept of conventional international law, a public interest can only be safeguarded if its protection is assumed authoritatively and goes hand in hand with the disregard of the consent of other States. This however ultimately exhibits the incoherence of the concept of conventional international law because the treaty in question must also be based on the consent of the States-parties. It is submitted that these inconsistencies are due to the distorting influence of the framework of obligation, which projects situations that may be regarded as in need of regulation, such as the situations at issue in the cases discussed, as within the complete discretion of the States concerned, both of the regulating States and of the regulated States. If, however, the exclusivity of the framework of obligation is discarded in favor of the reformulated framework, it may be seen that the situation between the third State

---

102 Roxburgh 1917, para 38; McNair 1930, pp. 112–114; Waldock 1962, pp. 77–81.

103 *International Status of South West-Africa*, Advisory Opinion of 11 July 1950, Separate Opinion Sir Arnold McNair, ICJ Reports 1950, 128, 153–155: 'From time to time it happens that a group of great Powers, or a large number of States both great and small, assume a power to create by multipartite treaty some new international regime or status, which soon acquires a degree of acceptance and durability extending beyond the limits of the actual contracting parties, and giving it an objective existence. This power is used when some public interest is involved, and its exercise often occurs in the course of the peace settlement at the end of a great war.'

104 Danilenko 1993, pp. 61–64.

105 Harvard Research in International Law 1935, Comment on Article 18 (a), pp. 922–923.

and the State-party, which is regarded as in need of regulation, is not characterized by mutual unlimited freedoms to act. Rather, this situation is characterized in terms of a dilemma, both sides having a power, but not an unlimited freedom to act so as to constitute this relationship. The role of the other States-parties involved may be viewed as connecting this relationship to the wider constituting of international society. This means that practical reasoning must address the question to what extent this relationship has a bearing on or affects the wider constituting of international society. On the other hand, practical reasoning cannot lead to a solution resulting from the wider constituting of international society being imposed on the sides involved. The connection between the constituting of the relationship and the wider constituting of international society is thus itself a matter of the constituting of international society pursuant to practical reasoning.

9.6 Conclusion

It is concluded that the foregoing considerations indicate that the concept of conventional international law should not be regarded either as contained within the framework of obligation or as contained within the framework of authorization. The framework of obligation gives rise to the problem that the concept of treaty must be regarded simultaneously as emanating from the common will of the States-parties and as restricting the freedom to act of the States-parties. Ultimately, this does not result in imposable obligations. Furthermore, it is presupposed that rules of conventional international law bind the States-parties. On the other hand, the framework of authorization is incapable of explaining the concept of conventional international law as emanating from the common will of the States-parties. Within that framework, the existence of rules of conventional international law is presupposed and the members of international society are not situated as having an inherent power to constitute international society.

This mutual incoherence of the framework of obligation and the framework of authorization can be overcome by the transition to the reformulated framework which combines elements of both. Thus, the restrictive function of the framework of obligation and the empowering function of the framework of authorization may be combined into a function of rules of conventional international law which is both restrictive and empowering. This reformulated function corresponds to a ground structure in which the members of international society are situated as having a power to act which is not an unlimited freedom to act. On the basis of this power to act, the members of international society constitute international society in the form of rules of conventional international law and are, thereby, simultaneously constituted as members of international society. These rules of conventional international law contain an empowering aspect in so far as they represent international society as constituted by the members of international society pursuant to their power to act. At the same time, these rules of conventional international law contain a restrictive aspect in so far as the members of international society cannot circumvent the common good formed by this structure of conventional international law, because they do not have an unlimited freedom to act. Acts to reconstitute the common good of international society must be directed at and proceed through this structure, taking the form of a process of practical reasoning about how these acts cohere with the common good of international society or diverge therefrom so as to further the common good of international society. Within this reformulated framework, the concept of conventional international law may be seen as both rigid—containing the common good of international society—and flexible—so as to propel the reconstituting of the common good of international society. Thereby, it gives shape to the middle ground, located between authority and consent, attracting both the public and the private sphere.

Chapter 10
The Concept of Customary International Law Situated Within the Framework of Obligation and the Framework of Authorization

10.1 Introduction

This chapter analyzes the concept of customary international law from the perspective of the mutual exclusivity of the framework of obligation and the framework of authorization. As will be described in Sect. 10.2, in contrast to the clearly demarcated concept of conventional international law, the concept of customary international law is commonly regarded as giving rise to general rules of public international law, derived from patterns in the practice of States corresponding to *opinio juris*.

As situated within the framework of obligation, the function of rules of customary international law is to restrict the freedom of States to act. At the same time, rules of customary international law are deemed to emanate from the exercise of the freedom of States to act, resulting in the formation of the practice of States. Conceived as consisting of rules inferred from the practice of States, the concept of customary international law cannot be situated within the framework of authorization. According to the framework of authorization, rules of customary international law would confer on States a power to act. That constellation precludes the possibility of seeing rules of customary international law as produced by a power of States to act, because that power of States to act must, in terms of unilateral causality, be seen as conferred by a rule of customary international law.

As will be argued in Sect. 10.3, however, when situated within the framework of obligation, it is not possible to identify conclusively rules of customary international law, derived from the practice of States, restricting the freedom of States to act, because a practice of States must always at the same time be regarded as resulting from a freedom of States to act. The latter perspective is diametrically opposed to viewing the practice of States as giving rise to or conforming to a rule of customary international law. Section 10.3 proceeds to consider several

J. A. Vos, *The Function of Public International Law*,
DOI: 10.1007/978-90-6704-861-3_10, © J. A. Vos, The Netherlands 2013

highlights in international jurisprudence that are commonly discussed in relation to the concept of customary international law, but which actually do not seem to confirm the view that rules of customary international law can be inferred from the practice of States. Section 10.4 concludes that the concept of customary international law may appropriately be resituated within the reformulated framework.

10.2 The Concept of Customary International Law

The concept of customary international law is commonly considered to consist of rules derived from patterns in the practice of States corresponding to *opinio juris*. Accordingly, pursuant to the 'secondary rules' of the concept of customary international law, developed in international jurisprudence and doctrine, the concept of customary international law consists of two elements:

(a) the practice of States;
(b) *opinio juris sive necessitatis*.

The practice of States is sometimes referred to as the material or objective element of the concept of customary international law. *Opinio juris sive necessitatis* is usually referred to as the psychological or subjective element of the concept of customary international law.[1]

In order to derive a rule of customary international law from the practice of States, this practice must satisfy a number of conditions. First, the practice of States must be consistent. This allows the identification of a pattern in the practice of States, which can be formulated as a rule. Second, the practice of States must be general in terms of the number of States participating in it.[2]

In order to determine whether the pattern identified in the practice of States reflects a rule of customary international law, reference is made to the subjective element. Thus, it is the function of the subjective element to indicate whether the pattern in the practice of States may be regarded as a rule of customary international law.

---

[1] *Asylum Case*, Judgment of 20 November 1950, ICJ Reports 1950, 266, 276; *North Sea Continental Shelf Cases*, Judgment of 20 February 1969, ICJ Reports 1969, 3, para 77; *Case Concerning Military and Paramilitary Activities in and against Nicaragua (Merits)*, Judgment of 27 June 1986, ICJ Reports 1986, 14, para 183.

Waldock 1962, pp. 42–45; Quadri 1964, pp. 323–326; Günther 1970, pp. 37–49; Mosler 1974, pp. 121–129; Weil 1992, pp. 164–172; Charney 1993, pp. 536–542; Danilenko 1993, p. 81; Wolfke 1993, pp. 40–51; Zemanek 1997, paras 273–274; Dinstein 2006, paras 63–64.

[2] *Asylum Case*, Judgment of 20 November 1950, ICJ Reports 1950, 266, 276; *North Sea Continental Shelf Cases*, Judgment of 20 February 1969, ICJ Reports 1969, 3, para 77; *Case Concerning Military and Paramilitary Activities in and against Nicaragua (Merits)*, Judgment of 27 June 1986, ICJ Reports 1986, 14, para 186.

Waldock 1962, pp. 44–45; Mosler 1974, pp. 121–125, 131–132; Weil 1992, pp. 164–167; Danilenko 1993, pp. 94–97; Villiger 1997, paras 34–36, 56–59; Kelly 2000, p. 452.

The States participating in the practice must recognize that it corresponds to a rule of customary international law.[3]

Commonly, it is considered that, if a majority of the States participating in the practice recognize that it corresponds to a rule of customary international law, it binds all the participating States.[4] Occasionally, however, the view is also advocated that a practice does not bind a participating State unless that State regards the practice as corresponding to a rule of customary international law.[5]

The view may also be held that a rule of customary international law derived from a pattern in the practice of States binds all States irrespective of whether those States participated in that practice. In this way, it is commonly assumed that rules of customary international law are rules of general international law.[6] In the *North Sea Continental Shelf Cases*, the ICJ observed in this respect that general or customary rules and obligations must, by their very nature, have equal force for all members of the international community and cannot therefore be the subject of any right of unilateral exclusion exercisable at will by any one of them in its own favor.[7] In support of this view, it may be considered that acts of States that did not participate actively in the pattern may be associated by regarding them as passive acts.[8] In addition, it may be considered that such passive acts signify *opinio juris*.[9]

On the other hand, international jurisprudence also supports the view that a rule of customary international law does not bind a State if, during the process of

3 *Case of the S.S. "Lotus"*, Judgment No. 9 of 7 September 1927, Series A.—No. 10, 28; *Asylum Case*, Judgment of 20 November 1950, ICJ Reports 1950, 266, 276; *North Sea Continental Shelf Cases,* Judgment of 20 February 1969, ICJ Reports 1969, 3, para 77; *Case Concerning Military and Paramilitary Activities in and against Nicaragua (Merits)*, Judgment of 27 June 1986, ICJ Reports 1986, 14, para 185.

Waldock 1962, pp. 45–49; Mosler 1974, pp. 125–129; Weil 1992, pp. 167–170; Danilenko 1993, pp. 98–103; Wolfke 1993, pp. 44–51; Villiger 1997, paras 65–68; Dinstein 2006, para 61.

4 Danilenko 1993, pp. 118–119; Villiger 1997, para 68; Dinstein 2006, para 72.

5 Strupp 1934, pp. 308–313; Günther 1970, pp. 127–132; Van Hooff 1983, pp. 85–116.

6 Henry 1928, pp. 83–84; Waldock 1962, pp. 40–41, 49–50; Akehurst 1974–1975, pp. 24, 29; Bos 1984, pp. 247–255; Weil 1992, pp. 186–189; Zemanek 1997, paras 273–277, pp. 312–319; Tomuschat 1999, Chap. IX, paras 32, 35–38; Dupuy 2002, pp. 168–179; Dinstein 2006, paras 42, 43, 47.

7 *North Sea Continental Shelf Cases*, Judgment of 20 February 1969, ICJ Reports 1969, 3, para 63.

8 Danilenko 1993, p. 95: 'It has to be emphasized here that general participation in practice does not mean general active participation. In many areas of relations the consolidation of the required general practice may be achieved through an active practice of a limited group of states, who are most interested in a particular matter, and a more or less tolerant attitude towards the emerging trends by all other members of the international community.'; Capotorti 1994, pp. 129–130: 'Même si un Etat s'abstient de l'action, dans des conditions telles que son abstention peut être qualifiée d'acquiescement, cela rentre dans la pratique susceptible de concourrir à la formation d'une norme coutumière.'; Villiger 1997, paras 48, 51.

9 Capotorti 1994, p. 132; Dinstein 2006, para 45.

formation, it has objected persistently to regarding the pattern in the practice of States as corresponding to a rule of customary international law binding it.[10]

Although, as just stated, rules of customary international law are commonly regarded as rules of general international law, it is nevertheless considered that the concept of customary international law, understood in this sense, does not preclude the existence of regional, local or bilateral customary international law.[11] Such rules of regional, local, or bilateral customary international law may be regarded as complementary to or as derogating from rules of general international law.[12]

10.3 The Concept of Customary International Law Situated Within the Framework of Obligation and the Framework of Authorization

It is submitted that the concept of customary international law, consisting of rules inferred from patterns in the practice of States, conforms to the framework of obligation. Pursuant to the framework of obligation, the function of rules of customary international law is to limit the freedom of States to act. Situated within the framework of obligation, the concept of customary international law is based on the assumption that in the absence of rules of customary international law, States have a freedom to act. The connection between these two propositions is formed by the proposition that rules of customary international law limiting the

---

[10] *Asylum Case*, Judgment of 20 November 1950, ICJ Reports 1950, 266, 277–278: 'But even if it could be supposed that such a custom existed between certain Latin-American States only, it could not be invoked against Peru which, far from having by its attitude adhered to it, has, on the contrary, repudiated it by refraining from ratifying the Montevideo Conventions of 1933 and 1939, which were the first to include a rule concerning the qualification of the offence in matters of asylum'; *Fisheries Case*, Judgment of 18 December 1951, ICJ Reports 1951, 116, 131: 'In any event the ten-mile rule would appear to be inapplicable as against Norway inasmuch as she has always opposed any attempt to apply it to the Norwegian coast.'

Mosler 1974, pp. 132–133; Charney 1985, pp. 1–5; Stein 1985, pp. 458–459; Weil 1992, pp. 189–201; Wolfke 1993, pp. 66–67; Villiger 1997, paras 43–46; Zemanek 1997, para 85; Dinstein 2006, paras 48–52.

[11] *Asylum Case*, Judgment of 20 November 1950, ICJ Reports 1950, 266, 276; *Case Concerning Right of Passage over Indian Territory (Merits)*, Judgment of 12 April 1960, ICJ Reports 1960, 6, 39–43; Separate Opinion Judge Wellington Koo, paras 18–21; Dissenting Opinion Judge Armand-Ugon, 82–84; Dissenting Opinion Judge Sir Percy Spender, 99–110; Dissenting Opinion Judge Chagla, 120–122; *Dispute Regarding Navigational and Related Rights*, Judgment of 13 July 2009, ICJ Reports 2009, 213, paras 141–144; Separate Opinion Judge Sepúlveda-Amor, paras 20–36.

[12] *Case Concerning Right of Passage over Indian Territory (Merits)*, Judgment of 12 April 1960, ICJ Reports 1960, 6, 43–44.

Cohen-Jonathan 1961, pp. 135–137; Wolfke 1993, pp. 88–90; Villiger 1997, paras 81–82; Zemanek 1997, para 84; Dinstein 2006, paras 47, 54.

freedom of States to act must be derived from the freedom of States to act resulting in patterns in the practice of States.

As analyzed from the perspective of critical theory of public international law, both the subjective element and the objective element are indispensible to the concept of customary international law. While the basis of the concept of customary international law is formed by the objective element, the subjective element is necessary so as to distinguish binding practice from non-binding practice. On the other hand, if the subjective element is merely regarded in terms of will or belief, it becomes indistinguishable from abstract consensus. Therefore, the subjective element must refer back to the objective element for the definition of the pattern which informs the content of the rule to be identified. When the focus returns to the objective element, it is commonly found that the practice of States does not admit the identification of a clear-cut pattern. Whereupon the focus again turns to the subjective element in order to find a criterion that may be applied to the practice of States. In this way, argument about customary international law is seen as circular and inconclusive.[13]

The perspective provided by critical theory of public international law is directed at a threefold distinction between the concepts of justice, law, and politics. It may be added that, within the framework of obligation, the practice of States itself is conceived in ambiguous terms. While mostly argument about customary international law is prevented from proceeding because of the impossibility of identifying a pattern in the practice of States, if such a pattern can be identified and is to be seen as reflecting a rule of customary international law, it must be viewed both as restricting the freedom of States to act and as emanating from the freedom of States to act. Consequently, in order to identify conclusively a rule of customary international law, the view of rules of customary international law as restricting the freedom of States to act must take precedence over the view of rules of customary international law as emanating from the freedom of States to act. However, in so far as such precedence is accorded, the concept of customary international law at the same time relinquishes its basis in the practice of States. Furthermore, as situated within the framework of obligation, the concept of customary international law projects the practice of States, in so far as it is not regulated by its rules-as a 'rechtsfreies Raum' (a non-legal area)-incoherently by the freedoms to act of the members of international society. At the same time, it relies on the assumption that this 'rechtsfreie Raum' can give rise to patterns from which rules may coherently be inferred, produced on the basis of the inconsistent freedoms to act of the members of international society.[14]

Hence, in view of the incoherence of the mutual exclusivity of the framework of obligation and the framework of authorization, it follows, it is submitted, that the concept of customary international law cannot be relied upon to identify conclusively rules of public international law capable of delimiting the freedom of

[13] Koskenniem 2005, pp. 410–438.

[14] Goldsmith and Posner 1999, pp. 1116–1120.

States to act. International jurisprudence superficially follows the common view that the concept of customary international law consists of an objective and a subjective element. However, as will be illustrated below, the instances in the jurisprudence of the PCIJ and the ICJ which are commonly associated with the concept of customary international law actually turn on considerations which fall outside of the concept of customary international law as thus conceived.

10.3.1 The Case of the S.S. "Lotus"

When deciding the dispute between France and Turkey about exclusive/concurrent criminal jurisdiction, the PCIJ examined whether a rule of public international law, according to which the flag State has exclusive jurisdiction in collision cases, could be inferred from a pattern in the practice of States. The Court analyzed this practice, consisting of four cases before national courts relating to three collisions on the high seas between ships of different nationalities. Two of those cases, the *Franconia – Strathclyde* case before a British court and the *Ortigia – Oncle Joseph* case before a French court, might be considered as supporting the principle of exclusive jurisdiction. The other two cases, the *Ekbatana – West Hinder* case before a Belgian court and the *Ortigia – Oncle Joseph* case before an Italian court, might be considered as supporting the principle of concurrent jurisdiction.

The Court observed that the practice of States as a whole, consisting of two cases supporting the principle of exclusive jurisdiction and two cases supporting the principle of concurrent jurisdiction, was inconsistent and did not permit the identification of a pattern from which a rule of customary international law could be derived.[15] Within the context of the view that the concept of customary international law consists of both an objective and a subjective element, this would have been sufficient to arrive at the conclusion that a rule of customary international law restricting the freedom of Turkey to assume concurrent jurisdiction, did not exist.[16] However, the PCIJ continued its reasoning, focusing on the absence of protests of the interested flag States in the cases supporting the principle of concurrent jurisdiction.

In the course of this reasoning, the Court drew an analogy between the two cases supporting the principle of concurrent jurisdiction and the practice of States with regard to the principle of concurrent territorial jurisdiction. It may be noted, in this connection, that concurrent territorial jurisdiction is considered to arise in a situation in which an act beginning in the territory of one State produces effects in the territory of another State, a typical example being a gunshot fired in State A

[15] *Case of the S.S. "Lotus"*, Judgment No. 9 of 7 September 1927, Series A.—No. 10, 29: 'It will suffice to observe that, as municipal jurisprudence is thus divided, it is hardly possible to see in it an indication of the existence of the restrictive rule of international law which alone could serve as a basis for the contention of the French Government.'

[16] Haggenmacher 1986, paras 30–31.

producing injury in State B. In such a situation, the principle of concurrent territorial jurisdiction is considered to provide that both States may exercise jurisdiction in respect of the act. A comparable situation would have been an act beginning onboard of ship A producing effects onboard of ship B. A collision between ships A and B would, however, seem different from an act beginning onboard of ship A producing effects onboard of ship B. The analogy with the principle of concurrent territorial jurisdiction, therefore, does not seem pertinent.

On the other hand, as has been pointed out by Haggenmacher, the absence of protests of the interested flag States in the two cases supporting the principle of concurrent jurisdiction was not irrelevant.[17] In addition to the inconsistency of the practice of States, the absence of *opinio juris* on the part of the interested flag States suggested the non-existence of a rule of customary international law restricting the freedom of States to assume concurrent jurisdiction.[18] As Günther has observed, the absence of the subjective element could have been derived from the inconsistency of the practice.[19] Conversely, the considerations relating to the absence of protests of the interested flag States in the cases supporting the principle of concurrent jurisdiction served to interpret the practice of States.[20]

Thus, within the framework of obligation, the inconsistency of the practice of States and the absence of *opinio juris* on the part of the interested flag States made it impossible to identify a rule of customary international law restricting the freedom of States to assume concurrent jurisdiction. Moreover, even if the interested flag States had protested, this would not have been sufficient to identify *opinio juris* on the part of the States assuming concurrent jurisdiction. Like the requirements of justice which the Court invoked, the Court found that the attitude of interested flag States towards the assumption of concurrent jurisdiction reinforced its interpretation of the practice of States in the sense that the assumption of concurrent jurisdiction was the appropriate solution in collision cases between ships of different nationalities. At the same time, however, this solution was based on the assumed freedom of Turkey to assume concurrent jurisdiction which, as such, was inconsistent with the freedom of France to assume exclusive jurisdiction.

---

[17] Haggenmacher 1986, para 31.

[18] *Case of the S.S. "Lotus"*, Judgment No. 9 of 7 September 1927, Series A.—No. 10, 29: 'On the other hand, the Court feels called upon to lay stress upon the fact that it does not appear that the States concerned have objected to criminal proceedings in respect of collision cases before the courts of a country other than that the flag of which was flown, or that they have made protests (…). This fact is directly opposed to the existence of a tacit consent on the part of States to the exclusive jurisdiction of the State whose flag is flown, such as the Agent for the French Government has thought it possible to deduce from the infrequency of questions of jurisdiction before criminal courts. It seems hardly probable, and it would not be in accordance with international practice, that the French Government in the *Ortigia – Oncle-Joseph case* and the German Government in the *Ekbatana-West-Hinder* case would have omitted to protest against the exercise of criminal jurisdiction by the Italian and Belgian Courts, if they had really thought that this was a violation of international law.'

[19] Günther 1970, pp. 65–66.

[20] Haggenmacher 1986, para 31.

10.3.2 The Asylum Case

In the *Asylum Case*, the ICJ was requested to resolve a dispute between Colombia and Peru, brought before the Court on the basis of the Act of Lima of August 31, 1949. The dispute related to the diplomatic asylum granted by Colombia to Haya de la Torre, accused by the authorities of Peru of the crime of military rebellion, in its embassy in Lima. The position of Colombia was formulated in two submissions: In the first submission, Colombia asserted that, as the State granting diplomatic asylum, it was competent to qualify unilaterally the nature of the offence, i.e., whether of a political or common nature, of which someone seeking diplomatic asylum was accused. In the second submission, Colombia asserted that the territorial State had an obligation to provide the guarantees necessary for the departure of Haya de la Torre from the territory. Peru submitted a counter-claim that the grant or maintenance of diplomatic asylum to Haya de la Torre violated Article 1, para 1, and Article 2, para 2, of the Havana Convention on Asylum of February 20, 1928.

Addressing this dispute in its Judgment of 20 November 1950, the ICJ adopted the view that diplomatic asylum derogates from the sovereignty of the territorial State.[21] According to the Court, a right to qualify unilaterally the nature of the offence could not be regarded as implied in the Convention on Asylum. Such a right, which would aggravate the derogation from the territorial sovereignty constituted by the exercise of diplomatic asylum, seemed moreover incompatible with the unusually restrictive terms of the Convention on Asylum.[22]

Subsequently, the ICJ examined the question whether such a right existed as regional or local customary international law. The Court stated that reaching this conclusion would require the establishment of a consistent practice expressing a right-obligation relation.[23] As part of this examination, the Court considered cases in which diplomatic asylum had in fact been granted and respected. With respect to this practice, the Court emphasized that it had not been shown that the right of unilateral qualification was invoked or that, if it was invoked, that it was exercised

---

[21] *Asylum Case*, Judgment of 20 November 1950, ICJ Reports 1950, 266, 274–275: 'In the case of diplomatic asylum, the refugee is within the territory of the State where the offence was committed. A decision to grant diplomatic asylum involves a derogation from the sovereignty of that State. It withdraws the offender from the jurisdiction of the territorial State and constitutes an intervention in matters which are exclusively within the competence of that State. Such a derogation from territorial sovereignty cannot be recognized unless its legal basis is established in each particular case.'

[22] *Asylum Case*, Judgment of 20 November 1950, ICJ Reports 1950, 266, 276.

[23] *Asylum Case*, Judgment of 20 November 1950, ICJ Reports 1950, 266, 276: 'The Party which relies on a custom of this kind must prove that this custom is established in such a manner that it has become binding on the other Party. The Colombian Government must prove that the rule invoked by it is in accordance with a constant and uniform usage practiced by the States in question, and that this usage is the expression of a right appertaining to the State granting asylum and a duty incumbent on the territorial State.'

by the State granting asylum as a right and respected by the territorial State as an obligation. In other words, the subjective element was absent.[24] The Court considered furthermore that, supposing such a right existed in customary international law, it could not bind Peru because Peru had repudiated it by not adhering to conventional international law conferring it.[25]

The ICJ adopted a similar approach with regard to the second submission of Colombia, according to which the territorial State had an obligation to provide the guarantees necessary for the departure of Haya de la Torre from the territory. Interpreting the text of the Convention on Asylum, the Court observed that admitting such an obligation would mean that the State granting diplomatic asylum could decide unilaterally that the conditions prescribed in Articles 1 and 2 of the Convention on Asylum had been fulfilled.[26] In this context, the ICJ made mention of the existence of a practice whereby the diplomatic representative who granted asylum immediately requested a safe-conduct without awaiting a request from the territorial State for the departure of the refugee. However, the Court observed that this practice could not be interpreted as implying that the territorial State was bound to accede to such a request. In other words, *opinio juris* with respect to that practice did not exist.[27]

As regards the counter-claim, the Court considered that it was well-founded in so far as it related to a violation of Article 2, para 2, of the Convention on Asylum, which provided as follows:

> Asylum may not be granted except in urgent cases and for the period of time strictly indispensable for the person who has sought asylum to ensure in some other way his safety.

Interpreting this provision, the Court noted the intention of the Convention on Asylum, which was to put an end to the abuses which had arisen in the practice of diplomatic asylum. According to the Court, this intention was reflected in the prohibitive and restrictive wording of Articles 1 and 2 of the Convention on Asylum. Furthermore, according to the Court, it was for Colombia to submit proof of facts to show that the condition posed by Article 2, para 2, had been fulfilled.[28]

Subsequently, the ICJ examined whether the danger of political justice by reason of the subordination of the Peruvian judicial authorities to the instructions of the Executive could be regarded as fulfilling the condition posed in Article 2, para 2, of the Convention on Asylum.[29] In the course of this examination, the Court made a

---

[24] *Asylum Case*, Judgment of 20 November 1950, ICJ Reports 1950, 266, 277: 'But it has not been shown that the alleged rule of unilateral and definitive qualification was invoked or – if in some cases it was in fact invoked – that it was (...) exercised by the States granting asylum as a right appertaining to them and respected by the territorial State as a duty incumbent on them and not merely for reasons of political expediency.'

[25] *Asylum Case*, Judgment of 20 November 1950, ICJ Reports 1950, 266, 277–278.

[26] *Asylum Case*, Judgment of 20 November 1950, ICJ Reports 1950, 266, 279.

[27] *Asylum Case*, Judgment of 20 November 1950, ICJ Reports 1950, 266, 279.

[28] *Asylum Case*, Judgment of 20 November 1950, ICJ Reports 1950, 266, 282.

[29] *Asylum Case*, Judgment of 20 November 1950, ICJ Reports 1950, 266, 283.

distinction between the regular operation of justice and arbitrary action by the government.[30] Thereupon, the Court observed that it had not been shown that decrees proclaiming and prolonging a state of siege implied the subordination of justice to the executive authority or that the suspension of certain constitutional guarantees entailed the abolition of judicial guarantees.[31] It could not be assumed, according to the Court, that revolution interferes with the administration of justice.[32] Otherwise, a conflict would arise with the tradition of non-intervention.[33] On this basis, the Court concluded that the requirement of urgency had not been fulfilled.[34]

Turning to the practice of States consisting of cases in which the territorial State had recognized diplomatic asylum granted against proceedings instituted by judicial authorities, the Court observed that those cases might be inspired by political considerations and did not reveal *opinio juris*.[35] More generally, the Court remarked that the institution of diplomatic asylum, as practiced in Latin America, owed its development, to a very great extent, to extra-legal factors. In support of this pronouncement, it pointed to the good-neighbor relations between the republics and the different political interests of the governments, which had favored the mutual recognition of diplomatic asylum outside of any clearly defined juridical system. Although the Convention on Asylum was intended to react to abuses, it did not limit the practice of diplomatic asylum as it might arise from agreements between interested governments inspired by mutual feelings of toleration and goodwill.[36]

In this respect, it may be asked how, if the institution of diplomatic asylum existed outside a clearly defined legal system, the Court could determine that Colombia had acted inconsistently with Article 2, para 2, of the Convention on Asylum. Although the Convention on Asylum was intended to restrict abuse of diplomatic asylum, it did not envisage its elimination. The Court laid upon Colombia the burden of proving that it had acted consistently with the Convention. This, however, was inconsistent with the framework of obligation. Within that

---

30 *Asylum Case*, Judgment of 20 November 1950, ICJ Reports 1950, 266, 284.

31 *Asylum Case*, Judgment of 20 November 1950, ICJ Reports 1950, 266, 284.

32 *Asylum Case*, Judgment of 20 November 1950, ICJ Reports 1950, 266, 286.

33 *Asylum Case*, Judgment of 20 November 1950, ICJ Reports 1950, 266, 285: 'The Court cannot admit that the States signatory to the Havana Convention intended to substitute for the practice of the Latin-American republics, in which considerations of courtesy, good-neighbourliness and political expediency have always held a prominent place, a legal system which would guarantee to their own nationals accused of political offences the privilege of evading national jurisdiction. Such a conception, moreover, would come into conflict with one of the most firmly established traditions of Latin America, namely, non-intervention. It was at the Sixth Pan-American Conference of 1928, during which the Convention on Asylum was signed, that the States of Latin America declared their resolute opposition to any foreign political intervention. It would be difficult to conceive that these same States had consented, at the very same moment, to submit to intervention in its least acceptable form, one which implies foreign interference in the administration of domestic justice and which could not manifest itself without casting some doubt on the impartiality of that justice.'

34 *Asylum Case*, Judgment of 20 November 1950, ICJ Reports 1950, 266, 287.

35 *Asylum Case*, Judgment of 20 November 1950, ICJ Reports 1950, 266, 286.

36 *Asylum Case*, Judgment of 20 November 1950, ICJ Reports 1950, 266, 286.

framework, a violation of an obligation incumbent on Colombia could only be derived from Article 2, para 2, of the Convention on Asylum, if it could be demonstrated that the circumstances in which asylum had been granted did not amount to urgency, as accepted by Colombia. It may further be observed that the instances of customary international law which the Court examined, were analyzed from the perspective of whether Peru had assumed an obligation. Thus, the Court found, inter alia, that the practice of States consisting of cases in which the territorial State had recognized diplomatic asylum granted against proceedings instituted by judicial authorities, did not amount to a rule of customary international law. That question, however, did not affect the right to grant asylum against proceedings instituted by judicial authorities that Colombia could derive, within the framework of obligation, from its freedom to act. If, as the ICJ suggested, the practice of diplomatic asylum could only operate on the basis of agreements between interested governments, this would effectively situate the States granting diplomatic asylum within the framework of authorization and eliminate the practice of diplomatic asylum which, to some extent, must depend on a unilateral act of the State granting diplomatic asylum.

There was, therefore, it is submitted, not a firm basis for the conclusion that Colombia had violated the Convention on Asylum. If the Court had not arrived at that conclusion, this would have left the resulting situation in the form of a dilemma: Colombia was justified in having accorded diplomatic asylum, but Peru was neither obliged to recognize it, nor to accord safe-conduct. This would have taken account of the extra-legal sphere in which the institution of diplomatic asylum existed. In the absence of agreement between the States concerned, however, no solution could be arrived at. Although in the course of its reasoning the Court repeatedly referred to the concept of customary international law, its insistence on the absence of political considerations as a precondition for the identification of its rules, effectively eliminated the possibility of identifying rules of customary international law.

It is interesting to consider how the ICJ subsequently dealt with this situation in the *Haya de la Torre Case*, when it addressed the question whether Colombia was required to surrender Haya de la Torre to Peru. In its Judgment of 13 June 1951, the Court observed that the Convention on Asylum did not give a complete answer to the question of the manner in which diplomatic asylum shall be terminated. The method prescribed for terminating asylum granted to persons accused of political crimes was the grant of a safe-conduct for the departure from the country. Under the terms of the Judgment of 20 November 1950 in the *Asylum Case*, safe-conduct could only be claimed if diplomatic asylum had been regularly granted and maintained and if the territorial State had required that the refugee be sent out of the country.

No provision was made in cases where the territorial State had not requested the departure of the refugee. Furthermore, no provision had been made for cases in which diplomatic asylum had not been regularly granted or maintained. From the fact that Article 1 of the Convention on Asylum provided for the surrender of persons accused of common crimes, the Court inferred that no such obligation could be derived from the terms of the Convention on Asylum with respect to persons accused of political crimes.[37] The Court added that the irregular character of the asylum granted entailed an obligation incumbent upon Colombia to terminate it, but, at the same time, that Colombia was not required to surrender the refugee. The ICJ remarked that these statements were not contradictory, because asylum could be terminated in more than one way. The Court concluded its Judgment by observing that it had thereby completed its task, giving practical advice as to how the asylum granted might be terminated would deviate from its judicial function. It limited itself to defining the legal relations between the parties, appealing once more to the considerations of courtesy and good-neighborliness which had always characterized relations between the Latin-American republics.[38]

With respect to these considerations, two observations seem particularly pertinent. First, it may be observed that, from the perspective of the Judgment in the *Haya de la Torre Case*, no practical consequence flowed from the answer to the question whether the asylum granted by Colombia was or was not consistent with Article 2, para 2, of the Convention on Asylum. In both cases, Colombia was not required to surrender the refugee to Peru. Second, although the Court clarified the legal relations between the parties, the resolution of the dispute was left to the field of international politics. Whether or not the asylum had been granted irregularly, both States could continue to insist on their respective positions; Colombia was not required to surrender the refugee and Peru was not required to grant a safe-conduct. Although both parties could thus insist, in a way, on their freedom to act, neither party could actually exercise it. If Colombia was required to terminate the asylum granted but not required to surrender the refugee, it required the cooperation of Peru for the exit of the refugee from the country. While Peru was not required to grant a safe-conduct, it could not require the surrender of the refugee either.

While thus defining the legal relations between the parties, the Court had at the same time defined the field of international politics from the perspective of public international law, situating the parties in terms of a dilemma; they could rely on their freedom to act, but at the same time required the cooperation of the other party for the exercise of that freedom to act. Ultimately, if the solution to the dilemma was to be propelled by considerations of mutual goodwill and good-neighborliness, this would mean that, within the context of the framework of obligation, the parties were compelled to reach an agreement.

10.3.3 The Fisheries Case

The *Fisheries Case*, brought by the United Kingdom against Norway on the basis of the Optional Clause, pertained to a dispute concerning the validity under

---

[37] *Haya de la Torre Case*, Judgment of 13 June 1951, ICJ Reports 1951, 71, 80–82.

[38] *Haya de la Torre Case*, Judgment of 13 June 1951, ICJ Reports 1951, 71, 81–83.

international law of the delimitation by Norway of its territorial sea on the basis of the method of straight baselines. As part of its argument relating to the invalidity of that delimitation, the United Kingdom contended that straight baselines could only be used if the mouth of a bay does not exceed ten miles. Norway contended that its use of the method of straight baselines was in conformity with international law.

Addressing this dispute, the ICJ considered that a rule of customary international law, providing that straight baselines may only be drawn if the mouth of a bay does not exceed ten miles, could not be derived from a pattern in the practice of States. The Court observed that, although some States might have adopted this limit, other States had adopted a different limit. Consequently, the practice of States did not satisfy the requirement of consistency.[39] The Court further observed that Norway had always opposed any attempt to apply such a rule to the Norwegian coast and that it could, therefore, in any event, not be invoked against Norway.[40] Thus, although the ICJ could have confined itself to rejecting the contention of the United Kingdom relating to the ten-mile rule in view of the inconsistency of the practice of States, it ascertained, in addition, the absence of the subjective element.[41] Specifically, with regard to the skjærgaard, a stretch of island formations along the Norwegian coast, the Court considered that the practice of States did not permit the formulation of a general rule of law, according to which the length of the baselines between those formations should not exceed ten miles.[42] In this light, the ICJ denied the existence of rules of customary international law by reference to which the validity of the delimitation by Norway of its territorial sea could be determined.

However, according to the Court, this did not mean that there were no principles of international law applicable to the delimitation by Norway of its territorial sea.[43]

[39] *Fisheries Case*, Judgment of 18 December 1951, ICJ Reports 1951, 116, 131: 'In these circumstances the Court deems it necessary to point out that although the ten-mile rule has been adopted by certain States both in their national law and in their treaties and conventions, and although certain arbitral decisions have applied it as between these States, other States have adopted a different limit. Consequently, the ten-mile rule has not acquired the authority of a general rule of international law.'

[40] *Fisheries Case*, Judgment of 18 December 1951, ICJ Reports 1951, 116, 131: 'In any event, the ten-mile rule would appear to be inapplicable as against Norway as she has always opposed any attempt to apply it to the Norwegian coast.'

[41] Haggenmacher 1986, para 36.

[42] *Fisheries Case*, Judgment of 18 December 1951, ICJ Reports 1951, 116, 131.

[43] *Fisheries Case*, Judgment of 18 December 1951, ICJ Reports 1951, 116, 132: 'It does not at all follow that, in the absence of rules having the technically precise character alleged by the United Kingdom Government, the delimitation undertaken by the Norwegian Government in 1935 is not subject to certain principles which make it possible to judge as to its validity under international law. The delimitation of sea areas has always an international aspect; it cannot be dependent merely upon the will of the coastal State as expressed in its municipal law. Although it is true that only the coastal State is competent to undertake it, the validity of the delimitation with regard to other States depends upon international law.'

The ICJ stated that the delimitation of the territorial sea had to be in conformity with the following criteria:

(a) baselines must not depart to any appreciable extent from the general direction of the coast;
(b) sea areas lying within baselines should be sufficiently closely connected to the land domain to be subject to the regime of internal waters; and
(c) certain economic interests peculiar to a region should be taken into account.

In the view of the Court, these criteria could be derived from certain basic considerations inherent in the nature of the territorial sea.[44]

It may, however, be questioned whether the validity of the delimitation of the territorial sea can be determined by reference to these principles and criteria. How can it be determined whether the baselines depart to any appreciable extent from the general direction of the coast and whether the sea areas lying within the baselines are sufficiently closely connected to the land domain to be subject to the regime of internal waters? What role is played by the economic interests? In terms of the framework of obligation, it would have to be established that the baselines depart to an appreciable extent from the general direction of the coast and that the sea areas lying within the baselines are not sufficiently closely connected to the land domain to be subject to the regime of internal waters, before the validity of the delimitation could be affected. These principles and criteria presuppose the existence of further standards by virtue of which these questions can be answered.

In its reasoning, the ICJ observed that the method of straight baselines had been used by several states so as to reflect the principle that the territorial sea must conform to the general direction of the coast and that other States had not objected thereto.[45] Specifically as regards the system of delimitation used by Norway, the Court made a similar observation[46] and emphasized the position adopted by the United Kingdom with respect thereto.[47] Thereby, the Court relied on the acquiescence of States with respect to the use of straight baselines, focusing

---

[44] *Fisheries Case*, Judgment of 18 December 1951, ICJ Reports 1951, 116, 133.

[45] *Fisheries Case*, Judgment of 18 December 1951, ICJ Reports 1951, 116, 129: 'The principle that the belt of territorial waters must follow the general direction of the coast makes it possible to fix certain criteria valid for any delimitation of the territorial sea; (…) in order to apply this principle, several States have deemed it necessary to follow the straight base-lines method and (…) they have not encountered objections of principle by other States.'

[46] *Fisheries Case*, Judgment of 18 December 1951, ICJ Reports 1951, 116, 136–137: 'The Court, having thus established the existence and the constituent elements of the Norwegian system of delimitation, further finds that this system was consistently applied by Norwegian authorities and that it encountered no opposition on the part of other States.'

[47] *Fisheries Case*, Judgment of 18 December 1951, ICJ Reports 1951, 116, 138–139: 'The Court notes that in respect of a situation which could only be strengthened with the passage of time, the United Kingdom Government refrained from formulating reservations. The notoriety of the facts, the general toleration of the international community, Great Britain's position in the North Sea, her own interest in the question, and her prolonged abstention would in any case warrant Norway's enforcement of her system against the United Kingdom.'

specifically on the system of delimitation adopted by Norway and the position with respect thereto adopted by the United Kingdom.

Thus, the ICJ based its reasoning with respect to the validity of the delimitation of the territorial sea undertaken by Norway on two strands. One strand of this reasoning consisted of principles and criteria derived from the nature of the territorial sea. Another strand of this reasoning consisted of acquiescence in the use of straight baselines by other States.[48] The strand consisting of acquiescence might be regarded as a kind of *communis opinio juris* with respect to the strand consisting of principles and criteria derived from the nature of the territorial sea.[49] Similarly, the use of those strands in the reasoning of the Court might be regarded as a rhetorical strategy, combining soft (principles and criteria) and hard (acquiescence) elements so as to produce a convincing result.[50]

It may be observed, however, that it is difficult to combine those strands coherently. In the strand relating to principles and criteria derived from the nature of the territorial sea, these principles and criteria should, as inherent, be sufficient in themselves to determine the validity of the delimitation undertaken by Norway. This appraisal should be independent of the views that other States might have of the validity of the system of delimitation used by Norway. Otherwise, these principles and criteria could not be regarded as inherent in the nature of the territorial sea. However, it does not seem possible to determine the validity of the delimitation simply by reference to these principles and criteria. Therefore, an external point of view, represented by the views of other States, was necessary to determine the validity of the delimitation. However, if the validity of the delimitation is made dependent on the question of whether other States have accepted it, this simultaneously subordinates the sovereignty of the State effecting the delimitation to the sovereignty of those other States and nullifies the view of the principles and criteria as inherent in the nature of the territorial sea. In so far as the two strands on which the reasoning is based are mutually exclusive, the rhetorical strategy must be regarded as incoherent.

It is submitted that these difficulties, presented by the incoherence of the mutual exclusivity of the framework of obligation and the framework of authorization, suggest, as a matter of practical reasoning, how a transition to the reformulated framework may be described. Clearly, the framework of authorization is unsuitable to address the situation presented. This would presuppose that the principles and rules identified by the ICJ are pre-existent and cannot be explained on the basis of acts of Norway, the United Kingdom, and other States. Indeed, it would leave those States without any power to act and, thereby, constitute international society. On the other hand, as we have seen, the principles and rules identified by the Court are, in themselves, insufficient for a delimitation of the freedom to act of Norway. That is not the same thing, however, as saying that nothing is inherent in

[48] Dupuy 2002, pp. 150–152.

[49] Haggenmacher 1986, paras 34, 37.

[50] Kennedy 1987, pp. 82–90.

the nature of the territorial sea. If these criteria are not determinate enough, that problem cannot be solved by anchoring their content in the consent of other States, because that would subject the sovereignty of the delimiting State to the sovereignty of those States and amount to saying that nothing is inherent in the nature of the territorial sea.

There are thus three elements: (a) the principles and rules; (b) the position of the delimiting State; and (c) the position of the other States. These elements may be resituated within the reformulated framework, which emerges if the mutual exclusivity of the framework of authorization and the framework of obligation is suppressed. The principles and rules may be regarded as informing the constituting of international society and inherent in so far as they relate to the relationship between the high seas and the territorial sea. Because these principles and rules do not in themselves establish validity, they must be related to the acts of the members of international society. Addressing, as the Court said, an international situation, they must relate to and be explicable pursuant to acts both of the delimiting State and of the other States. Within the reformulated framework, these acts emanate, not from an unlimited freedom to act, but from a power to act in the form of the constituting of international society. Most crucial is the function of these principles and rules. Within the reformulated framework, their function resides in the constituting of international society. They inscribe themselves in the dilemma in which the members of international society are situated; accordingly, they must reflect and give shape to the interests of both the delimiting State and the other States. Hence, within the reformulated framework, the international situation is no longer appropriately characterized in terms of delimitation. The role of the principles and rules is not to delimit the freedom to act of the coastal State, but to constitute the relationship between the high seas and the territorial sea and, therewith, between the coastal State and the other members of international society.

10.3.4 The North Sea Continental Shelf Cases

In the *North Sea Continental Shelf Cases*, two interrelated differences, submitted by separate special agreements, of 2 February 1967, concluded, on the one hand, between Denmark and the Federal Republic of Germany and, on the other hand, between the Federal Republic of Germany and The Netherlands, requesting the ICJ to identify the principles and rules of international law applicable to, respectively, the delimitation of the continental shelf between Denmark and the Federal Republic of Germany and the delimitation of the continental shelf between the Federal Republic of Germany and The Netherlands, were before the Court.

Denmark and The Netherlands contended that the method of equidistance should be considered as such a principle or rule, applicable unless special circumstances were present. The method of equidistance produces a line connecting points that are the same distance away from the nearest point on the baseline of the territorial sea of each of the States concerned. Denmark and The Netherlands contended further that the concavity of the coastline of the Federal Republic of Germany did not form a special circumstance detracting from the application of the method of equidistance.[51] In contrast, in view of that concavity, the Federal Republic of Germany argued that the delimitation should result in a just and equitable share of the continental shelf for each of the States concerned.[52] As argued by the Federal Republic of Germany, the application of the method of equidistance would result in cutting off the continental shelf of the Federal Republic of Germany, because of the convergence of the equidistance lines delimiting, respectively, the continental shelves of Denmark and the Federal Republic of Germany, and the continental shelves of the Federal Republic of Germany and The Netherlands.[53]

Denmark and The Netherlands argued that the method of equidistance was binding vis-à-vis the Federal Republic of Germany, either in the form of Article 6, para 2, of the Convention on the Continental Shelf, of 29 April 1958, or as a rule of customary international law. Article 6, para 2, of the Convention on the Continental Shelf provided:

> Where the same continental shelf is adjacent to the territories of two adjacent States, the boundary of the continental shelf shall be determined by agreement between them. In the absence of agreement, and unless another boundary is justified by special circumstances, the boundary shall be determined by application of the principle of equidistance from the nearest points of the baselines from which the breadth of the territorial sea of each State is measured.

The ICJ rejected the argument that, although the Federal Republic of Germany had not ratified the Convention on the Continental Shelf, it could nevertheless be considered as bound by Article 6, para 2, as a matter of conventional international law. According to the Court, only a very definite, very consistent course of conduct on the part of the Federal Republic of Germany could have justified such a conclusion.[54]

Subsequently, the Court examined the question whether a rule of customary international law could be derived from a practice consisting of agreements between States in which the method of equidistance had been adopted. The Court observed that, although States might have provided for the use of the method of equidistance in these agreements, this did not mean that they considered themselves obligated to use this method. In other words, in this practice of States the subjective element could not be identified.[55] Moreover, the practice consisted almost exclusively of delimitations between opposite States in which a median line was employed. The difference between delimitations between opposite States and delimitations between adjacent States, perceived by the Court, prevented this

[51] *North Sea Continental Shelf Cases*, Judgment of 20 February 1969, ICJ Reports 1969, 3, para 13.

[52] *North Sea Continental Shelf Cases*, Judgment of 20 February 1969, ICJ Reports 1969, 3, para 15.

[53] *North Sea Continental Shelf Cases*, Judgment of 20 February 1969, ICJ Reports 1969, 3, para 8.

[54] *North Sea Continental Shelf Cases*, Judgment of 20 February 1969, ICJ Reports 1969, 3, para 28.

[55] *North Sea Continental Shelf Cases*, Judgment of 20 February 1969, ICJ Reports 1969, 3, paras 76–78.

practice from being regarded as relevant for the delimitation of lateral boundaries.[56] Thus, although the Court stressed the absence of the subjective element, it could also have confined itself to considering that the practice was inconsistent or not sufficiently general.[57]

This negative result, however, did not mean that applicable principles and rules of international law could not be identified.[58] The ICJ stated that delimitation must be the result of agreement between the States concerned, which must be arrived at in accordance with equitable principles. The Court also required that the continental shelf of a State be the natural prolongation of its territory and not encroach upon the natural prolongation of the territory of another State.[59] The Court saw those requirements as emanating from rules of law.[60]

Examining these rules more closely, the ICJ arrived at the conclusion that, in the cases before the Court, the use of the principle of equidistance would be inequitable because it would result in treating the three States involved differently, although the coastlines of those States were comparable in length.[61] In this analysis, the concavity of the coastline of the Federal Republic of Germany was apparently treated as an incidental circumstance that should not influence the result.

With respect to this reasoning, it may first be observed that the Court simply asserted that those equitable requirements emanated from rules of law. Further, its consideration that the use of the method of equidistance would produce an inequitable result in the instant cases presupposed an understanding of the natural prolongation of the territories of the States involved, linked to the length of their respective coastlines. Apparently, the Court considered that it would be inequitable if a State would be deprived of the natural prolongation of its territory by reason of the concavity of its coastline. However, by virtue of what criteria could the Court determine the natural prolongation of the territory of the Federal Republic of Germany and consider, at the same time, that this natural prolongation did not encroach upon the natural prolongations of the territories of Denmark and The Netherlands?

---

56 *North Sea Continental Shelf Cases*, Judgment of 20 February 1969, ICJ Reports 1969, 3, para 79.

57 Haggenmacher 1986, para 45.

58 *North Sea Continental Shelf Cases*, Judgment of 20 February 1969, ICJ Reports 1969, 3, para 83: ‘But as between States faced with an issue concerning the lateral delimitation of adjacent continental shelves, there are still rules and principles of law to be applied; and in the present case it is not the fact either that rules are lacking, or that the situation is one for the unfettered appreciation of the Parties.’

59 *North Sea Continental Shelf Cases*, Judgment of 20 February 1969, ICJ Reports 1969, 3, para 85.

60 *North Sea Continental Shelf Cases*, Judgment of 20 February 1969, ICJ Reports 1969, 3, para 85: ‘On a foundation of very general precepts of justice and good faith, actual rules of law are here involved which govern the delimitation of adjacent continental shelves – that is to say, rules binding upon States for all delimitations; – in short, it is not a question of applying equity simply as a matter of abstract justice, but of applying a rule of law which itself requires the application of equitable principles (…)’

61 *North Sea Continental Shelf Cases*, Judgment of 20 February 1969, ICJ Reports 1969, 3, para 91.

Thus, a correction of the inequity identified by the Court, for example by means of the principle of the coastal front, which consists in drawing a straight baseline between the extreme points at either end of the coast of the State concerned, or a series of such lines, it might be argued, would encroach upon the natural prolongations of the territories of the adjacent States. This raises the fundamental question whether, if the natural prolongations of the territories of adjacent States intersect, one can actually speak of natural prolongations. It might be argued that, in this situation, none of those States could claim an original natural prolongation, which was to be delimited by means of the application of equitable principles. Might it not just as well be said that, in such a situation, the application of equitable principles would result in prolongations of the territories of the adjacent States, which would thereby, at the same time, be delimited? The Court had previously insisted that the delimitation of the continental shelf was not an issue of distributing shares in a pre-existing area.[62] Nevertheless, it also identified, as a factor to be taken account of, that delimitation according to equitable principles should result in a reasonable degree of proportionality between the extent of the continental shelf appertaining to the States concerned and the lengths of their respective coasts.[63]

Several of the dissenting Judges held that Article 6, para 2, of the Convention on the Continental Shelf, or the principle of equidistance, could be regarded as rules of customary international law. Judge Tanaka held the view that the principle of equidistance could be regarded as a rule of customary international law.[64] Judge Lachs considered that Article 6, para 2, and in particular the equidistance rule, had attained the status of generally accepted rules of international law.[65] Judge Sørensen held that Article 6, para 2, could be regarded as containing generally accepted rules of international law.[66]

As Judges Morelli and Sørensen observed, the view might also have been adopted that delimitation between opposite coasts and delimitation between adjacent coasts is not different.[67] If the Court had not dismissed that view, the practice of States could have been regarded as consistent and sufficiently general. However, the problem of identifying the subjective element would have remained. Judges Tanaka, Lachs and Sørensen all dispensed with the necessity of dealing with that element. To infer it from a practice of agreements providing for the method of equidistance is problematic, because it is by virtue of those agreements that the method of

---

62 *North Sea Continental Shelf Cases*, Judgment of 20 February 1969, ICJ Reports 1969, 3, paras 18–20.

63 *North Sea Continental Shelf Cases*, Judgment of 20 February 1969, ICJ Reports 1969, 3, para 98.

64 *North Sea Continental Shelf Cases*, Judgment of 20 February 1969, Dissenting Opinion Judge Tanaka, ICJ Reports 1969, 3, 174–179, 182.

65 *North Sea Continental Shelf Cases*, Judgment of 20 February 1969, Dissenting Opinion Judge Lachs, ICJ Reports 1969, 3, 225–232.

66 *North Sea Continental Shelf Cases*, Judgment of 20 February 1969, Dissenting Opinion Judge Sørensen, ICJ Reports 1969, 3, 247, 253.

67 *North Sea Continental Shelf Cases*, Judgment of 20 February 1969, Dissenting Opinion Judge Morelli, ICJ Reports 1969, 3, para 7; Dissenting Opinion Judge Sørensen, 250–252.

equidistance is regarded as obligatory; the point was to determine whether it would be binding in the absence of agreement.

In the course of its reasoning, the ICJ had denied the existence of a necessary connection between the concept of natural prolongation and the principle of equidistance, considering that the natural prolongation of the territory of a State may be closer to the territory of another State.[68] However, as Judges Tanaka and Morelli argued, the principle of equidistance may be regarded as intimately connected with the concept of the continental shelf.[69] If the natural prolongation of the territories of the adjacent States cannot be identified a priori, the argument that the application of the principle of equidistance results in the natural prolongations of the territories of those States, cannot easily be dismissed. Furthermore, from this perspective it is not easy to perceive why such a result would be inequitable.

Put together, the practice of States consisting of agreements concerning delimitations between opposite coasts on the basis of the principle of equidistance and agreements concerning delimitations between adjacent coasts on the basis of the principle of equidistance, as well as the close connection between the concept of the continental shelf and the principle of equidistance, might have been regarded as a strong indication of the principle and rules applicable to the delimitations at hand. Moreover, as Judge Tanaka argued, the assertion of a just and equitable share could not be substantiated.[70] In the circumstances, the assertion of a just and equitable share, put forward by the Federal Republic of Germany, merged with the element of consent required for the conclusion of agreements with the adjacent States.[71]

This points to a major problem in the solution arrived at by the Court: the connection which it identified, on the basis of rules of law, between equitable principles and agreement. For the essence of equitable principles would appear to be precisely that they operate independently of agreement. The Court thus adopted an approach fundamentally differing from its approach in the *Fisheries Case*. In the *Fisheries Case*, the Court, finding that delimitation always has an international aspect and should not be determined exclusively by the coastal State, tied the content of the principles and criteria to the assent of other States. In the *North Sea Continental Shelf Cases*, the Court discarded the applicability of the principle of equidistance and left the applicability of the principle of the coastal front to the consent of the coastal States involved.

The reformulated framework would, it is submitted, have thrown a different light on the situation at hand. From the perspective of the reformulated framework, the principles and rules identified by the Court would have been seen as elements informing the constituting of international society by the members of international society.

[68] *North Sea Continental Shelf Cases*, Judgment of 20 February 1969, ICJ Reports 1969, 3, paras 43–44.

[69] *North Sea Continental Shelf Cases*, Judgment of 20 February 1969, Dissenting Opinion Judge Tanaka, ICJ Reports 1969, 3, 179–181; Dissenting Opinion, Judge Morelli, paras 3–6.

[70] *North Sea Continental Shelf Cases*, Judgment of 20 February 1969, Dissenting Opinion Judge Tanaka, ICJ Reports 1969, 3, 187–191.

[71] Kennedy 1987, pp. 90–99.

They are, on the one hand, formed by the members of international society and, on the other hand, give form to the relationships between the members of international society. Fundamentally, their role, within the reformulated framework, of shaping the constituting of international society, replaces their role, within the framework of obligation, of delimiting freedom of action. From this perspective, all principles and rules involved, the principle of equidistance and the principle of the coastal front, as well as the 'natural' prolongation of the continental shelves and the just and equitable share, would have informed the process of constituting the international situation of the parties. That process of the constituting of international society may, in fact, be seen as a middle ground between a delimitation of natural prolongations which cannot pre-exist and a distribution of shares in a pre-existing area or, in other words, between the framework of obligation and the framework of authorization.

10.3.5 The Case Concerning Military and Paramilitary Activities in and Against Nicaragua (Merits)

In the *Case Concerning Military and Paramilitary Activities in and against Nicaragua (Merits)*, the ICJ departed from the premise that, for the purpose of the identification of a rule of customary international law, the practice of States and *opinio juris* should be considered.[72] With regard to the material element, the Court stated that it is not required that the practice of States be entirely consistent with the rule. According to the Court, it suffices if the practice of States is in general consistent with the rule and if instances of State conduct inconsistent with a given rule have generally been treated as breaches of that rule.[73]

Thereby, the ICJ discarded the conception that a rule of customary international law is derived from a pattern in the practice of States corresponding to *opinio juris*. In this conception, it is the role of the practice of States to determine the content of the rule to be derived from it. From this angle, it is impossible to derive a rule from an inconsistent practice of States. In the paragraphs referred to, the ICJ in fact presupposed the existence of a rule of customary international law. Only after the establishment of a rule of customary international law is it possible to determine whether the practice of States is in general consistent with the rule and whether the rule has been breached. Before the establishment of a rule of customary international law, those 'breaches' would appear to affect the perceived consistency of the practice so as to prevent the emergence of a rule of customary international law.[74]

---

[72] *Case Concerning Military and Paramilitary Activities in and against Nicaragua (Merits)*, Judgment of 27 June 1986, ICJ Reports 1986, 14, para 183.

[73] *Case Concerning Military and Paramilitary Activities in and against Nicaragua (Merits)*, Judgment of 27 June 1986, ICJ Reports 1986, 14, para 186.

[74] Charlesworth 1991, pp. 21–22.

This distortion of the material element may be illustrated with respect to the principle of non-use of force and the principle of non-intervention, which the Court identified in terms of customary international law. With respect to the principle of non-use of force, the ICJ presupposed the existence of a practice of abstention of the use of force by States[75] and dealt only with *opinio juris*.[76] With regard to the principle of non-intervention, the ICJ addressed the problem that the practice of States might be regarded as inconsistent in view of the existence of instances of foreign intervention for the benefit of forces opposed to the government of another State. Reverting to the framework of authorization—and inverting the relationship between law and politics—the Court considered that it had to examine whether a general right of States to intervene, directly or indirectly, with or without armed force, in support of an internal opposition in another State, had come into existence.[77] In this manner, the Court elliptically assumed that the principle of non-intervention already existed as customary international law[78] and that the envisaged practice of intervention could only be justified as a new general right or a new exception to the established principle of prohibition of intervention.[79] If it had followed the traditional conception, the existence of a practice of intervention might have rendered the practice of States as a whole inconsistent, thereby preventing the Court from identifying the principle of non-intervention as a matter of customary international law.[80]

Thus, notwithstanding the apparent centrality of the material element,[81] in the reasoning of the Court the traditional conception of the concept of customary international law, consisting of rules derived from a pattern in the practice of States corresponding to *opinio juris*, was suppressed. Concerned here with limitations of a freedom to use force and a freedom to intervene, the Court reduced the concept of customary international law to the subjective element, which it inferred mainly from the attitude of States towards General Assembly resolution 2625 (XXV).[82] According to the Court, the effect of consent to its text could be understood as an acceptance of the validity of the rule or set of rules

[75] Charlesworth 1991, pp. 18–19.

[76] *Case Concerning Military and Paramilitary Activities in and against Nicaragua (Merits)*, Judgment of 27 June 1986, ICJ Reports 1986, 14, paras 188–190.

[77] Charlesworth 1991, pp. 25–26.

[78] *Case Concerning Military and Paramilitary Activities in and against Nicaragua (Merits)*, Judgment of 27 June 1986, ICJ Reports 1986, 14, para 202.

[79] *Case Concerning Military and Paramilitary Activities in and against Nicaragua (Merits)*, Judgment of 27 June 1986, ICJ Reports 1986, 14, paras 206–209.

[80] Charlesworth 1991, pp. 19–21.

[81] *Case Concerning Military and Paramilitary Activities in and against Nicaragua (Merits)*, Judgment of 27 June 1986, ICJ Reports 1986, 14, para 186.

[82] Charlesworth 1991, pp. 23–24.

declared therein.[83] The difficulty with this approach is that consent to the text of the Declaration must then be based on the presumption that it is binding. Within the framework of obligation, consent does not itself endow an instrument with a binding character, but attaches to an instrument which is already regarded as having a binding character. The binding character of the Declaration is therefore presupposed. In para 70 of *Legality of the Threat or Use of Nuclear Weapons*, the Court modified its approach by noting that General Assembly resolutions, even if they are not binding, may sometimes have normative value. They can, according to the Court, in certain circumstances, provide evidence important for establishing the existence of a rule or the emergence of an *opinio juris*. To establish whether this is true of a given General Assembly resolution, it is necessary to look at its content and the conditions of its adoption; it is also necessary to see whether an *opinio juris* exists as to its normative character. Or, according to the Court, a series of resolutions may show the gradual evolution of the *opinio juris* required for the establishment of a new rule. According to the terms of this passage, General Assembly resolutions may be seen in a double light: while not binding, they may assist in establishing a rule or *opinio juris*. But in order to do this, their content and conditions of adoption must be examined and the existence of an *opinio juris* as to their normative character must also be established. This implies, it would appear, the necessity of referring to a further criterion so as to determine that such resolutions correspond to *opinio juris* held by the members of international society.[84] Under those conditions, such General Assembly resolutions would merely have accessory value and the existence of both the subjective and the objective element would still need to be established.

Doctrine would seem to confirm this inference. Zemanek, for example, attaches significance to the Friendly Relations Declaration as expressing *opinio juris*, but still requires that the subjective element be 'confirmed' in the practice of States.[85] Elsewhere, Zemanek described resolutions as expressing a consensus on principles, which still requires to be further implemented by means of specific rules of customary international law or conventional international law.[86] Even if the stronger view is followed, it would remain that the test whether a rule of customary international law has been formed by a resolution refers to the existence of both the subjective and the objective elements in the practice of States. A similar approach has been adopted by Sloan, who has answered the question whether General Assembly resolutions have become or may become a source of international law or, in other words, whether the General Assembly has attained or may

---

[83] *Case Concerning Military and Paramilitary Activities in and against Nicaragua (Merits)*, Judgment of 27 June 1986, ICJ Reports 1986, 14, paras 188, 203; Separate Opinion Judge Ago, para 7.

Weil 1992, pp. 172–179; Tomuschat 1999, Chap. V, para 4, Chap. VI, paras 5, 38, Chap. IX, para 41.

[84] Dinstein 2006, paras 83–91.

[85] Zemanek 1997, paras 53–55. A similar view is expressed by Dinstein 2006, paras 92–94.

[86] Zemanek 1997, paras 179, 259, 315.

attain a legislative or quasi-legislative role for the international community of States, by reference to the sources of international law.[87]

It may thus be observed that, from the point of view of the framework of obligation and from the point of view of its own premise that a rule of customary international law consists of both the material and the subjective element, the reasoning of the ICJ in the *Case Concerning Military and Paramilitary Activities in and against Nicaragua (Merits)* is problematic. It is explicable, however, by the fact that, within the framework of obligation, rules of customary international law cannot come into being against the development of the practice of States. Moreover, within the framework of obligation, there is no requirement that the development of the practice of States be directed at the common good of international society. If States consistently use force in international relations and intervene in their internal and external affairs, this would constitute the practice of States from which, if coupled with *opinio juris*, a rule of customary international law might be derived. Such a consistent practice certainly could not give rise to a rule of customary international law in the opposite direction, prohibiting the use of force and intervention. Against this background and in view of its reliance on the concept of customary international law, the ICJ could only identify a fundamental principle outlawing the use of force in international relations, the existence of which it had already accepted, by assuming *opinio juris* and discarding the objective element. In this way, the *Case Concerning Military and Paramilitary Activities in and against Nicaragua (Merits)* makes clear that, in order to arrive, within the context of the framework of obligation, at rules of customary international law oriented towards the common good of international society, the practice of States must, to some extent, be ignored. To the same extent, however, that step implies a transfer of power from the members of international society to political organs of international institutions in conjunction with the judicial function.

Resituated within the reformulated framework, the practice of States would lose its dual role of producing restrictive rules of customary international law and reflecting the freedom of States to act. Resituated within the reformulated framework, the practice of States emanates from the power of States to act so as to constitute (the common good of) international society. Within the reformulated framework, the practice of States is not directed at the freedom of States to act, but at the constituting of international society and the formation of the common good of international society. On the basis of the power to act of the members of international society so as to constitute (the common good of) international society, the element of *opinio juris*, whether held by States or contained in resolutions of (organs of) international institutions, is replaced by the process of practical reasoning about the constituting of (the common good of) international society. Because within the reformulated framework the concept of public international law is inherent in international society, there is no need to identify an element additional to the practice of States. At the same time, this constellation does not exclude a political

[87] Sloan 1987, pp. 95–105.

perspective, which may inform the formation of the common good of international society. That political perspective remains possible because, in comparison with the framework of obligation, the reformulated framework projects the concept of public international law in more flexible terms, operating in conjunction with the perspective of international politics.

10.3.6 The Case Concerning the Arrest Warrant of 11 April 2000

In the *Case Concerning the Arrest Warrant of 11 April 2000*, a dispute between the Democratic Republic of the Congo and Belgium was brought unilaterally before the Court by the Democratic Republic of the Congo. The Democratic Republic of the Congo contended that the issuance, by an investigating judge of a Belgian court, of an arrest warrant, in respect of war crimes and crimes against humanity, relating to the acting Minister of Foreign Affairs of the Democratic Republic of the Congo, Mr. Abdulaye Yerodia Ndombasi, and its international circulation, violated the rule of customary international law concerning the absolute inviolability and immunity from criminal process of incumbent foreign ministers.

In its reasoning with regard to that contention, the ICJ placed itself within the framework of customary international law. According to the Court, the extent of the immunities granted to Ministers for Foreign Affairs was dependent on the functions exercised by them.[88] After describing those functions, the Court immediately concluded that a Minister for Foreign Affairs, throughout the duration of his or her office, when abroad, enjoys full immunity from criminal jurisdiction and inviolability. The Court elaborated that this immunity and that inviolability protect the individual concerned against any act of authority of another State which would hinder him or her in the performance of his or her duties.[89]

It may be observed that, in this reasoning, although the Court indicated that it needed to consider the nature of the functions exercised by a Minister for Foreign Affairs in order to determine the extent of immunities accorded to Ministers for Foreign Affairs, the Court drew its conclusion with regard to the issue of immunity on the basis of its description of the functions of a Minister for Foreign Affairs. It did

[88] *Case Concerning the Arrest Warrant of 11 April 2000*, Judgment of 14 February 2002, ICJ Reports 2002, 3, paras 52–53: 'It is (…) on the basis of customary international law that the Court must decide the questions relating to the immunities of such Ministers raised in the present case. In customary international law, the immunities accorded to Ministers for Foreign Affairs are not granted for their personal benefit, but to ensure the effective performance of their functions on behalf of their respective States. In order to determine the extent of these immunities, the Court must therefore first consider the nature of the functions exercised by a Minister for Foreign Affairs.'

[89] *Case Concerning the Arrest Warrant of 11 April 2000*, Judgment of 14 February 2002, ICJ Reports 2002, 3, para 54.

not explain the connection between the extent of those immunities and the functions of a Minister for Foreign Affairs. It seemed to assume that the extent of those immunities flows automatically from the functions of a Minister for Foreign Affairs. It may also be observed that, although the ICJ put this reasoning in the context of the concept of customary international law, it did not refer either to the practice of States or to *opinio juris*.[90] Nevertheless, the decision of the Court with regard to the issue of immunity was broadly supported.[91] Only Judges Al-Khasawneh[92] and Van den Wyngaert[93] considered that the immunity of a Minister for Foreign Affairs does not extend to the case of war crimes or crimes against humanity.

Originally, the Democratic Republic of the Congo had also contended that the assumption of universal jurisdiction by the Belgian court was contrary to public international law. Subsequently, the Democratic Republic of the Congo abandoned this claim, prompting Belgium to invoke the *non ultra petita* rule. Thereby, the Court was prevented from dealing with the issue of universal jurisdiction.[94] Nonetheless, several judges addressed this question in their individual opinions.

In this connection, Judges Higgins, Kooijmans, Buergenthal and Van den Wyngaert adopted solutions on the basis of the reasoning followed in the *Case of the S.S. "Lotus"*. Judges Higgins, Kooijmans and Buergenthal took the view that international law does not prohibit the assumption of universal jurisdiction *in absentia*.[95] Similarly, Judge Van den Wyngaert considered that international law does not prohibit and permits the assumption of universal jurisdiction for war crimes and crimes against humanity.[96] Following the reasoning in the *Case of the S.S. "Lotus"*, these conclusions result if a rule of public international law prohibiting the assumption of universal jurisdiction with respect to certain crimes or in certain circumstances cannot be identified. It may, however, be observed that these conclusions seem to authorize the judicial intervention of a State in the 'internal' affairs of another State. Such a freedom to assume universal jurisdiction, inferred from the concept of sovereignty, would seem inconsistent with the

---

90 *Case Concerning the Arrest Warrant of 11 April 2000*, Judgment of 14 February 2002, Dissenting Opinion Judge Van den Wyngaert, ICJ Reports 2002, 3, paras 11–23.
Kamto 2002, pp. 519–523; Salmon 2002, pp. 513; Sands 2002, pp. 541; Schultz 2002, pp. 736.

91 *Case Concerning the Arrest Warrant of 11 April 2000*, Judgment of 14 February 2002, Separate Opinion Judge Koroma, ICJ Reports 2002, 3, para 5; Joint Separate Opinion Judges Higgins, Kooijmans and Buergenthal, para 83; Separate Opinion Judge Rezek, para 10; Separate Opinion Judge Bula Bula, paras 41, 48.

92 *Case Concerning the Arrest Warrant of 11 April 2000*, Judgment of 14 February 2002, Dissenting Opinion Judge Al-Khasawneh, ICJ Reports 2002, 3, para 8.

93 *Case Concerning the Arrest Warrant of 11 April 2000*, Judgment of 14 February 2002, Dissenting Opinion Judge Van den Wyngaert, ICJ Reports 2002, 3, para 10.

94 *Case Concerning the Arrest Warrant of 11 April 2000*, Judgment of 14 February 2002, ICJ Reports 2002, 3, paras 41–43.

95 *Case Concerning the Arrest Warrant of 11 April 2000*, Judgment of 14 February 2002, Joint Separate Opinion Judges Higgins, Kooijmans and Buergenthal, ICJ Reports 2002, 3, paras 53–58.

96 *Case Concerning the Arrest Warrant of 11 April 2000*, Judgment of 14 February 2002, Dissenting Opinion Judge Van den Wyngaert, ICJ Reports 2002, 3, paras 48–62.

freedom to act of the Democratic Republic of the Congo, similarly inferred from the concept of sovereignty. Put in this way, the question of universal jurisdiction in respect of war crimes and crimes against humanity suggests an inherent tension between respect for the principle of sovereign equality and the repression of war crimes and crimes against humanity.

With regard to the question of universal jurisdiction, President Guillaume followed a different type of reasoning. He considered that a right to assume universal jurisdiction could not be inferred from a development in conventional international law establishing the principle *aut dedere aut judicare*, which presupposes the presence of the person accused on the territory of the State concerned.[97] In the pertinent conventional international criminal law, the principle *aut dedere aut* judicare, it may be observed, is formulated as an obligation. If the reasoning of the *Case of the S.S. "Lotus"* is followed, this narrower obligation does not restrict the freedom of States to assume a wider jurisdiction. President Guillaume in fact reasoned on the basis that the pertinent conventional international criminal law should be read as containing a narrower authorization to assume universal jurisdiction in the circumstances triggering the principle *aut dedere aut judicare*, but not *in absentia*.

Judge Ranjeva focused on the principle of territoriality and considered that universal jurisdiction *in absentia* is inconsistent with international law, because the exercise of jurisdiction must have some connection with the territory concerned.[98] A similar position was adopted by Judge Rezek, who considered that international law does not allow the assertion of jurisdiction by a State having no particular connection with crimes under public international law.[99] The positions adopted by Judges Guillaume, Ranjeva and Rezek recognize that in the field of universal jurisdiction with respect to war crimes and crimes against humanity, relying on an inherent assumption of a freedom of States to act amounts to interference inconsistent with the principle of sovereign equality and requires something approaching an authorization from public international law. However, relying on rules of public international law to identify such an authorization involves relying on the incoherence of the framework of authorization and affects detrimentally the repression of war crimes and crimes against humanity. If, however, the framework of obligation is rejected, it also follows that the State represented by the Foreign Minister accused of war crimes and crimes against humanity, cannot derive

---

97 *Case Concerning the Arrest Warrant of 11 April 2000*, Judgment of 14 February 2002, Separate Opinion President Guillaume, ICJ Reports 2002, 3, paras 16–17.

98 *Case Concerning the Arrest Warrant of 11 April 2000*, Judgment of 14 February 2002, Declaration Judge Ranjeva, ICJ Reports 2002, 3, para 9: 'Territoriality as the basis of entitlement to jurisdiction remains a given, the core of contemporary positive international law.'

99 *Case Concerning the Arrest Warrant of 11 April 2000*, Judgment of 14 February 2002, Separate Opinion Judge Rezek, ICJ Reports 2002, 3, para 6: 'In no way does international law as it now stands allow for activist intervention, whereby a State seeks out on another State's territory, by means of an extradition request or an international arrest warrant, an individual accused of crimes under public international law but having *no factual connection with the forum State*.'

exclusive jurisdiction with respect to those war crimes and crimes against humanity from its freedom to act. Within the reformulated framework, there is no place for such an unlimited freedom to act.

In the *Case Concerning the Arrest Warrant of 11 April 2000*, the ICJ was concerned to identify a restriction of a freedom to exercise authority with respect to a representative of another State.[100] The Court located this restriction in a rule of customary international law without, however, deriving this rule from a practice of States corresponding to *opinio juris*. While the Court relied on the existence of a rule of customary international law, it seems that it effectively inferred the immunity from the concept of sovereignty itself. Had the issue remained before the Court, it would have been consistent to infer in a similar manner a right to assume universal jurisdiction in respect of war crimes and crime against humanity from the concept of sovereignty. If the situation at issue were transposed to the reformulated framework, both the right to assume universal jurisdiction and the immunity would be transformed into a power to act so as to constitute the common good of international society. Specifically, within that context, neither the institution of the State nor its representation can be understood in terms of exclusive jurisdiction in respect of war crimes or crimes against humanity.

10.3.7 The Concept of Customary International Law Resituated Within the Reformulated Framework

The final part of this section will elaborate how reasoning with respect to the concept of customary international law may be resituated within the reformulated framework. This is done with respect to the field of maritime delimitation and this discussion therefore seeks to develop further the points made above in connexion with the *Fisheries Case* and the *North Sea Continental Shelf Cases*.

Within the reformulated framework, no clear distinction can or has to be made between the concepts of justice and equity, on the one hand, and the concept of law, on the other hand. According to international jurisprudence, the main principle of customary international law relating to maritime delimitation is that it should be the reflection of an equitable solution.[101] The Court of Arbitration in the *Case Concerning the Delimitation of the Continental Shelf between the United Kingdom of Great Britain and Northern Ireland, and the French Republic* situated the combined equidistance/special circumstances rule, contained in Article 6 of the Convention on the Continental Shelf, within the context of equitable principles, so that both conventional international law and customary international law can be regarded as aiming at achieving an equitable solution pursuant to equitable

---

[100] Mahiou 2008, pp. 172–176.

[101] *Case Concerning the Continental Shelf*, Judgment of 24 February 1982, ICJ Reports 1982, 18, para 70.

principles.[102] This view has subsequently been endorsed by the ICJ in its Judgment in the *Case Concerning Maritime Delimitation in the Area between Greenland and Jan Mayen.*[103]

To be sure, there are some possible nuances as regards the relationship between Article 6 of the Convention on the Continental Shelf and customary international law. The Court of Arbitration has amalgamated them completely, regarding the equidistance/special circumstances rule as a single rule. In this light, it considered that the question whether special circumstances exist must be determined as a matter of law *proprio motu* by a tribunal, so that a burden of proof did not seem appropriate.[104] In contrast, in his Separate Opinion in the *Case Concerning Maritime Delimitation in the Area between Greenland and Jan Mayen*, Judge Shahabuddeen insisted that Article 6 of the Convention on the Continental Shelf consists of equidistance as the rule and special circumstances as an exception.[105]

For present purposes, it is important to remark that in the *North Sea Continental Shelf Cases*, the ICJ has insisted on the fact that the process of maritime delimitation is not a matter of apportioning shares in a previously undelimited area.[106] In the *Case Concerning the Continental Shelf*, the Court similarly remarked that maritime delimitation by means of equitable principles is not an operation of distributive justice.[107] The rejection of these perspectives may be inspired by the objections that can be levelled against the framework of authorization. If maritime delimitation were a matter of distributing shares in a previously undelimited area, the jurisdiction of the Court would have to be regarded in terms of property of this area and the transfer of parts thereof to the States concerned. The property of the Court in relation to this area would seem inexplicable in international legal terms.

In the *North Sea Continental Shelf Cases*, the Court rather opted for the view that the continental shelf is a natural prolongation of the territory of the State.[108] This approach is reminiscent of the framework of obligation. Like the assumption of a

---

[102] *Case Concerning the Delimitation of the Continental Shelf between the United Kingdom of Great Britain and Northern Ireland, and the French Republic*, Arbitral Award of 30 June 1977, XVIII Reports of International Arbitral Awards, 3-413, para 70.

[103] *Case Concerning Maritime Delimitation in the Area between Greenland and Jan Mayen*, Judgment of 14 June 1993, ICJ Reports 1993, 38, paras 46–48; Separate Opinion Judge Ajibola, 292–303.

Tanaka 2008, pp. 913–924.

[104] *Case Concerning the Delimitation of the Continental Shelf between the United Kingdom of Great Britain and Northern Ireland, and the French Republic*, Arbitral Award of 30 June 1977, XVIII Reports of International Arbitral Awards, 3-413, para 68.

[105] *Case Concerning Maritime Delimitation in the Area between Greenland and Jan Mayen*, Judgment of 14 June 1993, Separate Opinion Judge Shahabuddeen, ICJ Reports 1993, 38, 138–144.

[106] *North Sea Continental Shelf Cases*, Judgment of 20 February 1969, ICJ Reports 1969, 3, paras 18–20.

[107] *Case Concerning the Continental Shelf*, Judgment of 24 February 1982, ICJ Reports 1982, 18, para 71.

[108] *North Sea Continental Shelf Cases*, Judgment of 20 February 1969, ICJ Reports 1969, 3, para 19.

freedom of States to act, the view that the continental shelf constitutes the natural prolongation of the territory of a State becomes meaningless if these natural prolongations intersect and encroach upon one another. In that case, one cannot speak of the natural prolongations of the territories of the States concerned, precisely because in the overlapping area the presumed natural prolongations cancel each other out and disappear. Therefore, it might be said that, to some extent, this overlapping area acquires the characteristic of a previously undelimited area. To that qualification, the caveat must be added that this area may be seen as the joint property of the States concerned and does not fall as such within the jurisdiction of the Court. It follows that with the disappearance of those natural prolongations, we can no longer refer to the process involved in terms of delimitation.

It would appear that the ICJ may have sought to build a bridge between the framework of authorization and the framework of obligation, when, in its Judgment in *Maritime Delimitation in the Black Sea*, expounding its three-stage delimitation methodology,[109] it adhered to the 'magical formula' that the sharing out of the area is the consequence of the delimitation, not vice versa.[110] This formula may be characterized as magical, because it acknowledges that, after all, the process of maritime delimitation does involve an element of sharing. This element of sharing cannot, however, be the result of the delimitation, because delimitation involves limiting the natural prolongation of the territory of a State, which is assumed to belong already to that State, and would otherwise extend further. This excludes any element of sharing.

It is submitted that, when resituated within the reformulated framework, the elements of this magical formula can be explained in coherent terms. The States involved may be regarded as having a power to act in respect of the overlapping area. That power to act must be directed at the constituting of international society and of the common good of international society in the form of an equitable solution. That solution may consist, for example, in joint exploration and exploitation. The States involved may also exercise their power to act in the form of step by step cooperation along the lines of the *modus vivendi* at issue in the *Case Concerning the Continental Shelf.* It may also happen that the States involved are unable to overcome their dilemma situation. In that event, they may have recourse to the arbitral or judicial function; the role of that function is not to delimit, but to bring an additional perspective to the constituting of international society by the States involved. From that perspective, alternative equitable solutions, reflecting equitable principles, may be proposed and considered.

These proposed equitable solutions, reflecting equitable principles, cannot, within the reformulated framework, be imposed on the parties, but inscribe themselves within the constituting of international society by the members of

---

109 *Maritime Delimitation in the Black Sea*, Judgment of 3 February 2009, ICJ Reports 2009, 61, paras 115–122.

110 *Maritime Delimitation in the Black Sea*, Judgment of 3 February 2009, ICJ Reports 2009, 61, para 122; *Case Concerning Maritime Delimitation in the Area between Greenland and Jan Mayen*, Judgment of 14 June 1993, ICJ Reports 1993, 38, para 64.

international society. On the other hand, the members of international society cannot simply reject them by resorting to their freedom to act, because, within the reformulated framework, rejection leads back to the initial dilemma situation. From these perspectives, the delimitations arrived at, for example, in the *Case Concerning Maritime Delimitation in the Area between Greenland and Jan Mayen* and in the *Case Concerning the Delimitation of the Maritime Boundary between Guinea and Guinea Bissau*, may be seen as a possible equitable delimitation, informing the constituting of international society by the members of international society, which may be adopted by the parties pursuant to the process of practical reasoning. Alternatives to that possible equitable delimitation must likewise be guided by the process of practical reasoning. This process is neither exclusively a question of sharing nor exclusively a question of delimiting. The constituting of (the common good of) international society does not presuppose the existence of a common good, given ab extra, which can be shared by the members of international society, nor the pre-existence of competing 'natural' prolongations which can be delimited from each other. By the exercise of their power to act, the members of international society overcome their dilemma situation and constitute the area in question, which simultaneously involves an element of sharing and an element of delimitation.

10.4 Conclusion

On the basis of the preceding analysis, it is submitted that, if situated within the framework of obligation, it is not possible to infer coherently rules of customary international law from patterns in the practice of States which restrict the freedom of States to act. Even if a pattern can be identified in the practice of States, that pattern must at the same time be regarded as emanating from an exercise of the freedom of States to act. Turning to the apex of the framework of obligation, explaining the binding character of the concept of customary international law by reference to a basic norm of customary international law results in infinite regress.[111]

By suppressing the mutual exclusivity formed by the framework of obligation and the framework of authorization, the concept of customary international law may be resituated within the reformulated framework, projecting the practice of States in terms of the constituting of international society. This constituting of international society is done by acts based on a power to act in the form of the constituting of international society. Because the members of international society have such a power to act, rather than an unlimited freedom to act, they are situated in a dilemma situation, which requires that, in order to constitute international society, they must resort to a process of practical reasoning. As argued in the context of the analysis of the *Case Concerning Military and Paramilitary*

[111] Weil 1992, pp. 163–164; Dinstein 2006, para 67.

Activities in and against Nicaragua (Merits), this aspect ensures that the constituting of international society by the members of international society is directed at the common good of international society, without transferring power from the members of international society to (organs of) international institutions.

The analysis carried out in the context of the *Fisheries Case* demonstrated how, within the reformulated framework, a connection can be established between principles and rules, on the one hand, and the acts of the members of international society, on the other hand. The principles and rules in question cannot be regarded as pre-existent and must be related, to some extent, to the acts of the members of international society. They apply to an international situation which involves the members of international society and reflect the constituting of international society by the members of international society pursuant to their power to act. Both the acts of the delimiting State and the acts of the other States must be seen as contributing in this regard. Thereby, the principles and rules in question may be regarded as constituting a structure giving form to their international relationship. These principles and rules need not be fully determinate, because their role is not the delimitation of, for example, natural prolongations. The analysis carried out with respect to the *North Sea Continental Shelf Cases* confirmed that the basis of international society should not be seen in terms of the notion of agreement, because this would resituate international society within the framework of obligation and make the constituting of international society, in the form of equitable principles, dependent on the freedom to act of a member of international society. Nor does it seem coherent, as happened in the *North Sea Continental Shelf Cases*, to exclude certain considerations of justice or equity a priori. It follows, paradoxically, that, because they inform the constituting of international society by the members of international society, those rules and principles must to some extent be seen as inherent and to some extent as at the disposal of the members of international society.

How the transition from the framework of obligation to the reformulated framework resituates the concept of customary international law may, in conclusion, synoptically be described as follows. As situated within the framework of obligation, the concept of customary international law directs us to see the practice of States, whether it gives rise to a pattern or not, in non-legal, exclusively political terms. Within the terms set by the framework of obligation, that practice does not succeed in effecting the transition from practice to law. Conversely, if the concept of customary international law is reduced to the element of *opinio juris*, deduced from acts of organs of international institutions, it is seen in exclusively legal terms, detached from a political basis in the acts of the members of international society. The reformulated framework directs these divergent movements so as to converge on the middle ground, the constituting of (the common good of) international society. Within the reformulated framework, the acts of the members of international society, forming their practice, must *ab initio* be regarded as having both a political and a legal quality. There is, accordingly, no need for a later transition from a political to a legal sphere. At the same time, by envisaging the reconstituting of international society as inherent in the constituting of international society, the reformulated framework incorporates within itself the dilemma between stability and change.

Chapter 11
Conclusion to Part II

Part II has sought to analyze the traditional sources of public international law—general principles of law, conventional international law, and customary international law—from the perspective of the mutual exclusivity of the framework of obligation and the framework of authorization. Relying on the incoherence arising from the vertical structure of the concept of law underlying the concept of public international law, the argument has subsequently resituated the traditional sources of public international law within the reformulated framework developed in Part I.

Traditionally, the concept of general principles of law is regarded as a supplementary source of public international law, to which the judicial function may have recourse in order to fill gaps left by conventional international law and customary international law. In view of its relationship with the internal law of the State, the concept of general principles of law gives rise to the domestic analogy in the form of the transposition of general principles of private law and/or general principles of public law to the field of public international law. In this connection, it has been argued that even the transposition of general principles of private law involves the transposition of a public element, because, while applying to relations between individuals, general principles of private law are a part of public law. Fundamentally, the concept of general principles of law gives rise to a competition between the principle of good faith, on the one hand, and the assumption of a freedom of States to act, on the other hand or, as Lauterpacht formulated it, between the material and the formal completeness of the law. Within the framework of obligation, it is impossible to resolve this dilemma, the material completeness involving an exercise of judicial discretion and the formal completeness being internally inconsistent. This dilemma may be overcome, it was submitted, by rejecting the mutual exclusivity of the framework of obligation and the framework of authorization in transition to a reformulated framework, which combines the framework of obligation and the framework of authorization. In this reformulated framework, the function of rules of public international law is regarded as both enabling and restricting, corresponding to the power to act of the members of

J. A. Vos, *The Function of Public International Law*,
DOI: 10.1007/978-90-6704-861-3_11, © J. A. Vos, The Netherlands 2013

international society, which is distinguished from an unlimited freedom to act. In this manner, the dilemma posed by the concept of general principles of law is superseded by the reformulated framework. The *Corfu Channel Case (Merits)* has been put forward as affording an example of how the transition from the framework of obligation to the reformulated framework might bear on the practice of States. Within the framework of obligation, principles of humanity had to be resorted to in order to curb an undesirable freedom to act in the form of laying mines, regardless of whether the other party had a right of innocent passage. Within the reformulated framework, neither party can enforce a right, because it does not constitute an element of that structure. The reformulated framework propels the members of international society towards the constituting of the (common good of) international society. In its wake, this transition effaces the traditional distinction between the law of peace and the law of war.

As one of the main sources of public international law, the concept of conventional international law, consisting of text reflecting the common intentions of the parties, seems straightforward. However, while situated within the framework of obligation, the concept of conventional international law is problematic. Its axiomatic principle or rule that rules of conventional international law are binding—*pacta sunt servanda*—remains a matter of assumption. Furthermore, rules of conventional international law must at the same time be seen as both restricting the freedom of States to act and reflecting the exercise of that freedom to act. Resituated within the reformulated framework, the concept of conventional international law retains—in the form of text—its central place. Transiting to the reformulated framework, however, transforms the function of conventional international law into the constituting—in the form of textual principles and rules—of international society. Within the reformulated framework, principles and rules of conventional international law have both an enabling and a disabling aspect, which correspond to the power to act of the members of international society. On the basis of their power to act, the members of international society constitute (the common good of) international society in the form of principles and rules of conventional international law. In this way, the concept of conventional international law channels the activities of the members of international society, because they do not dispose of an unlimited freedom to act. Reforming a structure of conventional international law requires a process of practical reasoning so as to reconstitute international society. *Diversion of Water from the Meuse* has been put forward as affording a first example of how the transition from the framework of obligation to the reformulated framework might bear on the practice of States. Within the framework of obligation, rules of conventional international law are subject to a process of minimization, the existence of any gray areas translating into the residual freedom to act of States, so that the constituting of international society by the members of international society takes place outside the structure of conventional international law. Within the reformulated framework, the existence of any gray areas simply means that, to that extent, international society has not been constituted by the members of international society and that it remains for the members of international society to constitute, to that extent, international society.

The *Case Concerning the Gabčikovo-Nagymaros Project* has been put forward as affording a second example of how the transition from the framework of obligation to the reformulated framework might bear on the practice of States. Within the framework of obligation, the judicial function may uphold a structure of conventional international law, even though both parties to a bilateral treaty have diverted from it. To accommodate such a situation, the judicial function must simultaneously uphold and relax the principle/rule of *pacta sunt servanda*. The reformulated framework includes within itself both a degree of rigidity necessary to maintain a structure and a degree of flexibility necessary to reform it.

While situated within the framework of obligation, the concept of customary international law is problematic, because a pattern in the practice of States must be regarded simultaneously as restricting the freedom of States to act and as representing an exercise of the freedom of States to act. In so far as an exercise of the freedom of States to act necessarily includes political considerations, *opinio juris*, understood as excluding political considerations, cannot be identified. Resituated within the reformulated framework, the practice of States retains its central place. Transiting to the reformulated framework transforms the function of customary international law. Within the reformulated framework, the practice of States is understood as the constituting of international society, containing both an enabling and a disabling aspect. These aspects flow from the reformulated framework itself, which locates the concept of public international law as inherent in international society, directing the practice of States at the constituting of (the common good of) international society. The *Fisheries Case* has been put forward as affording an example of how the transition from the framework of obligation to the reformulated framework might bear on the practice of States. The ICJ realized that a three-fold connection had to be established between the principles and rules inferred from the nature of the territorial sea, the role of the delimiting State, and the roles of the other States. Within the framework of obligation, that connection could not be established coherently. Within the reformulated framework, those principles and rules are regarded as a structure reflecting the constituting of international society and addressing the international situation formed by the transition from the territorial sea to the high seas. As members of international society, the delimiting State and the other States participate, on the basis of their power to act, in the constituting of international society in the form of this structure. The reformulated framework thus entails a reciprocal relationship between structures of public international law and the members of international society.

Part III
Mutual Exclusivity and the Dichotomy Between Institutions and Community

Chapter 12
Introduction to Part III

It has been attempted to show in Part II how the vertical structure of the concept of law underlying the concept of public international law, in the form of the framework of obligation or the framework of authorization, distorts the sources of public international law: general principles of law, conventional international law, and customary international law. The discussion about the function of general principles of law resulted in the presentation of a choice between resort to general principles of law and reliance on the assumption of a freedom of States to act—between the material and the formal completeness of public international law—without, however, it being possible to indicate how to make such a choice. Resorting to a general principle of law involves the consequential problem that the assumption of a freedom of States to act creates a movement towards the identification and application of principles or rules by the judicial function, but that, at the same time, the fact that these principles and rules are not derivable from the free will of States leaves the judicial function without a basis in international society. It was submitted that the incoherence of the framework of obligation impels a movement to a reformulated framework.

It was argued that the situation of the concept of conventional international law within the framework of obligation partakes of this incoherence. Within the framework of obligation, the rule *pacta sunt servanda* ultimately remains a matter of assumption and the position that rules of conventional international law must both emanate from States as exercises of their freedom to act and restrict the freedom to act of States as subjects of conventional international law, excludes the possibility of identifying imposable rules of conventional international law which emanate from the freedom to act of States. The identification of such rules of conventional international law involves, in other words, privileging the view of States as subjects of conventional international law over the view of States as legislators of conventional international law.

Similarly, it was submitted that the concept of customary international law is distorted by the fact that the practice of States must at the same time be regarded as

J. A. Vos, *The Function of Public International Law*,
DOI: 10.1007/978-90-6704-861-3_12,

emanating from the freedom of States to act and as restricting the freedom of States to act in so far as the objective and subjective elements are present. Ultimately, this position involves identifying a rule of customary international law derived from the practice of States which must also be regarded as an exercise of the freedom of States to act and which cannot, therefore, contain, at the same time and exclusively, the subjective element.

It was submitted that, whereas the concept of general principles of law leads, more or less, automatically to the question of the function of public international law, the concepts of conventional international law and customary international law are adaptable to the reformulated framework described in Part I. Within this reformulated framework, the function of public international law is regarded as coterminous with the constituting of international society in the form of elements that are at the same time enabling and restricting. This corresponds to the initial situation of the members of international society as having a power to act, which is not an unlimited freedom to act. Because within the reformulated framework the concept of public international law is inherent in international society, there is no transition from a non-legal, or political, situation to a legal situation. At the same time, the constituting of international society by the members of international society is directed at the common good of international society. Conventional international law may be regarded as giving rise to part-structures, containing both principles and rules for particular areas.

In addition to the traditional main sources of public international law, Part III situates two essential features of the concept of public international law, the concept of international institution and the concept of international community, within the dichotomy formed by the framework of obligation and the framework of authorization. These features follow the common distinction between an 'organized' international community and an 'unorganized' international community. The concept of international institution may be said to have emerged out of an unorganized international community. At the same time, this unorganized international community remains important and complementary because of the (inherent?) 'deficiencies' of international institutions. At the same time, when analyzed from the perspective of the mutual exclusivity of the framework of obligation and the framework of authorization, both may be seen as incoherent. It will be argued that both the concept of international institution and the concept of international community may coherently be resituated within the reformulated framework derived from the incoherence of the mutual exclusivity of the framework of obligation and the framework of authorization. Resituated within the reformulated framework, both the concept of international institution and the concept of international community, transformed, for terminological purposes, into the concept of international society, may be seen as forming an integral part of the function of public international law understood as the constituting of (the common good of) international society. Within the reformulated framework, the constituting of international society by the members of international society takes place on the basis of their dilemma situation of having a power, but not a freedom to act. From that starting point, the constituting of international society takes the form of rules of public international law which, at the same time, constitute the members of international society as members of international society. The constituting of international society may take the form of rules of conventional international law and, in so far as it assumes a more permanent character, the form of international institutions. Organs of international institutions may be seen as managing the common good of international society entrusted to them. The question whether their management of the common good of international society conforms to the constituting of international society as envisaged by the members of international society is itself a question of the constituting of international society, reflecting the dialectical relationship between international institutions and international society. Rather than seeing the concept of international institution and the concept of international community as reciprocal remedies for deficiencies, the reformulated framework situates international institutions and international society as complementary elements of the constituting of international society.

Chapter 13
The Concept of International Institution Situated Within the Framework of Obligation and the Framework of Authorization

13.1 Introduction

The theory of law developed by Finnis formulates a circular relationship between rules and institutions in the sense that rules determine institutions which, in turn, determine rules. When situated within the framework of obligation, this circular relationship between rules and institutions is problematic, because the hierarchical, vertical structure of which the framework of obligation partakes, only allows unidirectional causality; if, on a higher level, rules determine institutions, it cannot simultaneously be admitted that institutions determine rules, unless these rules are situated at a lower level than the institution. In that hypothesis, however, a differentiation is made between higher level and lower level rules. When situated within the reformulated framework, this circular relationship between rules and institutions does not present a problem because, from that perspective, both rules and institutions are regarded as elements of the constituting of international society by the members of international society. Within the reformulated framework, the constituting of international society by the members of international society is seen in the first instance as giving rise to rules of public international law, which, since they address the dilemma situation of the members of international society of having a power to act, are both enabling and disabling. To the extent that the constituting of international society by the members of international society acquires a more durable form, these rules of public international law may transform into international institutions. From this angle, international institutions may be said to participate in the constituting of international society by the members of international society in the form of producing rules of public international law. These rules of public international law may be said to represent the common good of international society.

As situated within the framework of obligation, the concept of international institution may appear to demonstrate the proposition that rules give rise to institutions which, in turn, give rise to rules. It must be pointed out, however, that

DOI: 10.1007/978-90-6704-861-3_13,

the concept of international institution in a sense manifests the apex of the domestic analogy.[1] Following the example of individuals having proceeded, from the state of nature, to establish the institution of the State, States, on the international plane, may establish international institutions. This way of seeing international institutions assumes that the institution of the State and the internal law of the State may be explained coherently on the basis of social contract theory. Whereas the notion of a state of nature has actually been derived, in the theories of law/politics developed by Hobbes and Locke, from the international plane, the development of international institutions would seem to suggest that this international state of nature is not inherent, but may be transcended. Conversely, this would imply that, with the development of international institutions, a genuine example of a state of nature could no longer be pointed out.

This chapter seeks to situate the concept of international institution within the vertical structure of the concept of law underlying the concept of public international law, which unfolds itself in the forms of the framework of obligation and the framework of authorization. Section 13.2 will describe common features of the concept of international institution, whereupon Sect. 13.3 will situate the concept of international institution within the alternatives formed by the framework of obligation and the framework of authorization. Section 13.4 will conclude that the concept of international institution should not be seen as conforming to the mutual exclusivity of the framework of obligation and the framework of authorization, but should be resituated within the reformulated framework, which, in a way, combines the framework of obligation and the framework of authorization. When resituated within the reformulated framework, the concept of international institution may be seen in terms of the constituting of international society by the members of international society. This perspective entails seeing the concept of international institution as incorporating both an enabling and a disabling aspect. Forming part of the constituting of international society, the concept of international institution enables the members of international society to overcome the dilemma situation involved in their having a power, but not an unlimited freedom, to act. Along the enabling dimension, the members of international society may constitute international society in its more durable aspect in the form of international institutions. Because the members of international society cannot circumvent international institutions by relying on a, non-existent, freedom to act, international institutions represent at the

[1] The traditional sources of public international law have themselves also become linked to the development of international institutions. The transposability of general principles of public law to the international plane has been made dependent on the development of international institutions through which the concept of public international law would acquire a vertical structure. Treaties creating international organs or general rules, such as the Covenant of the League of Nations, have been characterized in terms of constitutional international law or international public law. In the *Case Concerning Military and Paramilitary Activities in and against Nicaragua (Merits), opinio juris* was derived from General Assembly resolution 2625 (XXV).

same time a disabling dimension. Reforming international institutions within the reformulated framework requires re-entering the cycle of practical reasoning directed at the constituting of (the common good of) international society.

13.2 The Concept of International Institution

The concept of international institution is commonly understood in terms of an entity—an intergovernmental organization—to which States have entrusted the attainment of common ends or interests.[2] This act of entrustment is commonly understood as entailing the bestowal of international personality on the intergovernmental organization,[3] which means, in the words of the ICJ in *Reparation for Injuries Suffered in the Service of the United Nations*, the capacity to possess international rights and duties.[4] In this way, international personality involves a separation between the international institution and the States by which it has been established.[5]

The constituent instrument of an international institution commonly circumscribes the purposes[6] and/or functions[7] of the intergovernmental organization. In

[2] *Certain Expenses of the United Nations (Article 17, paragraph 2, of the Charter)*, Advisory Opinion of 20 July 1962, ICJ Reports 1962, 151, 168; *Legality of the Use by a State of Nuclear Weapons in Armed Conflict*, Advisory Opinion of 8 July 1996, ICJ Reports 1996, 66, para 25.

[3] Weil 1992, pp. 101–110; Zemanek 1997, paras 141–144; Tomuschat 1999, Chap. IV, paras 3–9; Dupuy 2002, pp. 107–109.

[4] *Reparation for Injuries Suffered in the Service of the United Nations*, Advisory Opinion of 11 April 1949, ICJ Reports 1949, 174, 178–179.

[5] Bederman 1996, pp. 366–371; Klabbers 2002, pp. 52–59.

[6] Charter of the United Nations, Article 1; Constitution of the International Labour Organization, Article 1 (1); Constitution of the United Nations Educational, Scientific and Cultural Organization, Article I (1); Constitution of the Food and Agriculture Organization of the United Nations, Preamble; Constitution of the World Health Organization, Article 1; Articles of Agreement of the International Monetary Fund, Article I; Articles of Agreement of the International Bank for Reconstruction and Development, Article I; Constitution of the International Telecommunication Union, Article 1; Constitution of the Universal Postal Union, Article 1; Convention on International Civil Aviation, Article 44; Convention on the International Maritime Organization, Article 1; Convention of the World Meteorological Organization, Article 2; Statute of the International Atomic Energy Agency, Article II; Convention Establishing the World Intellectual Property Organization, Article 3; Constitution of the United Nations Industrial Development Organization, Article 1; Agreement Establishing the World Trade Organization, Article II, para 1.

[7] Charter of the United Nations, Article 60; Constitution of the United Nations Educational, Scientific and Cultural Organization, Article I (2); Constitution of the Food and Agriculture Organization of the United Nations, Article I; Constitution of the World Health Organization, Article 2; Convention on the International Maritime Organization, Articles 2 and 3; Statute of the International Atomic Energy Agency, Article III A; Convention Establishing the World Intellectual Property Organization, Article 4; Constitution of the United Nations Industrial Development Organization, Article 2; Agreement Establishing the World Trade Organization, Article III.

addition, the constituent instrument of an international institution commonly circumscribes the functions of the organs of the international institution[8] as well as the acts which may be adopted by those organs, including their legal effect.[9]

According to international jurisprudence, the powers of an international institution derive from the principle of attribution; an international institution has those

[8] Charter of the United Nations, Articles 10–17 (General Assembly), 24, para 1, (Security Council), 62–66 (Economic and Social Council), 87–88 (Trusteeship Council); Constitution of the International Labour Organization, Article 10 (International Labour Office); Constitution of the United Nations Educational, Scientific and Cultural Organization, Article IV (B) (General Conference), Article V(B) (Executive Board); Constitution of the Food and Agriculture Organization of the United Nations, Article IV (Conference), Article V, para 3 (Council); Constitution of the World Health Organization, Article 18 (World Health Assembly), Article 28 (Executive Board); Articles of Agreement of the International Monetary Fund, Article XII (2) (a) (Board of Governors); Article XII (3) (a) (Executive Board); Articles of Agreement of the International Bank for Reconstruction and Development, Article V, Section 2, para a (Board of Governors); Article V, Section 2, para a (Executive Directors); Constitution of the International Telecommunication Union, Article 8 (2) (Plenipotentiary Conference); Article 10 (3)–(4) (Council); Constitution of the Universal Postal Union, Article 17 (1) (Council of Administration); Article 18 (Postal Operations Council); Convention on International Civil Aviation, Article 49 (Assembly), Articles 54 and 55 (Council), Article 57 (Air Navigation Commission); Convention on the International Maritime Organization, Article 15 (Assembly), Article 21 (Council), Article 28 (Maritime Safety Committee), Article 33 (Legal Committee), Article 38 (Marine Environment Protection Committee), Article 43 (Technical Cooperation Committee); Convention of the World Meteorological Organization, Article 8 (World Meteorological Congress), Article 14 (Executive Council); Statute of the International Atomic Energy Agency, Article V D, E and F (General Conference), Article VI F (Board of Governors); Convention Establishing the World Intellectual Property Organization, Article 6, para 2 (General Assembly); Article 7, para 2 (Conference); Article 8, para 3 (Coordination Committee); Constitution of the United Nations Industrial Development Organization, Article 8, para 3 (General Conference), Article 9, para 4 (Industrial Development Board), Article 10, para 4 (Programme and Budget Committee); Agreement Establishing the World Trade Organization, Article IV, para 1 (Ministerial Conference), paras 2–4 (General Council), para 5 (Council for Trade in Goods/Council for Trade in Services/TRIPS Council).

[9] Charter of the United Nations, Articles 10, 11, paras 1 and 2, 13, para 1, 14 (General Assembly), 24, para 2, 25, 36, para 1, 37, para 2, 39, (Security Council), 62 and 63 (Economic and Social Council); Constitution of the International Labour Organization, Article 19, para 1 (General Conference); Constitution of the United Nations Educational, Scientific and Cultural Organization, Article IV, para 4 (General Conference); Constitution of the Food and Agriculture Organization of the United Nations, Articles IV, para 3, and XIV, paras 1 and 2; Constitution of the World Health Organization, Articles 19, 21 and 23 (World Health Assembly); Constitution of the International Telecommunication Union, Article 4 (3); Article 6 (1); Article 54; Constitution of the Universal Postal Union, Article 22 (1)–(4); Convention on International Civil Aviation, Articles 37 and 54, para l; Convention on the International Maritime Organization, Articles 2, paras a and b, 3, 15, paras i and j, 21, para b, 29, paras a and b, 34, para a, 39, paras a and b, 44, para a; Convention of the World Meteorological Organization, Articles 8, para b, 9, 14, para e; Statute of the International Atomic Energy Agency, Article V D; Convention Establishing the World Intellectual Property Organization, Article 7, para 2 (ii); Constitution of the United Nations Industrial Development Organization, Article 8, para 3, (d) and (e).

powers which the States by which the international organization has been established have given to it.[10] In *Legality of the Use by a State of Nuclear Weapons in Armed Conflict*, the ICJ referred in this connection to the principle of speciality.[11] The constituent instrument of an international institution is deemed to contain those powers.[12] In principle, these powers are set out expressly in that constitutive text.[13] It is commonly recognized, however, that international institutions may, in addition, have implied (subsidiary) powers in so far as these are necessary for the achievement of their objectives.[14] In *Legal Consequences for States of the*

---

[10] *Jurisdiction of the European Commission of the Danube between Galatz and Braila*, Advisory Opinion of 8 December 1927, Series B.—No. 14, 64: 'As the European Commission is not a state, but an international institution with a special purpose, it only has the functions bestowed upon it by the Definitive Statute with a view to the fulfilment of that purpose, but it has power to exercise these functions to their full extent, in so far as the Statute does not impose restrictions upon it.'

[11] *Legality of the Use by a State of Nuclear Weapons in Armed Conflict*, Advisory Opinion of 8 July 1996, ICJ Reports 1996, 66, para 25: 'International organizations are governed by the "principle of speciality", that is to say, they are invested by the States which create them with powers, the limits of which are a function of the common interests whose promotion those States entrust to them.'

Dupuy 2002, pp. 100, 103–104.

[12] *Competence of the International Labour Organization in Regard to International Regulation of the Conditions of Labour of Persons Employed in Agriculture*, Advisory Opinion of 12 August 1922, Series B.—No. 2, 23; *Competence of the International Labour Organization to Examine Proposals for the Organization and Development of the Methods of Agricultural Production as Well as Other Questions of a Like Character*, Advisory Opinion of 12 August 1922, Series B.—No. 3, 53–55; *Competence of the International Labour Organization to Regulate, Incidentally, the Personal Work of the Employer*, Advisory Opinion of 23 July 1926, Series B.—No. 13, 22–23; *Jurisdiction of the European Commission of the Danube between Galatz and Braila*, Advisory Opinion of 8 December 1927, Series B.—No. 14, 64; *Effect of Awards of Compensation Made by the United Nations Administrative Tribunal*, Advisory Opinion of 13 July 1954, Dissenting Opinion Judge Hackworth, ICJ Reports 1954, 47, 77; *Certain Expenses of the United Nations (Article 17, paragraph 2, of the Charter)*, Advisory Opinion of 20 July 1962, Separate Opinion Judge Sir Percy Spender, ICJ Reports 1962, 151, 184; *Legality of the Use by a State of Nuclear Weapons in Armed Conflict*, Advisory Opinion of 8 July 1996, ICJ Reports 1996, 66, para 19.

[13] *Jurisdiction of the European Commission of the Danube between Galatz and Braila*, Advisory Opinion of 8 December 1927, Series B.—No. 14, 64; *Legality of the Use by a State of Nuclear Weapons in Armed Conflict*, Advisory Opinion of 8 July 1996, ICJ Reports 1996, 66, para 25.

Klabbers 2002, pp. 63–67.

[14] *Competence of the International Labour Organization to Regulate, Incidentally, the Personal Work of the Employer*, Advisory Opinion of 23 July 1926, Series B.—No. 13, 18: 'It results from the consideration of the provisions of the Treaty that the High Contracting Parties clearly intended to give to the International Labour Organization a very broad power of co-operating with them in respect of measures to be taken in order to assure humane conditions of labour and the protection of workers. It is not conceivable that they intended to prevent the Organization from drawing up and proposing measures essential to the accomplishment of that end. The Organization, however, would be so prevented if it were incompetent to propose for the protection of wage-earners a regulative measure to the efficacious working of which it was found to be essential to include to some extent work done by employers. If such a limitation of the powers of the International Labour Organization, clearly inconsistent with the aim and the scope

Continued Presence of South Africa in Namibia (South-West Africa) Notwithstanding Security Council Resolution 276 (1970), the ICJ went so far as to recognize, in addition to the specific powers mentioned in Article 24, para 2, second sentence, of the UN Charter, general powers of the Security Council to discharge the responsibilities circumscribed in Article 24, para 1, of the UN Charter, i.e., the maintenance or restoration of international peace and security.[15] Since the constituent instrument of an international institution is a text of conventional international law, its interpretation follows, in principle, the rules of interpretation of conventional international law. Nevertheless, the special character of constituent instruments of international institutions should be taken into account as well.[16]

In *Certain Expenses of the United Nations (Article 17, paragraph 2, of the Charter)*, the ICJ addressed the question how it should be determined whether a power has been attributed to an international institution. The ICJ identified a presumption that action is not *ultra vires* the United Nations if it takes action

(Footnote 14 continued)
of Part XIII, had been intended, it would have been expressed in the Treaty itself. On the other hand, it is not strange that the Treaty does not contain a provision expressly conferring upon the Organization power in such a very special case as the present.'; *Reparation for Injuries Suffered in the Service of the United Nations*, Advisory Opinion of 11 April 1949, ICJ Reports 1949, 174, 180: '(…) the rights and duties of an entity such as the Organization must depend on its purposes and functions as specified or implied in its constituent documents and developed in practice.'; 182–183: 'Under international law, the Organization must be deemed to have those powers which, though not expressly provided in the Charter, are conferred upon it by necessary implication as being essential to the performance of its duties.'; *Effect of Awards of Compensation Made by the United Nations Administrative Tribunal*, Advisory Opinion of 13 July 1954, ICJ Reports 1954, 47, 56–58; *Certain Expenses of the United Nations (Article 17, paragraph 2, of the Charter)*, Advisory Opinion of 20 July 1962, Separate Opinion Judge Sir Percy Spender, ICJ Reports 1962, 151, 196; *Legality of the Use by a State of Nuclear Weapons in Armed Conflict*, Advisory Opinion of 8 July 1996, ICJ Reports 1996, 66, para 25: '[T]he necessities of international life may point to the need for organizations, in order to achieve their objectives, to possess subsidiary powers which are not expressly provided for in the basic instruments which govern their activities. It is generally accepted that international organizations can exercise such powers, known as "implied" powers.'

Zemanek 1997, paras 145–149; Klabbers 2001, pp. 295–297, 302–303; Klabbers 2002, pp. 67–73.

[15] *Legal Consequences for States of the Continued Presence of South Africa in Namibia (South-West Africa) Notwithstanding Security Council Resolution 276 (1970),* Advisory Opinion of 21 June 1971, ICJ Reports 1971, 16, para 110: 'As to the basis of the resolution, Article 24 of the Charter vests in the Security Council the necessary authority to take action such as that taken in the present case. The reference in paragraph 2 of this Article to specific powers of the Security Council under certain chapters of the Charter does not exclude the existence of general powers to discharge the responsibilities conferred in paragraph 1.'; Separate Opinion Judge Padilla Nervo, 118; Separate Opinion, Judge De Castro, 187.

Castañeda 1969, pp. 71–76.

[16] *Legality of the Use by a State of Nuclear Weapons in Armed Conflict*, Advisory Opinion of 8 July 1996, ICJ Reports 1996, 66, para 19.

which warrants the assertion that it was appropriate for the fulfillment of one of its purposes.[17] The ICJ further considered that the question whether an organ of an international institution has a power to adopt an act, is to be determined, in the first place at least, by the acting organ itself.[18] At the same time, however, the ICJ observed that the power conferred on the United Nations is not unlimited and that the Member States have retained their freedom of action in so far as they have not entrusted the United Nations with the attainment of common ends.[19]

These observations by the ICJ give some indications as regards the nature of the powers attributed to international institutions. In its jurisprudence, the PCIJ avoided taking a fixed position in respect of this question.[20] The ICJ commonly refers in its jurisprudence to powers conferred by States upon international

---

[17] *Certain Expenses of the United Nations (Article 17, paragraph 2, of the Charter)*, Advisory Opinion of 20 July 1962, ICJ Reports 1962, 151, 168: 'But when the Organization takes action which warrants the assertion that it was appropriate for the fulfillment of one of the stated purposes of the United Nations, the presumption is that such action is not *ultra vires* the Organization.'

[18] *Certain Expenses of the United Nations (Article 17, paragraph 2, of the Charter)*, Advisory Opinion of 20 July 1962, ICJ Reports 1962, 151, 168: 'In the legal system of States, there is often some procedure for determining the validity of even a legislative or governmental act, but no analogous procedure is to be found in the structure of the United Nations. Proposals made during the drafting of the Charter to place the ultimate authority to interpret the Charter in the International Court of Justice were not accepted; the opinion which the Court is in course of rendering is an *advisory* opinion. As anticipated in 1945, therefore, each organ must, in the first place at least, determine its own jurisdiction.'

[19] *Certain Expenses of the United Nations (Article 17, paragraph 2, of the Charter)*, Advisory Opinion of 20 July 1962, ICJ Reports 1962, 151, 168: 'These purposes are broad indeed, but neither they nor the powers conferred to effectuate them are unlimited. Save as they have entrusted the Organization with the attainment of these common ends, the Member States retain their freedom of action.'

[20] *Competence of the International Labour Organization in Regard to International Regulation of the Conditions of Labour of Persons Employed in Agriculture*, Advisory Opinion of 12 August 1922, Series B.—No. 2, 23: 'It was much urged in argument that the establishment of the International Labour Organization involved an abandonment of rights derived from national sovereignty, and that the competence of the Organization therefore should not be extended by interpretation. There may be some force in this argument, but the question in every case must resolve itself into what the terms of the Treaty actually mean, and it is from this point of view that the Court proposes to examine the question.'; *Competence of the International Labour Organization to Regulate, Incidentally, the Personal Work of the Employer*, Advisory Opinion of 23 July 1926, Series B.—No. 13, 22–23: 'So, in the present instance, without regard to the question whether the functions entrusted to the International Labour Organization are or are not in the nature of delegated powers, the province of the Court is to ascertain what it was the Contracting Parties agreed on.'

Bederman 1996, pp. 364–366; Klabbers 2002, pp. 60–63.

[21] *Reparations for Injuries Suffered in the Service of the United Nations*, Advisory Opinion of 11 April 1949, ICJ Reports 1949, 174, 182; *Certain Expenses of the United Nations (Article 17, paragraph 2, of the Charter)*, Advisory Opinion of 20 July 1962, ICJ Reports 1962, 151, 168; *Legality of the Use by a State of Nuclear Weapons in Armed Conflict*, Advisory Opinion of 8 July 1996, ICJ Reports 1996, 66, para 25.

institutions.[21] Its observations in *Certain Expenses of the United Nations (Article 17, paragraph 2, of the Charter)* suggest that the conferment of power by States to an international institution results in a corresponding limitation of their freedom of action because, in the view of the Court, States did not retain their freedom of action in so far as they had entrusted the attainment of common ends to the international institution. It would accordingly seem to follow that the power of an international institution emanates from a transfer of freedom of action by States to the international institution, involving a simultaneous transformation of this freedom of action into power. Conferment of power, according to this view, means transfer of power.

A similar point of view would seem to have been adopted by the Appellate Body of the Dispute Settlement Body of the WTO. In *EC – Measures Concerning Meat and Meat Products (Hormones)*, it stated that the standard of review to be applied by panels under the Agreement on the Application of Sanitary and Phytosanitary Measures, must reflect the balance established therein between the jurisdictional competences conceded by the WTO Members to the WTO and the jurisdictional competences retained by the WTO Members for themselves.[22]

13.3 The Concept of International Institution Situated Within the Framework of Obligation and the Framework of Authorization

It is submitted that the concept of international institution is incoherent if situated within the mutual exclusivity formed by the framework of obligation and the framework of authorization. According to the framework of obligation, the function of rules of public international law contained in a constituent instrument of an international institution and of rules of public international law adopted by an organ of an international institution, is to restrict the freedom of the Member States to act. In the absence of such rules of public international law, the Member States are regarded as having a freedom to act. According to the framework of authorization, the function of rules of public international law contained in a constituent instrument of an international institution and of rules of public international law adopted by an organ of an international institution, is to confer on the Member States a power to act. In the absence of such rules of public international law, the Member States are regarded as not having a power to act.

It would seem that the practice of States with regard to international institutions generally operates within the framework of obligation. For example, both Article 2,

---

[22] Report of the Appellate Body, *EC – Measures Concerning Meat and Meat Products (Hormones)*, WT/DS26/AB/R, WT/DS48/AB/R, para 115: 'The standard of review appropriately applicable in proceedings under the SPS Agreement, of course, must reflect the balance established in that Agreement between the jurisdictional competences conceded by the Members to the WTO and the jurisdictional competences retained by the Members for themselves.'

para 2, and Article 103 of the Charter of the United Nations reflect the view that the text of the UN Charter contains or may give rise to obligations. If the concept of international institution is situated within the framework of authorization, the international institution must be presupposed and cannot be explained as emanating from acts of States.

Within the framework of obligation, the concept of public international law is deemed to play a two-fold role.[23] First, the constituent instrument of an international institution is a text of conventional international law. Thereby, the Member States of the international institution are deemed to have limited their freedom to act.[24] At the same time, acts adopted by organs of international institutions may contain, as the case may be, non-binding or binding 'rules' of public international law.[25]

Situating, in this manner, the concept of international institution exclusively within the framework of obligation, however, seems to lead to an incoherent picture of the concept of international institution. If States transfer power to an international institution, it would follow—in line with the observations put forward by the ICJ in *Certain Expenses of the United Nations (Article 17, Paragraph 2, of the Charter)*—that, to that extent, those States no longer have a freedom to act: as a result of and to the extent of the transfer of power, the Member States of the international institution should be regarded as situated within the framework of authorization. Accordingly, rules of public international law adopted by the (organs of the) international institution should confer powers to act on the Member States, rather than contain restrictions of the freedom to act of the Member States. This perspective was exploited, to some extent, by the ICJ in *International Status of South-West Africa*:

> The authority which the Union Government exercises over the Territory is based on the Mandate. If the Mandate lapsed, as the Union Government contends, the latter's authority would equally have lapsed. To retain the rights derived from the Mandate and to deny the obligations thereunder would not be justified.[26]

---

[23] Pastor Ridruejo 1998, pp. 193–214.

[24] *Certain Expenses of the United Nations (Article 17, paragraph 2, of the Charter)*, Advisory Opinion of 20 July 1962, Dissenting Opinion Judge Bustamante, ICJ Reports 1962, 151, 304.

[25] *Certain Expenses of the United Nations (Article 17, paragraph 2, of the Charter)*, Advisory Opinion of 20 July 1962, Separate Opinion Judge Sir Gerald Fitzmaurice, ICJ Reports 1962, 151, 210; Dissenting Opinion President Winiarski, 232–234; *Legal Consequences for States of the Continued Presence of South Africa in Namibia (South-West Africa) Notwithstanding Security Council Resolution 276 (1970)*, Advisory Opinion of 21 June 1971, ICJ Reports 1971, 16, para 115: 'The decisions are consequently binding on all States Members of the United Nations, which are thus under obligation to accept and carry them out.'

Castañeda 1969, pp. 6–16; Zemanek 1997, paras 397–398 (ICAO, WHO); Tomuschat 1999, Chap. IX, paras 65–66 (General Assembly); Dupuy 2002, pp. 155–156 (ICAO, WHO), 156–157 (Security Council).

[26] *International Status of South-West Africa*, Advisory Opinion of 11 July 1950, ICJ Reports 1950, 128, 133.

More fundamentally, however, the notion of a transfer of power—and the concomitant transformation of the framework of obligation into the framework of authorization—itself gives rise to incoherence. First, in the case of a partial transfer of power, a problem of delimitation arises. In the case of a partial transfer of power, the power transferred to international institutions must be delimited from the power retained by the member States. As mentioned before, the ICJ distinguished in *Certain Expenses of the United Nations (Article 17, paragraph 2, of the Charter)* between powers conferred and freedoms of action retained.[27] Likewise, the Appellate Body of the Dispute Settlement Body of the WTO distinguished, in *EC – Measures Concerning Meat and Meat Products (Hormones)*, between jurisdictional competences conceded and jurisdictional competences retained.[28] Effecting the delimitation between the power of an international institution and the freedom to act of the Member States of the international institution requires, as mentioned before, interpretation of the text of the constituent instrument of the international institution.[29] As the PCIJ acknowledged with respect to the constituent instrument of the ILO, however, the texts of constituent instruments of international institutions do not contain precise or rigid limits.[30]

If, then, the interpretation of the constituent instrument adhered to by the organ of the international institution were decisive of itself, this would mean that the organ can delimit the freedoms to act retained by the Member States even though its power is regarded as deriving from a transfer of and transformation into power of those freedoms of the Member States to act. Furthermore, it would follow that entrusting the attainment of common aims or interests to the international institution and its organs, simultaneously involves the loss of control by the Member States over the acts of the international institution and its organs.[31] This would seem inconsistent with the notion of entrustment, which would appear to imply the retention of a measure of control. Conversely, if the interpretation of the constituent instrument adhered to by the Member States were decisive of itself, this would mean that the Member States can still delimit the power transferred to the international institution and its organs, even though the Member States were regarded as having already transferred power to the international institution and its organs. This would subject the acts of the international institution and its organs to total control by the Member States and seem inconsistent with the view that the

---

[27] *Certain Expenses of the United Nations (Article 17, paragraph 2, of the Charter)*, Advisory Opinion of 20 July 1962, ICJ Reports 1962, 151, 168.

[28] Report of the Appellate Body, *EC – Measures Concerning Meat and Meat Products (Hormones)*, WT/DS26/AB/R, WT/DS48/AB/R, para 115.

[29] Klabbers 2002, pp. 96–100.

[30] *Interpretation of the Convention of 1919 Concerning Employment of Women During the Night*, Advisory Opinion of 15 November 1932, Series A./B.—No. 50, 365, 375: 'An examination of the Opinions referred to above is sufficient to show that the limits of the sphere of the Labour Organization are not fixed with precision or rigidity in Part XIII, and a study of the text of Part XIII provides ample material for arriving at the same conclusion.'

[31] Castañeda 1969, pp. 122–123.

attainment of common aims or interests had been entrusted to the international institution and its organs.[32]

This dilemma was recognized by the PCIJ when, interpreting, in *Nationality Decrees Issued in Tunis and Morocco (French Zone)*, Article 15, para 8, of the Covenant of the League of Nations systematically in the light of Article 15 as a whole, it made the following observations:

> Article 15, in effect, establishes the fundamental principle that any dispute likely to lead to a rupture which is not submitted to arbitration in accordance with Article 13 shall be laid before the Council. The reservations generally made in arbitration treaties are not to be found in this Article.
>
> Having regard to this very wide competence possessed by the League of Nations, the Covenant contains an express reservation protecting the independence of States; this reservation is to be found in paragraph 8 of Article 15. Without this reservation, the internal affairs of a country might, directly they appeared to affect the interests of another country, be brought before the Council and form the subject of recommendations by the League of Nations. Under the terms of paragraph 8, the League's interest in being able to make such recommendations as are deemed just and proper in the circumstances with a view to the maintenance of peace must, at a given point, give way to the equally essential interest of the individual State to maintain intact its independence in matters which international law recognizes to be solely within its jurisdiction.[33]

The problem, it would appear, is that the competence to effect this delimitation cannot be located either exclusively in the organ of the international institution or in the Member States of the international institution.

The previous points about the alternation between the framework of obligation and the framework of authorization, pertaining to *International Status of South-West Africa*, and the wide competence that may be conferred on an organ of an international institution, pertaining to *Nationality Decrees Issued in Tunis and Morocco (French Zone)*, converge, in a way, in the reasoning of the PCIJ in *Article 3, Paragraph 2, of the Treaty of Lausanne (Frontier between Turkey and Iraq)*. In that advisory opinion, the Court examined whether the referral by Great Britain and Turkey, pursuant to Article 3, para 2, of the Treaty of Lausanne, of the determination of the frontier between Turkey and Iraq to the Council of the League of Nations, was to result in a decision binding on the Parties. The Court answered that the decision to be given by the Council was to be binding, inferring that character from the clear meaning of Article 3, para 2, of the Treaty of Lausanne and from the nature of a frontier.[34] Under Article 15 of the Covenant of the League of Nations, however, the powers of the Council were limited to the issuing of recommendations. While this

[32] *Certain Expenses of the United Nations (Article 17, paragraph 2, of the Charter)*, Advisory Opinion of 20 July 1962, ICJ Reports 1962, 151, 168; *Legality of the Use by a State of Nuclear Weapons in Armed Conflict*, Advisory Opinion of 8 July 1996, ICJ Reports 1996, 66, para 25. Klabbers 2002, pp. 202–206.

[33] *Nationality Decrees Issued in Tunis and Morocco (French Zone)*, Advisory Opinion of 7 February 1923, Series B.—No. 4, 24–25.

[34] *Article 3, paragraph 2, of the Treaty of Lausanne (Frontier between Turkey and Iraq)*, Advisory Opinion of 21 November 1925, Series B.—No. 12, 18–26.

aspect could have led the Court to revisit its interpretation of Article 3, para 2, of the Treaty of Lausanne, the Court reasoned that the Parties, pursuant to that provision, could have conferred additional powers on the Council by virtue of which its decision would be binding vis-à-vis the Parties.[35] It may be noted that the view that the powers of the Council under Article 15 of the Covenant of the League of Nations, which the PCIJ had characterized in *Nationality Decrees Issued in Tunis and Morocco (French Zone)* as very wide, were only minimum powers, and that the Parties could confer on the Council powers wider than those resulting from the strict terms of Article 15, would, in line with the approach adopted by the ICJ in *International Status of South-West Africa*, involve a reversion to the framework of authorization. From that point of view, the decision to be reached by the Council should, in turn, confer rights on the Parties and, in view of the mutual exclusivity of the framework of obligation and the framework of authorization, could not bind the Parties.

The question must also be addressed how powers that are subsequently transferred to an international institution can exist in the first place. As stated, the view adopted by the ICJ in *Certain Expenses of the United Nations (Article 17, paragraph 2, of the Charter)* suggests that the power of an international institution is derived from the freedom of States to act, which is transformed into power and simultaneously transferred to an international institution. The problem arises, however, that the framework of obligation cannot account for such a process of transformation. Within the framework of obligation, freedoms of States to act are pre-existent. The framework of obligation only accounts for the process whereby those freedoms of States to act may be restricted; such restrictions, resulting from the exercise of the freedoms of States to act, cannot transform those freedoms to act into powers that may be transferred. Thus, when Article 24 of the Charter of the United Nations provides that the Member States of the United Nations confer primary responsibility for the maintenance and restoration of international peace and security on the Security Council, it remains unclear how, before the transfer of that power, those States possessed, individually and/or collectively, that responsibility. To the contrary, individually and/or collectively, those States are regarded as merely having unlimited freedoms to act, which are problematic from the point of view of international peace and security and constitute the very reason for the conferment of the primary responsibility for the maintenance and restoration of

[35] *Article 3, Paragraph 2, of the Treaty of Lausanne (Frontier between Turkey and Iraq)*, Advisory Opinion of 21 November 1925, Series B.—No. 12, 26–28, 27: 'Though it is true that the powers of the Council, in regard to the settlement of disputes, are dealt with in Article 15 of the Covenant, and that, under that article, the Council can only make recommendations, which, even when made unanimously, do not of necessity settle the dispute, that article only sets out the *minimum* obligations which are imposed upon States and the minimum corresponding powers of the Council. There is nothing to prevent the Parties from accepting obligations and from conferring on the Council powers wider than those resulting from the strict terms of Article 15, and in particular from substituting, by an agreement entered into in advance, for the Council's power to make a mere recommendation, the power to give a decision which, by virtue of their previous consent, compulsorily settles the dispute.'

international peace and security on the Security Council. From the point of view of the framework of obligation, it remains difficult to see how these inconsistent freedoms to act, while providing the rationale for the existence of rules of public international law effecting their delimitation, can at the same time provide a coherent basis for the establishment of a structure capable of producing such rules.

On the basis of the above, it may be said that, in particular as recognized by the PCIJ in *Nationality Decrees Issued in Tunis and Morocco (French Zone)*, a balance has to be maintained between the position of the Member States and the position of the organs of international institutions. The vertical structure of the concept of law underlying the concept of public international law, however, makes the location of such a balance elusive. The framework of obligation, as applied to organs of international institutions, only affords the binary choice between non-binding and binding resolutions. Non-binding resolutions may be said to tilt the balance in favor of the Member States; binding resolutions may be said to tilt the balance in favor of the organs of international institutions. The combination of the characterization of the organs of international institutions as political with the characterization of their powers as discretionary, in the light of the legal personality of the international institution as a whole, would tend to transpose the problem of control, situated previously between the organs of international institutions and the Member States, to the interrelationship between (political and legal) organs of international institutions.[36] This issue may be illustrated further by returning to the position adopted by the ICJ in *Certain Expenses of the United Nations (Article 17, paragraph 2, of the Charter)* with respect to the question how it can be determined whether an (organ of an) international institution has power.

As described previously, in *Certain Expenses of the United Nations (Article 17, Paragraph 2, of the Charter)*, the ICJ identified a presumption that action is not *ultra vires* the United Nations if it takes action which warrants the assertion that it was appropriate for the fulfillment of one of its purposes.[37] This statement may be interpreted as a broad endorsement of the doctrine of implied powers. As formulated in Article 24, para 2, first sentence, of the UN Charter, the Security Council, when discharging its duties as described in para 1, shall act in accordance with the Purposes and Principles of the United Nations. According to this provision, the purposes and principles of the UN Charter should have the function of limiting the powers of the Security Council. By taking the appropriateness of action for the fulfillment of the purposes of the UN as a guiding criterion for determining the legality of acts of its organs, the Court has transformed the limiting function contained in the text of the UN Charter into a basis for extending the action of the UN.

A limitation of the powers of the Security Council has also been sought in Article 25 of the UN Charter, which provides that the UN Members agree to accept and carry out the decisions of the Security Council in accordance with the Charter.

---

[36] Zemanek 1997, paras 402–413.

[37] *Certain Expenses of the United Nations (Article 17, paragraph 2, of the Charter)*, Advisory Opinion of 20 July 1962, ICJ Reports 1962, 151, 168.

In his commentary, Delbrück has taken the view that the phrase 'in accordance with the Charter' is ambiguous, possibly referring to the way in which decisions have to be carried out or to the way in which decisions have to be adopted.[38] Seeing the former interpretation as rendering the phrase superfluous, Delbrück concluded that the phrase applies to the Security Council, albeit restricted to procedural issues.[39] Against this view, it has been remarked that Article 25 of the UN Charter unambiguously applies to the UN Members, describing how the decisions of the Security Council are to be implemented.[40] If, on the other hand, Article 25 of the UN Charter were applicable to the Security Council, there would seem to be no ground for restricting its scope of application to procedural issues. Its comprehensive application to the Security Council, extending to both substantive and procedural issues, would, as has also been observed,[41] seem inconsistent with the transferring moment stipulated in Article 24, para 1, of the UN Charter, which provides that, in order to ensure prompt and effective action by the UN, its Members confer on the Security Council primary responsibility for the maintenance of international peace and security, agreeing that, in carrying out this responsibility, the Security Council acts on their behalf. From this point of view, there seems to be no ground for minimizing, with Delbrück, the importance of this provision.[42] Directed at the transition of the international state of nature, it may be seen as incorporating the act of entrustment coupled with a transfer of power.

In the light of this act of entrustment, we may understand the ICJ's statement, in *Certain Expenses of the United Nations (Article 17, Paragraph 2, of the Charter)*, that the question whether an organ of the United Nations has power, is to be determined, in the first place at least, by the organ itself.[43] If that act is coupled with a transfer of power, however, the extent of which is to be determined by the organ, this would render that determination conclusive.[44] The Court's expression that this determination by the organ was to be made in the first instance, at least, appears to suggest that there might be a second instance in which the determination could be reviewed. As observed by Judge Fitzmaurice, the main question, therefore, resides in the provisional or final character of a determination by an organ of an international institution.[45] Seeing that determination as provisional, gives rise to exploring the consequential question how an act of an organ of an international institution could be reviewed. In this way, the question of the

---

[38] Delbrück 2002b, para 6.

[39] Delbrück 2002b, paras 17–18.

[40] Wood 2006, paras 18–19.

[41] Schilling 1995, pp. 93–96; Martenczuk 1999, pp. 534–546.

[42] Delbrück 2002a, para 11.

[43] *Certain Expenses of the United Nations (Article 17, paragraph 2, of the Charter)*, Advisory Opinion of 20 July 1962, ICJ Reports 1962, 151, 168.

[44] Klabbers 2002, pp. 185–192.

[45] *Certain Expenses of the United Nations (Article 17, paragraph 2, of the Charter)*, Advisory Opinion of 20 July 1962, Separate Opinion Judge Sir Gerald Fitzmaurice, ICJ Reports 1962, 151, 203.

relationship between organs of international institutions and Member states of international institutions entails the accessory question of judicial review of acts of organs of international institutions, which has arisen with respect to both advisory and contentious proceedings before the ICJ.

As regards advisory proceedings, it may be observed that the ICJ's position, in *Certain Expenses of the United Nations (Article 17, paragraph 2, of the Charter)*, that an organ of an international institution must itself, at least in the first instance, determine its competence, was informed precisely by its observation that the Charter of the United Nations did not foresee the possibility of judicial review. At the same time, this antecedent raises the question of how, in the absence of judicial review, a determination by an organ of an international institution of its competence, in the first instance, would not be conclusive. In this connection, it may be noted that, in these proceedings, the Court established its competence to consider the question whether certain expenditures were determined in conformity with the Charter.[46] Subsequently, the Court conducted an examination of the General Assembly and Security Council resolutions relating to UNEF and ONUC as well as the General Assembly resolutions authorizing expenditures for those operations.[47]

Similarly, in *Legal Consequences for States of the Continued Presence of South Africa in Namibia (South-West Africa) Notwithstanding Security Council Resolution 276 (1970)*, the Court acknowledged that it does not possess powers of judicial review or appeal in respect of decisions of the General Assembly and the Security Council, considering, moreover, that the validity or conformity with the UN Charter of General Assembly resolution 2145 (XXI) or of related Security Council resolutions was not the subject of the request for advisory opinion contained in Security Council resolution 284 (1970).[48] Notwithstanding this position, it subsequently proceeded to examine those resolutions, arriving at the conclusion

---

[46] *Certain Expenses of the United Nations (Article 17, paragraph 2, of the Charter)*, Advisory Opinion of 20 July 1962, ICJ Reports 1962, 151, 157: 'The rejection of the French amendment does not constitute a directive to the Court to exclude from its consideration the question whether certain expenditures were "decided on in conformity with the Charter", if the Court finds such consideration appropriate. It is not to be assumed that the General Assembly would thus seek to fetter or hamper the Court in the discharge of its judicial functions; the Court must have full liberty to consider all relevant data available to it in forming an opinion on a question posed to it for an advisory opinion.'

[47] *Certain Expenses of the United Nations (Article 17, paragraph 2, of the Charter)*, Advisory Opinion of 20 July 1962, ICJ Reports 1962, 151, 170–179.

Weil 1992, pp. 323–324; Tomuschat 1999, Chap. XI, para 49; Chemin 2006, pp. 55–59.

[48] *Legal Consequences for States of the Continued Presence of South Africa in Namibia (South-West Africa) Notwithstanding Security Council Resolution 276 (1970)*, Advisory Opinion of 21 June 1971, ICJ Reports 1971, 16, para 88.

that the decisions contained in Security Council resolution 276 (1970) were adopted in conformity with the purposes and principles of the Charter and in accordance with Articles 24 and 25 thereof.[49]

Several individual opinions stressed that it would be incompatible with the judicial function for the Court not to examine the validity of resolutions affecting a legal question addressed to it. In his Separate Opinion, Judge Petrén took the view that, since Security Council resolution 276 (1970) was based on antecedent resolutions, the Court could not pronounce on the legal consequences thereof without examining the validity of those antecedent resolutions.[50] Similarly, in his Separate Opinion, Judge Onyeama considered that the judicial function required the Court to examine, and not to assume, the validity of resolutions of the General Assembly and the Security Council, if those decisions affected the legal question addressed to the Court.[51] In his Separate Opinion, Judge Dillard also observed that if an organ

---

[49] *Legal Consequences for States of the Continued Presence of South Africa in Namibia (South-West Africa) Notwithstanding Security Council Resolution 276 (1970),* Advisory Opinion of 21 June 1971, ICJ Reports 1971, 16, para 115.

Weil 1992, pp. 323–324; Tomuschat 1999, Chap. XI, para 49; Chemin 2006, pp. 55–59.

[50] *Legal Consequences for States of the Continued Presence of South Africa in Namibia (South-West Africa) Notwithstanding Security Council Resolution 276 (1970),* Advisory Opinion of 21 June 1971, Separate Opinion Judge Petrén, ICJ Reports 1971, 16, 130–131: 'Since Security Council resolution 276 (1970) is based upon General Assembly resolution 2145 (XXI), and upon a series of subsequent resolutions of the General Assembly and Security Council, there can be no question of the Court being able to pronounce on the legal consequences of Security Council resolution 276 (1970) without first examining the validity of the resolutions upon which that resolution is itself based (…) So long as the validity of the resolution upon which resolution 276 (1970) is based has not been established, it is clearly impossible for the Court to pronounce on the legal consequences of resolution 276 (1970), for there can be no such legal consequences if the basic resolutions are illegal, and to give a finding as though there were such would be incompatible with the role of the court.'

[51] *Legal Consequences for States of the Continued Presence of South Africa in Namibia (South-West Africa) Notwithstanding Security Council Resolution 276 (1970),* Advisory Opinion of 21 June 1971, Separate Opinion Judge Onyeama, ICJ Reports 1971, 16, 143–145: 'The Court's powers are clearly defined by the Statute, and do not include powers to review decisions of other organs of the United Nations; but when, as in the present proceedings, such decisions bear upon a case properly before the Court, and a correct judgment or opinion could not be rendered without determining the validity of such decisions, the Court could not possibly avoid such a determination without abdicating its role of a judicial organ. (…) I do not conceive it as compatible with the judicial function that the Court will proceed to state the consequences of acts whose validity is assumed, without itself testing the lawfulness of the origin of those acts. I am therefore of the view that, whether an objection had been raised or not, the Court had a duty to examine General Assembly resolution 2145 (XXI) with a view to ascertaining its legal value; it had an equal duty to examine all relevant resolutions of the Security Council for the same purpose. (…) I conclude that in the present request, the Court had a duty to examine all General Assembly and Security Council resolutions which are relevant to the question posed to it, whether objections had been taken to them or not, in order to determine their validity and effect, and so that the Court can arrive at a satisfactory opinion.'

asks for an advisory opinion, the Court must examine a legal conclusion which affects the legal question posed.[52] In his Dissenting Opinion, Judge Gros expressed a similar view.[53]

In *Legal Consequences of the Construction of a Wall in the Occupied Palestinian Territory*, the Court examined whether the practice of the General Assembly of adopting recommendations while a dispute or situation was on the agenda of the Security Council, was in conformity with Article 12, para 1, of the UN Charter, which provides that while the Security Council is exercising in respect of any dispute or situation the functions assigned to it, the General Assembly shall not make any recommendation with regard to that dispute or situation unless the Security Council so requests. The Court found the accepted practice of the General Assembly, as it had evolved, to be consistent with Article 12, para 1, of the UN Charter, concluding that the General Assembly, in adopting resolution ES-10/14, seeking an advisory opinion from the Court, did not contravene the provisions of Article 12, para 1, of the UN Charter and, consequently, did not exceed its competence.[54]

In his Separate Opinion In *Certain Expenses of the United Nations (Article 17, paragraph 2, of the Charter)*, Judge Morelli adopted the position that the Court, if necessary, could examine the validity of resolutions antecedent to the resolutions to which the legal question addressed to it related.[55] Paradoxically, Judge Morelli also expressed the view that a determination by an organ of its competence has to be accepted as final.[56] These apparently inconsistent views expressed by Judge Morelli may be seen as reflecting the dilemma involved in the relationship between political organs of international institutions and the judicial function. In both *Certain Expenses of the United Nations (Article 17, paragraph 2, of the Charter)* and *Legal Consequences for States of the Continued Presence of South Africa in Namibia*

[52] *Legal Consequences for States of the Continued Presence of South Africa in Namibia (South-West Africa) Notwithstanding Security Council Resolution 276 (1970)*, Advisory Opinion of 21 June 1971, Separate Opinion Judge Dillard, ICJ Reports 1971, 16, 151: 'A court can hardly be expected to pronounce upon legal consequences unless the resolutions from which the legal consequences flow are themselves free of legal conclusions affecting the consequences. (…) There is, of course, nothing in the Charter which compels these organs to ask for an advisory opinion or which gives this Court (…) a power of review to be triggered by those who may feel their interests unlawfully invaded. But when these organs do see fit to ask for an advisory opinion, they must expect the Court to act in strict accordance with its judicial function. This function precludes it from accepting, without any enquiry whatever, a legal conclusion which itself conditions the nature and scope of the legal consequences flowing from it.'

[53] *Legal Consequences for States of the Continued Presence of South Africa in Namibia (South-West Africa) Notwithstanding Security Council Resolution 276 (1970)*, Advisory Opinion of 21 June 1971, Dissenting Opinion Judge Gros, ICJ Reports 1971, 16, para 18.

[54] *Legal Consequences of the Construction of a Wall in the Occupied Palestinian Territory*, Advisory Opinion of 9 July 2004, ICJ Reports 2004, 136, para 28.

[55] *Certain Expenses of the United Nations (Article 17, paragraph 2, of the Charter)*, Advisory Opinion of 20 July 1962, Separate Opinion Judge Morelli, ICJ Reports 1962, 151, para 2.

[56] *Certain Expenses of the United Nations (Article 17, paragraph 2, of the Charter)*, Advisory Opinion of 20 July 1962, Separate Opinion Judge Morelli, ICJ Reports 1962, 151, paras 8–10.

(South-West Africa) Notwithstanding Security Council Resolution 276 (1970), the Court insisted on the absence of powers of judicial review and yet proceeded, in view of the judicial function, to examine the legality of the relevant resolutions. These approaches can be reconciled in so far as it is recognized that, even if the Court examines the legality of an (antecedent) act in the context of advisory proceedings, those proceedings remain intended to assist the organ in the performance of its functions and cannot, in this way, affect that act.[57]

Thus, if the Court is specifically asked to examine the validity of an act and finds it to be *ultra vires*, that opinion cannot in itself invalidate that resolution. In *Constitution of the Maritime Safety Committee of the Inter-Governmental Maritime Consultative Organization*, the ICJ arrived at the conclusion that the Assembly had acted inconsistently with Article 28 (a) of the Convention for the Establishment of the Inter-Governmental Maritime Consultative Organization.[58] Although the ICJ declared in its Advisory Opinion the inconformity of the act of the Assembly, residing in its failure to elect Liberia and Panama to the Maritime Safety Committee, this declaration did not in itself affect the validity of that resolution, but advised the Assembly that it had acted unconstitutionally.

On the basis of these considerations, it is concluded that judicial review as such cannot be obtained in advisory proceedings. Even if the ICJ proceeds to examine the legality of acts adopted by an organ of an international institution, while insisting that it does not have powers of judicial review, this takes place within the context of advisory proceedings, which are intended to assist that organ. This position obtains both when antecedent resolutions may affect the legal question and when the legal question itself is directed at the validity of an act.

Turning now to contentious proceedings, in the *Cases Concerning Questions of Interpretation and Application of the 1971 Montreal Convention Arising from the Aerial Incident at Lockerbie (Provisional Measures)*, the ICJ took the view that it was not, at that stage, called upon to determine definitively the legal effect of Security Council resolution 748 (1992).[59] Nevertheless, by considering that, *prima*

---

[57] *Judgments of the Administrative Tribunal of the International Labour Organization upon Complaints Made against the United Nations Educational, Scientific and Cultural Organization*, Advisory Opinion of 23 October 1956, Dissenting Opinion Judge Córdova, ICJ Reports 1956, 77, 158–159; *Certain Expenses of the United Nations (Article 17, paragraph 2, of the Charter)*, Advisory Opinion of 20 July 1962, Separate Opinion Judge Sir Gerald Fitzmaurice, ICJ Reports 1962, 151, 202–203.

[58] *Constitution of the Maritime Safety Committee of the Inter-Governmental Maritime Consultative Organization*, Advisory Opinion of 8 June 1960, ICJ Reports 1960, 150, 171.

[59] *Case Concerning Questions of Interpretation and Application of the 1971 Montreal Convention arising from the Aerial Incident at Lockerbie (Provisional Measures)*, Order of 14 April 1992, ICJ Reports 1992, 3, paras 39–41: 'Whereas both Libya and the United Kingdom, as Members of the United Nations, are obliged to accept and carry out the decisions of the Security Council in accordance with Article 25 of the Charter; whereas the Court, which is at the stage of proceedings on provisional measures, considers that prima facie this obligation extends to the decision contained in resolution 748 (1992); and whereas, in accordance with Article 103 of the Charter, the obligations of the Parties in that respect prevail over their obligations under any other

facie, the decision contained in it was a decision within the meaning of Article 25 of the Charter of the United Nations which, by virtue of Article 103 of the Charter of the United Nations, prevailed over obligations arising under the Convention for the Suppression of Unlawful Acts Against the Safety of Civil Aviation, the Court gave legal effect to resolution 748 (1992), in so far as its presumed validity constituted a reason for not indicating provisional measures. These cases, brought by Libya against the United Kingdom and the United States, triggered the question whether the ICJ could examine the validity of a resolution of the Security Council in contentious proceedings. As a matter of judicial policy, the Court may have been desirous to avoid indicating provisional measures conflicting with resolution 748 (1992). It may also have had in view the discretion presumably enjoyed by the Security Council under Chap. VII of the UN Charter.[60] Nevertheless, in the phase of the preliminary objections, the Court appears to have adhered to a wider understanding of its jurisdiction, finding that the objection derived from resolution 748 (1992), advanced by the United Kingdom and the United States, did not have an exclusively preliminary character. This position may have implied that the Court considered that it did have jurisdiction to assess the validity of resolution

(Footnote 59 continued)
international agreement, including the Montreal Convention; Whereas the Court, while thus not at this stage called upon to determine definitively the legal effect of Security Council resolution 748 (1992), considers that, whatever the situation previous to the adoption of that resolution, the rights claimed by Libya under the Montreal Convention cannot now be regarded as appropriate for protection by the indication of provisional measures; Whereas, furthermore, an indication of the measures requested by Libya would be likely to impair the rights which appear prima facie to be enjoyed by the United Kingdom by virtue of Security Council resolution 748 (1992);'; *Case Concerning Questions of Interpretation and Application of the 1971 Montreal Convention arising from the Aerial Incident at Lockerbie (Provisional Measures)*, Order of 14 April 1992, ICJ Reports 1992, 114, paras 42–44: 'Whereas both Libya and the United States, as Members of the United Nations, are obliged to accept and carry out the decisions of the Security Council in accordance with Article 25 of the Charter; whereas the Court, which is at the stage of proceedings on provisional measures, considers that prima facie this obligation extends to the decision contained in resolution 748 (1992); and whereas, in accordance with Article 103 of the Charter, the obligations of the Parties in that respect prevail over their obligations under any other international agreements, including the Montreal Convention; Whereas the Court, while thus not at this stage called upon to determine definitively the legal effect of Security Council resolution 748 (1992), considers that, whatever the situation previous to the adoption of that resolution, the rights claimed by Libya under the Montreal Convention cannot now be regarded as appropriate for protection by the indication of provisional measures; Whereas, furthermore, an indication of the measures requested by Libya would be likely to impair the rights which prima facie appear to be enjoyed by the United States by virtue of Security Council resolution 748 (1992).'

[60] Tomuschat 1999, Chap. XI, para 49.

748 (1992).[61] It must in any event be observed, however, that the jurisdiction of the Court in these cases was based on Article 14, para 1, of the Convention for the Suppression of Unlawful Acts Against the Safety of Civil Aviation. Although the Court examined whether the conditions posed by this provision had been fulfilled, it does not seem to have considered whether the validity of resolution 748 (1992) was within its scope. In so far as the question of the validity or the invalidity of resolution 748 (1992) cannot be said to fall within the reach of Article 14, para 1, of the Convention for the Suppression of Unlawful Acts Against the Safety of Civil Aviation, the ICJ could not have dealt with that question. From that perspective, it may be said that the propriety of the indication of provisional measures should have been based solely on considerations derived from the provisions of the Convention for the Suppression of Unlawful Acts Against the Safety of Civil Aviation, even if such measures would have conflicted with resolution 748 (1992).

In this context, it may be mentioned that several constituent instruments of international organizations contain provisions for the referral of questions or disputes relating to the interpretation or application of those instruments to an organ of the international institution, arbitration, or the ICJ.[62] In so far as an appeal from those organs to an arbitral or judicial organ is foreseen, one could speak of review in these instances. The character of such proceedings does not seem to bear, however, on the issue of determining the validity or invalidity of an act of an organ of an international institution.

Therefore, although ICJ stated, in *Certain Expenses of the United Nations (Article 17, paragraph 2, of the Charter)*, that the question of its competence must be decided, in the first place at least, by an organ of an international institution itself, it would appear to follow from the preceding analysis that neither advisory proceedings nor contentious proceedings seem to constitute suitable avenues for reviewing this determination.[63] From the unsuitability of advisory or contentious proceedings for review, it would then—conversely—seem to follow that the provisional determination of its competence by an organ of an international institution would, automatically, become final.

---

[61] *Case Concerning Questions of Interpretation and Application of the 1971 Montreal Convention Arising from the Aerial Incident at Lockerbie (Preliminary Objections)*, Judgment of 27 February 1998, ICJ Reports 1998, 9, para 50; *Case Concerning Questions of Interpretation and Application of the 1971 Montreal Convention Arising from the Aerial Incident at Lockerbie (Preliminary Objections)*, Judgment of 27 February 1998, ICJ Reports 1998, 115, para 49.

[62] Constitution of the International Labour Organization, Article 37, para 1; Constitution of the United Nations Educational, Scientific and Cultural Organization, Article XIV, para 2; Constitution of the Food and Agriculture Organization of the United Nations, Article XVII, para 1; Constitution of the World Health Organization, Article 75; Articles of Agreement of the International Bank for Reconstruction and Development, Article IX, paras a and b; Convention on International Civil Aviation Organization, Article 84; Convention on the International Maritime Organization, Articles 69 and 70; Convention of the World Meteorological Organization, Article 29; Statute of the International Atomic Energy Agency, Article XVII A; Constitution of the United Nations Industrial Development Organization, Article 22, para 1.

[63] Klabbers 2002, pp. 235–243.

Against this background, the practice of an organ of an international institution, coupled with a teleological interpretation of its constituent instrument, may operate to broaden its competence in spite of objections on the part of the Member States.[64] Against this expansive trend, it might be argued that the subsequent practice of the parties can only be relied on to interpret a treaty if it establishes the agreement of the parties. More generally, it might be said that, if the exercise of competence by an organ of an international institution cannot be reviewed by the judicial function, then the Member States of the international institution may determine this question for themselves.[65] That position would, however, be inconsistent with the view that the attainment of common ends or interests has been entrusted by the Member States to the organ of the international institution, as involving a transfer of power, so that it would no longer be open to the Member States to adopt that position.[66]

Overall, this way of seeing the relationship between Members States of international institutions, political organs of international institutions, and the judicial function, in the light of the vertical structure of the concept of law underlying the concept of public international law, results in endowing the political organs with a discretionary power, which is disconnected, on the one hand, from the Members States of the international institution and, on the other hand, from the judicial function. These disjunctions are, it is submitted, produced by the distorting effect of the framework of obligation. Within the framework of obligation, even though the ICJ may exercise its judicial function to the full and examine the validity or invalidity of acts adopted by organs of international institutions, that activity must nevertheless at the same time be seen as assistance to the work of a political organ which is characterized by discretion. That characterization itself is, however, also a result of the framework of obligation. This discretionary power is deemed to originate in a transfer and transformation of the freedom to act of the members of international society. Against this background, the discretionary character of this power is informed by the view that it represents the transition from the international state of nature to organized international society. This view can only be maintained, however, if the view of this power as entrusted, conferred by the Member States, is downplayed. The framework of obligation forces the choice between international order and international legitimacy, by connecting the notion of entrustment of common purposes with the notion of a transfer of power. The

---

[64] *Certain Expenses of the United Nations (Article 17, paragraph 2, of the Charter)*, Advisory Opinion of 20 July 1962, Separate Opinion Judge Sir Percy Spender, ICJ Reports 1962, 151, 195–197.

Alvarez 2005, pp. 87–92.

[65] *Certain Expenses of the United Nations (Article 17, paragraph 2, of the Charter)*, Advisory Opinion of 20 July 1962, Separate Opinion Judge Sir Gerald Fitzmaurice, ICJ Reports 1962, 151, 202–205; Dissenting Opinion President Winiarski, 232.

Zemanek 1997, paras 150–160.

[66] *Certain Expenses of the United Nations (Article 17, paragraph 2, of the Charter)*, Advisory Opinion of 20 July 1962, Separate Opinion Judge Sir Percy Spender, ICJ Reports 1962, 151, 183.

reformulated framework, as envisaged here, does not operate on the basis of a transfer of power, but locates power to constitute international society both in the members of international society and in organs of international institutions.[67] As a matter of conventional international law, neither organs of international institutions, nor members of international society can claim an exclusive power of interpretation. As a consequence of the reformulated framework, both the power to act of the members of international society and the power to act of organs of international institutions are directed at the constituting of the common good of international society, which may metaphorically be situated between them—the middle ground. In this light, organs of international institutions must show how their acts contribute to the constituting of the common good of international society. At the same time, organs of international institutions are part of the constituting of international society by the members of international society and cannot be circumvented pursuant to a non-existent freedom to act. The relationship between organs of international institutions and the members of international society thus being itself an aspect of the constituting of international society, it may be informed from the perspective of the judicial function. If the relationship between law and politics is seen in terms of perspectives rather than in terms of a distinction, it may be said that the activities of political organs of international institutions are directed at the formation of the common good of international society, whereas the judicial function addresses the coherence of the constituting of international society.

Thus, if the concept of international institution is situated within the reformulated framework, which in a way combines the framework of obligation and the framework of authorization, the relationship between the members of international society and (organs of) international institutions is transformed. Pursuant to the basic framework, the members of international society have a power to act which is not an unlimited freedom to act. The members of international society may transcend this dilemma situation by resorting to practical reasoning about the constituting of international society. This constituting of international society may take the more permanent form of international institutions assuming both an enabling role and a disabling role. As thus situated, international institutions are a part of the constituting of international society to which the members of international society have entrusted the management of the common good of international society. The question whether the management of the common good by organs of international institutions is taken care of coherently, in the view of the members of international society, is itself a matter of practical reasoning. There is no transfer of power involved; the power to act of both organs of international institutions and the members of international society is directed at the constituting of the common good of international society. Within this context, organs of international institutions must demonstrate, pursuant to the process of practical reasoning, how they have executed the tasks entrusted to them by

[67] Klabbers 2002, pp. 202–206.

the members of international society, in conjunction with the constituting of international society by the members of international society.

Correspondingly, the acts of the members of international society in the field constituted by the international institution must be directed at the constituting or reconstituting of the international institution. The enabling aspect thus forms at the same time the disabling aspect. For the members of international society there is no alternative to channelling their acts through the international institution, because they cannot resort to a non-existent unlimited freedom to act. The reconstituting of international society, the reforming of international institutions, like the constituting of international society, must proceed on the basis of practical reasoning directed at the common good of international society. In this way, the constituting of international society and of international institutions may be regarded as having, simultaneously, a political and a legal aspect. In this way the circular relationship between rules and institutions, which was regarded as problematic within the framework of obligation, finds a natural environment within the reformulated framework. Within the reformulated framework, movement is essential, because the power to act situates the members of international society in a dilemma situation. Proceeding from this dilemma situation, the members of international society may constitute international society in the form of rules of public international law. On the basis of these rules, the members of international society may proceed to establish international institutions so as to give international society a durable form. And from that position, international institutions may participate in the constituting of international society in the form of rules, which are both enabling and disabling, addressing the dilemma situations of the members of international institutions. Within the reformulated framework, the concept of international institution and the concept of public international law flow into each other.

The approach of the ICJ, in *International Status of South-West Africa*, to the question concerning the international status of the Territory of South-West Africa and the international obligations of the Union of South Africa arising therefrom, that had been submitted to the Court by General Assembly resolution 338 (IV), may illustrate more elaborately how the analysis from the perspectives of the framework of obligation and the framework of authorization may be fruitful. This general question had been subdivided into three particular questions, the first of which was as follows:

> Does the Union of South Africa continue to have international obligations under the Mandate for South-West Africa and, if so, what are those obligations?

Beginning its examination of this question, the Court observed that the Mandates System, created by Article 22 of the Covenant of the League of Nations, gave practical effect to two principles, the principle of non-annexation and the principle that the well-being and development of 'non self-governing' peoples formed a sacred trust of civilization. Accordingly, a tutelage was to be established for these peoples, which was to be entrusted to advanced nations and exercised by them as mandatories on behalf of the League. On this basis, the Principal Allied and Associated Powers proposed the terms of a Mandate to be conferred upon his

Britannic Majesty, which was to be exercised on his behalf by the Government of the Union of South Africa. His Brittanic Majesty, for and on behalf of the Government of the Union of South Africa, agreed to accept the Mandate and to exercise it on behalf of the League in accordance with the proposed terms. On 17 December 1920, the Council of the League of Nations, confirming the Mandate, defined its terms. In accordance with these terms, the Union of South Africa, as Mandatory, on the one hand, was to have full power of administration and legislation and, on the other hand, was to observe a number of obligations, while the Council of the League of Nations was to supervise the administration and see to it that these obligations were fulfilled.[68]

The Court then turned to the contention advanced on behalf of the Government of the Union of South Africa that the Mandate had lapsed because the League of Nations had ceased to exist. Rejecting that contention, the Court observed:

> The Mandate was created, in the interest of the inhabitants of the territory, and of humanity in general, as an international institution with an international object – a sacred trust of civilization. (...) The international rules regulating the Mandate constituted an international status for the Territory recognized by all the Members of the League of Nations, including the Union of South Africa.[69]

It then proceeded to observe:

> The authority which the Union Government exercises over the Territory is based on the Mandate. If the Mandate lapsed, as the Union Government contends, the latter's authority would equally have lapsed. To retain the rights derived from the Mandate and to deny the obligations thereunder would not be justified.[70]

It seems as if, at that point, the Court was focusing on the framework of authorization. Indeed, if the power of administration held by the Union of South Africa was derived from the Mandate and if the Mandate had lapsed, the Union of South Africa could no longer be regarded as having retained that right. The Court did not, however, draw that conclusion, which would have raised the question to what entity that right had reverted. Rather, the Court was focusing on the alternatives of maintaining the Mandate or placing the territory under the trusteeship system pursuant to Article 77, para 1 (a), of the UN Charter. While the purpose of the trusteeship system, according to Article 76 (b) of the UN Charter, was to promote the progressive development towards self-government or independence of each territory and its peoples, the placement of such territories under the system was dependent on agreement. The Court's invocation of South Africa's reliance on the rights derived from the Mandate formed an element in the demonstration that the Mandate had not lapsed so as to identify the obligations incumbent on South Africa.

---

[68] *International Status of South-West Africa*, Advisory Opinion of 11 July 1950, ICJ Reports 1950, 128, 131–132.

[69] *International Status of South-West Africa*, Advisory Opinion of 11 July 1950, ICJ Reports 1950, 128, 132.

[70] *International Status of South-West Africa*, Advisory Opinion of 11 July 1950, ICJ Reports 1950, 128, 133.

The subsequent reasoning bears out that the Court was not concerned with denying the rights of the Union of South Africa, but with emphasizing the continuity of the Mandate and of the obligations of the Union of South Africa thereunder. It distinguished two kinds of international obligations assumed by the Union of South Africa. One kind was directly related to the administration of the Territory, corresponding to the sacred trust of civilization referred to in Article 22 of the Covenant of the League of Nations. The other kind was related to the machinery for implementation and was linked to the supervision and control of the League of Nations, corresponding to the securities for the performance of the trust referred to in Article 22 of the Covenant of the League of Nations.[71] With respect to the first group of obligations, the very essence of the sacred trust of civilization, the Court found that their *raison d'être* and original object remained and that, since their fulfillment did not depend on the existence of the League of Nations, they could not have been brought to an end merely because this supervisory organ had ceased to exist.[72] In respect of the second group of obligations, the Court found that the General Assembly was legally qualified to exercise the supervisory functions previously exercised by the League of Nations with regard to the administration of the Territory. Consequently, the Union of South Africa was under an obligation to submit to supervision and control of the General Assembly and to render annual reports to it.[73] Thus, notwithstanding the disappearance of the League of Nations, the Mandate and the obligations thereunder had continued to exist and the General Assembly had taken over the supervisory functions from the Council of the League of Nations.

Rhetorically, the Court, having distinguished the two groups of obligations as relating to, respectively, the sacred trust of civilization and supervision, focused on the irrelevance of the disappearance of the supervisory organ so as to justify the continuing character of the Mandate. At the same time, however, as the substitution of the General Assembly for the Council of the League of Nations demonstrated, the Court regarded both the sacred trust of civilization and supervision as essential.[74] Directed at refuting the argument that the Mandate had involved a cession of territory or a transfer of sovereignty,[75] the Court's approach was shaped entirely by the framework of obligation.

While it might thus be said that the position adopted by the Court that the Mandate had not lapsed was informed by the voluntary character of trusteeship

---

[71] *International Status of South-West Africa*, Advisory Opinion of 11 July 1950, ICJ Reports 1950, 128, 133.

[72] *International Status of South-West Africa*, Advisory Opinion of 11 July 1950, ICJ Reports 1950, 128, 133–136.

[73] *International Status of South-West Africa*, Advisory Opinion of 11 July 1950, ICJ Reports 1950, 128, 136–138.

[74] *International Status of South-West Africa*, Advisory Opinion of 11 July 1950, ICJ Reports 1950, 128, 133, 136.

[75] *International Status of South-West Africa*, Advisory Opinion of 11 July 1950, ICJ Reports 1950, 128, 132.

agreements concluded on the basis of Chap. XII of the UN Charter, it does not seem coherent. Principally, it gives rise to the question how the Mandate could have continued to exist while its legal basis, Article 22 of the Covenant of the League of Nations, had disappeared. To this effect, the Court relied on antecedent principles, valid *dehors* the Covenant of the League of Nations, international rules regulating the Mandate and the view of the Mandate as an international institution. Placed within the framework of obligation, those principles, rules, and institutions would have to be seen as emanating from and restricting the freedom to act of the members of the international community, including the Mandatory. It is, however, difficult to fit the concept of trust, whereby the international community, as *cestui que trust*, had entrusted to the Union of South Africa, as trustee, the well-being of the inhabitants of the Territory, as beneficiary,[76] into that framework. This is not simply a matter of the transposability to the international plane of private law concepts, which the Court declined in this instance. Rather, it involves the issue that the framework of obligation which informed the principles, rules and institutions identified by the Court, which endows the members of the international community with freedoms to act, cannot explain how a right can be conferred by the members of the international community on a Mandatory.

The Separate Opinions of Sir Arnold McNair and Judge Read differed from the majority position to the extent that the United Nations had not, in their view, succeeded the League of Nations in respect of the supervision of the Mandate. In their view, even though the United Nations could not exercise administrative supervision with respect to the Mandate, the former Members of the League of Nations could initiate judicial supervision on the basis of Article 7 of the Mandate.[77]

The second question addressed to the Court by the General Assembly was formulated as follows:

> Are the provisions of Chapter XII of the Charter applicable and, if so, in what manner, to the Territory of South-West Africa.

Relying on Articles 75, 77, and 79 of the UN Charter, the Court found that, while Chap. XII of the UN Charter was applicable in the sense that the Territory might be placed thereunder by means of a Trusteeship Agreement, there was no obligation to negotiate and conclude a Trusteeship Agreement.[78]

The Dissenting Opinions appended to the Advisory Opinion mainly diverged therefrom in respect of the view of the majority that Chap. XII of the UN Charter did not contain an obligation to transform the Mandate by placing it under the Trusteeship System. Judges Krylow and De Visscher found that Chap. XII of the

[76] Castañeda 1969, p. 128.

[77] *International Status of South-West Africa*, Advisory Opinion of 11 July 1950, Separate Opinion Sir Arnold McNair, ICJ Reports 1950, 128, 157–162; Separate Opinion Judge Read, 164–173.

[78] *International Status of South-West Africa*, Advisory Opinion of 11 July 1950, ICJ Reports 1950, 128, 138–140.

UN Charter gave rise to an obligation to negotiate with a view to concluding a trusteeship agreement,[79] Judges Guerrero, Zoričić and Badawi Pasha declaring that they concurred in the views expressed by Judge De Visscher. Judge Alvarez even identified, under the new international law, an obligation to conclude a trusteeship agreement.[80]

These diverging positions as regards the import of Chap. XII of the UN Charter may be explained, it is submitted, by the contradictory nature of the provisions of Chap. XII of the UN Charter. While, on the one hand, the text of those provisions suggests that there was a compelling expectation that Mandate territories would be brought under the Trusteeship System, the emphasis on the instrument of agreement, on the other hand, negated this expectation. The position adopted by the Court with respect to the first question seems to have been determined to a significant extent by its answer to the second question.

The third question addressed by the General Assembly to the ICJ was as follows:

> Has the Union of South Africa the competence to modify the international status of the Territory of South-West Africa, or, in the event of a negative reply, where does the competence rest to determine and modify the international status of the Territory.

With respect to this question, the Court found that the competence to determine and modify the international status of South-West Africa rested with the Union of South Africa acting with the consent of the United Nations. Whereas previously, pursuant to Article 7, para 1, of the Mandate, the consent of the Council of the League of Nations had been required for any modification of the terms of the Mandate, the Court considered that by analogy with Chap. XII of the UN Charter, which gave the General Assembly the authority to approve alterations and modifications of Trusteeship Agreements, the consent of the United Nations would now be required for the modification of the international status of South-West Africa.[81]

Like the first part of the Court's answer to the first question, the answer of the Court to the third question was unanimous.[82] It was motivated by the concern that the competence to modify the status of the Territory should not rest with the Mandatory alone. The Court accordingly found that it rested with the Mandatory in conjunction with the United Nations. To all intents and purposes, therefore, the Court treated the Mandate as if the United Nations had automatically succeeded

---

[79] *International Status of South-West Africa*, Advisory Opinion of 11 July 1950, Dissenting Opinion Judge De Visscher, ICJ Reports 1950, 128, 186–190; Dissenting Opinion Judge Krylov, 191–192.

[80] *International Status of South-West Africa*, Advisory Opinion of 11 July 1950, Dissenting Opinion Judge Alvarez, ICJ Reports 1950, 128, Section VII.

[81] *International Status of South-West Africa*, Advisory Opinion of 11 July 1950, ICJ Reports 1950, 128, 141–143.

[82] *International Status of South-West Africa*, Advisory Opinion of 11 July 1950, Separate Opinion Sir Arnold McNair, ICJ Reports 1950, 128, 162–163.

thereto. Declining to identify an obligation on the part of the Mandatory to bring the Mandate under the International Trusteeship System, the Court applied, by analogy, the provisions of Chap. XII of the UN Charter relating to alterations and amendments as if the Mandate formed part of the International Trusteeship System.

The ICJ's approach in *International Status of South-West Africa*, inspired by the framework of obligation, acquires its full significance when compared and contrasted with its subsequent approach in *Legal Consequences for States of the Continued Presence of South Africa in Namibia (South-West Africa) Notwithstanding Security Council Resolution 276 (1970)*, in which the Court responded to the question formulated in para 1 of Security Council resolution 284 (1970):

> What are the legal consequences for States of the continued presence of South Africa in Namibia, notwithstanding Security Council resolution 276 (1970)?

After first establishing, in paras 42–54 of the Advisory Opinion, that the so-called "C" Mandate, which applied to the Territory of South-West Africa, could not be equated with annexation, the ICJ, in two sections (paras 55–72; 73–83), reiterated the answer to the two parts of the first question that had been given by the Court in *International Status of South-West Africa*. In the course of its reasoning, the Court stressed, particularly in para 81, the interrelated nature of the sacred trust and the supervision thereof. In that paragraph, the Court then situated these interconnected elements within the framework of authorization, referring to the passage on page 133 of *International Status of South-West Africa*, in which it had observed that the authority of South Africa over the Territory was derived from the Mandate.[83] Relying on the same passage, the Court then also situated, in

[83] *Legal Consequences for States of the Continued Presence of South Africa in Namibia (South-West Africa) Notwithstanding Security Council resolution 276 (1970)*, Advisory Opinion of 21 June 1971, ICJ Reports 1971, 16, para 81:

> Thus, by South Africa's own admission, "supervision and accountability" were of the essence of the Mandate, as the Court had consistently maintained. The theory of the lapse of the Mandate on the demise of the League of Nations is in fact inseparable from the claim that there is no obligation to submit to the supervision of the United Nations, and vice versa. Consequently, both or either of the claims advanced, namely that the Mandate has lapsed and/or that there is no obligation to submit to international supervision by the United Nations, are destructive of the very institution upon which the presence of South Africa in Namibia rests, for:
>
> The authority which the Union Government exercises over the Territory is based on the Mandate. If the Mandate lapsed, as the Union Government contends, the latter's authority would equally have lapsed. To retain the rights derived from the Mandate and to deny the obligations thereunder could not be justified (*I.C.J. Reports 1950*, p. 133; cited in *I.C.J. Reports 1962*, p. 333).

para 105 of *Legal Consequences for States of the Continued Presence of South Africa in Namibia (South-West Africa) Notwithstanding Security Council resolution 276 (1970)*, General Assembly resolution 2145 (XXI), which had revoked the Mandate, within the framework of authorization.

Between those two paragraphs, the Court dealt with two objections that had been raised. First, in paras 87–95, the Court addressed the question whether the General Assembly, by adopting resolution 2145 (XXI), had acted *ultra vires*. A key element in its reasoning was its observation in para 91 that one of the fundamental principles governing the international relationship established between all Members of the United Nations and South Africa, as Mandatory, is that a party which disowns or does not fulfill its own obligations cannot be recognized as retaining the rights which it claims to derive from the relationship. Subsequently, in paras 94–95, it treated the Mandate as an international agreement having the character of a treaty or convention. In this way, the Court relied both on the framework of authorization and the framework of obligation. The framework of authorization, inspired by the passage in *International Status of South-West Africa*, determined the effect of breach of the Mandate seen as an agreement. The framework of obligation served as the prism through which the Court determined that South Africa had breached the Mandate, seen as an agreement.

The Court then turned, in paras 96–103, to the objection that the Covenant of the League of Nations had not conferred on the Council the power to terminate a Mandate for misconduct of the mandatory. In that respect, however, the ICJ identified and relied on a general principle of law (paras 96, 98, and 101) that a right of termination on account of breach must be presumed to exist in respect of all treaties. The resulting position was that the Mandate had been validly terminated by virtue of General Assembly resolution 2145 (XXI). Accordingly, the right to administer the Territory had reverted to the General Assembly, as an organ of the United Nations representing the Members of the United Nations. Against this background, the issues of coherence signalled previously with respect to the Court's approach in *International Status of South-West Africa*, may now be amplified. First, if, by virtue of the general principle of law identified by the Court, the Council of the League of Nations had disposed of a right to terminate the Mandate, and if, by virtue of the exercise of that right, the right to administer the Territory would have reverted to the Council as an organ of the League of Nations, the role of the Council and of the League of Nations as a whole were not as minimal as the Court suggested in *International Status of South-West Africa*, in order to support the continued existence of the Mandate and the transfer of the supervisory functions to the United Nations. Second, in its answer to the third question, in *International Status of South-West Africa*, the ICJ had found that the competence to modify the Mandate rested with the Mandatory acting with the consent of the United Nations. The general principle of law identified by the Court in *Legal Consequences for States of the Continued Presence of South Africa in Namibia (South-West Africa) Notwithstanding Security Council resolution 276 (1970)*, located the competence to modify the Mandate in the United Nations. Between the approaches of *International Status of South-West Africa* and *Legal*

Consequences for States of the Continued Presence of South Africa in Namibia (South-West Africa) Notwithstanding Security Council resolution 276 (1970), therefore, the competence to modify and terminate the Mandate shifted from the Mandatory, acting with the consent of the United Nations, to the United Nations; consent had turned into a power. Third, the approaches of the Court in *International Status of South-West Africa* and *Legal Consequences for States of the Continued Presence of South Africa in Namibia (South-West Africa) Notwithstanding Security Council resolution 276 (1970)*, are marked by the contrast between the framework of obligation and the framework of authorization. The reasoning in *International Status of South-West Africa* inscribed itself within the framework of obligation, although it appeared to rely on the framework of authorization. That appearance inspired the turn, in *Legal Consequences for States of the Continued Presence of South Africa in Namibia (South-West Africa) Notwithstanding Security Council resolution 276 (1970)*, to the framework of authorization. That turn made it possible to see the revocation of the Mandate by General Assembly resolution 2145 (XXI) as conforming to the concept of public international law.

In dealing with the problematique at issue in these advisory opinions, the reformulated framework advocated here would see the relationship between organs of international institutions and the members of international institutions neither in terms of a power to confer rights nor in terms of a power to impose obligations. The basic problem that the Court had to deal with, was how to account for both rights and obligations while working within the mutual exclusivity of the framework of obligation and the framework of authorization. The reformulated framework situates the members of international society in the position of a dilemma: by virtue of that framework, the members of international society have a power to act which is not a freedom to act; the extent of the power to act of the members of international society is indeterminate. In other words, the members of international society have a right to act, but also, at the same time, an obligation, which position corresponds to rights/obligations of the other members of international society. To overcome this dilemma situation, the members of international society must constitute international society pursuant to the process of practical reasoning. This process gives rise to rules of public international law which do not contain either rights or obligations but both. Those rules, constituted by the members of international society, constitute at the same time the relationships between the members of international society and characterize them in terms of rights/obligations. Accordingly, those rules have both an enabling aspect and a disabling aspect.

The process of practical reasoning may also give rise to international institutions, which are based on rules of public international law and in turn give rise to rules of public international law. They are constituted by the process of practical reasoning and constitute, in turn, that process. Accordingly, the relationship between organs of international institutions and the members of international society is not characterized by the notion of a transfer of powers, but may appropriately be seen in terms of the concept of trust, whereby the organ of the international institution may be seen as a trustee, while the members of international society may be seen as both cestui que trust and as beneficiary. The notion of authority can thus neither be located exclusively in the organ of the international institution nor exclusively in the members of international society. The role of the organ of the international institution, as trustee, consists of informing the process of the formation of the common good of international society by the members of international society. Because the members of international society cannot circumvent the organ of the international institution, not having, within the reformulated framework, a freedom to act, they cannot simply revoke the trust and leave it there. That would throw the members of international society back into the dilemma situation. Reforming organs of international institutions thus requires re-entering the cycle of practical reasoning directed at the constituting of international society. In this way, the power to constitute international society may be seen as dispersed within the system, neither located exclusively in the members of international society nor located exclusively in organs of international institutions. Moreover, the power to constitute international society is directed at the structure of international society, consisting of relations between the members of international society and between the organs of international institutions and the members of international society.

13.4 Conclusion

On the basis of this examination, it is concluded that the framework of obligation and the framework of authorization are insufficient to explain coherently the concept of international institution. Within the framework of authorization, the concept of international institution is presupposed and cannot be explained as emanating from acts of States. Within the framework of obligation, it is attempted to link the achievement of common purposes of States with the limitation of their freedom to act. The resulting situation, however, is characterized by two extremes, neither of which can be accepted. If it is considered that the Member States have transferred power to (organs of) international institutions, it is no longer possible for them to determine whether the (organs of) international institutions have exceeded their competence. On the other hand, to admit that those Member States may, collectively or individually, determine whether those (organs of) international institutions have remained within their competence, would in itself be inconsistent with the notion that States have entrusted the attainment of common ends or interests to international institutions by means of a transfer of power.

Together, these considerations relating to the incoherence of the mutual exclusivity of the framework of obligation and the framework of authorization, point to a number of requirements relating to the concept of international institution. The incoherence of the framework of authorization points to the requirement of a connection between the concept of international institution and acts of members of international society. The incoherence of the framework of obligation points to the requirement that the concept of international institution should not be seen in terms of a transfer of power, pursuant to which power is located either exclusively at the level of the international institution or located exclusively at the level of the members of international society. It is submitted that the reformulated framework, as developed in Part I, satisfies these requirements and constitutes a framework within which the concept of international institution may be situated coherently. The concept of international institution may thus be seen as a structure forming a part of the constituting of international society by the members of international society. As such, international institutions represent both an enabling aspect, in the form of constituting international society, and a disabling aspect, in so far as acts of members of international society must conform to or reform that structure. As situated within the reformulated framework, it may synoptically be said, with Finnis, that rules of public international law determine international institutions and that international institutions determine rules of public international law. The constituting of international society in the form of international institutions takes place on the ground work of rules of public international law and, in turn, gives rise to rules of public international law. The relationship between the concept of public international law and the concept of international institution thus becomes inherently circular.

This approach diverges from the view that the Charter of the United Nations may fruitfully be regarded as (a part of) the constitution of the international community. Dupuy, for example, has put forward the view that, in view of the representativeness of the General Assembly and the Security Council and in view of the material principles contained in Articles 1 and 2, combined with the hierarchical effect of Article 103, the UN Charter may be regarded as, respectively, the organic and material constitution of the international legal order,[84] supplemented by the concept of *jus cogens*.[85] Such a view would appear to imply that the notion of constitution, as applied to the international plane, is characterized by strengthening and directed at the establishment of a vertical structure.

In contrast, as applied to the internal sphere of the institution of the State, the notion of constitution may be seen as characterized by dispersing power and directed at the establishment of a horizontal structure. If social contract theory does not succeed in explaining the institution of the State and the internal law of the State coherently, it would follow that the notion of constitution presupposes the existence of the institution of the State; its purpose is to divert its powers into three branches and to enumerate the fundamental rights of the subjects of the internal law of the State.[86] If it is attempted to explain the constitution of a State as emanating from a social contract concluded by individuals in order to exit the state of nature, the problem arises that fundamental rights, in this perspective, can only be explained as rights which those individuals have retained; this would imply that

[84] Dupuy 2002, pp. 215–244.

[85] Dupuy 2002, pp. 299–307.

[86] Paulus 2001, pp. 285–328.

those individuals have, to that extent, not really exited the state of nature. This replicates exactly the pattern identified if the concept of international institution is situated within the framework of obligation. On the other hand, if fundamental rights are explained as conferred, in the form of the constitution, by the institution of the State, those rights cannot really be characterized as fundamental; to the contrary, this would imply that the institution of the State is presupposed in terms of the framework of authorization. One way or another, therefore, the notion of constitution and its transposition to the international plane give rise to the problem that they inscribe themselves within the vertical structure of the concept of law underlying the concept of public international law. This conclusion leaves the existing plurality of States, described in Sect. 4.12, unexplained. Seeing the concept of public international law in terms of the constituting of international society, rather than connecting it to the notion of constitution, opens the door, it is submitted, to explaining and reforming the existing plurality of States, both on the international plane and in the internal sphere of the State.

Chapter 14
The Concept of *Jus Cogens* and the Concept of Obligation *Erga Omnes* Situated Within the Framework of Obligation and the Framework of Authorization

14.1 Introduction

The concept of international institution, dealt with in the previous chapter, refers the protection of the common aims or interests of the members of international society to the establishment of intergovernmental organizations and the concomitant creation of organs. Alongside the development of intergovernmental organizations, a second movement has taken place which locates the protection of the common or public interests of States in the 'unorganized' concept of international community. Descriptively, the concept of international community (community of States) has long since formed a part of international jurisprudence.[1] However, with the development of the concept of *jus cogens* and the concept of obligation *erga omnes* within the concentric circle of the international community (of States) as a whole, the concept of international community has aspired to acquire a normative meaning. A peremptory norm of general international law is defined as a norm accepted and recognized by the international community of States as a whole as a norm from which no derogation is permitted. An obligation *erga omnes* is defined as an obligation towards the international community as a whole. In these definitions, it is the international community (of States) as a whole which recognizes and accepts a norm of general international law as a peremptory norm from which no derogation is permitted and to which an obligation *erga omnes* is owed.

Sections 14.2 and 14.3 will describe, respectively, the concept of *jus cogens* and the concept of obligation *erga omnes*, as situated within the concentric circle of the international community (of States) as a whole. Section 14.4 will then tentatively describe the relationship between both concepts. Subsequently, it will be argued in Sect. 14.5 that the concept of the international community (of States) as a whole as situated within the mutual exclusivity of the framework of obligation or the framework of authorization must be analyzed as incoherent. Sections 14.6 and 14.7

---

[1] *Fisheries Case*, Judgment of 18 December 1951, ICJ Reports 1951, 116, 138–139; *North Sea Continental Shelf Cases*, Judgment of 20 February 1969, ICJ Reports 1969, 3, para 63.

J. A. Vos, *The Function of Public International Law*,
DOI: 10.1007/978-90-6704-861-3_14,

deepen this argument with respect to third States and the bilateral structure of public international law. It will subsequently be concluded in Sect. 14.8 that the concept of international community may appropriately be resituated within the reformulated framework, which transcends the mutual exclusivity of the framework of obligation and the framework of authorization. As resituated and transformed within this reformulated framework, the concept of international community may be seen in terms of the constituting of (the common good of) international society by the members of international society, which, thereby, are constituted as members of international society.

14.2 The Concept of *Jus Cogens*

The concept of *jus cogens* became a part of the concept of public international law on the basis of Articles 53 and 64 of the Vienna Convention on the Law of Treaties. Those articles deal with the eventuality of conflict between a treaty and a peremptory norm of general international law. Article 53 deals with the situation of a treaty which, at the time of its conclusion, conflicts with a peremptory norm of general international law. Article 53, first sentence, declares that such a treaty is void. Article 64 deals with the situation of an existing treaty which conflicts with an emerging peremptory norm of general international law and declares that such a treaty becomes void and terminates.

Article 53, second sentence, defines a peremptory norm of general international law as a norm accepted and recognized by the international community of States as a whole as a norm from which no derogation is permitted and which can be modified only by a subsequent norm of general international law having the same character. In this definition, the terms ‘accepted’ and ‘recognized’ have been inspired by the descriptions of customary international law and general principles of law in Article 38, para 1, (b) and (c), of the Statute of the ICJ.[2] Derogation, in this context, takes the form of conventional international law.

Those provisions of the Vienna Convention on the Law of Treaties look at the concept of *jus cogens* from the perspective of conventional international law. Recognizing an unlimited freedom of States to conclude treaties, regardless of their content, was deemed unacceptable. Traditionally, such a freedom was inferred from the freedom of contract of States. Articles 53 and 64 of the Vienna Convention on the Law of Treaties aim to avoid this result by declaring that a treaty which conflicts with *jus cogens* is or becomes void. For this purpose, Article 53, second sentence, defines the concept of *jus cogens*; its function is to restrict the freedom of States to conclude treaties.[3]

---

[2] Yasseen 1976, pp. 40–41.

[3] Schwarzenberger 1965, pp. 460–461: ‘In the absence of clear evidence of international *jus cogens*, the freedom of contract of the subjects of international law is unlimited. (…) The rules of international customary law (…) are prohibitory rules.’; Virally 1966, pp. 9–12: ‘(…) le *jus*

As defined in Article 53, second sentence, the basis of the concept of *jus cogens* is formed by the concept of general international law. Bearing in mind the identity between the concepts of general international law and customary international law, established by the ICJ in the *North Sea Continental Shelf Cases*, this would imply that the basis of *jus cogens* is formed by customary international law. With regard to such rules, the ICJ remarked in the *North Sea Continental Shelf Cases* that general or customary rules and obligations must, by their very nature, have equal force for all members of the international community and cannot, therefore, be the subject of any right of unilateral exclusion, exercisable at will by any one of them in its own favour.[4] At the same time, however, the ICJ remarked that, in the absence of *jus cogens*, rules of international law can, by agreement, be derogated from in particular cases or as between particular parties.[5]

From this perspective, a peremptory norm of general international law is to be regarded as a norm of general international law with special characteristics. Those special characteristics emanate from the acceptance and recognition of that norm of general international law, by the international community of States as a whole, as a norm from which no derogation is permitted. The recognition and acceptance by the international community of States as a whole, transform a norm of general international law, from which derogation is permitted, into a peremptory norm of general international law, from which no derogation is permitted.[6]

In other words, in the absence of the recognition and acceptance, by the international community of States as a whole, of a norm of general international law as a peremptory norm of general international law, that norm of general

(Footnote 3 continued)
cogens présente un caractère prohibitif (...) le *jus cogens* introduit une limitation à l'autonomie de la volonté des Etats, c'est-à-dire à leur liberté contractuelle, considérée traditionnellement comme absolue, parce qu'elle représente un des attributs les plus essentiels de la souveraineté. Sous cet aspect, le *jus cogens* pourrait être considéré comme une atteinte à la souveraineté des Etats.'; Schwelb 1967, pp. 948–949, 951, 963–964; Marek 1968, pp. 439–440: 'Notre examen ne portera que sur la liberté de déterminer le contenu du contrat, en d'autres termes sur la question de savoir s'il existe en droit international des règles impératives venant limiter cette liberté (...) De tout temps le droit international, s'il existe, n'a fait que [limiter la volonté souveraine des Etats]; autrement il n'existerait pas. Cette limitation de la volonté souveraine des Etats peut être relativement faible; elle n'en reste pas moins l'essence même du droit international. (...) Par définition, tout droit – comme tout ordre normatif – est une limite à la liberté de ses sujets. Par le fait même de poser des règles, il ordonne, il permet et il interdit.'; Mosler 1968, pp. 14–22; Barberis 1970, p. 26: 'L'objet de notre étude consiste à rechercher si, dans le domaine des normes réglant le droit conventionnel, il y en a qui interdisent aux Etats de déroger par la voie de traité à certaines règles juridiques. Il s'agit donc de savoir s'il y a des normes limitant la liberté contractuelle des Etats. En droit des gens il y a un principe selon lequel une conduite est permise dans la mesure où elle n'est pas juridiquement interdite. Par conséquent les Etats ont la liberté de donner aux conventions n'importe quel contenu et de déroger à n'importe quelle norme dans la mesure où il n'existe pas une norme juridique interdisant de le faire.'; Rozakis 1976, pp. 15–19, 27–30; De Hoogh 1991, pp. 185–187; Weil 1992, pp. 263–266.

[4] *North Sea Continental Shelf Cases*, Judgment of 20 February 1969, ICJ Reports 1969, 3, para 63.

[5] *North Sea Continental Shelf Cases*, Judgment of 20 February 1969, ICJ Reports 1969, 3, para 72.

[6] Dupuy 2002, pp. 275–277.

international law is to be regarded as *jus dispositivum*. The recognition and acceptance by the international community of States as a whole, of that norm of general international law as a peremptory norm of general international law turns it into *jus cogens*.[7]

The view that a peremptory norm of general international law is to be regarded as a norm of general international law with special characteristics, appears to have led to a doctrinal confusion regarding the question whether the concept of *jus cogens* is applicable to unilateral acts of States.[8] Clearly, following the reasoning of the ICJ in the *North Sea Continental Shelf Cases*, a norm of general international law applies to unilateral acts of States and a peremptory norm of general international law applies to bilateral acts of States. From this perspective, *jus cogens* does not apply to unilateral acts of States and its raison d'être is limited to bilateral acts of States.[9] It may also be remarked, however, that the existence of a peremptory norm of general international law implies the existence of an underlying norm of general international law which applies to unilateral acts of States.[10]

The concept of *jus cogens* is also commonly associated with the existence of an *ordre public* in public international law.[11] Initially, Lauterpacht linked the concept of *jus cogens* with the existence of an international public policy. Sometimes the existence of an international *ordre public* is connected to the question whether the concept of *jus cogens* applies to unilateral acts of States. These perspectives appear to set up an opposition between the international community, regarded as incorporating the

---

[7] Verdross 1937, pp. 571–572: 'Our starting-point is the uncontested rule that, as a matter of principle, states are free to conclude treaties on any subject whatsoever. All we have to investigate, therefore, is whether this rule does or does not admit certain exceptions. The answer to this question depends on the preliminary question, whether general international law contains rules which have the character of *jus cogens*. For it is obvious that if general international law consists *exclusively* of non-compulsory norms, states are always free to agree on treaty norms which deviate from general international law, without by doing so, violating general international law. If, on the other hand, general international law does contain also norms which have the character of *jus cogens*, things are very different. For it is the quintessence of norms of this character that they prescribe a certain, positive or negative behavior unconditionally; norms of this character, therefore, cannot be derogated from by the will of the contracting parties.'; Verdross 1966, p. 55: 'For this purpose it seems to me necessary to point out that, according to the general opinion of writers and jurists of international law, the power of states to conclude international treaties is in *principle* unlimited. They are in principle competent to enter into international agreements on any subject whatever. The problem arises, however, if under general international law there are exceptions to this principle. Hence the question is whether all norms of general international law may be repealed by treaty provisions in relations among the contracting parties, or whether there are norms of general international law restricting the freedom of states to conclude treaties. In other words the question is whether all norms of international law have the character of *jus dispositivum* or if there exist some norms having the character of *jus cogens* too, from which no derogation is permitted by an agreement *inter partes*.'; Weil 1992, pp. 263–266.

[8] Gómez Robledo 1981, pp. 192–204.

[9] Marek 1968, pp. 439–441; Mosler 1968, pp. 22–26; Weil 1992, pp. 281–282.

[10] Suy 1967, pp. 70–76; Paulus 2001, pp. 351–354.

[11] Dupuy 2002, pp. 280–283.

common or public interest, and the individual members of the international community, understood, bilaterally or unilaterally, as representing private interests.

The raison d'être of the concept of *jus cogens* also seems to imply a departure from the traditional non-hierarchical relationship between customary international law and conventional international law. Whereas the concept of general international law as *jus dispositivum* might be regarded as suggesting that conventional international law is hierarchically superior in so far as States may derogate from it, the concept of *jus cogens* is clearly situated above conventional international law in so far as States are not permitted to derogate from it.[12] Nevertheless, even the concept of *jus dispositivum* might be regarded as situated hierarchically above conventional international law, because it is by virtue of these norms that States are permitted to derogate from them. From this perspective, it may be observed that both *jus dispositivum* and *jus cogens* presume the existence of general or customary international law applicable to unilateral acts of States.

14.3 The Concept of Obligation *Erga Omnes*

The concept of obligation *erga omnes* became part of the concept of public international law by the Judgment of the ICJ in the *Case Concerning the Barcelona Traction, Light and Power Company, Limited (New Application: 1962; Second Phase)*, in which the ICJ drew an essential distinction between obligations of a State vis-à-vis another State in the field of diplomatic protection and obligations of a State towards the international community as a whole, which the Court characterized as obligations *erga omnes*. By their very nature, the Court said, obligations *erga omnes* are the concern of all States and all States, in view of the importance of the rights involved, can be held to have a legal interest in their protection.[13]

The Court added that obligations *erga omnes* derive, for example, from the outlawing of acts of aggression, of genocide, and from the principles and rules concerning the basic rights of the human person, including protection from slavery

---

[12] Gómez Robledo 1981, pp. 192–204. In so far as the concept of *jus cogens* is seen as sustained by both customary international law and conventional international law, the hierarchy may be located in the vertical relationship between norms of *jus cogens* and other norms; Rozakis 1976, pp. 19–24.

[13] *Case Concerning the Barcelona Traction, Light and Power Company, Limited (New Application: 1962; Second Phase)*, Judgment of 5 February 1970, ICJ Reports 1970, 3, para 33: 'In particular, an essential distinction should be drawn between the obligations of a State towards the international community as a whole, and those arising vis-à-vis another State in the field of diplomatic protection. By their very nature, the former are the concern of all States. In view of the importance of the rights involved, all States can be held to have a legal interest in their protection, they are obligations *erga omnes*.'

and racial discrimination.[14] As regards the corresponding rights of protection, the Court observed that some had entered into the body of general international law and that others are conferred by international instruments of a universal or quasi-universal character.[15]

In its description of the concept of obligation *erga omnes*, the Court connected the concept of obligation *erga omnes* to the concept of the international community as a whole; obligations *erga omnes* were characterized by the Court as obligations towards the international community as a whole. The Court also remarked that, by their very nature, obligations *erga omnes* are the concern of all States and that all States, in view of the importance of the rights involved, can be held to have a legal interest in their protection. These statements have been interpreted as meaning that the legal interest which all States can be held to have in the protection of the rights involved is equivalent to a right on the part of individual States to institute proceedings before an international court or tribunal. In other words, the concept of obligation *erga omnes* should be regarded as conferring *locus standi* on individual members of the international community as a whole.[16] In an expansive interpretation, this *locus standi* is also seen as conferring extra-judicial standing to adopt countermeasures.[17] This would mean that the corresponding rights of protection to which the Court referred are rights of States as members of the international community, which correspond to an obligation *erga omnes*.

In support of this interpretation, it might be considered that the Court, when locating the corresponding rights of protection, was referring to the dispute settlement clauses contained in Article IX of the Convention on the Prevention and Punishment of the Crime of Genocide, Article 10 of the Supplementary Convention on the Abolition of Slavery, the Slave Trade, and Institutions and Practices Similar to Slavery, and Article 22 of the International Convention on the Elimination of all Forms of Racial Discrimination.

Furthermore, the context of the description of the concept of obligation *erga omnes* in paras 33–34 of the Judgment also points in this direction. The Court contrasted the concept of obligation *erga omnes* with obligations arising in the field of diplomatic protection. With regard to obligations arising in the field of

---

[14] *Case Concerning the Barcelona Traction, Light and Power Company, Limited (New Application: 1962; Second Phase)*, Judgment of 5 February 1970, ICJ Reports 1970, 3, para 34: 'Such obligations derive, for example, in contemporary international law, from the outlawing of acts of aggression, and of genocide, as also from the principles and rules concerning the basic rights of the human person, including protection from slavery and racial discrimination.'

[15] *Case Concerning the Barcelona Traction, Light and Power Compnay, Limited (New Application: 1962; Second Phase)*, Judgment of 5 February 1970, ICJ Reports 1970, 3, para 34: 'Some of the corresponding rights of protection have entered into the body of general international law (...); others are conferred by international instruments of a universal or quasi-universal character.'

[16] Annacker 1994a, pp. 138–148, 162–165; Frowein 1994, pp. 427–429; Coffman 1996, pp. 296–299; Paulus 2001, pp. 364–379; Tams 2005, pp. 158–197.

[17] Tams 2005, pp. 198–251.

diplomatic protection, the Court stated that all States cannot be held to have a legal interest in their observance and that, in order to bring a claim, a State must establish its right to do so.[18] Apparently, with respect to obligations arising in the field of diplomatic protection, the Court regarded a legal interest as equivalent to a right.

At the same time, however, this interpretation gives rise to several problems. First, it might appear to be contradicted by para 91 of the Judgment, in which the ICJ seemed to recognize that the existence of a right of a State to bring a claim against another State with respect to infringement of human rights was dependent on conventional international law, while noting that such a right had not been established at the universal level.[19] This apparent contradiction between paras 33–34 and 91 might be explicable along the lines of a distinction between human rights and basic human rights or along the lines of a distinction between universal and regional law. Such an explanation would not, however, suffice in itself to establish the existence of rights of individual members of the international community in respect of obligations *erga omnes.*

In paras 33–34, the ICJ seemed to draw a clear distinction between legal interests and rights. In para 33, it inferred a legal interest of States in the protection of the rights involved from the importance of those rights. In para 34, it located the corresponding rights of protection in the body of general international law and in international instruments of a universal or quasi-universal nature. With regard to the body of general international law, the Court referred to page 23 of *Reservations to the Convention on the Prevention and Punishment of the Crime of Genocide.* The text on that page is not about rights of protection appertaining to States vis-à-vis obligations *erga omnes*; it relates to rights of existence of human groups. This would mean that the corresponding rights of protection envisaged by the Court are not rights of States, but rights of the beneficiaries of obligations *erga omnes.* Such an interpretation might explain why the Court distinguished between general international law and international instruments. The Convention on the Prevention and Punishment of the Crime of Genocide, as an instrument of international criminal

[18] *Case Concerning the Barcelona Traction, Light and Power Company, Limited (New Application: 1962; Second Phase)*, Judgment of 5 February 1970, ICJ Reports 1970, 3, paras 32, 35–36.

[19] *Case Concerning the Barcelona Traction, Light and Power Company, Limited (New Application: 1962; Second Phase)*, Judgment of 5 February 1970, ICJ Reports 1970, 3, para 91: 'With regard more particularly to human rights, to which reference has already been made in paragraph 34 of this Judgment, it should be noted that these also include protection against denial of justice. However, on the universal level, the instruments which embody human rights do not confer on States the capacity to protect the victims of infringements of such rights irrespective of their nationality. It is therefore still on the regional level that a solution to this problem has had to be sought; thus, within the Council of Europe, of which Spain is not a member, the problem of admissibility encountered by the claim in the present case has been resolved by the European Convention on Human Rights, which entitles each State which is a party to the Convention to lodge a complaint against any other contracting State for violation of the Convention, irrespective of the nationality of the victim.'

law, does not stipulate, but rather presupposes rights of beneficiaries. Determining the object and purpose of the Convention on the Prevention and Punishment of the Crime of Genocide, the Court identified, on page 23 of *Reservations to the Convention on the Prevention and Punishment of the Crime of Genocide*, the right of existence of human groups. The reference to international instruments would then comprise the Supplementary Convention on the Abolition of Slavery, the Slave Trade and Institutions and Practices Similar to Slavery and the International Convention on the Elimination of all Forms of Racial Discrimination. This interpretation would imply that the Court was not referring to Article IX of the Convention on the Prevention and Punishment of the Crime of Genocide.

Yet, an interpretation which solely focuses on the rights of beneficiaries does not seem fully satisfactory either. First, if seen as an element of a legal relationship, an obligation *erga omnes* should be complemented by a right. If this right is located in the corresponding right of protection of beneficiaries of an obligation *erga omnes*, there is no legal relationship at the international plane, particularly not in respect of the international community as a whole. Second, it then remains unclear what legal consequences should be attached to the statements of the Court that obligations *erga omnes* are the concern of all States and that all States have a legal interest in the protection of the rights involved. Moreover, with respect to the first example of an obligation *erga omnes*, aggression, it would be difficult to distinguish between a right of protection of a beneficiary and a right to act in the form of individual or collective self-defence. At the international plane, the concept of collective self-defence seems the clearest example of a right corresponding to an obligation *erga omnes*, but, as it devolves standing on beneficiaries, it blurs the distinction between right and legal interest.

In the *Case Concerning East Timor*, the ICJ endorsed the characterization of the right of peoples to self-determination as a norm/right *erga omnes*.[20] The Court did not identify a relationship between the right *erga omnes* and the international community as a whole, alternating between the qualification of the norm of self-determination as a principle or right. The characterization of the right of peoples to self-determination in the *Case Concerning East Timor* seems to support the interpretation of the corresponding rights of protection, as referred to by the Court in the *Case Concerning the Barcelona Traction, Light and Power Company, Limited (New Application: 1962; Second Phase)*, in the sense of the rights of the beneficiaries of an

---

[20] *Case Concerning East Timor*, Judgment of 30 June 1995, ICJ Reports 1995, 90, para 29: 'In the Court's view, Portugal's assertion that the right of peoples to self-determination, as it evolved from the Charter and from United Nations practice, has an *erga omnes* character, is irreproachable. The principle of self-determination of peoples has been recognized by the United Nations Charter and in the jurisprudence of the Court (...); it is one of the essential principles of contemporary international law. However, the Court considers that the *erga omnes* character of a norm and the rule of consent to jurisdiction are two different things. Whatever the nature of the obligations invoked, the Court could not rule on the lawfulness of the conduct of a State when its judgment would imply an evaluation of the lawfulness of the conduct of another State which is not a party to the case. Where this is so, the Court cannot act, even if the right in question is a right *erga omnes*.'

obligation *erga omnes*. From that standpoint, in the wake of the question of consent to jurisdiction, the reasoning of the Court would also have given rise to a question about the relationship between the right of peoples to self-determination and the *locus standi* of States in respect of a violation of such a right *erga omnes*.

In his Dissenting Opinion, Judge Weeramantry developed the distinction between the concept of obligation *erga omnes* and the concept of right *erga omnes*. Judge Weeramantry characterized the concept of obligation *erga omnes* as an obligation of a State towards all other States, which have a legal interest in the observance of that obligation.[21] With respect to the obligation *erga omnes* of Australia towards all States to respect the right of peoples to self-determination, Judge Weeramantry concluded that both Portugal, as the administering Power of East Timor, and East Timor would have a legal interest in the observance of that duty and that Australia was in breach of that duty *erga omnes* towards East Timor.[22] It may be observed that this interpretation of the concept of obligation *erga omnes* diverges from the description put forward by the ICJ in the *Case Concerning the Barcelona Traction, Light and Power Company, Limited (New Application: 1962; Second Phase)*. Judge Weeramantry regarded obligations *erga omnes* as obligations towards all States and included East Timor within that category. At the same time, Judge Weeramantry considered that Australia was in breach of the obligation *erga omnes* to recognize the right of self-determination appertaining to East Timor. This would suggest that Judge Weeramantry was of the opinion that, within the concept of obligation *erga omnes*, a direct obligation-right relation existed between Australia and East Timor, the intended beneficiary of the obligation *erga omnes*. This would mean that an obligation *erga omnes* gives rise both to rights on the part of other States and to rights of beneficiaries. This construction, it may be observed, would render the rights attributed to other States superfluous; the rationale of the rights of other States would seem to reside in the absence of rights of beneficiaries. If a direct obligation-right relation existed between Australia and East Timor, there would seem to be no need for the existence of a legal interest on the part of other States in the observance of the obligation *erga omnes* to respect the right of peoples to self-determination.

Judge Weeramantry considered that, in the instant case, an obligation *erga omnes* could co-exist with a right *erga omnes*, suggesting that such a right is opposable to all States.[23] It would seem, however, that if the beneficiary of an

[21] *Case Concerning East Timor*, Judgment of 30 June 1995, Dissenting Opinion Judge Weeramantry, ICJ Reports 1995, 90, 214: 'In *Barcelona Traction*, the Court was (...) dealing with obligations that are *owed erga omnes*. In that case, the Court was spelling out that, where a State has an obligation towards all other States, each of those other States has a legal interest in its observance.'

[22] *Case Concerning East Timor*, Judgment of 30 June 1995, Dissenting Opinion Judge Weeramantry, ICJ Reports 1995, 90, 214, 215.

[23] *Case Concerning East Timor*, Judgment of 30 June 1995, Dissenting Opinion Judge Weeramantry, ICJ Reports 1995, 90, 215: 'However, this case has stressed the obverse aspect of *rights* opposable *erga omnes*—namely, the *right erga omnes* of the people of East Timor to the recognition of their self-determination and permanent sovereignty over their natural resources. The claim is based on the opposability of the right to Australia.'

obligation *erga omnes* is regarded at the same time as having a right *erga omnes*, there would be no need for linking the obligation *erga omnes* to rights of other States; it would be sufficient for the beneficiary to rely on its own right *erga omnes*. Moreover, the simultaneous exercise of rights of other States corresponding to the obligation *erga omnes* might interfere with the exercise of the right *erga omnes*. From this point of view, it would seem to follow that obligations *erga omnes* and rights *erga omnes* must be regarded as mutually exclusive.

Nevertheless, in its Judgment in the *Case Concerning Application of the Convention on the Prevention and Punishment of the Crime of Genocide (Preliminary Objections),* the ICJ further developed the *erga omnes* concept, referring simultaneously to the rights and obligations contained in the Convention on the Prevention and Punishment of the Crime of Genocide as rights and obligations *erga omnes*. The Court made this determination in the context of the question of the territorial scope of the obligation to prevent and to punish the crime of genocide, arriving at the conclusion that this obligation is not limited territorially.[24]

With regard to this reasoning, it may be observed that the text of the Convention on the Prevention and Punishment of the Crime of Genocide mainly contains obligations of States to punish individuals which have committed acts of genocide. The reference to rights may perhaps be understood as pertaining indirectly to the right of existence of human groups identified in *Reservations to the Convention on the Prevention and Punishment of the Crime of Genocide*. The implicit line of

[24] *Case Concerning Application of the Convention on the Prevention and Punishment of the Crime of Genocide (Preliminary Objections)*, Judgment of 11 July 1996, ICJ Reports 1996, 595, para 31: '(…) as to the territorial problems linked to the application of the Convention, the Court would point out that the only provision relevant to this, Article VI, merely provides for persons accused of one of the acts prohibited by the Convention to "be tried by a competent tribunal of the State in the territory of which the act was committed…". It would also recall its understanding of the object and purpose of the Convention, as set out in its Opinion of 28 May 1951 (…):

> The origins of the Convention show that it was the intention of the United Nations to condemn and punish genocide as 'a crime under international law' involving a denial of the right of existence of entire human groups, a denial which shocks the conscience of mankind and results in great losses to humanity, and which is contrary to moral law and to the spirit and aims of the United Nations (Resolution 96 (I), December 11th, 1946). The first consequence arising from this conception is that the principles underlying the Convention are principles which are recognized by civilized nations as binding on States, even without any conventional obligation. A second consequence is the universal character both of the condemnation of genocide and of the co-operation required 'in order to liberate mankind from such an odious scourge' (Preamble to the Convention). (*I.C.J. Reports*, 1951, p. 23.)

It follows that the rights and obligations enshrined by the Convention are rights and obligations *erga omnes*. The Court notes that the obligation each State thus has to prevent and to punish the crime of genocide is not territorially limited by the Convention.'; *Case Concerning Armed Activities on the Territory of the Congo (New Application: 2002; Jurisdiction of the Court and Admissibility of the Application)*, Judgment of 3 February 2006, ICJ Reports 2006, 3, para 64.

argument would then have been that human groups must be protected within or without the territorial limits of the State, because they enjoy rights *erga omnes*.

In overview, up to this point, it would seem that, in spite of the initial emphasis of the link between obligations *erga omnes* and the international community as a whole, the emphasis in ICJ jurisprudence has shifted more and more to the intended beneficiaries of obligations *erga omnes*, which are characterized more and more in terms of rights *erga omnes*.

This interim conclusion would correspond to some extent to a third interpretation of the concept of obligation *erga omnes*, according to which it is an obligation to which all States are subject, which, so to speak, extends its effects *erga omnes*. This is an interpretation very much in line with the statement of the ICJ in *Reservations to the Convention on the Prevention and Punishment of the Crime of Genocide* that the principles underlying the Convention on the Prevention and Punishment of the Crime of Genocide are principles recognized by civilized nations as binding on States even without any conventional obligation. In fact, the characterization of obligations *erga omnes* as obligations towards the international community as a whole in a sense also presupposes that all members of the international community as a whole are subject to such obligations.[25] This approach must nevertheless be distinguished from the concept of rights *erga omnes*, in so far as the concept of rights *erga omnes* situates the intended beneficiaries in a direct right-obligation relationship with the State.

Yet, in *Legal Consequences of the Construction of a Wall in the Occupied Palestinian Territory*, the ICJ returned to its original conception of obligations *erga omnes*, when determining the legal consequences for other States of the internationally wrongful acts flowing from Israel's construction of a wall in the Occupied Palestinian Territory.[26] The Court observed that Israel had violated obligations *erga omnes*, namely the obligation to respect the right of the Palestinian people to self-determination and certain of its obligations under international humanitarian law.[27] As regards the right of peoples to self-determination, the Court identified obligations on the part of all States not to recognize the illegal situation resulting from the construction of the wall, not to render aid or assistance in maintaining that situation, and to see to it that any impediment to the exercise of the right of peoples to self-determination is brought to an end.[28]

As regards international humanitarian law, the Court observed that rules of international humanitarian law which are so fundamental to the respect of the

---

[25] *Case Concerning Application of the Convention on the Prevention and Punishment of the Crime of Genocide (Preliminary Objections)*, Judgment of 11 July 1996, Dissenting Opinion Judge Kreća, ICJ Reports 1996, 595, para 101.

[26] *Legal Consequences of the Construction of a Wall in the Occupied Palestinian Territory*, Advisory Opinion of 9 July 2004, ICJ Reports 2004, 136, para 154.

[27] *Legal Consequences of the Construction of a Wall in the Occupied Palestinian Territory*, Advisory Opinion of 9 July 2004, ICJ Reports 2004, 136, para 155.

[28] *Legal Consequences of the Construction of a Wall in the Occupied Palestinian Territory*, Advisory Opinion of 9 July 2004, ICJ Reports 2004, 136, paras 156, 159.

human person and 'elementary considerations of humanity' that they are to be observed by all States because they constitute intransgressible principles of international customary law, incorporate obligations which are essentially of an *erga omnes* character.[29] In addition, the Court interpreted Common Article 1 to the Geneva Conventions in the sense that it requires States Parties to ensure that Parties to a conflict comply with their provisions.[30] As Judges Higgins and Kooijmans observed, this is an extensive interpretation,[31] which may be contrasted with its approach to Common Article 1 in para 220 of the *Case Concerning Military and Paramilitary Activities in and against Nicaragua (Merits).* Whereas in the *Case Concerning Military and Paramilitary Activities in and against Nicaragua (Merits),* the Court relied on this provision so as to identify the obligations flowing from Common Article 3, in *Legal Consequences of the Construction of a Wall in the Occupied Palestinian Territory*, the Court used it so as to identify the obligations of the members of the international community as a whole in reaction to breaches of international humanitarian law. More generally, it may be observed that, having focused initially, in *Case Concerning the Barcelona Traction, Light and Power Company, Limited (New Application: 1962; Second Phase),* on the link between an obligation *erga omnes* and the international community as a whole, and subsequently, in the *Case Concerning East Timor*, on the beneficiary of an obligation *erga omnes*, the Court now seems to have reverted to an interpretation of the concept of obligation *erga omnes* which stresses its relationship with the international community as a whole. Curiously, in this process of transversion and reversion, the rights of protection appertaining to members of the international community as a whole, if they were such, have transformed into obligations.

14.4 The Relationship Between the Concept of *Jus Cogens* and the Concept of Obligation *Erga Omnes*

The various descriptions given of the concept of obligation *erga omnes* seem to converge at least in so far as they focus on unilateral acts of States. That does not mean, however, that the concept of obligation *erga omnes* would be irrelevant for bilateral acts of States. If the understanding of obligations *erga omnes* as conferring *locus standi* on individual States is followed, they may be analyzed as consisting of pairs of bilateral relations between States. A bilateral treaty

29 *Legal Consequences of the Construction of a Wall in the Occupied Palestinian Territory*, Advisory Opinion of 9 July 2004, ICJ Reports 2004, 136, para 157.

30 *Legal Consequences of the Construction of a Wall in the Occupied Palestinian Territory*, Advisory Opinion of 9 July 2004, ICJ Reports 2004, 136, paras 158, 159.

31 *Legal Consequences of the Construction of a Wall in the Occupied Palestinian Territory*, Advisory Opinion of 9 July 2004, Separate Opinion Judge Higgins, ICJ Reports 2004, 136, paras 36–39; Separate Opinion Judge Kooijmans, paras 37–51.

purporting to derogate from this structure could not affect the bilateral relations remaining between the treaty partners and the other members of the international community. In this respect, the concept of *jus cogens* and the concept of obligation *erga omnes* might be said to have similar effects, except for a technical difference. According to the concept of *jus cogens*, the bilateral treaty which conflicts with a peremptory norm of general international law is or becomes void. According to the concept of obligation *erga omnes*, a conflict would arise between the bilateral treaty and the other bilateral relations. Nevertheless, it may be pointed out that, pursuant to a combined interpretation of Article 2, para 1 (g), and Article 65, para 1, of the Vienna Convention on the Law of Treaties, the nullity of a treaty can only be claimed by the parties.[32] From this perspective, the *Case Concerning East Timor* could be seen as an attempt by Portugal to obtain, by recourse to the concept of obligation *erga omnes*, the 'invalidity' of the Timor Gap Treaty concluded between Australia and Indonesia, so as to surpass the reach of the Vienna Convention on the Law of Treaties.

On the other hand, while the concept of *jus cogens* relates to bilateral acts of States and the concept of obligation *erga omnes* relates to unilateral acts of States, it has already been argued in Sect. 14.2 that the applicability of a peremptory norm of general international law to a bilateral act of States presupposes its applicability to unilateral acts of States. The perspectives described in Sects. 14.2 and 14.3 relating, respectively, to *jus cogens* and obligations *erga omnes*, would in fact seem to converge on the point that the essence of both notions resides in the question whether all members of the international community are subject to obligations which are essential for the protection of the interests of the intended beneficiaries and, concomitantly, for the protection of the interests of the international community (of States) as a whole.[33]

This conclusion harmonizes with the prevailing doctrinal view that, notwithstanding the differences that may be identified, the concept of *jus cogens* and the concept of obligation *erga omnes* are similar, although the category of obligations *erga omnes* is regarded as broader and encompassing that of *jus cogens*.[34] It may also be noted that in respect of the requirement of consent to jurisdiction, both

---

[32] Rozakis 1976, pp. 115–122; Gómez Robledo 1981, pp. 155–162; Paulus 2001, pp. 348–350.

[33] Rozakis 1976, pp. 15–19; Dupuy 2002, pp. 299–307.

[34] MacDonald 1987, pp. 135–139; Gaja 1989, pp. 158–159; De Hoogh 1991, pp. 193–194; Annacker 1994b, pp. 49–50; Frowein 1994, pp. 405–406; Byers 1997, pp. 229–238; Paulus 2001, pp. 413–416; Dupuy 2002, pp. 377–387; Study Group 2006, paras 404–406.

notions are treated similarly by the ICJ.[35] In view of these characteristics, both concepts may be subsumed under the notion of an international public order.[36]

14.5 The Concept of *Jus Cogens* and the Concept of Obligation *Erga Omnes* Situated Within the Framework of Obligation and the Framework of Authorization

The concept of the international community (of States) as a whole may be regarded as forming a concentric circle around the concept of *jus cogens* and the concept of obligation *erga omnes*.[37] Norms of *jus cogens* are the result of the recognition and acceptance, by the international community of States as a whole, of a norm of general international law as a peremptory norm of general international law. Obligations *erga omnes* are obligations of States towards the international community as a whole. *Jus cogens* and obligations *erga omnes* are deemed to reflect the common or public interest of the international community (of States) as a whole.[38]

The question then arises how the public or common interest of the international community (of States) as a whole is formed. In *Reservations to the Convention on the Prevention and Punishment of the Crime of Genocide*, the ICJ seemed to suggest that a common or public interest may arise in the absence of the existence of individual interests.[39] However, it would seem that the concept of common or public interest must at least to some extent be connected to the individual interests of the

---

[35] *Case Concerning Armed Activities on the Territory of the Congo (New Application: 2002; Jurisdiction of the Court and Admissibility of the Application)*, Judgment of 3 February 2006, ICJ Reports 2006, 3, para 64: 'The Court observes, however, as it has already had occasion to emphasize, that "the *erga omnes* character of a norm and the rule of consent to jurisdiction are two different things" (...), and that the mere fact that rights and obligations *erga omnes* may be at issue in a dispute would not give the Court jurisdiction to entertain that dispute. The same applies to the relationship between peremptory norms of general international law (*jus cogens*) and the establishment of the Court's jurisdiction: the fact that a dispute relates to compliance with a norm having such a character, which is assuredly the case with regard to the prohibition of genocide, cannot of itself provide a basis for the jurisdiction of the Court to entertain that dispute. Under the Court's Statute that jurisdiction is always based on the consent of the parties.'

[36] Tomuschat 1999, Chap. II, paras 37–41, 43–45.

[37] Weil 1992, pp. 261–262, 282–284, 306–312.

[38] Mosler 1968, p. 37; Rozakis 1976, pp. 27–30; Annacker 1994b, p. 31; Bleckmann 1995, p. 32; Carillo Salcedo 1997, pp. 586, 592; Delbrück 1998, p. 27.

[39] *Reservations to the Convention on the Prevention and Punishment of the Crime of Genocide*, Advisory Opinion of 28 May 1951, ICJ Reports 1951, 15, 23: 'In such a convention the contracting States do not have any interest of their own; they merely have, one and all, a common interest, namely, the accomplishment of those high purposes which are the *raison d'être* of the convention.'

members of the international community (of States) as a whole. Otherwise, the common or public interest of the international community (of States) as a whole would not be explicable on the basis of acts of the members of the international community (of States) as whole and remain a matter of presumption. Accordingly, it seems impossible to see the concept of common or public interest of the international community (of States) as a whole as entirely disconnected from the individual interests of the members of the international community (of States) as a whole.

According to an opposite approach, the concept of the public or common interest of the international community (of States) as a whole is regarded as the sum of the individual interests of the members of the international community (of States) as a whole.[40] This approach relies on a metaphor, according to which—pre-given—individual interests are susceptible to addition so as to result in a total common or public interest. It seems questionable, however, whether individual interests can be regarded in such harmonious terms. In particular, this view assumes that individual interests are complementary and excludes the possibility that individual interests compete with each other. This approach relies on the primacy and concordance of individual interests and sees no independent role for the common or public interest.

Commonly, the concept of common or public interest of the international community (of States) as a whole is regarded as situated within the framework of obligation. Accordingly, the common or public interest of the international community (of States) as a whole is intended to restrict the freedom to act of the members of the international community (of States) as a whole.[41] However, the problem then arises that while the common or public interest of the international community (of States) as a whole must at least in part be derived from the individual interests of the members of the international community of States as a whole, the common or public interest of the international community (of States) as a whole is also expected to restrict the freedom to act of the members of the international community (of States) as a whole. When situated within the framework of obligation, the common or public interest of the international community (of States) as a whole must be regarded at the same time as emanating from and as restricting the acts of the members of the international community (of States) as a whole. These movements, however, are mutually exclusive. These movements, however, are mutually exclusive.

With regard to the concept of *jus cogens* this problem arises as follows. The formation of a peremptory norm of general international law is dependent on the recognition and acceptance by the international community of States as a whole of

---

[40] Annacker 1994a, pp. 136–137; 1994b, p. 32.

[41] *Reservations to the Convention on the Prevention and Punishment of the Crime of Genocide*, Advisory Opinion of 28 May 1951, Joint Dissenting Opinion Judges Guerrero, Read, Hsu Mo, and Sir Arnold McNair, ICJ Reports 1951, 15, 46: '(…) an undeniable fact that the tendency of all international activities in recent times has been towards the promotion of the common welfare of the international community with a corresponding restriction of the sovereign power of individual States.'

Annacker 1994a, p. 31; Carillo Salcedo 1997, p. 588.

a norm of general international law as a peremptory norm of general international law. Thus, by means of the acts of recognition and acceptance, a peremptory norm of general international law emanates from the exercise of the freedom to act of the members of the international community of States as a whole. At the same time, the function of a peremptory norm of general international law is to limit the freedom of members of the international community of States as a whole to act bilaterally.[42] If a peremptory norm of general international law limiting the freedom to act bilaterally of members of the international community of States as a whole is formed by other members of the international community of States as a whole,[43] this gives rise to two issues of incoherence. First, those members of the international community of States as a whole are limiting not their freedom to act, but the freedom to act of other members of the international community of States as a whole. Second, this would mean that the freedom to act of those members of the international community of States as a whole is regarded as superior to the freedom to act of the members acting bilaterally, inconsistently with the principle of sovereign equality.[44]

Similar problems arise with regard to the concept of obligation *erga omnes*. As noted, the ICJ described an obligation *erga omnes* as an obligation towards the international community as a whole, considering that an obligation *erga omnes* is the concern of all States and that all States, in view of the importance of the rights involved, have a legal interest in their protection. The ICJ located the corresponding rights of protection in general international law or in international instruments of a universal or quasi-universal character.

The structure of fulfilment of obligations *erga omnes* has been analyzed in particular in the doctrinal work of Annacker. She envisages two possibilities of perceiving the character of the rights corresponding to an obligation *erga omnes*: (i) those rights are subjective rights of the individual members of the international community as a whole; or (ii) those rights are objective rights resulting from the violation of a norm of public international law.[45] A similar distinction has been made by Paulus.[46]

Whatever approach is adopted in regard of the characterization of those corresponding rights of individual members of the international community as a

---

[42] Mosler 1968, p. 18: 'Es ist aber unbestritten, dass die Gemeinschaft der Staaten (…) die Rolle des Gesetzgebers im Völkerrecht übernehmen kann. Wenn das richtig ist, kann die Staatengemeinschaft auch bestimmen, daß die frei gestalteten Beziehungen zwischen den Staaten eingeschränkt sind. (…) Sie können bestimmen, daß gewisse Rechtssätze der grundsätzlich freigestalteten Beziehung zwischen einzelnen Mitgliedern der Völkerrechtsgemeinschaft vorgehen.'; MacDonald 1987, pp. 129–135.

[43] Yasseen 1976, pp. 40–41; Rozakis 1976, pp. 73–84.

[44] Gómez Robledo 1981, pp. 104–108; Weil 1992, p. 273. This tension is highlighted when conventional international law is treated as a possible source of general international law; Rozakis 1976, pp. 66–73; Gómez Robledo 1981, pp. 96–100.

[45] Annacker 1994a, pp. 138–148; Annacker 1994b, pp. 53–65.

[46] Paulus 2001, pp. 379–386.

whole, it must be observed that attributing rights to individual members of the international community as a whole cannot take place within the framework of obligation, which features only obligations and infers rights from the assumption of a freedom to act. Conferring rights on individual members of the international community as a whole presupposes the applicability of the framework of authorization. At the same time, however, the concept of obligation *erga omnes* operates within the framework of obligation. Thus, accepting the existence of a right corresponding to an obligation *erga omnes* involves relying simultaneously on the framework of obligation and the framework of authorization, in disregard of their mutual exclusivity. A parallel may perhaps be drawn here with the differentiation between integral, interdependent and reciprocal obligations, developed by Fitzmaurice. The concept of integral obligation is characterized by the fact that the breach of an obligation by a State does not relieve another State from a similar obligation.[47] Similarly, the concept of obligation *erga omnes* is characterized by the fact that all States are subject to obligations to the international community as a whole. However, like the concept of obligation *erga omnes*, the concept of integral obligation does not allocate a clear position to rights. Moreover, attributing rights to individual members of the international community as a whole undermines the very concept of the international community as a whole, because it fragments the common or public interest of the international community as a whole into individual interests of the members of the international community as a whole.[48]

In fact, the concept of obligation *erga omnes* seems to presuppose the existence of an authority above States imposing obligations on States and conferring rights on States.[49] It presupposes that an authority above States determines obligation-right and right-obligation relationships between States, which correspond to the public or common interest of the international community as a whole. Such a presupposition is inconsistent with the horizontal structure of public international law, characterized by the absence of authority above States, and envisages this authority as representative of the international community as a whole while simultaneously excluding States from the political process constitutive of that community. Bleckmann has finely remarked that obligations in the common interest establish rights of all States as members of the international community and that rights in the common interest establish obligations for all States as members of the international community.[50] However, although obligations in the common interest seem to presuppose rights in

---

47 Fitzmaurice 1957b, paras 124–126; 1958b, para 91; Dupuy 2002, pp. 135–146.

48 *South West Africa Cases (Preliminary Objections)*, Judgment of 21 December 1962, Joint Dissenting Opinion of Sir Percy Spender and Sir Gerald Fitzmaurice, ICJ Reports 1962, 319, 550–552.

Weil 1992, pp. 282–291, 293–303; Zemanek 1997, paras 529, 603, 558–559, 612.

49 Tomuschat 1999, Chap. V, para 2, Chap. VII, paras 33–34, Chap. IX, para 5; Dupuy 2002, pp. 263–265, 307–310.

50 Bleckmann 1995, p. 32: 'If in fact the obligations in the common interest establish rights of all States of the public international law community, then, as the other side of the coin, a right in the common interest must obligate all States.'

the common interest and rights in the common interest seem to presuppose obligations in the common interest, it must be observed that in both branches of this argument the obligations and rights in the common interest, to which the corresponding rights and obligations in the common interest are connected, are themselves presupposed. Moreover, pursuant to the mutual exclusivity of the framework of obligation and the framework of authorization, obligations in the common interest cannot co-exist with rights in the common interest and rights in the common interest cannot co-exist with obligations in the common interest.

On the basis of these observations, it is concluded that the concept of the international community as a whole cannot be situated coherently within the mutual exclusivity formed by the framework of obligation and the framework of authorization. Instead, the concept of the international community as a whole should be resituated within the reformulated framework, which combines the framework of obligation and the framework of authorization. Within this reformulated framework, the relationship between rights and obligations may be connected to the power to act of the members of international society to constitute international society. This power to act has both an enabling aspect and a disabling aspect. It has an enabling aspect in so far as the members of international society may constitute (the common good of) international society. It has a disabling aspect in so far as the members of international society cannot circumvent the common good of international society by resorting to a non-existent freedom to act. From this perspective, it may be said that the power to act of the members of international society can be characterized simultaneously as a right-obligation. At the same time, rules of public international law may be characterized as simultaneously establishing right-obligation and obligation-right relationships between members of international society, incorporating the common good of international society.

Resituating the concept of the international community as a whole within the reformulated framework also addresses the driving concerns behind the concepts of *jus cogens* and obligation *erga omnes*. As remarked previously, the point of these concepts is to subject all States to community obligations which restrict the freedom of States to act unilaterally and detrimentally to the public or common interest of the international community as a whole by, for example, acts of genocide or racial discrimination. Within the reformulated framework, States, as members of international society, would not have such a freedom to act unilaterally, externally or internally, in the first place. Within the reformulated framework, the constituting of (international) society by the members of (international) society is based on their power to act and must be directed at the common good of (international) society.

14.6 The Concept of the International Community (of States) as a Whole and the Position of Third States

The problems encountered in the context of the concept of the international community as a whole may also be illustrated from the perspective of third States. Protecting the common or public interest of the international community (of States) as a whole presupposes that peremptory norms of general international law and obligations *erga omnes* apply unconditionally to all States.[51]

However, if the rule *pacta tertiis nec nocent nec prosunt* is taken into consideration, it may be perceived that from the perspective of the States-parties to a bilateral treaty, all other members of the international community of States as a whole are third States, which can neither benefit from nor be injured by the treaty. Within the framework of obligation, States are regarded as having a freedom to act bilaterally, the exercise of which assumes the form of conventional international law. The text of a treaty is considered to limit the freedom to act of the States-parties *inter se*. The notion that a treaty is void if it conflicts with a peremptory norm of general international law accepted and recognized by the international community of States as a whole seems inconsistent with that freedom of States to act bilaterally. Moreover, it seems to presuppose that the common or public interest of the international community of States as a whole is not sufficiently protected by the operation of the rule *pacta tertiis nec nocent nec prosunt*. Furthermore, from the perspective of the framework of obligation, the point may be made that if the text of a treaty limits the freedom to act of States *inter se*, it is difficult to envisage how it could detrimentally affect the interests of other States at all. Yet again, from this perspective, it may accordingly be observed that the concept of *jus cogens* seems principally directed, not at the bilateral freedom of States to act, but at their unilateral freedom to act.

As situated within the framework of obligation, a freedom of States to act bilaterally in respect of other States disregards the freedom of those other States to act.

---

[51] Virally 1966, pp. 13–14: 'Le fait que le *jus cogens* soit constitué exclusivement de normes de droit international général souligne, en effet, qu'il présente un caractère d'universalité (...) En d'autres termes, on constate que la notion qui nous occupe conduit nécessairement à la conception d'une société internationale universelle, dotée de ses valeurs propres et pouvant invoquer, à son profit, un véritable intérêt général, qui doit l'emporter sur les intérêts particuliers de ses membres: il s'agit donc d'une société internationale à laquelle les Etats ne sont pas libres de s'ouvrir ou de se refuser.'; Coffman 1996, pp. 296–299; Ragazzi 1997, *passim*; De Wet 2000, pp. 192–193: 'Such a constitutional outlook on the Charter and other peremptory norms offers a coherent explanation of current developments in international law by emphasizing the growing interest of the international community as a whole over those of individual states. (...) It is also an almost logical consequence that norms of such fundamental importance such as *jus cogens* would apply to the international community as a whole. (...) It could therefore be concluded that a norm from which no derogation is permitted because of its fundamental nature will normally be applicable *erga omnes*, i.e. all members of the legal community.'

It is in order to protect this freedom that peremptory norms of general international law are invoked. Accordingly, the principle of sovereignty[52]; the principle of independence[53]; the principle of sovereign equality[54]; the rule *pacta tertiis nec nocent nec prosunt*[55]; the principle of the freedom of the high seas[56]; and principles protecting the common interests of third States, such as the freedom of the seas,[57] have commonly been put forward as peremptory norms of general international law. To suggest, however, that these principles or rules may be seen as peremptory norms of general international law seems superfluous and inconsistent with the framework of obligation. Within that framework, third States are already regarded as having a freedom to act derived from the concepts of sovereignty and independence. Therefore, their protection, as members of the international community (of States) as a whole, against a freedom to act bilaterally, would not require the identification of these principles or rules as peremptory norms of general international law. Such peremptory norms of general international law are based on and presuppose the freedom of third States to act and therefore involve circular reasoning.

14.7 The Bilateral Structure of Public International Law?

As indicated in Sect. 14.2, rules of general international law are generally seen in terms of *jus dispositivum*. This perspective informs the view of the structure of general international law as bilateral in the sense that rules of general international law give rise to bilateral relations between States, from which States can derogate bilaterally. The rationale of the concept of *jus cogens* resided in the elimination of such bilateral derogation.

In previous sections, the incoherence of the concept of *jus cogens* as situated within the framework of obligation has been explored. It would also seem fruitful, however, to examine more closely the assumption that, as situated within the framework of obligation, the structure of rules of general international law is bilateral. On the face of it, it would seem possible to say that the framework of obligation does not see rules of public international law as establishing a relationship between members of international society at all, since it is merely directed at limiting the freedom of States to act. To the extent that it is assumed, however, that rules of general international law establish a network of relations between States, the character of the relations comprised by the network, bilateral or otherwise, may be examined. Generally, it would seem possible to analyze such a

52 Virally 1966, pp. 12–13.

53 Marek 1968, p. 449.

54 Virally 1966, p. 12; Touret 1973, pp. 180–184.

55 Verdross 1966, pp. 58–59; Mosler 1968, p. 37; Barberis 1970, pp. 36–37.

56 Verdross 1937, p. 572.

57 Mosler 1968, p. 37.

network of relations established by rules of general international law in terms of bilateral relations between States, the smallest possible relational element. Furthermore, it would seem difficult to see why States could not abrogate such bilateral relations by means of a bilateral treaty.

It would not follow, however, that such a bilateral treaty could thereby detrimentally affect the interests of the international community as a whole, so that recourse must be had to the concept of *jus cogens* in order to protect those interests. That conclusion does not follow, because the two States involved simultaneously remain a part of the network established by general international law by means of bilateral relations with other States. If, for example, States A, B and C jointly adopt measures for the conservation and sustainable management of the living resources of the high seas, which subsequently take the form of customary international law, the network of relations thereby established may be broken down into the bilateral relations A–B, A–C and B–C. If, subsequently, B and C agree to abrogate the measures, this cannot affect, as such, the remaining bilateral relations A–B and A–C. There seems, consequently, to be no warrant for the automatic view that the concept of general international law must be regarded as *jus dispositivum*, if that is taken to mean that States could derogate from a rule of customary international law simply by concluding a bilateral treaty. Such a conclusion would involve disregarding the continuing existence of other bilateral relations. From the perspective of the framework of authorization, the concept of *jus dispositivum* may be seen as involving the assumption of a hierarchical permission to derogate. From the perspective of the framework of obligation, the concept of *jus dispositivum* may be seen as derived from the freedom of States to act unilaterally and, by extension, bilaterally.

Hence, in a triangular relationship A–B–C, all three bilateral relationships A–B, A–C and B–C must be taken into account. Such a situation was at issue in the *Case Concerning Territorial and Maritime Dispute between Nicaragua and Honduras in the Caribbean Sea*, in which the ICJ effected a maritime delimitation between Nicaragua and Honduras, while taking into account the interests of a third State, Colombia. Bilaterally, Colombia and Honduras had concluded the Treaty of 2 August 1986 on Maritime Delimitation, which might be regarded as curtailing the rights of Nicaragua, but which could not, as *res inter alios acta*, affect the rights of Nicaragua. Having effected a maritime delimitation between Honduras and Nicaragua,[58] the ICJ examined whether that delimitation could affect the rights of Colombia as a third State. With respect to the Treaty of 2 August 1986 on Maritime Delimitation between Honduras and Colombia, the Court observed that the maritime delimitation it had arrived at would not actually prejudice the rights of Colombia, because the delimitation line adopted by the Court and the delimitation

[58] *Case Concerning Territorial and Maritime Dispute between Nicaragua and Honduras in the Caribbean Sea*, Judgment of 8 October 2007, ICJ Reports 2007, 659, paras 283–305.

line agreed between Honduras and Colombia diverged.[59] It may be questioned, however, whether that reasoning was sufficient to harmonize the relations N–H and H–C because, conceivably, the attribution to Nicaragua of the maritime area in question might indirectly reduce the rights of Colombia derived from the Treaty of 2 August 1986 on Maritime Delimitation between Honduras and Colombia.

The Court also examined whether the delimitation it had arrived at could affect the rights of Colombia as a third State by reference to the 1928 Barcenas-Esguerra Treaty between Nicaragua and Colombia. The Court observed in this respect that, in any event, the delimitation line it had adopted would not cross the line that might be derived from the 1928 Barcenas-Esguerra Treaty and could not, therefore, affect the rights of Colombia.[60] Here, also, it may be questioned whether that reasoning was sufficient to harmonize the relations H–N and N–C because, conceivably, the attribution to Nicaragua of the maritime area in question might indirectly reduce the rights Colombia derived from the 1928 Barcenas-Esguerra Treaty. Nevertheless, with respect to both treaties, it may also be observed that if it is examined whether the delimitation effected between Nicaragua and Honduras affects, on the one hand, the treaty between Honduras and Colombia and, on the other hand, the treaty between Nicaragua and Colombia, this would assume that Colombia can derive rights from both treaties even if Nicaragua and Honduras, respectively, were not a party to them. Synoptically, it may be said that, while it is necessary to take all three bilateral relationships into account, it is also necessary to relate these three bilateral relationships to each other, so as to form a coherent community of interest.

A parallel may be drawn here with the recourse by the PCIJ to the notion of a community of interest in the *Case Relating to the Territorial Jurisdiction of the International Commission of the River Oder*, on which it relied in order to explain that the internationalization of the Oder extended into the territory of the last upstream State, Poland, even though it could not be said, in the terms of Article 331 of the Treaty of Versailles, that those parts provided more than one State with access to the sea. The Court famously stated:

> But when consideration is given to the manner in which States have regarded the concrete situations arising out of the fact that a single waterway traverses or separates the territory of more than one State, and the possibility of fulfilling the requirements of justice and the considerations of utility which this fact places in relief, it is at once seen that a solution of the problem has been sought not in the idea of a right of passage in favour of upstream States, but in that of a community of interest of riparian States. This community of interest

---

[59] *Case Concerning Territorial and Maritime Dispute between Nicaragua and Honduras in the Caribbean Sea*, Judgment of 8 October 2007, ICJ Reports 2007, 659, para 316.

[60] *Case Concerning Territorial and Maritime Dispute between Nicaragua and Honduras in the Caribbean Sea*, Judgment of 8 October 2007, ICJ Reports 2007, 659, para 315.

> in a navigable river becomes the basis of a common legal right, the essential features of which are the perfect equality of all riparian States in the user of the whole course of the river and the exclusion of any preferential privilege of any one riparian State in relation to the other.[61]

The Court derived this idea from the principles of international river law, as developed from Articles 108 and 109 of the Final Act of the Congress of Vienna.[62] As fitted within the framework of obligation, however, it was difficult to reconcile with the freedom to act of Poland. Within the light of the reformulated framework, the idea of such a community of interest may be seen as informing the constituting of international society by the members of international society. Applied to the triangular relationship composed of three pairs of bilateral relationships, it may be said, in mutually constitutive terms, that, together, the three pairs of bilateral relationships must be directed at the formation of the triangular whole; at the same time, the formation of this triangular whole is not pre-given, but results from the adjustment of the bilateral relationships.

14.8 Conclusion

When situated within the framework of obligation or the framework of authorization, the concept of the international community (of States) as a whole, seen as forming a concentric circle around the concept of *jus cogens* and the concept of obligation *erga omnes*, does not permit, it is submitted, the identification of coherent relations between States. A peremptory norm of general international law, resulting from the acceptance and recognition by the international community of States as a whole of a norm of general international law as a norm from which no derogation is permitted, presupposes that such a norm can be imposed on States exercising their bilateral freedom to act in the form of conventional international law. This amounts to considering that the recognition and acceptance of the members of the international community of States as a whole override the consent of the States-parties to the treaty. Such a result implies a hierarchy of sources of public international law which must, at the same time, remain based in the sovereignty and independence of States.

However, the necessity of resorting to the concept of *jus cogens* is brought about by the assumption of a freedom of contract of States, which includes a freedom to conclude treaties damaging the interests of third States, or of the international community of States as a whole, and treaties relating to internal situations. Paradoxically, this freedom of contract forms both an extension and a

---

[61] *Case Relating to the Territorial Jurisdiction of the International Commission of the River Oder*, Judgment No. 16 of 10 September 1929, Series A.—No. 23, 27.

[62] *Case Relating to the Territorial Jurisdiction of the International Commission of the River Oder*, Judgment No. 16 of 10 September 1929, Series A.—No. 23, 26–29.

limitation of the freedom to act unilaterally. It follows from the incoherence of the framework of obligation, however, that this assumption cannot be maintained.

With respect to the concept of obligation *erga omnes*, it may be observed that the assumption that such obligations bind all members of the international community as a whole is derived from the concept itself. It would seem incoherent if State A owed an obligation *erga omnes* to all other States, if not all of those other States owed a similar obligation to State A. In its Judgment in the *Case Concerning the Barcelona Traction, Light and Power Company, Limited (New Application: 1962; Second Phase)*, the ICJ identified the relationship between the concept of obligation *erga omnes* and the sources of public international law, by indicating that the corresponding rights of protection were located in general international law and conventional international law. In doctrine, the most common assumption also seems to be that obligations *erga omnes* emanate from rules of customary international law or conventional international law. However, if those explanations are followed, it must be assumed that all States have, in a general or specific way, consented to such norms and, more importantly, that such norms are at the free disposition of States.

A major problem with regard to the concept of obligation *erga omnes* is presented by the question how such obligations can be enforced. The only practical possibility seems to be that other members of the international community as a whole must have corresponding rights of protection, which may be characterized as subjective or objective. However, this position entails a fragmentation of the public or common interest of the international community as a whole by giving it a private aspect. In addition, from the perspective of the function of law, it may be pointed out that the attribution of rights to individual members of the international community as a whole presupposes the applicability of the framework of authorization, whereas the concept of obligation *erga omnes* assumes the operation of the framework of obligation. Within the vertical structure of the concept of law underlying the concept of public international law, however, those frameworks are mutually exclusive. Consequently, there is a disjunction: the freedom to act projects the requirement of obligations protecting the common or public interest of the international community as a whole; the rights required to enforce such obligations reveal the tension between the common or public interest of the international community as a whole and the private interests of the individual members of the international community as a whole, while operating within the framework of authorization.

It may be noted that in the *Case of the S.S. "Lotus"*, the PCIJ made use of the concept of the community of States in a descriptive sense, while at the same time characterizing States as independent communities.[63] It made those observations while endorsing the framework of obligation, thereby attributing a freedom to act to States while, at the same time, excluding the possibility of considering the concept of community of States in a normative sense. The development of a super-normative

---

[63] *Case of the S.S. "Lotus"*, Judgment No. 9 of 7 September 1927, Series A.—No. 10, 16, 18.

category, consisting of the concepts of *jus cogens* and obligation *erga omnes*, reverses this relationship in so far as it locates normativity in the international community of States as a whole, restricting the freedom of States to act in the form of aggression, genocide, slavery and racial discrimination. Reflecting this development, the principle of non-use of force has been characterized in ICJ jurisprudence in terms of *jus cogens*[64] or a cardinal principle of customary international law.[65] To the extent that this international community of States as a whole is seen as established, however, those independent communities must be seen as restricted. If and when this international community of States as a whole is fully constituted, the super-State will have assumed its form and absorbed the independent communities.

The concept of obligation *erga omnes* gives insight into the possibility of envisaging relations between all members of the international community, seen in terms of rights and obligations, which pervade both the international plane and the internal sphere of States. Transposed to the reformulated framework, the members of international society are characterized in their initial dilemma situation in terms of a right/obligation to constitute (the common good of) international society. The constituting of international society takes the form of rules of public international law which consist, between pairs of members of international society, simultaneously of both an obligation-right and a right-obligation relationship. In this way, the concept of public international law will not be split between the independent communities and the international community of States as a whole, but constitute the centre at which the activities of the international community as a whole and of the independent communities converge. Within the reformulated framework, the constituting of international society by the members of international society and of the common good of international society in the form of rules of public international law, are coterminous. Situated within the reformulated framework, the concept of public international law does not assume the character of *jus cogens* because, while formed by the members of international society and forming the members of international society, its function is not to restrict bilateral or unilateral acts, but to incorporate the structure of international society.

---

[64] *Case Concerning Military and Paramilitary Activities in and against Nicaragua (Merits)*, Judgment of 27 June 1986, ICJ Reports 1986, 14, para 190; Separate Opinion President Nagendra Singh, 153.

[65] *Case Concerning Military and Paramilitary Activities in and against Nicaragua (Merits)*, Judgment of 27 June 1986, Separate Opinion Judge Sette-Camara, ICJ Reports 1986, 14, 199–200.

Chapter 15
Conclusion to Part III

Part III has sought to extend the analysis derived from the incoherence of the mutual exclusivity of the framework of obligation and the framework of authorization, resulting in the reformulated framework, developed in Part I and applied to the sources of public international law in Part II, to international society, considered in its 'organized' and 'unorganized' forms: the concept of international institution and the concept of international community.

Dealing with international society in its organized form, Chap. 13 considered the concept of international institution as situated within the mutual exclusivity of the framework of obligation and the framework of authorization. It was argued that, as situated within the framework of obligation, the concept of international institution is essentially seen in terms of a transfer of power, which is located either at the Member States or at the organs of international institutions. This movement parallels the transition from a state of nature to the institution of the State propounded by social contract theory and gives rise to a dilemma: so long as States have not transferred power to the international institution, they have not succeeded in exiting the international state of nature; as soon as they have transferred power to the international institution, they can no longer control its acts. If it is up to the Member States to determine whether the international institution has exceeded its power, no transfer of power can be said to have taken place. If it is up to the international institution to determine whether it has exceeded its power, then States have succeeded in exiting the international state of nature but have, as Kant recognized, at the same time ceased to be sovereign and independent States. Paradoxically, while the upward movement inherent in the concept of international institution is impelled by the vertical structure of the concept of law underlying the concept of public international law, this same structure compels this movement not to succeed. In *Reparation for Injuries Suffered in the Service of the United Nations*, the ICJ observed that the United Nations is not a super-State. In *Interpretation of the Agreement of 25 March 1951 between the WHO and Egypt*, the ICJ confirmed this view with respect to

J. A. Vos, *The Function of Public International Law*, 275
DOI: 10.1007/978-90-6704-861-3_15, © J. A. Vos, The Netherlands 2013

international organizations in general.[1] From the perspective of the function of public international law, the important point is that the vertical structure of the concept of law underlying the concept of public international law—which Lauterpacht, not coincidentally, termed the super-State of law—requires international institutions to approximate the super-State.

It is submitted that this impossible dichotomy between the sovereignty and independence of States and the super-State can be avoided by resituating the concept of international institution within the reformulated framework as developed in Part I. Within this reformulated framework, States, as members of international society, are situated in terms of a dilemma, as having a power to act which is not an unlimited freedom to act. On the basis of this premise, States, as members of international society, constitute international society in the form of rules of public international law. Part of this constituting of international society may be regarded as taking the form of international institutions. As such, they correspond to an enabling factor, because they are part of international society as constituted by States. At the same time, they represent a disabling factor, because States cannot act outside of these channels. As thus situated, a relationship between institutions and rules may be formulated along the lines suggested by Finnis: rules determine institutions and institutions determine rules. On the basis of the initial situation, as developed by rules, international institutions have been constituted, which may, in turn give rise to rules. In both movements, rules have both an enabling and a disabling aspect, which ensure that rules produced by organs of international institutions do not have a non-binding character, because they inform the constituting of international society by the members of international society. At the same time, those rules cannot have a binding character, because the question whether they contribute coherently to the constituting of international society by the members of international society remains a question of the constituting of international society, to be addressed in terms of the dialectical process of practical reasoning.

Dealing with international society in its unorganized form, Chap. 14 considered the concept of international community as situated within the mutual exclusivity of the framework of obligation and the framework of authorization, and as concentrically comprising the concept of *jus cogens* and the concept of obligation *erga omnes*. The concept of *jus cogens* and the concept of obligation *erga omnes* may be seen as representing an attempt to adapt the vertical notion of common or public interest to the horizontal structure of public international law, in the course of which this common or public interest is transformed into the acceptance of and recognition by the international community of States as a whole and into the existence of obligations towards the international community as a whole. With respect to the concept of *jus cogens*, this movement ultimately results in the position that the recognition by and acceptance of the members of the international

[1] *Interpretation of the Agreement of 25 March 1951 between the WHO and Egypt*, Advisory Opinion of 20 December 1980, ICJ Reports 1980, 73, para 37.

community of States as a whole takes precedence over the freedom to act of other members of the international community of States as a whole. While this precedence may seem entirely justified in the light of the common or basic values protected by those norms, it does not fit coherently into the framework of obligation. The concept of obligation *erga omnes* in a way avoids this problem by assuming the existence of obligations reflecting the common or public interest. It shifts the focus to the beneficiaries of such obligations and to the members of the international community as a whole which may invoke the rights corresponding to these obligations. However, in the very moment that these rights are attributed to individual States, the concept of the international community as a whole disintegrates, because it can no longer be determined whether those States exercise these rights in accordance with the public or common interest of the international community. In terms of the function of public international law, this fragmentation is compounded because, in order to identify those rights, those States must revert to the framework of authorization which cannot coexist with the framework of obligation which informs the concept of obligation *erga omnes*.

When resituated within the reformulated framework as developed in Part I, the concept of the international community as a whole, transformed, for purposes of terminological harmony, into the concept of international society, may be said to be constituted by the members of international society and constituting, in turn, the members of international society as members of international society. Within the reformulated framework, the concept of international society transforms the dichotomy between rights and obligations, characteristic of the concept of obligation *erga omnes*, into the power to act of the members of international society, which may be described in terms of the combination of a right and an obligation. The members of international society have to some extent a right to act, but the extent of this right is indeterminate, because all members of international society must be deemed to have the same right; to that extent, the right contains within itself, so to speak, an obligation. Together, they may be regarded as a right-obligation, which accurately characterizes the power to act of the members of international society. This basic position corresponds to a transformation of the function of rules of public international law; within the reformulated framework, rules of public international law may be seen as containing rights-obligations, which have both an enabling and a disabling aspect so as to establish coherent relations between the members of international society. In so far as the members of international society constitute international society out of this initial situation of international society, rules of public international law may be said to be directed at and to reflect the common good of international society. In sum, within the reformulated framework, public international law and international society are mutually constitutive: the concept of public international law is seen as inherent in the concept of international society. At the same time, the concept of international society is seen as inherent in the concept of public international law. Both are coterminous.

Chapter 16
Conclusion: The Function of Public International Law as the Constituting of International Society Pursuant to Practical Reasoning

The argument presented in the preceding chapters was propelled by the aim to overcome the dilemma posed by the dichotomy between mainstream public international law and critical theory of public international law. Mainstream public international law sees itself as a matter of imposing limitations on States but at the same time sees itself as based on the consent of States. In the words of the PCIJ in *Mavrommatis Palestine Concessions*, when dealing with the phrase 'international obligations accepted by the Mandatory', appearing in Article 11 of the Mandate for Palestine, it may be said that, in a sense, the whole body of international law has been accepted by States.[1] Critical theory pointed out that, viewed in this way, rules of public international law must simultaneously fulfill two contradictory requirements: to restrict the freedom to act of States and, at the same time, to constitute an exercise of that freedom to act. But, while this criticism seems persuasive, critical theory of public international law did not provide an alternative conception. Its suggestion that the concept of public international law should rather be seen in terms of practical reasoning, left open the point that practical reasoning might, as much as international legal argument, be eclipsed by politics.

To initiate this analysis, it was argued as a first step that the traditional view of a contrast between the horizontal structure of public international law and the vertical structure of the internal law of the State is actually a false contrast, which distorts the framework within which the concept of public international law actually operates. That framework, it was argued, may be characterized as not having a horizontal but a vertical structure. The classical horizontal structure of public international law was analyzed as inscribing itself within this vertical structure. This followed from the definition of the concept of public international law in terms of governing or regulating relations between States and the assumption of freedoms of States to act derived from the concepts of sovereignty and independence. The delegation of the legislative function to States, in view of

---

[1] *Mavrommatis Palestine Concessions*, Judgment No. 2 of 30 August 1924, Series A.—No. 2, 24.

DOI: 10.1007/978-90-6704-861-3_16,

the absence of authority above States, in the form of their consent to rules of public international law is likewise a reflection of this vertical structure. By deriving in this way the horizontal structure of public international law from this vertical structure, it may be seen how consent and the freedom of States to act are brought together in the sovereignty and independence of States.

Returning to the dichotomy between mainstream public international law and critical theory of public international law, it could be said that, although critical theory of public international law, on the one hand, explored and exploited the extremities of the concept of public international law, by identifying ascending and descending patterns, it did not, on the other hand, go far enough, because it also relied on the vertical structure of the concept of law underlying the concept of public international law, by transposing the liberal doctrine of politics to the international plane, so as to subsume law into politics. The paradox here is that, from its perspective, critical theory of public international law could not go further, because, by exploring and exploiting the extremities of the concept of public international law, it went to the limits of mainstream public international law.

The solution that critical theory of public international law put forward to resolve the dichotomy between ascending and descending patterns—practical reasoning, reasoning about the resolution of practical problems here and now—was not intended to be a real solution, which would redeem the concept of public international law. Rather, it was designed to make the concept of public international law more transparent in terms of politics. But, all the same, the subsumption of law into politics revolving around the notion of practical reasoning results in the disappearance of the legal aspect. Critical theory of public international law thus makes a double move: while jettisoning the dividing line between law and politics, law is subsumed into politics because politics is viewed as having a primary and absolute character. The argument presented here also revolves around the notion of practical reasoning and accepts the unfruitfulness of attempting to delimit law from politics. It maintains, however, that it does not necessarily follow that, thereby, law is subsumed into politics. It is possible for social situations to have both legal and political aspects, without the one aspect being absorbed by the other. This result may be achieved by resituating the process of practical reasoning in another framework. That framework may be found by focusing on the function of public international law. Thereby, the possibility opens up of broadening the conceptual field within which mainstream public international law operates. In this way, the dichotomy between mainstream public international law and critical theory of public international law may be transcended. Focusing on the function of public international law allows one to identify the vertical structure of the concept of law underlying the concept of public international law and to bisect it into two forms: the framework of obligation and the framework of authorization.

According to the framework of obligation, rules of law contain obligations which restrict the freedom to act of the subjects of the law. It is based on the assumption that in the absence of rules of law, the subjects of the law have a freedom to act in respect of each other. The concept of obligation and the concept of freedom to act thus exclude each other.[2] However, as regards the concept of public international law, rules of public international law containing obligations are linked to the assumption of a freedom of States to act in the sense that it is considered that rules of public international law containing obligations emanate from the exercise of the freedom of States to act. This renders the concept of public international law incoherent because rules of public international law containing obligations are thus viewed at the same time as restricting the freedom of States to act and as emanating from the freedom of States to act.[3] These movements are, however, mutually exclusive; a rule of public international law cannot at the same time be regarded as restricting a freedom of States to act and as emanating from a freedom of States to act. In the former case, A (restriction) determines B (freedom to act), whereas in the latter case, B determines A. These propositions cannot simultaneously be adhered to. As a result, rules of public international law do not succeed in restricting the freedom of States to act.

It would appear, however, that if the existence of rules of public international law containing obligations cannot coherently be explained on the basis of the assumption of a freedom to act of States, there remains no other way to explain the existence of such rules of public international law. The assumption of a freedom to act of States explains both the existence and the function of rules of public international law delimiting those freedoms, but those explanations are not coherent; to the extent that their existence is presumed,[4] their basis in the freedom of States to act is relinquished. At the same time, however, the assumption of a freedom to act of States itself appears to be inconsistent, because the freedom of State A to act in respect of State B and the freedom of State B to act in respect of State A cannot coherently coexist.[5] On these grounds, it was concluded that the framework of obligation must be rejected as an exclusive frame of reference; accordingly, the function of rules of public international law cannot consist exclusively in restricting the freedom of States to act.

According to the framework of authorization, on the other hand, rules of public international law contain rights by virtue of which States can act. The framework of authorization is based on the assumption that in the absence of rules of public

[2] Hüning 1998, pp. 101–104.

[3] *Railway Traffic between Lithuania and Poland (Railway Sector Landwarów-Kaisiadorys)*, Advisory Opinion of 15 October 1931, Series A./B.—No. 42, 108, 112: '(...) a Resolution was adopted by the Council on December 10th, 1927, with the concurrence of the two Parties concerned.'; 116: 'The two Governments concerned being bound by their acceptance of the Council's Resolution (...)'; *Voting Procedure on Questions Relating to Reports and Petitions Concerning the Territory of South-West Africa*, Advisory Opinion of 7 June 1955, Separate Opinion Judge Klaestad, ICJ Reports 1955, 67, 87: 'When the Union of South Africa, by a concurrent vote in the Council, gave an expression of its acceptance of a Resolution concerning reports and petitions relating to the Territory of South-West Africa, the Union Government became, by reason of that acceptance, legally bound to comply with the Resolution.'

[4] Weil 1992, pp. 66–81.

[5] Hüning 1998, pp. 83–84.

international law, States do not have a power to act. By its terms, the perspective of authorization does not and cannot explain the existence of rules of public international law by reference to acts of States, precisely because such acts are dependent on prior rules of public international law containing rights. Therefore, the perspective of authorization presupposes the existence of rules of public international law conferring rights. At the same time, the assumption that States do not have a power to act in the absence of rules of public international law implies that they are not recognized as active, political, members of international society. The framework of authorization portrays international society as inanimate; in fact, the framework of authorization does not even convey a clear need for rules of public international law, because the members of international society could remain indefinitely in this inanimate state. From this perspective, they may be compared to the marionettes of a puppet player. Such a view would seem wholly inconsistent with the characterization of international society as consisting of sovereign and independent States. On those grounds, it was concluded that the function of rules of public international law does not consist exclusively in conferring powers on States.

It is important to emphasize that both the framework of obligation and the framework of authorization presuppose the existence of rules of public international law. Within the framework of obligation those rules of public international law are explained as both emanating from and as restricting the freedom of States to act. But because rules of public international law cannot sufficiently be explained as emanating from the freedom to act of States, it follows, in the absence of any other explanation, that they are presupposed. Moreover, it is singularly important to emphasize that their character is presupposed. In respect of the framework of obligation, it is presupposed that rules of public international law are binding; that rules of public international law contain obligations. In respect of the framework of authorization, it is presupposed that rules of public international law are authorizing; that rules of public international law contain rights.

These configurations of the framework of obligation and the framework of authorization convey, it was maintained, their incoherence. This incoherence arises in two ways. First, the framework of obligation and the framework of authorization contain within themselves inconsistent assumptions. The framework of obligation assumes the coexistence of inconsistent freedoms to act of the members of society. At the same time, it seeks to remedy this situation, by inferring rules containing obligations from those inconsistent freedoms to act. Although the social necessity for rules containing obligations is made clear, the framework of obligation does not succeed in making the restrictive aspect prevail. The incoherence residing in the inconsistent coexistence of freedoms to act is transposed to the rules of public international law created pursuant to the exercise of those freedoms to act. The framework of authorization assumes the coexistence of non-existent powers to act. But in that situation, the need for rules of law does not arise. Both in the absence and in the presence of rules containing rights, society does, in fact, not exist; everything is coordinated by a third party, which cannot be explained by virtue of acts of the members of society. The second way in which incoherence arises is that both frameworks as a whole depend on and are validated by a basic rule which determines the characteristics of all the other rules without being explained itself. This is crucial because this means that behind those frameworks, a phantom entity is presupposed which ultimately determines the character of those frameworks without being explained by them, by virtue of acts of the members of society or in any other way. This phantom entity is, it is suggested, the institution of the State. Both at the international plane and in the internal sphere, this entails incoherence: at the international plane, it is inconsistent with the horizontal structure of public international law (if that horizontal structure is seen as actually inscribing itself within a vertical structure, as is maintained here, the incoherence pertains to the presupposition of that super-State); in the internal sphere, it is inconsistent with the idea that the institution of the State and the internal law of the State can be the result of acts of members of society.

In theory of public international law, the framework of obligation and the framework of authorization have been described as coexistent in the practice of States.[6] Actually, it is crucial to recognize that the framework of obligation and the framework of authorization are mutually exclusive. One cannot simultaneously adhere to the view that rules of public international law exclusively contain obligations and to the view that rules of public international law exclusively contain rights. Similarly, one cannot simultaneously adhere to the assumption that, in the absence of rules of public international law, States have a freedom to act and to the assumption that, in the absence of rules of public international law, States do not have a power to act.

The final step in the analysis is that the mutual exclusivity and the incoherence of both frameworks can be transformed into what has been termed a reformulated framework. This step can be taken because, if both frameworks are incoherent, that incoherence must also affect the point of mutual exclusivity and there remains, in fact, no ground to maintain it. When that step is taken, it may be seen that both frameworks are actually opposites of each other: the disabling function of the framework of obligation is the opposite of the enabling function of the framework of authorization; the concept of obligation is the opposite of the concept of right; the assumption that, in the absence of rules of law, the members of society have a freedom to act is the opposite of the assumption that, in the absence of rules of law, the members of society do not have a power to act. When the mutual exclusivity separating both frameworks is removed, all of these aspects may be seen as forming part of a single framework: the reformulated framework. This reformulated framework acquires its characteristics because all those aspects, as opposites, constitute its extremities: disabling, enabling, obligation, right, freedom to act, no power to act.

By locating these aspects of both frameworks at the extremities of the reformulated framework, it can be described how the reformulated framework operates. In a sense, each element of the reformulated framework must form a mean

[6] Bleckmann 1978, *passim*.

between the extremities defined by these aspects. Accordingly, within the reformulated framework, the function of rules of public international law may be described as both enabling and disabling. Similarly, rules of public international law may be said to contain, at the same time, both rights and obligations. Concurrently, the basic position of the members of international society in respect of each other may be described in terms of a power to act which is not an unlimited freedom to act. Against this background, the creation of rules of public international law mediates between the framework of authorization and the framework of obligation. The framework of authorization could not explain the existence of rules of public international law. This deficiency informed the attractiveness of the framework of obligation, but that framework located the rule-making function too closely to the members of international society, merging the existence of rules of public international law and the exercise of the freedom to act of the members of international society into each other. Within the reformulated framework, the members of international society partly retain the role of creating rules of public international law. But the character of that role changes: it is no longer directed at restricting their freedom to act, but at the constituting of international society so as to exit their dilemma situation of having a power to act but not an unlimited freedom to act. That dilemma situation explains the need for rules of public international law as also the character of those rules, which must correspond to that dilemma situation. In order to transcend it, rules of public international law must have both enabling and disabling aspects, contain both rights and obligations.

This reformulated framework, as described above, has been derived from an analysis of the mutual exclusivity and the incoherence of the framework of obligation and the framework of authorization. In the course of the analysis in the preceding chapters, elements have been identified which may be transcribed to it. The first to be mentioned in this respect is the 'objective structural framework' identified by Judge Shahabuddeen in his Dissenting Opinion in *Legality of the Threat or Use of Nuclear Weapons.*[7] In his probing search to protect international society against the threat or use of nuclear weapons, Judge Shahabuddeen considered the framework of obligation, the framework of authorization, and what he termed an objective structural framework, formed by sovereignties, which provides limits to the freedom of action of the members of international society. While Judge Shahabuddeen ultimately opted for the framework of authorization, his objective structural framework approximated the reformulated framework as it has been described here. The difference is that, while the objective structural framework is seen as formed by sovereignties and thereby containing limits, the reformulated framework situates multiple sovereignties in the position of a

[7] *Legality of the Threat or Use of Nuclear Weapons*, Advisory Opinion of 8 July 1996, Dissenting Opinion Judge Shahabuddeen, ICJ Reports 1996, 226, 392: 'The existence of a number of sovereignties side by side places limits on the freedom of each State to act as if the others did not exist. These limits define an objective structural framework within which sovereignty must necessarily exist; the framework, and its defining limits, are implicit in the reference in "*Lotus*" to "co-existing independent communities".'

dilemma, characterized by a power to act which is not, however, an unlimited freedom to act.

Two further transcribable elements are furnished by the theories of law developed by MacCormick and Finnis. MacCormick described the concept of law in terms of legal reasoning, which must satisfy the requirements of coherence and consistency. Finnis suggested that the concept of law is oriented towards the common good and consists of practical reasoning about the common good. As said before, the reformulated framework also revolves around the notion of practical reasoning. But in the reformulated framework, practical reasoning is a vehicle for the members of (international) society to exit their dilemma situation of having a power to act which is not an unlimited freedom to act. That process should satisfy the requirement of consistency, that is, not entail contradictions, but, in comparison to the theory of legal reasoning developed by MacCormick, the requirement of coherence is more flexible, because it is not situated within the framework of authorization, but in the hybrid reformulated framework. Within the context of the reformulated framework, it may be understood in the sense that the constituting of (international) society requires coherence between constitutive acts. Because the process of practical reasoning operates as a vehicle for exiting the dilemma situation of the members of (international) society, it may at the same time be said that it is directed, in this sense, at the common good of (international) society. The common good is, accordingly, informed by the process of practical reasoning and, in turn, informs that process. From this perspective, the common good of international society may be seen as coterminous with the constituting of (international) society.

Two more transcribable elements are furnished by the theories of public international law developed by Kratochwil and Allott. Kratochwil saw the concept of public international law as a form of practical reasoning on the basis of topoi, or starting points for argument.[8] But while it remains situated within the framework of obligation, the process of practical reasoning seems too much informed by politics and too little constraining. Within the reformulated framework, as it is directed at the constituting of international society, the process of practical reasoning must be both enabling and disabling. Its flexible character allows the members of international society to constitute international society. At the same time, international society as thus constituted is disabling, because the members of international society cannot resort to a, non-existing, freedom to act. This angle connects to the theory of public international law developed by Allott, which revolves around the notion of the self-constituting of (international) society. As said before, within the reformulated framework, the process of practical reasoning operates as a vehicle for exiting the dilemma situation of the members of (international) society. Since it is directed at the common good of (international) society, it may be said that, thereby, the members of international society constitute international society. Similar to the

[8] Kratochwil 1989, pp. 34–39, 205–248.

theory of public international law developed by Allott,[9] the reformulated framework sees the concept of public international law as inherent in international society. The difference is that the theory of public international law developed by Allott was situated within the framework of authorization: public international law was inherent in international society in the sense that international society delegated power-rights to the members of international society. Within the reformulated framework, practical reasoning about the common good of international society in itself gives rise to the constituting of international society in the form of rules of public international law, so that the members of international society are not seen as beneficiaries of power-rights, but as involved in the constituting of international society. The formation of rules of public international law and the constituting of international society are, accordingly coterminous.

It may be observed that this description of the reformulated framework is essentially circular. International society is constituted by the members of international society in the form of rules of public international law pursuant to a process of practical reasoning. At the same time, this process constitutes the members of international society as members of international society. If the members of international society desire to reform international society, they must return to the process of practical reasoning, because they cannot rely on an unlimited freedom to act which the reformulated framework does not admit. Accordingly, the constituting of international society and the reconstituting of international society flow into each other.

In connection with the circularity of the reformulated framework and in consequence of its hybrid character, the rules of public international law to which it gives rise do not contain exclusively either obligations or rights. Since a rule of public international law is created by two or more members of international society so as to overcome their dilemma situation, it must be both enabling and disabling; enabling with a view to the constituting of international society and disabling in so far as it is limited to international society as thus constituted. Moreover, to the extent that this process does not involve all members of international society, it must at the same time define their relations with the other members of international society in the form of interlinked rights and obligations.[10] Schematically, the constituting of international society inherently involves the (re)creation of mutual legal relations consisting, at a minimum, of a right-obligation relation paired with an obligation-right relation between members A and B. For individual members of international society, it follows that a rule of public international law must simultaneously contain both a right and an obligation.

Resituating the sources of public international law within the reformulated framework may be represented in terms of a layered structure, which proceeds from principles to rules to acts. Accordingly, it may be said that, within the reformulated framework, general principles of law and (general) principles of

[9] Allott 1990, para 11.11.

[10] Chinkin 1993, pp. 39–44.

international law may be regarded as topoi for the practical reasoning of the members of international society about the common good of international society. Such general principles may be inferred both from the reformulated framework and from the rules of public international law formed by the members of international society. Conventional international law may be positioned as a transition between principles and rules of public international law. Consisting of texts containing both principles and rules, conventional international law may be regarded as a formal way of the constituting of international society. The concept of customary international law may be positioned as a transition between rules of public international law and acts of the members of international society. Consisting of the acts of the members of international society, customary international law may be regarded as an informal way of the constituting of international society. This is not, it may be noted, a transition from an international situation of fact to a rule of international law.[11] It represents the transition from the dilemma situation of the members of international society to the constituting of international society. This representation of the resituating of the sources of public international law within the reformulated framework does not imply the existence of a hierarchy. Within the reformulated framework, general principles of (international) law, conventional international law, and customary international law may be seen as mutually constituting and informing each other.

From this perspective, international institutions may be regarded as both forming a part of and informing the reformulated framework and may be regarded, as was suggested by Finnis, in a circular relationship with rules, in the sense that rules of public international law may give rise to international institutions and international institutions may give rise to rules of public international law. While remaining problematic within the framework of obligation, within the reformulated framework this circular relationship is essential. The constituting of international society pursuant to the process of practical reasoning may give rise to the establishment of international institutions. The relationship between those international institutions and the members of internationals society may not, however, be described in terms of a transfer of power. By themselves, international institutions may be regarded as a more permanent form of the constituting of international society by its members. Organs of international institutions may be entrusted by the members of international society with the task of managing the common good of international society.

[11] *Case of the S.S. "Lotus"*, Judgment No. 9 of 7 September 1927, Dissenting Opinion Judge Nyholm, Series A.—No. 10, 60–61: 'The reasoning of the judgment appears to be that, failing a rule of positive law, the relations between States in the matter under consideration are governed by an absolute freedom. If this reasoning is followed out, a principle of public international law is set up that where there is no special rule, absolute freedom must exist. The basis of this reasoning appear to be that it is vaguely felt that, even outside the domain of positive public international law, the situation of fact as regards relations between nations in itself embodies a principle of public international law. But that is a confusion of ideas. In considering the existing situation of fact, a distinction should be drawn between that which is merely an international situation of *fact* and that which constitutes a rule of international *law*. The latter can be created only by a special process and cannot be deduced from a situation which is merely one of fact.'

The question whether those organs execute this task in conformity with their trust constitutes an aspect of the constituting of international society. In this dialogue, neither the organs of international institutions nor the members of international society can impose their views on the other. The resulting situation has to be addressed as a matter of the constituting of international society pursuant to practical reasoning. Within the reformulated framework, in other words, resolutions of organs of international institutions may not be seen in terms of the dichotomy between non-binding and binding. Within the reformulated framework, resolutions of organs of international institutions occupy the middle ground between the terms of this distinction, which the framework of obligation excluded.

Likewise, the concept of international community should neither exclusively be seen in a normative sense nor exclusively in a descriptive sense. Transplanted to the reformulated framework, the constituting of international society takes place on the basis of the ground structure and takes the form of rules of public international law.

Concomitantly, within the reformulated framework, the position of an international court or tribunal is markedly different. Within the framework of obligation, an international court or tribunal was caught by the dilemma of having to restrict the freedom of States to act,[12] but being restricted by the law as determined by the parties as legislators. Within the reformulated framework, the function of an international court or tribunal is to take part in the constituting, on the basis of practical reasoning, of international society by the members of international society. From that angle, legal relations identified by a court or tribunal represent possible ways of the constituting of international society between members of international society. While not binding for the parties, they may be regarded as representing a spectrum within which international society may be constituted. A party may put forward an alternative way of constituting international society, but must do so on the basis of practical reasoning; it is not sufficient simply to reject the alternatives proposed pursuant to the judicial function. In its Order in the *Case of the Free Zones of Upper Savoy and the District of Gex*, the PCIJ famously said that the judicial settlement of international disputes is simply an alternative to the direct and friendly settlement of such disputes between the parties.[13] Within the framework of obligation, however, as the same Order also made clear, both judicial settlement and direct settlement of disputes are ultimately dependent on

[12] *Judgments of the Administrative Tribunal of the International Labour Organization upon Complaints Made against the United Nations Educational, Scientific and Cultural Organization*, Advisory Opinion of 23 October 1956, Dissenting Opinion Judge Córdova, ICJ Reports 1956, 77, 160.

[13] *Case of the Free Zones of Upper Savoy and the District of Gex*, Order of 19 August 1929, Series A.—No. 22, 13; 'Whereas the judicial settlement of international disputes, with a view to which the Court has been established, is simply an alternative to the direct and friendly settlement of such disputes between the Parties; as consequently it is for the Court to facilitate, so far as is compatible with its Statute, such direct and friendly settlement.'; *Mavrommatis Palestine Concessions*, Judgment No. 2 of 30 August 1924, Dissenting Opinion Judge Pessôa, Series A.—No. 2, 88, 91.

Weil 1992, pp. 152–153.

the free will of the parties.[14] The reformulated framework eliminates the possibility of a simple refusal to cooperate. As members of international society, States have no alternative to the constituting of international society. The role of the judicial function is to mark out one or more possible ways to constitute international society.

In this light, judical creativity, which is acknowledged to be unavoidable,[15] but which also bears within itself the danger of detachment between the judicial function and the law of (international) society,[16] fulfills an essential but also limited role. Within the reformulated framework, judicial creativity is of the essence of the judicial function.[17] But, at the same time, it is bounded because the extent to which it will actually shape (international) society will be dependent on the underlying practical reasoning. In this way, two primordial—and contradictory—values in the process of judicial reasoning, rigidity and flexibility,[18] can both be accounted for.

By the same token, the reformulated framework dissolves the opposition between public international law and international politics. This is a prime characteristic of mainstream public international law, reflected in the classical distinction between legal and political disputes.[19] But, as critical theory of public international law maintains, because of the dependence of the formation of a rule of public international law on the exercise of the freedom of States to act, the concept of public international law easily dissolves into the field of international politics. In *The Function of Law in the International Community*, Lauterpacht contended that all acts of States can inevitably be brought under a rule of public international law.[20] It must be noted, however, that this absorption of the field of international politics by the concept of public international law was not self-standing and depended on the assumption of a vertical structure of the concept of public international law and of the concept of law in general. Within the reformulated framework, there is no distinction between the field of international politics and the concept of public international law, because within the reformulated framework—founded on the dilemma situation of the members of international society as having a power to act, but not an unlimited freedom to act—the concept of public international law is inherent; the members of international society must resort to the process of practical reasoning in order to exit the dilemma situation of having a power to act which is not a freedom to act. That

---

[14] *Case of the Free Zones of Upper Savoy and the District of Gex*, Order of 19 August 1929, Series A.—No. 22, 18; *Mavrommatis Palestine Concessions*, Judgment No. 2 of 30 August 1924, Series A.—No. 2, 18.

[15] Lauterpacht 1933, Chap. V, para 21; Weil 1992, pp. 141–143; Zemanek 1997, paras 245, 609.

[16] Weil 1992, pp. 245–260.

[17] *Case of the Free Zones of Upper Savoy and the District of Gex*, Order of 19 August 1929, Series A.—No. 22, 15.

[18] Kolb 2006, para 8.

[19] Mosler 1974, pp. 288–292; Virally 1983, pp. 232–234.

[20] Lauterpacht 1933, part III, para 9.

power to act, directed at the constituting of international society and the formation of the common good of international society, contains both legal and political aspects. The legal aspect may be said to be directed at the coherence of the constituting of international society; the political aspect may be said to be directed at the formation of the common good of international society.

This reformulated framework, it may be observed, is not *ipso facto* coherent. The coherence of the reformulated framework is dependent on the coherence of the process of practical reasoning which gives rise to the constituting of international society. Practical reasoning about the common good of international society can only constitute international society in the form of legal relations if it is coherent. This requirement is implicit in the metaphor that practical reasoning is a form of constituting legal relations between members of international society. Legal relations cannot be constituted if based on incoherent practical reasoning. But the coherence of this reformulated framework is only relative and not absolute; the process of practical reasoning between the members of international society may give rise to several ways of constituting international society. The resulting degree of coherence is a reflection of the quality of the mutual obligation-right and right-obligation relations which are established between the members of international society. To the extent that the constituting of international society is deemed incoherent, it may give rise to the reconstituting of international society pursuant to the process of practical reasoning.

A requirement of coherence is not, of course, unknown to the framework of obligation.[21] In *Diversion of Water from the Meuse*, The Netherlands was precluded from complaining about the so-called Neerhaeren Lock, which had been constructed by Belgium and through which water was diverted from the river Meuse, as violating a bilateral treaty concluded between The Netherlands and Belgium, because The Netherlands had previously constructed a similar lock, the Bosscheveld Lock.[22] This part of the judgment was emphatically supported in the Dissenting Opinion of Judge Anzilotti[23] and in the Separate Opinion of

---

[21] Elias 1980, pp. 296–302.

[22] *Diversion of Water from the Meuse*, Judgment of 28 June 1937, Series A./B.—No. 70, 4, 25: 'The Court cannot refrain from comparing the case of the Belgian lock with that of The Netherlands lock at Bosscheveld. Neither of these locks constitutes a feeder, yet both of them discharge their lock-water into the canal, and thus take part in feeding it with water otherwise than through the treaty feeder, though without producing an excessive current in the Zuid-Willemsvaart. In these circumstances, the Court finds it difficult to admit that The Netherlands are now warranted in complaining of the construction and operation of a lock of which they themselves set an example in the past.'

[23] *Diversion of Water from the Meuse*, Judgment of 28 June 1937, Dissenting Opinion Judge Anzilotti, Series A./B.—No. 70, 4, 50: 'I am convinced that the principle (…) *inadimplenti non est adimplendum* (…) is so just, so equitable, so universally recognized, that it must be applied in international relations also. In any case, it is one of these "general principles of law recognized by civilized nations" which the Court applies in virtue of Article 38 of its Statute.'

Judge Hudson.[24] But, as has been seen, requiring coherence from the applicant had the effect of pushing the matter out of the purview of public international law and entrusting the mutual cooperation of the parties to their respective freedoms to act.

On the side of the respondent, the *Case of the S.S. "Wimbledon"* and the *Corfu Channel Case (Merits)* might be explained by the fact that the respondent governments had not appeared consistent in their pleadings with respect to certain aspects. However, strictly speaking, within the framework of obligation, coherence can only be required if a rule of public international law to that effect can be identified, for example in the form of the notion of estoppel. That issue, however, triggers the question whether legitimate expectations or detrimental reliance of other members of international society justified the requirement of coherence.[25] More fundamentally, however, inconsistency in the form of self-contradiction cannot, within the framework of obligation, suffice to establish an obligation, which would require an affirmative assertion on the part of the State in its capacity as legislator. Within the reformulated framework, in contrast, the requirement of coherence is situated at the heart of the concept of public international law and that requirement itself is informed by the process of practical reasoning.

If the delineated transition from the incoherence of the mutual exclusivity of the framework of obligation and the framework of authorization to the reformulated framework can be effected, on the basis of practical reasoning, the function of public international law would be transformed: it would no longer exclusively be a matter of restricting freedoms to act by means of obligations or of conferring powers to act by means of rights, but both at the same time. Within the reformulated framework, a rule of public international law contains, in respect of any member of international society, both an obligation and a right, which merge into each other. By forming such rules of public international law, the members of international society constitute at the same time international society, in the form of both enabling and disabling aspects. This transformation would conclusively answer the question of whether States, in the absence of a restrictive rule of public international law, would have a freedom to commit acts of genocide. Within the reformulated framework, the members of international society do not have such a freedom, not to mention the question of whether such acts could be regarded as directed at the constituting of international society and at the formation of the common good of international society. Because the reformulated framework excludes such a freedom, it need not produce a corresponding restrictive rule of public international law.

---

[24] *Diversion of Water from the Meuse*, Judgment of 28 June 1937, Separate Opinion Judge Hudson, Series A./B.—No. 70, 4, 76–77: 'Article 38 of the Statute expressly directs the application of "general principles of law recognized by civilized nations", and in more than one nation principles of equity have an established place in the legal system. (…) It must be concluded, therefore, that under Article 38 of the Statute, if not independently of that Article, the Court has some freedom to consider principles of equity as part of the international law which it must apply.'

[25] Koskenniemi 2005, pp. 355–364.

Not only would States not have such a freedom to act within the reformulated framework, but the reformulated framework also reconstitutes the members of international society in their internal sphere. Similar to the external constituting of international society, the internal constituting of the members of international society may take place in accordance with the reformulated framework. This would envisage the members of society as constituting society pursuant to a power to act, thereby constituting rules and institutions and rules. The institutions of society are then not conceived in terms of authority in respect of the members of society, but as managing the common good of society, constituted by the members of society, and entrusted to them. In such a constellation, both externally and internally, the relevance of the question of a freedom to commit acts of genocide is thus eliminated.

Metaphorically, the transition from the incoherence of the framework of obligation and the framework of authorization to the reformulated framework may perhaps aptly be described by returning to the notion of a traffic light to which President Bedjaoui referred in his Declaration appended to *Legality of the Threat or Use of Nuclear Weapons*. President Bedajoui remarked that the Court had neither given the red light of prohibition nor the green light of authorization. In terms of the framework of obligation, the function of public international law cannot exclusively consist in regulating traffic by means of a red light. In order to prevent chaos, the light should always be red, stopping traffic indefinitely. In terms of the framework of authorization, the function of public international law cannot exclusively consist in regulating traffic by means of a green light; in order to create movement, traffic should be operated by the light. As envisaged by the reformulated framework, traffic lights at an intersection always combine, for different directions, green and red lights, so that traffic can flow both smoothly and safely in all directions. Thereby, traffic lights, simultaneously based on a combination of and forming a combination of the framework of obligation and the framework of authorization, may be seen in terms of the constituting of (international) society.

Table of Cases

International Court of Justice

Case Concerning Application of the International Convention on the Elimination of All Forms of Racial Discrimination (Preliminary Objections), Judgment of 1 April 2011, not yet reported.

Accordance with International Law of the Unilateral Declaration of Independence in respect of Kosovo, Advisory Opinion of 22 July 2010, not yet reported.

Dispute Regarding Navigational and Related Rights, Judgment of 13 July 2009, ICJ Reports 2009, 213.

Maritime Delimitation in the Black Sea, Judgment of 3 February 2009, ICJ Reports 2009, 61.

Case Concerning Certain Questions of Mutual Assistance in Criminal Matters, Judgment of 4 June 2008, ICJ Reports 2008, 177.

Case Concerning Territorial and Maritime Dispute between Nicaragua and Honduras in the Caribbean Sea, Judgment of 8 October 2007, ICJ Reports 2007, 659.

Case Concerning Application of the Convention on the Prevention and Punishment of the Crime of Genocide, Judgment of 26 February 2007, ICJ Reports 2007, 43.

Case Concerning Armed Activities on the Territory of the Congo (New Application: 2002; Jurisdiction of the Court and Admissibility of the Application), Judgment of 3 February 2006, ICJ Reports 2006, 3.

Legal Consequences of the Construction of a Wall in the Occupied Palestinian Territory, Advisory Opinion of 9 July 2004, ICJ Reports 2004, 136.

Case Concerning Oil Platforms (Merits), Judgment of 6 November 2003, ICJ Reports 2003, 161.

Case Concerning the Arrest Warrant of 11 April 2000, Judgment of 14 February 2002, ICJ Reports 2002, 3.

Case Concerning Kasikili/Sedudu Island, Judgment of 13 December 1999, ICJ Reports 1999, 1045.

Case Concerning the Land and Maritime Boundary between Cameroun and Nigeria (Preliminary Objections), Judgment of 11 June 1998, ICJ Reports 1998, 275.

Case Concerning the Gabčíkovo-Nagymaros Project, Judgment of 25 September 1997, ICJ Reports 1997, 7.

J. A. Vos, *The Function of Public International Law*,

DOI: 10.1007/978-90-6704-861-3,

(continued)

Case Concerning Questions of Interpretation and Application of the 1971 Montreal Convention Arising from the Aerial Incident at Lockerbie (Preliminary Objections), Judgment of 27 February 1998, ICJ Reports 1998, 115.

Case Concerning Questions of Interpretation and Application of the 1971 Montreal Convention Arising from the Aerial Incident at Lockerbie (Preliminary Objections), Judgment of 27 February 1998, ICJ Reports 1998, 9.

Case Concerning Application of the Convention on the Prevention and Punishment of the Crime of Genocide (Preliminary Objections), Judgment of 11 July 1996, ICJ Reports 1996, 595.

Legality of the Threat or Use of Nuclear Weapons, Advisory Opinion of 8 July 1996, ICJ Reports 1996, 226.

Legality of the Use by a State of Nuclear Weapons in Armed Conflict, Advisory Opinion of 8 July 1996, ICJ Reports 1996, 66.

Case Concerning East Timor, Judgment of 30 June 1995, ICJ Reports 1995, 90.

Case Concerning Maritime Delimitation in the Area between Greenland and Jan Mayen, Judgment of 14 June 1993, ICJ Reports 1993, 38.

Case Concerning Questions of Interpretation and Application of the 1971 Montreal Convention arising from the Aerial Incident at Lockerbie (Provisional Measures), Order of 14 April 1992, ICJ Reports 1992, 114.

Case Concerning Questions of Interpretation and Application of the 1971 Montreal Convention arising from the Aerial Incident at Lockerbie (Provisional Measures), Order of 14 April 1992, ICJ Reports 1992, 3.

Case Concerning Military and Paramilitary Activities in and against Nicaragua (Merits), Judgment of 27 June 1986, ICJ Reports 1986, 14.

Case Concerning the Continental Shelf, Judgment of 24 February 1982, ICJ Reports 1982, 18.

Interpretation of the Agreement of 25 March 1951 between the WHO and Egypt, Advisory Opinion of 20 December 1980, ICJ Reports 1980, 73.

Legal Consequences for States of the Continued Presence of South Africa in Namibia (South West Africa) Notwithstanding Security Council Resolution 276 (1970), Advisory Opinion of 21 June 1971, ICJ Reports 1971, 16.

Case Concerning the Barcelona Traction, Light and Power Company, Limited (New Application: 1962; Second Phase), Judgment of 5 February 1970, ICJ Reports 1970, 3.

North Sea Continental Shelf Cases, Judgment of 20 February 1969, ICJ Reports 1969, 3.

South West Africa Cases (Second Phase), Judgment of 18 July 1966, ICJ Reports 1966, 6.

South West Africa Cases (Preliminary Objections), Judgment of 21 December 1962, ICJ Reports 1962, 319.

Certain Expenses of the United Nations (Article 17, Paragraph 2, of the Charter), Advisory Opinion of 20 July 1962, ICJ Reports 1962, 151.

Constitution of the Maritime Safety Committee of the Inter-Governmental Maritime Consultative Organization, Advisory Opinion of 8 June 1960, ICJ Reports 1960, 150.

Case Concerning Right of Passage over Indian Territory (Merits), Judgment of 12 April 1960, ICJ Reports 1960, 6.

Judgments of the Administrative Tribunal of the International Labour Organization upon Complaints Made against the United Nations Educational, Scientific and Cultural Organization, Advisory Opinion of 23 October 1956, ICJ Reports 1956, 77.

Voting Procedure on Questions Relating to Reports and Petitions Concerning the Territory of South-West Africa, Advisory Opinion of 7 June 1955, ICJ Reports 1955, 67.

Effect of Awards of Compensation Made by the United Nations Administrative Tribunal, Advisory Opinion of 13 July 1954, ICJ Reports 1954, 47.

Fisheries Case, Judgment of 18 December 1951, ICJ Reports 1951, 116.

Haya de la Torre Case, Judgment of 13 June 1951, ICJ Reports 1951, 71.

Reservations to the Convention on the Prevention and Punishment of the Crime of Genocide, Advisory Opinion of 28 May 1951, ICJ Reports 1951, 15.

Asylum Case, Judgment of 20 November 1950, ICJ Reports 1950, 266.

International Status of South-West Africa, Advisory Opinion of 11 July 1950, ICJ Reports 1950, 128.

Interpretation of Peace Treaties with Bulgaria, Hungary and Romania (First Phase), Advisory Opinion of 30 March 1950, ICJ Reports 1950, 65.

Competence of the General Assembly for the Admission of a State to the United Nations, Advisory Opinion of 3 March 1950, ICJ Reports 1950, 3.

Reparation for Injuries Suffered in the Service of the United Nations, Advisory Opinion of 11 April 1949, ICJ Reports 1949, 174.

Corfu Channel Case (Merits), Judgment of 9 April 1949, ICJ Reports 1949, 4.

Permanent Court of International Justice

Diversion of Water from the Meuse, Judgment of 28 June 1937, Series A./B.—No. 70, 4.

Interpretation of the Convention of 1919 Concerning Employment of Women During the Night, Advisory Opinion of 15 November 1932, Series A./B.—No. 50, 365.

Case of the Free Zones of Upper Savoy and the District of Gex, Judgment of 7 June 1932, Series A./B.—No. 46, 96.

Railway Traffic between Lithuania and Poland (Railway Sector Landwarów-Kaisiadorys), Advisory Opinion of 15 October 1931, Series A./B.—No. 42, 108.

Case Relating to the Territorial Jurisdiction of the International Commission of the River Oder, Judgment No. 16 of 10 September 1929, Series A.—No. 23.

Case of the Free Zones of Upper Savoy and the District of Gex, Order of 19 August 1929, Series A.—No. 22.

Jurisdiction of the European Commission of the Danube between Galatz and Braila, Advisory Opinion of 8 December 1927, Series B.—No. 14.

Case of the S.S. "Lotus", Judgment No. 9 of 7 September 1927, Series A.—No. 10.

Competence of the International Labour Organization to Regulate, Incidentally, the Personal Work of the Employer, Advisory Opinion of 23 July 1926, Series B.—No. 13.

Case Concerning Certain German Interests in Polish Upper Silezia (Merits), Judgment No. 7 of 25 May 1926, Series A.—No. 7.

Article 3, Paragraph 2, of the Treaty of Lausanne (Frontier between Turkey and Iraq), Advisory Opinion of 21 November 1925, Series B.—No. 12.

Mavrommatis Palestine Concessions, Judgment No. 2 of 30 August 1924, Series A.—No. 2.

Case of the S.S. "Wimbledon", Judgment No. 1 of 17 August 1923, Series A.—No. 1.

Nationality Decrees Issued in Tunis and Morocco (French Zone), Advisory Opinion of 7 February 1923, Series B.—No. 4.

Competence of the International Labour Organization to Examine Proposals for the Organization and Development of the Methods of Agricultural Production as Well as Other Questions of a Like Character, Advisory Opinion of 12 August 1922, Series B.—No. 3.

Competence of the International Labour Organization in Regard to International Regulation of the Conditions of Labour of Persons Employed in Agriculture, Advisory Opinion of 12 August 1922, Series B.—No. 2.

Arbitral Awards

Case Concerning the Delimitation of the Maritime Boundary between Guinea and Guinea-Bissau, Arbitral Award of 14 February 1985, XIX Reports of International Arbitral Awards, 149–196.

Case Concerning the Air Service Agreement of 27 March 1946 between the United States of America and France, Arbitral Award of 9 December 1978, XVIII Reports of International Arbitral Awards, 417–493.

Case Concerning the Delimitation of the Continental Shelf between the United Kingdom of Great Britain and Northern Ireland, and the French Republic, Arbitral Award of 30 June 1977, XVIII Reports of International Arbitral Awards, 3–413.

Lac Lanoux Case, Arbitral Award of 16 November 1957, XII Reports of International Arbitral Awards, 281–317.

Island of Palmas Case, Arbitral Award of 4 April 1928, II Reports of International Arbitral Awards, 829–871.

Report of the International Committee of Jurists Entrusted by the Council of the League of Nations with the Task of Giving an Advisory Opinion upon the Legal Aspects of the Ålands Islands Question, 5 September 1920, League of Nations Official Journal, Special Supplement No. 3, October 1920.

World Trade Organization

Report of the Appellate Body, *European Communities – Customs Classification of Frozen Boneless Chicken Cuts*, WT/DS269/AB/R, WT/DS286/AB/R.

Report of the Appellate Body, *EC – Measures Concerning Meat and Meat Products (Hormones)*, WT/DS26/AB/R, WT/DS48/AB/R.

Report of the Appellate Body, *European Communities – Customs Classification of Certain Computer Equipment*, WT/DS62/AB/R, WT/DS68/AB/R, WT/DS69/AB/R.

Report of the Appellate Body, *United States – Import Prohibition of Certain Shrimp and Shrimp Products*, WT/DS58/AB/R.

Report of the Appellate Body, *Japan – Taxes on Alcoholic Beverages*, WT/DS8/AB/R, WT/DS10/AB/R, WT/DS11/AB/R.

Report of the Appellate Body, *United States – Standards for Reformulated and Conventional Gasoline*, WT/DS2/AB/R.

References

Advisory Committee of Jurists (1920) Procès-Verbaux of the proceedings of the committee (16 June–24 July 1920). Van Langenhuysen, The Hague
Akande D (1997) Nuclear weapons, unclear law? Deciphering the nuclear weapons advisory opinion of the International Court. British Year B Int Law LXVIII:165–218
Akehurst M (1974–1975) Custom as a source of international law. British Year B Int Law XLVII:1–53
Akehurst M (1976) Equity and general principles of law. Int Comp Law Q 25:801–825
Alexidze L (1981) Legal nature of *jus cogens* in contemporary international law. Recueil des Cours 172:219–270
Allott P (1990) Eunomia—new order for a new world. Oxford University Press, Oxford
Allott P (1992) Reconstituting humanity—new international law. Eur J Int Law 3:219–252
Allott P (1999) The concept of international law. Eur J Int Law 10:31–50
Alvarez J (2005) International organizations as law-makers. Oxford University Press, Oxford
Amerasinghe C (1999) Theory with practical effects: is international law neither fish nor fowl? Reflections on the characterization of international law. Archiv des Völkerrechts 37:1–24
Anand R (1986) Sovereign equality of States in international law. Recueil des Cours 197:9–228
Annacker C (1994a) The legal régime of *erga omnes* obligations in international law. Austrian J Public Int Law 46:131–166
Annacker C (1994b) Die Durchsetzung von erga omnes Verpflichtungen vor dem Internationalen Gerichtshof. Verlag Dr. Kovać, Hamburg
Arrangio-Ruiz G (1997) The 'federal analogy' and UN Charter interpretation: a crucial issue. Eur J Int Law 8:1–28
Barberis J (1970) La liberté de traiter des états et le jus cogens. Zeitschrift für ausländisches öffentliches Recht und Völkerrecht 30:19–45
Basdevant J (1936) Règles générales du droit de la paix. Recueil des Cours 58:471–692
Bederman D (1996) The souls of international organizations: legal personality and the lighthouse at Cape Spartel. Va J Int Law 36:275–377
Bergbohm C (1877) Staatsverträge und Gesetze als Quellen des Völkerrechts. Verlag von C. Mattiesen, Dorpat
Bleckmann A (1978) Die Handlungsfreiheit der Staaten—System und Struktur der Völkerrechtsordnung. Österreichische Zeitschrift für öffentliches Recht und Völkerrecht 29:173–196
Bleckmann A (1985) The subjective right in public international law. Ger Yearb Int Law 28:144–162
Bleckmann A (1995) General theory of obligations under public international law. Ger Yearb Int Law 38:26–40

J. A. Vos, *The Function of Public International Law*,
DOI: 10.1007/978-90-6704-861-3,

Blondel A (1968) Les Principes Généraux de Droit devant la Cour Permanente de Justice Internationale et la Cour Internationale de Justice. In: Recueil de'Études de Droit International en Hommage à Paul Guggenheim, Genève, pp 201–236

Bos M (1984) A methodology of international law. North-Holland Publishing Company, Amsterdam

Bruns V (1929) Völkerrecht als Rechtsordnung I. Zeitschrift für ausländisches öffentliches Recht und Völkerrecht I:1–56

Bruns V (1933) Völkerrecht als Rechtsordnung II. Zeitschrift für ausländisches öffentliches Recht und Völkerrecht III:445–487

Byers M (1997) Conceptualizing the relationship between *jus cogens* and *erga omnes* rules. Nordic J Int Law 66:211–239

Castañeda J (1969) Legal effects of United Nations resolutions. Columbia University Press, New York

Capotorti F (1994) Cours Général de Droit International Public. Recueil des Cours 248:9–344

Carillo Salcedo J (1997) Reflections on the existence of a hierarchy of norms in international law. Eur J Int Law 8:583–595

Castberg F (1933) La Méthodologie du Droit International. Recueil des Cours 43:309–383

Charlesworth H (1991) Customary international law and the Nicaragua Case. Aust Yearb Int Law 11:1–31

Charney J (1985) The persistent objector rule and the development of customary international law. British Yearb Int Law 56:1–24

Charney J (1993) Universal international law. Am J Int Law 87:529–551

Chemain R (2006) Le contrôle des actes de l'organisation. In: Chemain R, Pellet A (eds) La Charte des Nations Unies, Constitution Mondiale? Pedone, Paris, pp 45–63

Cheng B (1953) General principles of law as applied by international courts and tribunals. Stevens & Sons Limited, London

Cheng B (1965) United Nations resolutions on outer space: 'instant' international customary law? Indian J Int Law 5:23–48

Chinkin C (1993) Third parties in international law. Clarendon Press, Oxford

Christenson G (1988) *Jus cogens*: guarding interests fundamental to international society. Va J Int Law 28:585–648

Coffman P (1996) Obligations erga omnes and the absent third state. Ger Yearb Int Law 39:285–333

Cohen-Jonathan G (1961) La coutume locale. Annuaire Français de Droit International 7:119–140

D'Amato A (1970) On consensus. Can Yearb Int Law VIII:104–122

D'Amato A (1971) The concept of custom in international law. Cornell University Press, Ithaca

Danilenko G (1993) Law-making in the international community. Kluwer Law International, The Hague

De Vattel E (1916) Le Droit des Gens, ou Principes de la Loi Naturelle. Appliqués à la Conduite et aux Affaires des Nations et des Souverains, Washington

De Visscher C (1933) Contribution à l'Étude des Sources du Droit International. Revue de Droit International et de Législation Comparée:395–420

De Wet E (2000) Judicial review as an emerging general principle of law and its implications for the International Court of Justice. Neth Int Law Rev XLVII:181–210

Degan V (1990) Customary process in international law. Finnish Yearb Int Law I:1–78

Degan V (1992) General principles of law (a source of general international law). Finnish Yearb Int Law III:1–102

Degan V (1997) Sources of international law. Kluwer Law International, The Hague

Dekker I, Werner W (2003) The completeness of international law and Hamlet's dilemma—*Non Liquet*, the Nuclear Weapons case, and legal theory. In: Dekker I, Post H (eds) On the foundations and sources of international law. TMC Asser Press, The Hague, pp 5–30

Delbrück J (1998) 'Laws in the public interest'—some observations on the foundations and identification of *erga omnes* norms in international law. In: Götz et al. (eds) Liber Amicorum Günther Jaenicke—Zum 85. Geburtstag. Springer, Berlin, pp 17–36
Delbrück J (2001) Structural changes in the international system and its legal order: international law in the era of globalization. Schweizerische Zeitschrift für internationales und europäisches Recht:1–36
Delbrück J (2002a) Article 24. In: Simma B (ed) The charter of the United Nations: a commentary. Oxford University Press, Oxford, pp 442–452
Delbrück J (2002b) Article 25. In: Simma B (ed) The charter of the United Nations: a commentary. Oxford University Press, Oxford, pp 452–464
Dewitt Dickinson E (1920) The equality of States in international law. Harvard University Press, Cambridge
Dinstein Y (2006) The interaction between customary international law and treaties. Recueil des Cours 322:243–428
Dunoff J, Trachtman J (1999) Economic analysis of international law. Yale J Int Law 24:1–59
Dupuy P (1997) The constitutional dimension of the charter of the United Nations revisited. Max Planck Yearb U N Law 1:1–33
Dupuy P (2002) L'Unité de l'ordre juridique international: Cours général de droit international public (2000). Recueil des Cours 297:9–487
Dworkin R (1998) Law's empire. Hart Publishing, Oxford
Dyzenhaus D (2005) The rule of (administrative) law in international law. Law Contemp Probl 68:127–166
Elias O, Lim C (1997) 'General principles of law', 'Soft' law and the identification of international law. Neth Yearb Int Law XXVIII:3–49
Elias O, Lim C (1998) The paradox of consensualism in international law. Kluwer Law International, The Hague
Elias T (1980) The doctrine of intertemporal law. Am J Int Law 74:285–307
Fassbender B (1998) The United Nations Charter as constitution of the international community. Colombia J Transnatl Law 36:529–619
Fastenrath U (1991) Lücken im Völkerrecht—Zu Rechtscharakter, Quellen, Systemzusammenhang, Methodenlehre und Funktionen des Völkerrechts. Duncker & Humblot, Berlin
Fastenrath U (1993) Relative normativity in international law. Eur J Int Law 4:305–340
Favre A (1968) Les Principes Généraux du Droit, Fonds Commun du Droit des Gens. In: Recueil d'Études de Droit International en Hommage à Paul Guggenheim, Genève, pp 366–390
Finnis J (1980) Natural law and natural rights. Clarendon Press, Oxford
Fitzmaurice G (1957a) The general principles of international law considered from the standpoint of the rule of law. Recueil des Cours 92:1–227
Fitzmaurice G (1957b) Second report on the law of treaties. Yearb Int Law Comm II:16–70
Fitzmaurice G (1958a) Some problems regarding the formal sources of international law. In: Van Asbeck F et al (eds) Symbolae Verzijl. Nijhoff, The Hague, pp 153–176
Fitzmaurice G (1958b) Third report on the law of treaties. Yearb Int Law Comm II:20–46
Friedmann W (1964) The changing structure of international law. Stevens & Sons, London
Frowein J (1983) Die Verpflichtungen erga omnes im Völkerrecht und ihre Durchsetzung. In: Bernardt R (ed) Völkerrecht als Rechtsordnung—Internationale Gerichtsbarkeit—Menschenrechte; Festschrift für Hermann Mosler. Springer, Berlin, pp 241–262
Frowein J (1994) Reactions by not directly affected states to breaches of public international law. Recueil des Cours 248:345–437
Gaja G (1981) *Jus cogens* beyond the Vienna convention. Recueil des Cours 172:271–316
Gaja G (1989) Obligations *erga omnes,* International crimes and *jus cogens*: a tentative analysis of three related concepts. In: Weiler J et al (eds) International crimes of state: a critical analysis of the ILC's Draft Article 19 on State Responsibility. De Gruyter, Berlin, pp 151–160
Gardiner R (2008) Treaty interpretation. Oxford University Press, Oxford
Gilson B (1984) The conceptual system of sovereign equality. Peeters, Leuven

Goldsmith J, Posner E (1999) A theory of customary international law. Univ Chic Law Rev 66:1113–1177
Goldsmith J, Posner E (2000) Understanding the resemblance between modern and traditional customary international law. Va J Int Law 40:639–672
Gomez Robledo A (1981) Le *Ius cogens* international: sa Genèse, sa nature, ses fonctions. Recueil des Cours 172:9–217
Graf Vitzthum W (1997) Begriff, Geschichte und Quellen des Völkerrechts. In: Graf Vitzthum W et al. (eds) Völkerrecht. De Gruyter, Berlin, pp 1–100
Grapin P (1934) Valeur internationale des principes généraux du droit—Contribution à l'étude de l'article 38 § 3 du statut de la cour permanente de justice internationale. Domat-Montchrestien, Paris
Grotius H (1964) De jure belli ac pacis. Oceana Publications, New York
Günther H (1970) Zur Entstehung von Völkergewohnheitsrecht. Duncker & Humblot, Berlin
Hackel V (2000) Kants Friedensschrift und das Völkerrecht. Duncker & Humblot, Berlin
Haggenmacher P (1986) La doctrine des deux éléments du droit coutumier dans la Pratique de la Cour Internationale. Revue Générale de Droit International Public 90:5–125
Hannikainen L (1988) Peremptory norms (jus cogens) in international law—historical development, criteria, present status. Finnish Lawyer's Publishing Company, Helsinki
Härle E (1935) Les principes généraux de droit et le droit des gens. Revue de Droit International et de Législation Comparée:663–687
Hart H (1994) The concept of law: Clarendon law series. Clarendon Press, Oxford
Harvard research in international law (1935) Draft convention on the law of treaties. Am J Int Law 29 (special supplement)
Henry N (1928) Le 'Lotus' à la cour de La Haye. Revue de Droit International 2:65–134
Hobbes T (1996) Leviathan. Cambridge University Press, Cambridge
Hohfeld W (1913) Some fundamental legal conceptions as applied in judicial reasoning. Yale Law J 23:16–59
Hohfeld W (1917) Fundamental legal conceptions as applied in judicial reasoning. Yale Law Journal 27:710–770
Van Hooff G (1983) Rethinking the sources of international law. Kluwer, Deventer
De Hoogh A (1991) The relationship between *jus cogens*, obligations *erga omnes* and international crimes: peremptory norms in perspective. Austrian J Public Int Law 42:183–214
Hüning D (1998) Freiheit und Herrschaft in der Rechtsphilosophie des Thomas Hobbes. Duncker & Humblot, Berlin
Kadelbach S (1992) Zwingendes Völkerrecht. Duncker & Humblot, Berlin
Kamto M (2002) Une troublante 'immunité totale' du Ministre des affaires étrangères (sur un aspect de l'arrêt du 14 février 2002 dans l'affaire relative au mandat d'arrêt du 11 avril 2000). Revue Belge de Droit International XXXV:518–530
Kant I (1991a) On the common saying: 'this may be true in theory, but it does not apply in practice' (In: Kant I, Political Writings). Cambridge University Press, Cambridge, pp 61–92
Kant I (1991b) Perpetual peace: a philosophical sketch (In: Kant I, Political Writings). Cambridge University Press, Cambridge, pp 93–130
Kant I (1996) The metaphysics of morals. Cambridge University Press, Cambridge
Kelly J (2000) The twilight of customary international law. Va J Int Law 40:449–543
Kelsen H (1960) Reine Rechtslehre. Deuticke, Wien
Kennedy D (1980) Theses about international law discourse. Ger Yearb Int Law 23:353–391
Kennedy D (1986) Primitive legal scholarship. Harv Int Law J 27:1–98
Kennedy D (1987a) International legal structures. Nomos Verlagsgesellschaft, Baden-Baden
Kennedy D (1987b) The move to institutions. Cardozo Law Rev 8:841–988
Kennedy D (1999) The disciplines of international law and policy. Leiden J Int Law 12:9–133
Kennedy D (2000) When renewal repeats: thinking against the box. N Y J Int Law Politics 32:335–500

Kingsbury B, Krisch N, Stewart R (2005) The emergence of global administrative law. Law Contemp Probl 68:15–61
Kingsbury B (2009) The concept of 'law' in global administrative law. Eur J Int Law 20:23–57
Klabbers J (1996) The concept of treaty in international law. Kluwer Law International, The Hague
Klabbers J (1997) De derde in het volkenrecht: graadmeter voor structuurveranderingen. Ars Aequi 46:112–119
Klabbers J (1998) Clinching the concept of sovereignty: Wimbledon Redux. Austrian Rev Int Eur Law 3:345–367
Klabbers J (2001) The life and times of the law of international organizations. Nordic J Int Law 70:287–317
Klabbers J (2002) An introduction to international institutional law. Cambridge University Press, Cambridge
Kolb R (1998a) La bonne foi en droit international public. Revue Belge de Droit International 31:661–732
Kolb R (1998b) The formal source of *ius cogens* in public international law. Zeitschrift für öffentliches Recht 53:69–105
Kolb R (2000) Le droit international est-il un droit primitif? Zeitschrift für öffentliches Recht 55:101–114
Kolb R (2001) La règle résiduelle de liberté en droit international public ('Tout ce qui n'est pas interdit est permis')—aspects Théoriques. Revue Belge de Droit International 34:100–127
Kolb R (2006) Interprétation et création du droit international. Bruylant, Brussels
Kooijmans P (1964) The doctrine of the legal equality of states—an inquiry into the foundations of international law. Sijthoff, Leiden
Korhonen O (1996) New international law: silence, defence or deliverance? Eur J Int Law 7:1–28
Koskenniemi M (1990) The politics of international law. Eur J Int Law 1:4–32
Koskenniemi M (2005) From Apology to Utopia—the structure of international legal argument. Cambridge University Press, Cambridge
Koskenniemi M (2009) The politics of international law—20 years later. Eur J Int Law 20:7–19
Kratochwil F (1989) Rules, norms, and decisions—on the conditions of practical and legal reasoning in international relations and domestic affairs. Cambridge University Press, Cambridge
Küntzel W (1935) Ungeschriebenes Völkerrecht—Ein Beitrag zu der Lehre von den Quellen des Völkerrechts, Gräfe und Unzer
Lammers J (1980) General principles of law recognized by civilized nations. In: Kalshoven et al. (eds) Essays on the development of the international legal order in memory of Haro F. van Panhuys. Sijthoff & Noordhoff, Alphen aan den Rijn/Rockville, pp 53–75
Lauterpacht H (1927) Private law sources and analogies of international law (with special reference to international arbitration). Longmans, Green and Co. Ltd., London
Lauterpacht H (1933) The function of law in the international community. Clarendon Press, Oxford
Lauterpacht H (1936) The Covenant as the "higher law". British Yearb Int Law 17:54–65
Lejbowicz A (1999) Philosophie du droit international—L'impossible capture de l'humanité. Presses Universitaires de France, Paris
Locke J (1988) Two treatises of government. Cambridge University Press, Cambridge
MacCormick N (1994) Legal reasoning and legal theory. Clarendon Press, Oxford
MacDonald R (1987) Fundamental norms in contemporary international law. Can Yearb Int Law XXV:115–149
Mahiou A (2008) Le droit international ou la dialectique de la rigueur et de la flexibilité—Cours général de droit international public. Recueil des Cours 337:9–516
Marek K (1968) Contribution à l'étude du *jus cogens* en droit international. In: Recueil d'Études de Droit International en Hommage à Paul Guggenheim, Genève, pp 426–459

Marmo L (1958) Il diritto internazionale e la distinzione tra diritto pubblico e privato—spunti critici introduttivi allo studio delle organizzazioni internazionali. Giuffrè, Milano

Martenczuk B (1999) The security council, the international court and judicial review: what lessons from Lockerbie? Eur J Int Law 10:517–547

McDougal M, Feliciano F (1987) International coercion and world public order: the general principles of the law of war. In: McDougal M et al. (eds) Studies in world public order. New Haven Press, New Haven, pp 237–334

McDougal M, Lasswell H (1987) The identification and appraisal of diverse systems of public order. In: McDougal M et al. (eds) Studies in world public order. New Haven Press, New Haven, pp 3–41

McNair A (1930) The functions and differing legal character of treaties. British Year B Int Law XI:100–118

McNair A (1961) The law of treaties. Clarendon Press, Oxford

Mosler H (1968) Ius Cogens im Völkerrecht. Schweizerisches Jahrbuch für internationales Recht XXV:9–40

Mosler H (1974) The international society as a legal community. Recueil des Cours 140:1–320

Mosler H (1976) Völkerrecht als Rechtsordnung. Zeitschrift für ausländisches öffentliches Recht und Völkerrecht 36:6–49

Mosler H (1992) General principles of law. Encycl Public Int Law 2:511–527

Onuf N (1994) The constitution of international society. Eur J Int Law 5:1–19

Ost F, Van de Kerchove M (2002) De la pyramide au réseau?—pour und théorie dialectique du droit. Publications des facultés universitaires Saint-Louis, Bruxelles

Pastor Ridruejo J (1998) Le droit international à la veille du vingt et unième siècle: Normes, faites et valeurs—Cours général de droit international Public. Recueil des Cours 274:9–308

Paulus A (2001) Die internationale Gemeinschaft im Völkerrecht—Eine Untersuchung zur Entwicklung des Völkerrechts im Zeitalter der Globaliserung. Verlag C.H. Beck, München

Quadri R (1964) Cours général de droit international public. Recueil des Cours 113:237–483

Ragazzi M (1997) The concept of international obligations *erga omnes*. Clarendon Press, Oxford

Raftopoulos E (1990) The inadequacy of the contractual analogy in the law of treaties. Publications of the Hellenic Institute of International and Foreign Law, Athens

Rawls J (1999a) A theory of justice. Harvard University Press, Cambridge

Rawls J (1999b) The law of peoples with "The idea of public reason revisited". Harvard University Press, Cambridge

Rawls J (2005) Political liberalism. Columbia University Press, New York

Reuter P (1995) Introduction to the law of treaties. Kegan Paul International, London

Ripert G (1933) Les règles du droit civil applicables aux rapports internationaux (Contribution à l'étude des principes généraux du droit visés au statut de la Cour Permanente de Justice Internationale). Recueil des Cours 44:565–664

Roxburgh R (1917) International conventions and third states. Longmans, Green and Co, London

Rousseau J (2001) Du contrat social. GF Flammarion, Paris

Rozakis C (1976) The concept of *jus cogens* in the law of treaties. North-Holland Publishing Company, Amsterdam

Salmon J (2002) Libres propos sur l'arrêt du 14 février 2002 dans l'affaire relative au Mandat d'arrêt du 11 avril 2000. Revue Belge de Droit International XXXV:512–517

Sands P (2002) What is the ICJ for? Revue Belge de Droit International XXXV:537–545

Schilling T (1995) Die 'Neue Weltordnung' und die Souveränität der Mitglieder der Vereinten Nationen. Archiv des Völkerrechts 33:67–106

Schultz N (2002) Ist Lotus verblüht? Anmerkungen zum Urteil des IGH vom 14. Februar 2002 im Fall betreffend den Haftbefehl vom 11. April 2000 (Demokratisch Republik Kongo gegen Belgien). Zeitschrift für ausländisches öffentliches Recht und Völkerrecht 62:703–758

Schwarzenberger G (1965) International *jus cogens*? Texas Law Rev 43:455–478

Schwelb E (1967) Some aspects of international *jus cogens* as formulated by the International Law Commission. Am J Int Law 61:946–975

Scobbie I (1990) Towards the elimination of international law: some radical skepticism about skeptical radicalism. British Year B Int Law LXI:339–362
Simma B (1994) From bilateralism to community interest in international law. Recueil des Cours 250:217–384
Siorat L (1958) Le problème des lacunes en droit international—contribution à l'étude des sources du droit et de la fonction judiciaire. Pichon & Durand-Auzias, Paris
Sloan B (1987) General assembly resolutions revisited (forty years later). British Year B Int Law LVIII:39–150
Sørensen M (1960) Principes de droit international public. Recueil des Cours 101:1–254
Spiermann O (2005) International legal argument in the Permanent Court of International Justice—the rise of the international judiciary. Cambridge University Press, Cambridge
Spiropoulos J (1928) Die allgemeinen Rechtsgrundsätze im Völkerrecht—Eine Auslegung von Artikel 38(3) des Statuts des Ständigen Internationalen Gerichtshofs. Verlag des Instituts für internationales Recht, Kiel
Stein T (1985) The approach of the different drummer: the principle of the persistent objector in international law. Harv Int Law J 26:457–482
Stone J (1959) *Non liquet* and the function of law in the international community. British Year B Int Law XXXV:124–161
Strupp K (1934) Les règles générales du droit de la paix. Recueil des Cours 47:257–595
Study Group of the International Law Commission (2006) Fragmentation of international law: difficulties arising from the diversification and expansion of international law, A/CN.4/L.682
Suy E (1967) The concept of jus cogens in international law. In Carnegie endowment for international peace, The concept of jus cogens in international law: papers and proceedings, Conference on international law, Lagonissi (Greece), 3–8 April 1966, Geneva, pp 17–77
Tams C (2005) Enforcing obligations *erga omnes* in international law. Cambridge University Press, Cambridge
Tanaka Y (2008) Reflections on maritime delimitation in the *Nicaragua/Honduras* Case. Zeitschrift für ausländisches öffentliches Recht und Völkerrecht 68:903–937
Tomuschat C (1993) Obligations arising for states without or against their will. Recueil des Cours 241:195–374
Tomuschat C (1995) Die internationale Gemeinschaft. Archiv des Völkerrechts 33:1–20
Tomuschat C (1999) International law: ensuring the survival of mankind on the eve of a new century: general course on public international law. Recueil des Cours 281:9–438
Tönnies F (2001) Community and Civil Society. Cambridge University Press, Cambridge
Touret D (1973) Le principe de l'égalité souveraine des états—fondement du droit international. Revue Générale de Droit International Public 77:136–199
Triepel H (1899) Völkerrecht und Landesrecht. Verlag von C.L. Hirschfeld, Leipzig
Verdross A (1935) Les principes généraux du droit dans la jurisprudence internationale. Recueil des Cours 52:191–251
Verdross A (1937) Forbidden treaties in international law—comments on Professor Garner's report on 'The Law of Treaties'. Am J Int Law 31:571–577
Verdross A (1966) Jus dispositivum and Jus cogens in International Law. Am J Int Law 60:55–63
Verdross A (1968) Les principes généraux de droit dans le système des sources du droit International Public. In: Recueil d'études de droit international en hommage à Paul Guggenheim, Genève, pp 521–530
Villiger M (1997) Customary international law and treaties—a manual on the theory and practice of the interrelation of sources. Kluwer Law International, The Hague
Virally M (1966) Réflexions sur le 'jus cogens'. Annuaire Français de Droit International XII:5–29
Virally M (1968) Le rôle des 'principes' dans le développement du droit International. In: Recueil d'études de droit international en hommage à Paul Guggenheim, Genève, pp 531–554
Virally M (1983) Panorama du droit international contemporain: Cours général de droit international public. Recueil des Cours 183:9–382

Vitanyi B (1982) Les positions doctrinales concernant le sens de la notion de 'Principes généraux de droit reconnus par les nations civilisées'. Revue Générale de Droit International Public 86:48–116

Waldock H (1962) General course on public international law. Recueil des Cours 106:1–251

Weil P (1983) Towards relative normativity in international law? Am J Int Law 77:413–442

Weil P (1992) Le droit international en quête de son identité. Recueil des Cours 237:11–370

Wood M (2006) The UN Security Council and international law—The Security Council's powers and their limits. Hersch Lauterpacht Memorial Lectures. www.lcil.cam.ac.uk

Yaseen M (1976) L'interprétation des traités d'après la convention de vienne sur le droit des traités. Recueil des Cours 151:1–114

Zemanek K (1997) The legal foundations of the international system: general course on public international law. Recueil des Cours 266:9–335

Zotiades G (1967) Staatsautonomie und die Grenzen der Vertragsfreiheit im Völkerrecht. Österreichische Zeitschrift für öffentliches Recht XVII:90–112

MIX
Papier aus verantwortungsvollen Quellen
Paper from responsible sources
FSC® C105338

If you have any concerns about our products,
you can contact us on
ProductSafety@springernature.com

In case Publisher is established outside the EU,
the EU authorized representative is:
Springer Nature Customer Service Center GmbH
Europaplatz 3, 69115 Heidelberg, Germany

Printed by Libri Plureos GmbH
in Hamburg, Germany